Personality Theory
a book of readings

edited by
André Kukla

Canadian Scholars' Press Inc.   Toronto   1996

Personality Theory: A Book of Readings
edited by André Kukla

First published in 1996 by
Canadian Scholars' Press Inc.
180 Bloor Street West, Suite 402
Toronto, Ontario   M5S 2V6

Canadian Cataloguing in Publication Data

Main entry under title:

Personality theory

ISBN 1-55130-085-0

1. Personality.   I. Kukla, André, 1942–

BF698. P47   1996   155.2   C95-932846-7

Page layout by Brad Horning

Printed and bound in Canada

TABLE OF CONTENTS

INTRODUCTION

The word "personality" does not have the same meaning in everyday speech as it does in the phrase "personality theory", or "theories of personality". In everyday speech, our "personality" refers to an integrated collection of relatively stable and enduring psychological characteristics. An "anxious" personality is one that causes its possessor to exhibit frequent or intense anxiety. Similarly, we speak of introverted, aggressive, friendly, or interesting personalities. This way of talking is based on the idea that the explanation for much of human behavior is to be given by specifying some internal property of the behaving agent. There are, indeed, some personality theories that endorse this idea. But there are others that explicitly reject it. B. F. Skinner, for one, locates the causes of behavior entirely in the external environment: what causes anxious behavior according to Skinnerians is not an inner trait of anxiety-proneness, but rather the presence in the world of anxiety-producing stimuli. Nevertheless, Skinner's views on these matters count as a theory of personality.

What makes a psychological theory a *personality* theory is the breadth of its explanatory scope. Personality theories are attempts to construct an overall conception of the person. They are *general theories of human nature.* Some of these theories posit the existence of something like the "personality" of everyday speech. Others deny its existence — there are personality theories which say that there are no personalities. This is an unfortunate verbal knot. A few decades ago, there was a laudable attempt on the part of some personality psychologists to change the name of their field to *personology*. If the new name had caught on, we would have been able to say that theories of personology are general theories of the person, which would have made immediate sense and saved both reader and writer the trouble of these first two paragraphs. It seems, however, that we are stuck with the knot.

The field of personality psychology has some unique properties among the subdisciplines of psychology. All the other areas are defined in terms of the psychological *processes* that they concern themselves with. Perceptual psychology studies the process of perception, social psychologists study social processes, and so on. Suppose that these areas have done their job maximally well — that perceptual psychologists have learned everything that can be learned by the study of perceptual processes in isolation from other processes, that social psychologists have likewise learned everything about isolated social processes, etc. This is, of course, far from being true. But even if it were true, we could not say that the work of psychology as a whole would be finished. There would still be the task of figuring out how these isolated process accounts fit together to make a whole person. For example, the question of how perceptual and social processes *interact* is a problem that transcends the disciplinary boundary between perceptual and social psychology. One theory about this interrelationship is that our perception of the world is largely determined by our biological endowment, so that perceptual processes are relatively uninfluenced by social forces. Another theory is that we see what society teaches us to expect to see. The personality theorist is the person whose professional task it is to worry about global, cross-disciplinary issues of this kind. Each of the process areas of psychology strives to construct a piece of the jig-saw puzzle of human nature; the personality theorist is the one who tries to put the pieces together into a coherent picture.

Before we get to the substance of our inquiry, we need to say a little about the nature of theoretical work. Scientific work involves both *observing* the world and *thinking* about our observations. The former comprises the *empirical* part of science; the latter comprises its *theoretical* part. The two lines of work do not, of course, proceed in isolation from each other. But any given investigation may contribute exclusively to the empirical or to the theoretical part of science. If the contribution is empirical, its ultimate aim is the acquisition of new data about the world. If it is theoretical, its aim is to arrive at a better understanding of the data that we already have. Both endeavors require special methods and skills. The methods of empirical work are routinely studied in undergraduate courses devoted to the process areas of psychology. Indeed, most undergraduate psychology programs include an entire course in methods of empirical research. The teaching of methods of theoretical research, however, is far more haphazard. Theoretical work being what this book is all about, it seems advisable to begin with an overview of the nature and scope of theoretical research (chapter 1).

Conceptions of human nature have varied drastically over the centuries. Most of these conceptions can be categorized as belonging to one of two major families — the *materialist* theories and the *dualist* theories. According to materialism, persons are physical objects, no different in principle from stones or clouds. To be sure, human beings are more *complicated* than stones and clouds — they have more articulated parts and complex connections among those parts. Nevertheless, according to materialists, persons are subject to the same natural laws as other physical objects. If we knew all the laws of physics and had enough time to make all the necessary calculations, we might in principle be able to predict all of a person's behavior, just as we can predict the future motions of the planets in their orbits. It is only the enormously greater complexity of the physical processes that produce behavior which makes this goal impractical — at present.

This materialist picture comes into direct conflict with the personality theory implicit in the Judeo-Christian religious tradition. According to the tradition, human beings are, or have, souls which are capable of surviving the dissolution of the body. This is an example of a dualist view. According to dualism, persons are compounds of two elements — a physical body, and an immaterial element, such as the soul, which inhabits the body and drives it around. Since the second element is immaterial, its activity is not necessarily or obviously subject to the laws of physics. Many (but not all) dualists believe that the immaterial element is able to influence the behavior of the body by exercising the faculty of *will*, and that this faculty is unconstrained by physical law. The hypothesis that we have free will has the consequence that human behavior is unpredictable, even in principle. To subscribe to this kind of dualism is therefore to believe that there cannot be a science of human behavior.

Dualism is not the exclusive province of the religious. There are also secular dualists, who tend to speak of the immaterial portion of a person as the *mind*, rather than the soul. Unlike souls, minds are not usually thought to be capable of surviving the dissolution of the body. In this respect, the mind is like the brain. But dualists believe that the mind is not *identical* to the brain either. According to secular dualism, mental processes such as perceptions, imaginings, feelings, and thoughts cannot be identified with physical processes in the brain.

The combination of dualism and freedom of the will received its quintessential expression in the writings of René Descartes (chapter 2). Descartes wrote in the seventeenth century, about two hundred years before psychology established itself as an independent and systematic field of inquiry. He thus belongs to the pre-history of personality theory. In the eighteenth and nineteenth centuries, Descartes' analysis of the relationship between mind and body became so firmly entrenched that it came to be regarded as common sense. Not surprisingly, the first systematic psychological theories were Cartesian through and through ("Cartesian" is an adjectival form of Descartes' name). Additionally, many of the more modern theories of personality can best be understood as *reactions* to one aspect or another of Cartesianism. In sum, it is impossible to understand the development of personality theory to the present day without reading a little Descartes.

The first systematic psychological theory goes by the name of *introspectionism*. The psychology of introspectionism was founded by Wilhelm Wundt in the 1870s. We will read an account by the foremost American introspectionist, E. B. Titchener (chapter 3). True to their Cartesian heritage, introspectionists were dualists who made no attempt to discover the laws of behavior. Psychology in the nineteenth century was exclusively a science of mental life. In this respect, it diverged greatly from the behavioristic psychology that succeeded it. Introspectionist conceptions of how to do empirical research were also drastically different from their successors'. Introspectionists did not "run subjects". Instead, they induced mental processes *in themselves* by means of various experimental arrangements, and then tried to describe the resultant mental states as accurately as they could. The descriptions of such "intro-spections", or lookings-within, were the observational data upon which psychologists of the nineteenth century tried to build theories.

The introspectionists were strongly influenced by the then-current atomic theory of matter. The atomic theory promised to reduce the innumerable varieties of physical substances to various combinations of relatively few elementary substances. The introspectionists supposed that psychology should try to perform the same sort of reduction in the second realm of the mental. Introspective research was aimed at discovering the elementary "atoms of experience", out of which the countless varieties of human experiences could be formed. A complex experience like nostalgia might be analyzed as a compound of a certain kind of thought and a certain kind of feeling. These thoughts and feelings, as well as sensations and images, were to be analyzed in turn until the experiential atoms were reached that could not be further broken down. This project was often described as discovering the *structure* of human experience, and introspectionism as a whole is often referred to as *structuralism*. The former name is inspired by its method of research, the latter by its substantive goal.

The judgment of history is that introspectionism was not a fruitful enterprise. Despite half a century of effort, no surprising new discoveries about experience were made. Even more seriously, introspectionists seemed unable to agree about mundane and unsurprising principles. By the early years of the twentieth century, dissatisfaction with the introspectionist theory had become widespread. At more or less the same time, there arose three new psychological theories — the *phenomenological*, the *behavioral*, and the *psychoanalytic* — which came to dominate the first 75 years of the twentieth century. Each of the three psychologies can be understood as a different reaction to the failure of introspectionism. Each one blamed the failure on a different part of the introspective enterprise. Moreover, each of the three diagnoses gained favor with a different geographical or professional group. Psychoanalysis captured the allegiance of most clinical psychologists, but never made much headway in the universities. Among academic psychologists, those in the English-speaking world went overwhelmingly over to the behaviorist side, while psychologists on the continent of Europe favored phenomenology.

Phenomenology is the theory that remained closest to its introspective forebears. Like introspectionists before them, phenomenologists regarded the study of conscious experience to be the sole occupation of psychology. What the phenomenologists objected to in introspectionism was its *structuralism* — its attempt to explain human experiences as compounds of atomic experiences. Phenomenology is the least familiar of the twentieth-century schools among North American students and psychologists. The exception is *Gestalt* psychology, a branch of phenomenology whose European founders migrated to the United States in the 1930s. We will read the definitive phenomenological critique of introspective psychology by Wolfgang Köhler, one of the luminaries of Gestalt psychology (chapter 4).

The psychoanalytic objection to introspectionism was that its subject matter and methodology were incomplete. Psychoanalysts conceded that conscious experience is a proper subject for psychological investigation and that introspection is an appropriate tool for its study. But, it was claimed, conscious introspection leaves out of account the most important aspect of mental life — the *un*conscious. According to Freud, most of what happens to us — indeed, most of conscious experience itself — is determined by inner forces that are simply not available to introspection (this is what it means to call them unconscious). Thus the method of introspection needs to be supplemented by other techniques which permit us to infer the nature of unconscious mental processes. Chapter 5 presents one of Freud's most succinct summaries of the principles of psychoanalysis. Chapter 6 is an account of the main supplementary method which Freud believed could give us knowledge of unconscious mental processes — dream analysis.

The most thoroughgoing repudiation of introspectionism is to be found in the principles of behaviorism. According to its founding manifesto by J. B. Watson (chapter 7), the problem with introspectionism was that it had adopted an illegitimate subject-matter: mental life. It wasn't surprising, Watson argued, that psychologists could not agree about the most basic facts of the field, when the facts they were trying to establish were about so elusive a phenomenon as consciousness. If psychology was to develop a solid foundation of agreed-upon lore, it would have to emulate the other successful sciences in studying some aspect of the *physical* world. The aspect of the physical world which could be claimed for psychology was *behavior* — the physical movements through space and time of the limbs and bodies of living organisms. The movements are *responses*; the physical settings in which they take place are *stimuli*; and a theory which follows the behaviorist recipe is a *stimulus-response* or *S-R* theory.

There are two major phases in the development of S-R theory. The first is associated with Clark Hull, the second with B. F. Skinner. Hull's own writings are replete with mathematical technicalities that are no longer worth working through. His views are therefore represented by a secondary source (chapter 8). This is followed by a famous critique by Robert W. White (chapter 9). White also demonstrates that Hull's theory turns out to have remarkably many points of agreement with classical psychoanalytic theory — and many of the same shortcomings. White's article thus serves as a critical appraisal of Freud's views as well as Hull's. Skinner's version of S-R theory (chapter 10) is followed by an analysis from his most influential critic, the linguist Noam Chomsky (chapter 11).

The critiques of White and Chomsky are addressed to two specific formulations of S-R theory. In addition, there is the broader question of the validity of behaviorism itself — the view that psychological theories should avoid all references to the mental. Watson never gave any clear reason why the study of mental life was doomed to failure. He simply noted that it *had* failed in the hands of the introspectionists. But introspectionism was a complex enterprise involving many assumptions and methods, any one of which might have been at the root of its demise. Indeed, we saw that phenomenologists and psychoanalysts did locate the cause of the failure elsewhere. It was left to a later generation of behaviorists to construct positive arguments for behaviorism. These fall into two broad categories — the *methodological* and the *metaphysical*. Methodological behaviorism is the view that there is something about mental events — their inaccessibility to public observation — that renders them unsuitable as scientific data. Methodological behaviorists do not necessarily deny the dualism of the physical and the mental. What they deny is that there can be a science of the mental. *Metaphysical* behaviorism is the view that there can be no science of mental events because mental events do not exist. Metaphysical behaviorists explicitly reject the dualism of introspective psychology in favor of a militant materialism. We will read the classical account of the subtlest version of this thesis, by the philosopher Carl Hempel (chapter 12). According to Hempel, a mentalistic claim like "John is angry" may be true; but such statements are merely abbreviations for much longer statements that are entirely about behavior. On this view, what we call mental events do exist, but they are merely behavioral events differently described.

Phenomenology, psychoanalysis, and behavioral psychology were the dominant theories of human nature through most of the twentieth century. However, there now exists a third-generation theoretical approach which goes by the name of *cognitive science*. Cognitive science in some ways represents a synthesis of its predecessors. From psychoanalysis, it inherits the emphasis on unconscious mental processes. Its preferred methodology, however, is the controlled experiment which was imported into psychology by the behaviorists. Finally, it shows some sympathy for the phenomenological practice of treating first-person reports of conscious experiences as data. An overview of cognitive science is given by Jerry Fodor (chapter 13). Fodor's article also discusses the shortcomings of Hempel's brand of behaviorism, which he calls "logical behaviorism".

If one tried to summarize cognitive science's most central tenet in a single sentence, it might be this: human mental activity can be precisely duplicated on a properly programmed computer. This proposition, if true, has enormously significant consequences for our understanding of human nature. One of these is that human mental activity must be compatible with materialism. Not surprisingly, the development of cognitive science is interwoven with that of the related field of artificial intelligence (AI) research. We will read a modern analysis of the relationship between psychology (cognitive-science style), philosophy, and AI research (chapter 14). Then comes an account of what has and has not been accomplished in AI (chapter 15).

The last two readings comprise a critique of contemporary cognitive science and AI. Searle's famous "Chinese room argument" is an attempt to refute the basic principle that human mentality can be captured in a computer program (chapter 16). The final article by Nagel suggests that the current cognitive science paradigm may be unable to deal with one particular aspect of mental life — conscious experience itself (chapter 17). Indeed, Nagel argues that it may be impossible to accommodate conscious experience in any theoretical framework that adheres to a materialist (or "physicalist") line. Which brings us back to Descartes . . .

1

NONEMPIRICAL ISSUES IN PSYCHOLOGY

André Kukla

University of Toronto

"You don't mean to say, Monsieur Poirot, that you would undertake to solve a case without moving from your chair, do you?"
"That is exactly what I do mean — granted the facts were placed before me. I regard myself as a consulting specialist."
(Christie, 1984, p. 106)

Empiricism is a doctrine that admits of degrees. At one end of the continuum stands Plato, who regarded all sensory experiences as impediments to the apprehension of reality. At the other end is Skinner, who considers logic to be a branch of the empirical science of behavior (Skinner, 1974, pp. 109-110). In comparison to most times and most places, the last few centuries in the English-speaking world have been marked by a relative extreme of the empiricist temper. But the pendulum has begun to swing the other way. Evidence of the decline of radical empiricism has been noted in virtually every academic discipline, from physics (Bohm, 1971) to jurisprudence and literary criticism (Michaels, 1980). Among philosophers of science, everyone now seems to agree that the role of empirical research in scientific progress was vastly overestimated by the logical positivists of the previous generation. In psychology, the postempiricist attitude is evident in the work of social psychological theorists like Gergen (1985) who emphasize the contractual nature of knowledge, in the rationalist theories of Chomsky (1968) and his followers, and in the largely a priori enterprise of artificial intelligence research. There are profound — perhaps irreconcilable — differences between these several research paradigms. But they have all contributed to the same change in the prevailing intellectual climate. Many of us are now

Kukla, A. May 1989. "Nonempirical Issues in Psychology" in *American Psychologist*, 44(5), pp. 785-794. © May 1989 by the American Psychological Association. Reprinted (or Adapted) with permission.

ready to concede that *scientific* work is a much broader category of activity than *empirical* work, that is, that there is plenty for an armchair psychologist to do.

My aim in this article is to present an updated job description for armchair psychologists, or as they less contentiously be called, theoretical psychologists. I will delineate several types of activities that share the following pair of characteristics: (a) they are indispensable for the advancement of psychological knowledge, and (b) they do not involve empirical research. Most of these activities have their counterparts in the other sciences as well. There are two reasons, however, for relating the discussion to psychology. First, I think that many of the ideas to be discussed will come as news, particularly to psychologists, because psychology has been the most aggressively empiricist of all academic disciplines. Second, I will argue for the exercise of nonempirical methods of research — far more so than, say, geology or bacteriology. The irony of the second point in light of the first poses an interesting historical problem that will only fleetingly be touched on here.

Some caveats before we begin: I have not taken great care to make my catalog of nonempirical issues exhaustive or exclusive. The idea of a catalog is merely an organizational device for allowing me to talk about various important aspects of an emergent theoretical tradition in psychology. I will discuss these issues roughly in order of their familiarity. The reader should not be greatly disappointed if we begin with nonempirical tasks whose nature and scope are already well-understood by the vast majority of psychologists. Before we reach the end, we will be discussing proposals that call for drastic revisions of received empiricist views.

THEORY CONSTRUCTION AND THE DERIVATION OF EMPIRICAL CONSEQUENCES

To begin with, there is the nonempirical activity of *theory construction*: Given a set of data, obtain a set of principles that *explains* the data in accordance with some notion of proper scientific explanation. To be sure, theories are or ought to be amenable to empirical test. But first we must have a theory to test. Data do not yield up theories of themselves, nor will theories emerge by adding more data to the lot. There is no alternative but to invent a theory. Furthermore, the claim that a particular invention is a viable candidate for empirical testing requires an *argument*. For example, if we adhere to a hypothetico-deductive model of scientific explanation, we need to show that the known fact can be deduced from the theory. none of this work requires us to break the contact between armchair and backside.

Establishing the criteria for a proper scientific explanation is also a nonempirical task. But I see this activity as belonging to the philosophy of science rather than to science itself. I do not think it is very important to draw clear boundaries between science and philosophy. But I do wish to make the point that given any plausible line of demarcation, there will be many significant nonempirical tasks that fall squarely within the province of science. The construction of theories to explain bodies of data is the first example of such a task.

A second example is *the derivation of new empirical consequences from existing theories*. The confirmation or disconfirmation of a new prediction is a matter for empirical research. But the process of *obtaining* the prediction to be tested is not itself an empirical activity. Until quite recently, psychological theories were usually so simple in structure that deriving consequences from them — as well as constructing them in the first place — was a fairly trivial activity. There were few *hidden* consequences of psychological theories, as compared, say, to theories of physics. This state of affairs led to a vast underestimation of the substantiality of theoretical issues in psychology. One symptom of this underestimation was the virtual nonexistence of theoretical psychology as an organized subdiscipline. Who needs a specialist to derive consequences from the Frustration-Aggression Hypothesis?

The situation is very different in physics, where a substantial proportion of scientists make theory construction and the derivation of consequences from existing theories their sole professional occupation. In physics, the derivation of a new theoretical consequence is routinely considered to be an important scientific development, even if nobody knows how to submit the consequence to empirical test. A recent example is the discovery that black holes are a consequence of general relativity theory. No one has as yet found any empirical confirmation of the existence of black holes. Yet their derivation is regarded as a scientific advance, *sans* supporting data, simply by virtue of its *being* a consequence of an important theory. Such a derivation may not provide additional support for the theory; but it enhances our *understanding* of the theory by exposing some of its unexpected ramifications.

Of course it might have been the case that the subject matter of psychology does not lend itself to nontrivial theoretical formulation. This depressing possibility has been effectively laid to rest by the advent of artificial intelligence (AI). The term "AI" has (at least) two distinct senses, which Searle (1980) called *weak* and *strong* AI. Until further notice, I will use "AI" to refer to the weak enterprise. (Weak) AI is essentially a style of theory construction and hypothesis derivation. The AI researcher begins with a mental capacity and tries to find a sequence of elementary computations that generates that capacity. Within the metatheoretical framework of computational psychology, the resultant program is treated as a *theory* of the capacity (Boden, 1977). The theory/program can then be used to derive predictions that could never have been obtained by "hand." There are only two respects in which AI research differs from traditional theoretical work in psychology. First, it makes use of special conceptual tools that take some effort to master, second, it sometimes arrives at nonobvious results.

The nonempirical character of AI research has been noted by Dennett (1978) and by Longuet-Higgins (1981). Newell and Simon (1981) have argued for the contrary claim that AI is an empirical science. Their arguments, however, are defective (Kukla, 1989). One of them is that AI research is empirical because it is not ordinarily known whether a program will do the job it was designed to do until one runs it and *sees*. But the need to run the program on a computer arises only because of our mental limitations. In principle, we could know exactly how any given program will perform simply by running it through in our heads. The only problem is that we get confused and run out of time. These problems, however, do not alter the nonempirical character of the AI enterprise. If there were no paper and no pencils, it might have been impossible to derive the existence of black holes from general relativity theory — or for that matter to construct the theory in the first place. But this does not mean that theoretical physics is an empirical activity in any significant sense. The reliance of AI on powerful computers to obtain its results does not differ in essence from the traditional dependence of the theoretical on the more primitive information process in devices of paper and pencil.[1] Longuet-Higgins (1981) concluded a similar analysis of AI with the following description of its status:

> It is perhaps time that the title "artificial intelligence" were replaced by something more modest and less provisional.... Might one suggest, with all due deference to the psychological community, that "theoretical psychology" is really the right heading under which to classify artificial intelligence studies of perception and cognition.... The task of the theoretician is to formulate hypotheses and to elicit their logical implications as carefully as he can, with due attention to matters of internal consistency and predictive power.... The time has come, it seems, when the task of theory construction is altogether too intricate to be consigned to spare moments away from the laboratory; it is at least as much of a discipline as good experimentation. (p. 200)

In sum, AI is armchair psychology made respectable again by the acquisition of the symbolic prerequisite of big-time science: expensive equipment. But computers are incidental to the AI enterprise. Their only function is to speed up deduction.

COHERENCE ANALYSIS

The armchair analysis of an existing theory does not always have to result in a new empirical consequence. We may undertake such an analysis in order to investigate the *logical coherence* of the theory. For example, we may try to discover whether the theory contains internal inconsistencies. If it can be shown that a theory T entails both a proposition P and it negation *not-P*, the T is falsified just as surely as if one of its consequences were shown to be false by empirical means. Analysis may also reveal formal weaknesses that fall short of outright inconsistency. A theory may be guilty of circularity, infinite regress, ambiguity, non sequitur, or nonindependence among its fundamental assumptions. These lesser theoretical errors do not necessarily show the principles of the theory to be false, but they do indicate the need for remedial work.

Laudan (1977) called this type of scientific task a *conceptual problem.*[2] According to Laudan, we can distinguish two types of conceptual problems. There are *internal conceptual problems*, which arise when a theory *T* exhibits internal inconsistencies (or circularities, etc.), and *external conceptual problems*, which arise "when *T* is inconsistent with another theory or doctrine, *T*, which proponents of *T* believe to be rationally well founded" Laudan, 1977, p. 49). The second theory, *T*, that is involved in an external conceptual problem may be a broader or more fundamental theory than *T*, as when *T* is criticized for violating a basic methodological tenet of science.

A psychological example of an internal conceptual problem is Hartmann's (1958) critique of the classical psychoanalytic account of the development of the ego. Essentially, Freud's position was that we begin to acquire knowledge about the world (i.e., develop an ego) because knowledge proves to be instrumental in gratifying our instinctive needs (Freud, 1926/1962). Hartmann argued that this account is incoherent, for we could never discover the instrumental value of knowledge unless we were engaged in the enterprise of acquiring knowledge *beforehand.* Therefore, both the capacity and the propensity to acquire knowledge (i.e., the possession of an ego) must be an innate endowment. It is superfluous to investigate Freud's hypothesis by empirical means, because this hypothesis can be proven false on logical grounds alone.

In contrast, consider Skinner's (1959) charge that psychoanalytic theory has no explanatory force. Here the inconsistency is not within the theory itself, but rather between the theory and the putative principles of scientific explanation. Hence Skinner's is an external conceptual critique. Another is Chomsky's (1959) charge that Skinnerian reinforcement theory has no explanatory force.

In principle, there can be any number of competing theories that survive the rigors of an analysis for coherence. It is up to empirical research to make a selection from among the survivors. But the preselective potential of coherence has not been fully exploited in the history of psychology — to say the least.

LOGICALLY NECESSARY TRUTHS

There are portions of every theory whose truth can be established by nonempirical means because they deal with logical necessities. The classic textbook example of a logically necessary truth is "Bachelors are unmarried." An example with a more psychological flavor is "The reinforcer of a response R does not terminate before the onset of R." Such *necessary propositions* are to be distinguished from *contingent propositions* like "The average bachelor weighs 160 lbs." Contingent propositions are true in some possible worlds and false in some possible worlds (Bradley & Swartz, 1979). Thus we must look at the actual world to see whether a particular contingency is satisfied therein. But necessary propositions are either true in all possible worlds or false in all possible worlds. Thus it is redundant to try to ascertain their truth value by observing the actual world. In cases where their truth or falsehood is not evident by inspection, the issue is settled by the a priori methods of proof and refutation.

There are two nonempirical tasks relating to necessary propositions. The first is to distinguish the logically necessary from the contingent components of a theory. The second is to discover brand-new necessary truths. Without the first activity, we may very well waste time and effort in useless empirical investigations of logical necessities. There is nothing to stop us from doing this. We *could* establish that bachelors are unmarried by doing a survey. The data would undoubtedly yield a gratifyingly high level of statistical significance. Smedslund (1984) has made the claim that *all* psychological generalizations are logical necessities, and hence that none of them are in need of empirical confirmation. No doubt Smedslund has overstated his case (Vollmer, 1984). But it is certainly true that *some* necessary propositions have been put forth in the guise of contingent claims about the world. For instance, consider the law of effect. If we employ Skinner's (1953) definition of positive reinforcement as any event that increases the probability of a preceding response, it is clear that the (weak) law of effect becomes a necessary truth. Meehl's (1950) famous discussion of the problem, in which he strove to disentangle the necessary from the contingent elements in the law of effect, is a paradigm of the first of our two types of nonempirical tasks relating to necessary propositions. A more contemporary issue of the same type concerns the question of whether human beings are rational. Kahneman and Tversky have presented voluminous evidence purporting to show that people routinely employ various irrational heuristics in judgment and decision making (e.g., Kahneman & Tversky, 1972; Tversky & Kahneman, 1973). According to Cohen (1981), however, the rationality of human judgment is a logically necessary truth — that is, there is a connection of meaning between the concept of rationality and actual human judgments. Cohen did not question the empirical validity of Kahneman and Tversky's data. The central issue is whether the several heuristics discovered by Kahneman and Tversky are actually irrational. Clearly, this issue cannot be settled by further empirical research. What it calls for is a deeper analysis of the concept of rationality.

The second nonempirical task relating to necessary propositions is the discovery of new ones. We do not differentiate the necessary from the contingent merely to consign the former to oblivion. The discovery of necessary truths by a priori analysis is important for at least two reasons. To begin with, necessary truth is after all a species of truth and is thus worth knowing for its own sake. The discovery of a new necessary truth represents an increment of knowledge just as surely as the discovery of a new contingent fact. Here again, the simplicity of most historical psychological theories may lead to the erroneous impression that necessary truths are always trivial and uninsightful, like "Bachelors are unmarried." But this view is clearly untenable when applied to necessary propositions generally. After all, logic and mathematics are as difficult and as full of surprises as any field; yet logical and mathematical propositions are paradigmatically necessary. I will discuss some instances of nonobvious necessities in psychology later in this section.

The second reason for trying to discover necessary truths may strike a more sympathetic chord in an empiricist's heart. The reason is that there are issues of *contingent fact* that can only be resolved by a priori research into the truth and falsehood of necessary propositions. I will give a contrived example of what I mean, followed by a real example drawn from certain contemporary research problems. First consider the following proposition: Fermat's mathematical intuitions were never wrong. Let us call this proposition *F*. *F* makes a certain claim about the history of Fermat's mental processes. This claim is undeniably contingent: Maybe Fermat never made a mistake, but maybe he did. Now let us suppose that we are already in possession of all the empirical data that are relevant to the truth or falsehood of *F*. Depending on how these data come out, it may very well be the case that we still will not know whether *F* is true until we discover whether Fermat's Last Theorem is provable. But the only way to find out whether Fermat's Last Theorem is provable is to try to prove it. In this case, the only way to establish the truth of a contingent proposition is to prove a necessary one. There is nothing about this situation that creates any new problems for an empiricist theory of knowledge. It is not as though the truth of a contingent proposition were being established without recourse to *any* empirical data. It is just that in this hypothetical case the relevant data are already in, but we are still stuck on a difficulty in reasoning from the data to the desired conclusion. It is important to keep in mind that such a situation may arise — that the obstacle keeping us from acquiring a piece of *contingent* knowledge about the world may be removable only by a priori analysis.

A realistic example of the same situation is provided by the enterprise of *strong* AI. Strong AI is an attempt to substantiate what Newell and Simon (1981) called the Physical Symbol System Hypothesis — the hypothesis that purely physical systems are capable of every sort of human intelligence. Strong AI proceeds, just like weak AI, by constructing programs that can perform various intelligence tasks. The new twist is that the discovery of such a program is interpreted as evidence in favor of the Physical Symbol System Hypothesis. The idea is that if we can get a computer to do something, then we know for sure that a purely physical system can do it; and if we can get a computer to do anything, then the Physical Symbol System Hypothesis must be true. Now the Physical Symbol System Hypothesis is clearly a contingent proposition. Nevertheless, researchers in the area of strong AI are no more engaged in empirical research than their colleagues working in weak AI. Their work is a sustained attempt to establish the truth-value of propositions like the following: There exists a program that can alphabetize lists of names; there exists a program that can write summaries of longer texts; and so on. But these propositions are not themselves contingent. The claim that there is a program that can perform in a predetermined manner is either *necessarily* true or *necessarily* false, and the actual construction of the program is an a priori proof of the corresponding existence claim. Such claims are in fact the examples of nonobvious necessities in psychology that were promised earlier on. In sum, it is true that strong AI researchers are interested in a contingent hypothesis. But this interest is not attended to by any sort of empirical work. Strong AI research is nonempirical despite its bearing on the Physical Symbol System Hypothesis, just as a person who tries to prove Fermat's Last Theorem is doing mathematics even though the result of his or her work might bear on the psychohistorical hypothesis that Fermat never made mistakes.

Before leaving the topic of necessary truths, some mention must be made of the fact that the necessary-contingent distinction has come in for some philosophical criticism. The seminal work here is Quine's (1953). One consequence of Quine's semantic theory is that *any* belief might be abandoned on the basis of observational evidence. Even the laws of logic and supposedly defintional truths like "Bachelors are unmarried" are not exempt. If Quine's view is right, then certain traditional ideas about the nature and status of a priori scientific work stand in need of revisions. But this revision would not affect the relative *importance* of a priori work. Quine's view amounts to the assertion that necessity and contingency form a continuum rather than a dichotomy. Both empirical observation and a priori argument continue to be appropriate methods for settling scientific disputes. In the traditional view, the empirical investigator and the a priori analyst divide up the class of propositions between them, the former dealing with contingencies and the latter with logical necessities. In the Quinean view, the empirical researcher and the analyst both take upon themselves the privilege of addressing any and every question of truth by their respective methods. However, as we approach the "necessary" end of the continuum, changes of belief by empirical means require increasing global disconfirmations of our expectations about the world, and as we approach the "contingent" end, changes of belief by a priori argument require increasingly global a priori adjustments throughout our belief system. Nevertheless, "any statements can be held true come what may, if we make drastic enough adjustments elsewhere in the system" (Quine, 1953, p. 43). Evidently, this view leads to a reconstruction of what is accomplished by a priori analysis (as well as by empirical research), but it does not entail any decrement in its scope. Finally, it should be noted that Quine's theory has by no means obtained universal assent among linguists and philosophers of science. See Chomsky (1969) and Searle (1987) for particularly vigorous critiques.

CONCEPTUAL INNOVATION

Still another type of nonempirical task is *the construction of new conceptual schemes*. This activity is usually run together with theory construction. But one may construct a new theory out of old concepts, and one may also construct new concepts without promulgating a new theory about them.

A contrived example will once again help to make my point. Suppose no one had ever thought to classify matter into solids, liquids, and gases. Suppose now that somebody came along who made these distinctions. One would have to consider this move a scientific advance. After all, many important scientific laws are applicable only to one of these categories of matter and so presumably could not be formulated until the appropriate category system was in place. However, the proposer of the solid-liquid-gas conceptual scheme need not have made any new empirical discoveries, nor even any substantial empirical claims. Indeed, the proposer need not have said anything that could be construed as true or false because concepts per se are neither true nor false (is "dog" true or false?). It makes no sense to ask for empirical confirmation of new conceptual schemes. Their construction is a nonempirical activity.

It might be objected that the proposal of a new conceptual scheme commits the proposer at least to the empirical claim that there *exist* phenomena that fall under the posited concepts. But this is simply not the case. The set of all unicorns is presumably empty, but this fact foes not invalidate the concept of a unicorn (whatever it might mean to invalidate a concept). Indeed the term "unicorn" plays a crucial role in expressing a zoological fact that was established only after centuries of field research, namely, that there are no unicorns. The unfounded view that scientific concepts must be nonempty is a special case of the more general idea that the theoretical importance of a concept is a function of it numerosity. This idea might appropriately be called the *factor analysis fallacy*, after its most infamous perpetrator. In fact, the discovery that a particular category has no members can have enormous theoretical significance. Suppose for example, that after the periodic table of the elements had been erected, it had been fond that there were no elements in nature with prime atomic numbers. Without a doubt, physical theorists would have immediately become preoccupied with the task of accounting for these gaps in the periodic table. Less fancifully, consider the current interest in the question of whether cognitive functions are "modular" (Fodor, 1983). Certainly, the concept of a cognitive module was invented and refined because it was thought that many cognitive functions would turn out to be modular. But if continued research were to persuade us that cognitive functions are *never* modular, it will still not have been a waste of time to devise the concept of a module. The concept will still have been a vehicle for the discovery of an important and nonobvious fact about cognitive architecture, namely that it is nonmodular. Indeed, Fodor devoted a large part of his book on the subject to developing the thesis that central processes like reasoning and belief fixation are nonmodular.

It is true that new conceptual schemes are generally presented in conjunction with new substantive theories. It often happens, however, that the theory comes to be repudiated while the conceptual innovation lives on. The most famous case in the history of science is probably Copernicus's heliocentric theory. The conceptual component of the Copernican revolution was a switch to describing the motions of the heavenly bodies relative to the sun as opposed to the earth.[3] Like all conceptual proposals, there is no question of truth or falsehood involved in this move. It is not a mistake to describe planetary motions relative to the earth, or to Venus, or to any other body. The *empirical* component of Copernicanism was the assertion that, in terms of the new conceptual scheme, the planetary orbits are circular. This empirical thesis was false. In fact, the geocentric scheme of Ptolemy, according to which the planets revolve about the earth in epicycles, provided about as good a fit with observational data as the Copernican system (Kuhn, 1970, p. 156). Nevertheless, the work of Copernicus is rightly considered to be an enormously important scientific advance. The advance, however, was *conceptual*, not empirical. Copernicus introduced a manner of talking about planetary motion that made Kepler's theory of elliptical orbits and the subsequent Newtonian synthesis feasible. *Empirically*, Ptolemaic astronomy was as close to the truth as Copernican astronomy. But its conceptual scheme was less fruitful. The correct description of planetary motion relative to the earth is so complex that not even Newton could have extracted the Law of Universal Gravity from it.

It is arguable that Freud's contribution plays the same role in psychology as Copernicus's in the physical sciences. Even if all of Freud's empirical claims turn out to be false, his place in the history of psychology is secure on the basis of his conceptual innovations alone. Foremost among these, of course, is the concept of unconscious mental processes, without which contemporary cognitive psychology would go out of business. Freud (1917/1973a) himself was quite aware of the conceptual side of his work and of the importance of conceptual innovation generally. He described his major contribution as a move "to extend the concept of 'psychical'" (p. 363); and in discussing his "conception of...the basic instincts of mental life", he wrote:

> I have a particular reason for using the word "conception" here. These are the most difficult problems that are set to us, but their difficulty does not lie in any insufficiency of observations; what present us with these riddles are actually the commonest and most familiar of phenomena. Nor does the difficulty lie in the recondite nature of the speculations to which they give rise; speculative consideration plays little part in this sphere. But it is truly a matter of conceptions — that is to say, of introducing the right abstract ideas, whose application to the raw material of observation will produce order and clarity in it. (Freud, 1933/1973b, p. 113)

These remarks put into perspective the accusations of unfalsifiability that have been leveled against psychoanalytic theory from its earliest days. To the extent that the psychoanalytic contribution is conceptual — and it is at least partly that on Freud's own account — there is no question of falsifying or verifying it.

The examples of Copernicus's and Freud's work show that even after the contingent hypotheses of new theories are completely repudiated, the conceptual schemes devised to *express* these hypotheses may live on. It is a small step from here to the realization that one may legitimately offer a new conceptual scheme to the scientific world without putting forward any new hypotheses in the first place. One may propose a manner of conceptualizing phenomena in which certain new and interesting theoretical options can be delineated without necessarily having to take sides with respect to these options. In such a case, the reflex request to "see the data" is clearly misplaced. Conceptual proposals may be *suggested* by certain observations, but their scientific value does not always depend on the data's coming out any particular way. Mendeleev's periodic table and Linnaeus's biological taxonomies are examples of conceptual proposals that were relatively unencumbered by new empirical commitments. Yet both of them proved to be indispensable for the later development of important scientific theories.

The invention of "solid," "liquid," and "gas" is a particularly feeble type of conceptual innovation. Given any statement about solids, liquids, or gases, there exists an equivalent but longer statement in our old, unenriched vocabulary; that is, these concepts are *reducible* to the more fundamental concepts of volume, shape, and time. But there can also be new concepts that are *not* reducible to the old conceptual scheme. If Davidson (1970), Fodor (1974), and other token identity theorists are correct, the introduction of mentalistic concepts into a previously physicalistic language would constitute such an innovation. And if Kuhn (1970) and Feyerabend (1978) are correct, then *most* new scientific concepts are not reducible to their predecessors. Regardless of the fate of these particular examples, it is incontrovertible that there exist *some* concepts that cannot be reduced to *some* other concepts, and therefore that radical conceptual innovation is possible.[4] I will discuss only one of a number of interesting consequences that follow from the possibility of such a radical conceptual change. Suppose that a branch of science is complete in the sense that (a) we know the truth values of all the propositions that can be expressed in its conceptual scheme, and (b) we have a theory that provides a perfect explanation for all the true propositions. In this situation, it would appear that there is nothing more to be done — the enterprise is finished. In fact, however, it is still possible for someone to contrive a new way of conceptualizing the phenomena of the science that proves to be irreducible to the old conceptual scheme. The result would be that the apparently completed enterprise would be thrown open again, for we would now be able to express new hypotheses that have no equivalent formulation in the old scheme. In this case, conceptual innovation would create new questions for research where there were no questions before.

In addition to creating new hypotheses, there is a sense in which conceptual innovation can provide us with contingent information about the world without our having to do any new empirical research. Consider once again the effect of introducing the concepts, "solid," "liquid," and "gas" into our language describing the physical world. As soon as this conceptual innovation is made, we can begin to recite a long list of brand-new contingent facts without rising from our armchair. Water is liquid, pencils are solid, and so on. It would be absurd to submit these "hypotheses" to empirical tests — to stick a pencil in a cup and note whether it maintains its shape. Of course, we rely here on *prior* observation: We have seen what happens to pencils in cups many times before. Perhaps it can be said that we "implicitly" knew that pencils are solid, but that our old conceptual scheme failed to call our attention to this implicit knowledge. Be that as it may, we have an increment in the *explicitly represented data base of science* as a result of a purely conceptual proposal. The situation is even more striking in the case of new concepts that are irreducible to the old scheme. Here we previously lacked the *expressive power* to formulate our implicit knowledge; hence there was no possibility whatever of that knowledge entering into our data base. In this manner, a judiciously wrought taxonomy of cognitive structures or psychological traits could throw a large amount of contingent psychological information into our laps *prior* to any further empirical research. This is not the first time we have encountered the possibility of enlarging our contingent knowledge by nonempirical operations. In the previous section we saw that a contingent claim like Newell and Simon's Physical Symbol System Hypothesis might be established by proving necessary truths. In both cases, the manner in which the increment in contingent knowledge takes place does not pose any fundamental difficulties for an empiricist theory of knowledge. But it does give us some idea of the potential fruitfulness of nonempirical methods in furthering the aims of science.

THE CONTINGENT A PRIORI

This article began with the observation that empiricism comes in various degrees. There is, however, a natural place to draw the line between empiricists and rationalists. This dividing point was located by Kant (1781/1929) in terms of a pair of distinctions of which we have already made frequent use. First, there are *necessary* as opposed to *contingent* propositions. The former are either true in all possible worlds or false in all possible worlds, whereas the latter are true in some possible worlds and false in some possible worlds.[5] Second, there is *empirical* knowledge (Kant called it "a posteriori" knowledge), which requires observation or experiment for its justification, as opposed to *a priori* knowledge, which does *not* require observation or experiment for its justification. *Empiricism* may be identified as the view that only necessary propositions can be known a priori; *rationalism* is the view that there is some contingent a priori knowledge. These definitions give a more precise sense to the previous claim that nothing in my analysis so far has given us cause to abandon an empiricist theory of knowledge.

If rationalism were to be true, then of course a priori analysis would play an even more important role in science than has been demonstrated so far. I think that rationalism is true. I will argue that there are viable candidates for contingent a priori status. Indeed, there is a type of contingent a priori introduced by Kripke (1972), the existence of which is widely acknowledged in contemporary philosophical circles. Kripke's candidate is a technical and almost incidental consequence of his formal work in modal logic. Certainly, it does not pose a significant challenge to the empiricist's world view (Evans, 1979). Nevertheless, it forces us to recognize that there are hidden complexities in the relation between the contingent and the a priori.

The type of contingent a priori that *does* challenge the empiricist's world view is related to what Kuhn (1970) called a "paradigm" and what Lakatos (1978) called the "hard core" of a research program. According to both Kuhn and Lakatos, scientific theories inevitably contain some propositions that are too basic to be submitted to empirical test, even though these propositions are not logically necessary truths. The need for such presuppositions was seen by Kant, who argued that a presuppositionless stance leads inexorably to absolute skepticism about all knowledge claims. Granted that one has to begin with empirically unfounded presuppositions, it might be hoped that these assumptions are only provisional on the outcome of empirical research; that is, every scientific belief is either verifiable or falsifiable in the long run. Kuhn and Lakatos presented a number of compelling reasons for rejecting this point of view. I will discuss only one of these reasons here.

One can suppose that run-of-the-mill scientific hypothesis may be overturned by the weight of accumulated evidence But it is incoherent to suppose that *the rules whereby hypotheses are overturned* can themselves be overturned. The attempt to submit methodological principles to empirical test must inevitably involve the logical fallacy of begging the question (Kuhn, 1977). Yet methodological principles entail contingent claims about the world: They tell us how we must proceed in order to arrive at the facts in this actual world. The most famous argument to the effect that a methodological rule is beyond the reach of empirical verification or falsification is undoubtedly Hume's (1739/1964) disquisition on the "Principle of the Uniformity of Nature," which is referred to nowadays as the principle of induction. In its simplest form, this principle asserts that the observation of past regularities gives us grounds for predicting that the same regularities will recur in the future. An assumption of this type is involved whenever a researcher generalizes from a set of particular experimental results. The principle of uniformity makes a contingent claim about the world because for any observed regularity there is a possible world where that regularity ceases to obtain as of today. Nevertheless, Hume argued, it is impossible to offer empirical evidence in support of the principle of uniformity without lapsing into circularity. For example, it will not help to point to the past successes of inductive reasoning, because these past successes give us no indication that success will continue to be forthcoming unless we *assume* the validity of the principle of uniformity in the first place.

Empiricists might object that if a presupposition is unverifiable and unfalsifiable, then it should not count as an instance of contingent a priori *knowledge*, because we actually have no basis for asserting that it is true. Let us conceded the point and refer to such presuppositions as contingent a priori *beliefs*. The important point is that we *must* adopt some contingent beliefs on a priori grounds if we are to engage in anything like a scientific enterprise. This argument does not logically force empiricists to give up their point of view. They have a choice: Either give up empiricism, or give up science.

The principle of uniformity is an example of a presupposition that underlies all or most scientific theories. There are also more specific presuppositions that constitute the "hard core" of specific research traditions. As an example from psychology, consider the disagreement between behaviorists and phenomenologists over the status of introspective reports (Kukla, 1983). According to the former, a subject S's report of n experience E yields the observational datum "S *reported* that he or she had experience E" (Brody & Oppenheim, 1966). According to phenomenologists, the same event yields the datum "S *experienced* E" (Kohler, 1947). This disagreement cannot be settled by performing another experiment, because both parties to the dispute would systematically interpret the results of any experiment in accordance with their own methodological precepts. As Kuhn (1970) put it, "each paradigm will be shown to satisfy more or less the criteria that it dictates for itself and to fall short of a few of those dictated by its opponents" (pp. 109-110).[6]

Another Kantian insight is that scientific presuppositions are rarely, if ever, explicitly laid out at the beginning of a scientific enterprise. One has to work backward from what scientists actually say and do to the system of presuppositions that seems to warrant these practices. Kant referred to this procedure as *transcendental deduction*. The major difference between the Kantian and the Kuhn-Lakatos treatment of scientific presuppositions is that Kant believed that there exists a unique set of presuppositions underlying all possible scientific theories. Kuhn and Lakatos, however, have persuasively argued that disagreements at the presuppositional level are ubiquitous in the history of science. These two claims are not incompatible: From a Kuhnian perspective, Kant's universal contingent a priori principles may be features of a superordinate paradigm that is shard by every scientific theory. In any case, another task for the theoretical psychologist is to transcendentally deduce the specific ("Kuhnian") presuppositions underlying current psychological theories. A noteworthy example of this sort of work is Fodor's (1975, 1980) elucidation of the "computational" theory of mind, which is presupposed by most contemporary research in cognitive psychology. Fodor's (1975) name for this activity is "speculative psychology" (p. vii). Formally, the practice of speculative psychology is similar to the task of formulating first-order theories to account for bodies of data. Here, however, the first-order theories themselves play the role of the "data" to be accounted for by a more fundamental second-order theory. More precisely, a second-order theory of speculative psychology accounts for the *range* of first-order theories that are considered to be viable candidates on a priori grounds.

How does one evaluate the claims of competing second-order theories? Not very easily. There is always the test of logical coherence. This is the level at which adherents to different paradigms usually argue with one another, each one maintaining that the other's position is internally inconsistent, or that it is inconsistent with the broader presuppositions of science as a whole. Of course, there is no guarantee that only a single system of presuppositions will pass the test of coherence. The question of whether there is a rational basis for choosing between two coherent paradigms has been the most heatedly debated issue in the philosophy of science of the past generation, with Kuhn (1970, 1977) and Feyerabend (1978) taking the irrationalist side against Lakatos (1978) and Laudan (1977, 1984). From a Kuhnian perspective, empirical work undertaken within, say, the computational paradigm leads only to more refined computational theories, just as stimulus-response (S-R) research leads only to more refined S-R theories. The differences *between* S-R theory and computational theory are too fundamental to be settled by empirical means. This is what it means to say that they are different paradigms. Even Laudan, who is most sanguine about the empirical resolution of paradigmatic differences, views the relation between second-order theories and data to be very indirect. Finally, it must be noted that the problem of how to choose between coherent paradigms is purely hypothetical in psychology. Discounting a few degenerate positions such as absolute skepticism, it has proven to be enormously difficult to construct *any* a priori framework for psychology that is free of major conceptual difficulties.

THE PRAGMATIC A PRIORI

If theoretical psychologists have the job of discovering the presuppositions of psychological theories, whose task is it to discover the more general "Kantian" presuppositions underlying the whole of science? It would seem natural to assign this task to the philosophers. What is interesting for a psychologist, however, is that these a priori constraints on all scientific theories are largely cognitive and social in nature. At lease on the face of it, there are all sorts of exotic physical environments in which we could conduct the business of science more or less as usual. Indeed, it is not clear that there even needs to be a physical world for science to exist, for disembodied spirits might be able to do a kind of scientific research. But there could not be anything like science unless there exist beings who possess a certain type of *mental equipment* and *social organization*. Thus, the proposition that people do in fact possess that type of mental equipment and social organization must be presupposed by any scientific theory whatever. At the same time, this proposition belongs squarely to the science of psychology (and to sociology, though I will not pursue this line of inquiry here). For reasons that are not worthy of the lengthy justification they would require, I have come to call this category of contingent a priori the *pragmatic a priori*.

Pragmatic a priori beliefs do not play the same role in psychology as the presuppositions of particular psychological theories. There is a sense in which we are free to reject the presuppositions of any particular theory and search for alternatives, but the pragmatic a priori imposes constraints that must be adhered to by all conceivable theories in psychology. The presuppositions of particular theories can neither be confirmed nor disconfirmed by experiment. The relation between empirical research and the pragmatic a priori is more peculiar. If we were to submit a pragmatic a priori proposition to empirical test, we would not have to wait for the outcome of the experiment, because *the truth of the hypothesis would follow logically from the fact that it was being tested*. In sum, the presuppositions of particular theories are *optional*, whereas pragmatic a priori propositions are *mandatory* — given, of course, that we are doing science.

The most fundamental — and most famous — pragmatic a priori proposition is the conclusion of Descartes's (1641/1968) *cogito* argument. Descartes established the contingent psychological fact *that there are mental processes* on the grounds that it is a logical consequence of his being embarked on a project of assessing the justifiability of various beliefs. However this project may turn out in detail, the very fact that it is begun already warrants the conclusion that mental processes exist. Indeed, it is a pragmatic a priori truth that mental processes of a very high order of intelligence exist; this is half the joke behind the name of Lilly Tomlin's stage play, *The Search for Intelligent Life in the Universe*.

How much can psychology hope to establish via the pragmatic a priori route? This is a largely unexplored question. Perhaps we can get nothing more out of this kind of analysis than a few obvious existential generalizations, but it is also prima facie possible that a fairly detailed picture of our mental (and social) life can be deduced from the very existence of the scientific enterprise. Consider, for example, the various theories of cognitive consistency that assert that belief systems follow some dynamic rules for eliminating overt inconsistencies (e.g., Feestinger, 1957; Heider, 1958). These theories have generated an enormous amount of empirical research. But a close analysis may show that it is incoherent to suppose that empirical research might *disconfirm* the basic postulate of consistency theory because the concept of disconfirmation has meaning only in relation to consistent systems. Theories of cognitive consistency are contingent theories; nevertheless, some of the empirical research they have inspired may be just as redundant as research into logically necessary truths.

In AI terms, the investigation of pragmatic a priori truths is more or less equivalent to the project of building an artificial scientist. What types of structures and processes are presupposed by the capacity to gather data, formulate explanatory theories, submit these theories to empirical test, and revise them in the light of new results? Like all matters relating to AI, this issue calls for analysis rather than empirical research. Whatever the results of this analysis may be, however, we can be sure of the contingent truth that these structures and processes are realized in *us* — because we too are capable of gathering data, formulating theories, and so on. To be sure, there may be more than one way to build an artificial scientist, in which case the question of whether we are built like artificial scientist *A* or artificial scientist *B* can only be settled by empirical research. This possibility dictates a slight elaboration of the previous claim. Let S_1, S_2 . . ., S_n represent all the (as yet undiscovered) systems that are capable of behaving like scientists. Then the disjunctive statement "*We* are either an S_1 or an S_2 . . . or an S_n" is a pragmatic a priori truth of psychology. The amount of detail about our mental apparatus that is supplied by this disjunction depends on the heterogeneity of the set $S = (S_1, S_2, . . ., S_n)$. This set might of course be infinite; it might even fail to be recursively enumerable. But seeing as the number of systems currently known to belong to S is zero, it seems premature to worry that S might be too large. At present, *nobody knows* how much of cognitive psychology can be derived from a purely a priori analysis of science.

FINAL POINTS

The foregoing discussion has touched on a number of unresolved controversies in the philosophy of science and the philosophy of language. The issues involved are difficult, and my treatment of them has been less that definitive. However, I think that at least one point has been established beyond reasonable doubt: It is inappropriate to pass a global judgment on the status of armchair psychology as a whole. Each of the nonempirical tasks discussed earlier has a different logical character and a different relation to empirical work. One might wish to question the validity or importance of these tasks one at a time. But there is no chance that any single empiricist argument will dispose of the lot.

I will close with a few words about the relative importance of theoretical analysis as compared to empirical research in psychology. The range of opinions on this issue among contemporary psychologists is as vast as the gulf between Plato and Skinner. On the one side, we have the view expressed by Christensen-Szalanki and Beach (1983) that journals should not publish commentaries on articles "because they seldom contain new data" (p. 1400). According to these authors,

> Criticism and proposal of alternative interpretations of results can be valuable, but without supporting evidence, the matter often boils down to being merely a difference of opinion.... It seems to us that psychologists should spend more time collecting data and testing hypotheses and less time advocating their favorite opinions. (pp. 1400-1401)

There is a perverse pleasure in encountering one's straw person in the real world. Evidently, Christensen-Szalanki and Beach believe that the only discernible scientific activity besides "collecting data" is giving vent to unfounded "opinions." The diametrically opposite view that psychology presently has *no need whatever* for new data is at least initially more plausible. Not surprisingly, this sentiment is often expressed in AI circles. Boden (1977) put it this way:

> For many [AI researchers] ... visual, reasoning or language-understanding programs ... quite clearly cannot do many things which people can do; no further experimentation is needed to show this. Such experiments will only be needed when the programs concerned are powerful enough to give a close approximation to human behavior, so close as to make discriminatory experimental tests appropriate. (p. 37)

If we substitute *theories* for *programs* and *explain* for *do* in this passage, we get a general call for a hiatus in empirical research. I think that this argument is inconclusive. Theoretical progress often requires that we resolve *particular* matters of fact, even though we are surrounded on all sides by facts that are beyond the purview of our current theories. This history of science would be incomprehensible if this were not so, for humanity has always possessed empirical information that systematic science could not yet explain. Nevertheless, the need to investigate novel matters of fact arises only when we already have a well-articulated theory in place that focuses attention on selective details. This is why, despite the exhortations of Christensen-Szalanki and Beach, we should resist the temptation to publish our laundry bills and grocery lists. When theory does not play a selective role, our data-gathering activities belong to the realm of journalism rather than science. Psychology has committed more than its share of journalism over the years. But there is cause for optimism about the future.

NOTES

[1] See Teller (1980) and Detlefsen and Luker (1980) for closely related critiques of Tymoczko's (1979) argument that computer proofs of mathematical theorems have changed mathematics into an empirical science.

² Laudan distinguished conceptual problems from *empirical problems*, by which he meant the task of constructing theories to account for bodies of empirical data. One would have thought that an "empirical problem" is the problem of submitting theoretical claims to empirical test. But Laudan forgot to mention this task in his informal taxonomy of scientific problems. Such is the rationalistic temper of the contemporary philosophy of science!

³ This is a drastically oversimplified description of Copernicus's conceptual innovation. Kuhn (1970, pp. 149-150) pointed out that Copernicus also changed the definition of "earth."

⁴ Fodor (1975) has argued that one could not acquire such a radically new concept from experience; that is, that all irreducible concepts must be innately represented in the internal code of "mentalese." But there is nothing in Fodor's argument that rules out the possibility of introducing a brand-new irreducible concept into *English*. The corresponding representation in mentalese might never have been given a public label before.

⁵ The distinction between necessary and contingent propositions in terms of possible-world semantics is a modernized version of the Kantian distinction between "analytic" and "synthetic" propositions (Bradley & Swartz, 1979).

⁶ Laudan (1984) argued, *contra* Kuhn, that methodological disagreements can *sometimes* be resolved by empirical means, but he did not attempt to maintain that such disagreements can *always* be settled empirically — even in principle.

REFERENCES

Boden, M. (1977). *Artificial intelligence and natural man*. New York: Harvester Press.

Bohm, D. (1971). Quantum theory as an indication of a new order in physics. Part A: The development of new orders as shown through the history of physics. *Foundations of Physics, 1*, 359-381.

Bradley, R. & Swartz, N. (1979). *Possible worlds: An introduction to logic and its philosophy*. Indianapolis, IN: Hackett.

Brody, N. & Oppenheim, P. (1966) Tension in psychology between the methods of behaviorism and phenomenology. *Psychological Review, 73*, 295–305.

Chomsky, N. (1959). Review of Skinner's "Verbal behavior." *Language, 35*, 26–58.

Chomsky, N. (1968). *Language and mind*. New York: Harcourt Brace Jovanovich.

Chomsky, N. (1969). Some empirical assumptions in modern philosophy of language. In S. Morgenbesser, P. Suppes, & M. White (Eds.), *Philosophy, science and method: Essays in honor of Ernest Nagel* (pp. 260–285). New York: St. Martin's Press.

Christensen-Szalanki, J. J. J., & Beach, L. R. (1983). Publishing opinions: A note on the usefulness of commentaries. *American Psychologist, 38*, 1400–1401.

Christie, A. (1984). *Hercule Poirot's casebook*. New York: Dodd Mead.

Cohen, L. J. (1981). Can human irrationality be experimentally demonstrated? *The Behavioral and Brain Sciences, 4*, 317–331.

Davidson, D. (1970). Mental events. In L Forster & J. W. Swanson (Eds.), *Experience and theory* (pp. 79–101). Amherst, MA: University of Massachusetts Press.

Dennett, D. (1978). *Brainstorms: Philosophical essays on mind and psychology*. Montgomery, VT: Bradford.

Descartes, R. (1968) Meditations. In E. Haldane & G. Ross (Eds.), *The philosophical works of Descartes*. Cambridge, England: Cambridge University Press. (Original work published 1641)

Detlefsen, M. & Luker, M. (1980). The four color map theorem and mathematical proof. *Journal of Philosophy, 77*, 803–820.

Evans, G. (1979). Reference and contingency. *Monist, 62*, 161–189.

Festinger, L. (1957). *A theory of cognitive dissonance*. Stanford, CA: Stanford University Press.

Feyerabend, P. (1978). *Against method*. London: Verso.

Fodor, J.A. (1974). Special sciences (or: The disunity of science as a working hypothesis). *Synthesis, 28*, 97-115.

Fodor, J. A. (1975). *The language of thought*. Cambridge, MA: Harvard University Press.

Fodor, J. A. (1980). Methodological solipsism considered as a research strategy in cognitive psychology. *The Behavioral and Brain Sciences, 3*, 63–73.

Fodor, J. A. (1983). *The modularity of mind*. Cambridge, MA: MIT Press.

Freud, S. (1962) The question of lay-analysis. In J. Strachey (Ed.), *Sigmund Freud: Two short accounts of psycho-analysis* (pp. 91–70).

Freud, S. (1973a). *Introductory lectures on psychoanalysis*. Middlesex, England: Penguin Books. (Original work published 1917)

Freud, S. (1973b). *New introductory lectures on psychoanalysis*. Middlesex, England: Penguin Books. (Original work published 1933)

Gergen, K. J. (1985). The social constructionist movement in modern psychology. *American Psychologist, 40*, 266–275.

Hartmann, H. (1958). *Ego psychology and the problem of adaptation*. New Tork: International Universities Press.

Heider, F. (1958). *The psychology of interpersonal relations*. New York: Wiley.

Hume, D. (1964). *A treatise on human nature*. Oxford, England: Clarendon Press. (Original work published 1739)

Kahneman, D., & Tversky, A. (1972) Subjective probability: A judgment of representativeness. *Cognitive Psychology, 3*, 430–454.

Kant, I. (1929). *Critique of pure reason*. London: Macmillan. (Original work published 1781)

Kohler, W. (1947). *Gestalt psychology: An introduction to new concepts in modern psychology*. New York: Livewright.

Kripke, S. A. (1972). *Naming and necessity*. Cambridge, MA: Harvard University Press.

Kuhn, T. S. (1970). *The structure of scientific revolutions* (2nd ed.). Chicago: University of Chicago Press.

Kuhn, T. S. (1977). *The essential tension*. Chicago: University of Chicago Press.

Kukla, A. (1983). Toward a science of experience. *Journal of Mind and Behavior, 4*, 231–246.

Kukla, A. (1989). Is AI an empirical science? *Analysis, 49*, 56–60.

Lakatos, I. (1978). *The methodology of scientific research programmes*. Cambridge, England: Cambridge University Press.

Laudan, L. (1977). *Progress and its problems*. Berkeley: University of California Press.

Laudan, L. (1984). *Science and values*. Berkeley: University of California Press.

Longuet-Higgins, H. C. (1981). Artificial intelligence — a new theoretical psychology? *Cognition, 10*, 197–200.

Meehl, P. E. (1950). On the circularity of the law of effect. *Psychological Bulletin, 47*, 52–75.

Michaels, W. B. (1980). Against formalism: Chickens and rocks. In L. Michaels & C. Ricks (Eds.), *The state of the language* (pp. 410–420). Berkeley: University of California Press.

Nevell, A., & Simon, H. A. (1981). Computer science as empirical inquiry: Symbols and search. In J. Haugeland (Ed.), *Mind design: Philosophy, psychology, artificial intelligence* (pp. 35–66). Cambridge, MA: MIT Press.

Quine, W. V. O. (1953). Two dogmas of empiricism. In W. V. O. Quine (Ed.), *From a logical point of view* (pp. 20–46). Cambridge, MA: Harvard University Press.

Searle, J. R. (1980). Minds, brains and programs. *The Behavioral and Brain Sciences, 3*, 417–424.

Searle, J. R. (1987). Indeterminacy, empiricism, and the first person. *Journal of Philosophy, 84*, 123–146.

Skinner, B. F. (1953). *Science and human behavior*. New York: Macmillan.

Skinner, B. F. (1959). A critique of psychoanalytic concepts and theories. In B. F. Skinner (Ed.), *Cumulative record* (pp. 185–194). New York: Appleton-Century-Crofts.

Skinner, B. F. (1974). *About behaviorism*. New York: Knopf.

Smedslund, J. (1984). What is necessarily true in psychology? In J. R. Royce & L. P. Mos (Eds.), *Annals of theoretical psychology* (Vol. 2, pp. 241–272). New York: Plenum Press.

Teller, P. (1980). Computer proof. *Journal of Philosophy, 77*, 797–803.

Tversky, A., & Kahneman, D. (1973). Availability: A heuristic for judging frequency and probability. *Cognitive Psychology, 5*, 207–232.

Tymoczko, T. (1979). The four color map theorem and mathematical proof. *Journal of Philosophy, 76*, 57–83.

Vollmer, F. (1984). On the limitations of commonsense psychology. In J. R. Royce & L. P. Mos (Eds.), *Annals of theoretical psychology* (Vol. 2, pp. 279–286). New York: Plenum Press.

2

THE MEDITATIONS

Réné Descartes

FIRST MEDITATION
What can be called in Question

Some years ago now I observed the multitude of errors that I had accepted as true in my earliest years, and the dubiousness of the whole superstructure I had since then reared on them; and the consequent need of making a clean sweep for once in my life, and beginning again from the very foundations, if I would establish some secure and lasting result in science. But the task appeared enormous, and I put it off till I should reach such a mature age that no increased aptitude for learning anything was likely to follow. Thus I delayed so long that now it would be blameworthy to spend in deliberation what time I have left for action. Today is my chance; I have banished all care from my mind, I have secured myself peace, I have retired by myself; at length I shall be at leisure to make a clean sweep, in all seriousness and with full freedom, of all my opinions.

To this end I shall not have to show they are all false, which very likely I could never manage; but reason already convinces me that I must withhold assent no less carefully from what is not plainly certain and indubitable than from what is obviously false; so the discovery of some reason for doubt as regards each opinion will justify the rejection of all. This will not mean going over each of them — an unending task; when the foundation is undermined, the superstructure will collapse of itself; so I will proceed at once to attack the very principles on which all my former beliefs rested.

Descartes, R. Meditations 1, 2 and 6. In P. Geach and E. Anscombe (Eds.), *Descartes: Philosophical Writings*. London: Thomas Nelson & Sons, 1963. © Thomas Nelson & Sons.

What I have so far accepted as true *par excellence*, I have got either from the senses or by means of the senses. Now I have sometimes caught the senses deceiving me; and a wise man never entirely trusts those who have once cheated him.

'But although the senses may sometimes deceive us about some minute or remote objects, yet there are many other facts as to which doubt is plainly impossible, although these are gathered from the same source: e.g. that I am here, sitting by the fire, wearing a winter cloak, holding this paper in my hands, and so on. Again, these hands, and my whole body — how can their existence be denied? Unless indeed I likened myself to some lunatics, whose brains are so upset by persistent melancholy vapours that they firmly assert they are kings, when really they are miserably poor; or that they are clad in purple, when really they are naked; or that they have a head of pottery, or are pumpkins, or are made of glass; but then they are madmen, and I should appear no less mad if I took them as a precedent for my own case.'

A fine argument! As though I were not a man who habitually sleeps at night and has the same impressions (or even wilder ones) in sleep as these men do when awake! How often, in the still of the night, I have the familiar conviction that I am here, wearing a cloak, sitting by the fire — when really I am undressed and lying in bed! 'But now at any rate I am looking at this paper with wide-awake eyes; the head I am now shaking is not asleep; I put out this hand deliberately and consciously; a sleeping man would have no such distinct experiences.' As though I did not recall having been formerly deceived by just such reflections (*cogitationibus*) during sleep! When I reflect (*cogito*) more carefully on this, I am bewildered; and my very bewilderment confirms the idea of my being asleep.

'Well, suppose I am dreaming, and these particulars, that I open my eyes, shake my head, put out my hand, are incorrect; suppose even that I have no such hand, no such body; at any rate it has to be admitted that the things that appear in sleep are like painted representations, which cannot have been formed except in the likeness of real objects. So at least these general kinds of things, eyes, head, hands, body, must be not imaginary but real objects. Painters themselves, even when they are striving to create sirens and satyrs with the most extraordinary forms, cannot give them wholly new natures, but only mix up the limbs of different animals; or even if they did devise something so novel that nothing at all like it had ever been seen, something wholly fictitious and unreal, at least they must use real colours in its make-up. Similarly, even if these general kinds of things, eyes, head, hands and so on, could be imaginary, at least it must be admitted that some simple and more universal kinds of things are real, and are as it were the real colours out of which there are formed in our consciousness (*cogitatione*) all our pictures of real and unreal things. To this class there seem to belong: corporeal nature in general, and its extension; the shape of extended objects; quantity, or the size and number of these objects; place for them to exist in, and time for them to endure through; and so on.

'At this rate we might be justified in concluding that whereas physics, astronomy, medicine, and all other sciences depending on the consideration of composite objects, are doubtful; yet arithmetic, geometry, and so on, which treat only of the simplest and most general subject-matter, and are indifferent whether it exists in nature or not, have an element of indubitable certainty. Whether I am awake or asleep, two and three add up to five, and a square only has four sides; and it seems impossible for such obvious truths to fall under a suspicion of being false.'

But there has been implanted in my mind the old opinion that there is a God who can do everything, and who made me such as I am. How do I know he has not brought it about that, while in fact there is no earth, no sky, no extended objects, no shape, no size, no place, yet all these things should appear to exist as they do now? Moreover, I judge that other men sometimes go wrong over what they think they know perfectly well; may not God likewise make me go wrong, whenever I add two and three, or count the sides of a square, or do any simpler thing that might be imagined? 'But perhaps it was not God's will to deceive me so; he is after all called supremely good.' But if it goes against his goodness to have so created me that I am always deceived, it seems no less foreign to it to allow me to be deceived sometimes; and this result cannot be asserted.

Perhaps some people would deny that there is a God powerful enough to do this, rather than believe everything else is uncertain. Let us not quarrel with them, and allow that all I have said about God is fiction. But whether they ascribe my attaining my present condition to fate, or to chance, or to a continuous series of events, or to any other cause, delusion and error certainly seem to be imperfections, and so this ascription of less power to the source of my being will mean that I am more likely to be so imperfect that I always go wrong. I have no answer to these arguments; I am obliged in the end to admit that none of my former ideas are beyond legitimate doubt; and this, not from inconsideration or frivolity, but for strong and well-thought-out reasons. So I must carefully withhold assent from them just as if they were plainly false, if I want to find any certainty.

But it is not enough to have observed this; I must take care to bear it in mind. My ordinary opinions keep on coming back; and they take possession of my belief, on which they have a lien by long use and the right of custom even against my will. I shall never get out of the habit of assenting to and trusting them, so long as I have a view of them answering to their real nature; namely, that they are doubtful in a way, as has been shown, but are yet highly probable, and far more reasonably believed than denied. So I think it will be well to turn my will in the opposite direction; deceive myself, and pretend they are wholly false and imaginary; until in the end the influence of prejudice on either side is counterbalanced, and no bad habit can any longer deflect my judgment from a true perception of facts. For

I am sure no danger or mistake can happen in the process, and I cannot be indulging my scepticism more than I ought; because I am now engaged, not in action, but only in thought.

I will suppose, then, not that there is a supremely good God, the source of truth; but that there is an evil spirit, who is supremely powerful and intelligent, and does his utmost to deceive me. I will suppose that sky, air, earth, colours, shapes, sounds and all external objects are mere delusive dreams, by means of which he lays snares for my credulity. I will consider myself as having no hands, no eyes, no flesh, no blood, no senses, but just having a false belief that I have all these things. I will remain firmly fixed in this meditation, and resolutely take care that, so far as in me lies, even if it is not in my power to know some truth, I may not assent to falsehood nor let myself be imposed upon by that deceiver, however powerful and intelligent he may be. But this plan is irksome, and sloth brings me back to ordinary life. I am like a prisoner who happens to enjoy an imaginary freedom during sleep, and then begins to suspect he is asleep; he is afraid to wake up, and connives at the agreeable illusion. So I willingly slip back into my old opinions, and dread waking up, in case peaceful rest should be followed by the toil of waking life, and I should henceforth have to live, not in the light, but amid the inextricable darkness of the problems I raised just now.

SECOND MEDITATION

The Nature of the Human Mind: it is better known than the Body

Yesterday's meditation plunged me into doubts of such gravity that I cannot forget them, and yet do not see how to resolve them. I am bewildered, as though I had suddenly fallen into a deep sea, and could neither plant my foot on the bottom nor swim up to the top. But I will make an effort, and try once more the same path as I entered upon yesterday; I will reject, that is, whatever admits of the least doubt, just as if I had found it was wholly false; and I will go on until I know something for certain — if it is only this, that there is nothing certain. Archimedes asked only for one fixed and immovable point so as to move the whole earth from its place; so I may have great hopes if I find even the least thing that is unshakably certain.

I suppose, therefore, that whatever things I see are illusions; I believe that none of the things my lying memory represents to have happened really did so; I have no senses; body, shape, extension, motion, place are chimeras. What then is true? Perhaps only this one thing, that nothing is certain.

How do I know, however, that there is not something different from all the things I have mentioned, as to which there is not the least occasion of doubt? — Is there a God (or whatever I call him) who gives me these very thoughts? But why, on the other hand, should I think so? Perhaps I myself may be the author of them.

— Well, am *I*, at any rate, something? — 'But I have already said I have no senses and no body — ' At this point I stick; what follows from this? Am I so bound to a body and its senses that without them I cannot exist? — 'But I have convinced myself that nothing in the world exists — no sky, no earth, no minds, no bodies; so am not I likewise non-existent?' But if I did convince myself of anything, I must have existed. 'But there is some deceiver, supremely powerful, supremely intelligent, who purposely always deceives me.' If he deceives me, then again I undoubtedly exist; let him deceive me as much as he may, he will never bring it about that, at the time of thinking (*quamdiu cogitabo*) that I am something, I am in fact nothing. Thus I have now weighed all considerations enough and more than enough; and must at length conclude that this proposition 'I am', 'I exist', whenever I utter it or conceive it in my mind, is necessarily true.

But I do not yet sufficiently understand what is this 'I' that necessarily exists. I must take care, then, that I do not rashly take something else for the 'I', and thus go wrong even in the knowledge that I am maintaining to be the most certain and evident of all. So I will consider afresh what I believe myself to be before I happened upon my present way of thinking; from this conception I will subtract whatever can be in the least shaken by the arguments adduced, so that what at last remains shall be precisely the unshakably certain element.

What, then, did I formerly think I was? A man. But what is a man? Shall I say 'a rational animal'? No; in that case I should have to go on to ask what an animal is and what 'rational' is, and so from a single question I should fall into several of greater difficulty; and I have not now the leisure to waste on such subtleties. I will rather consider what used to occur to me spontaneously and naturally whenever I was considering the question 'what am I?' First came the thought that I had a face, hands, arms — in fact the whole structure of limbs that is observable also in a corpse, and that I called 'the body'. Further, that I am nourished, that I move, that I have sensations (*sentire*), that I am conscious (*cogitare*); these acts I assigned to the soul. But as to the nature of this soul, either it did not attract my attention, or else I fancied something subtle like air or fire or aether mingled among the grosser parts of my body. As regards 'body' I had no doubt, and I thought I distinctly understood its nature; if I had tried to describe my conception, I might have given this explanation: 'By *body* I mean whatever is capable of being bounded by some shape, and comprehended by some place, and of occupying space in such a way that all other bodies are excluded; moreover of being perceived by touch, sight, hearing, taste, or smell; and further, of being moved in various ways, not of itself but by some other body that touches it.' For the power of self-movement, and the further powers of sensation and consciousness (*sentiendi, vel cogitandi*), I judged not to belong in any way to the essence of body (*naturam corporis*); indeed, I marvelled even that there were some bodies in which such faculties were found.

What am I to say now, when I am supposing that there is some all-powerful and (if it be lawful to say this) malignant deceiver, who has taken care to delude me about everything as much as he can? Can I, in the first place, say I have the least part of the characteristics that I said belonged to the essence of body? I concentrate, I think, I consider; nothing comes to mind; it would be wearisome and futile to repeat the reasons. Well, what of the properties I ascribed to the soul? Nutrition and locomotion? Since I have no body, these are mere delusions. Sensation? This cannot happen apart from a body; and in sleep I have seemed to have sensations that I have since realised never happened. Consciousness (*cogitare*)? At this point I come to the fact that there is consciousness (*or* experience: *cogitatio*); of this and this only I cannot be deprived. *I* am, *I* exist; that is certain. For how long? For as long as I am experiencing (*cogito*), maybe, if I wholly ceased from experiencing (*ab omni cogitatione*), I should at once wholly cease to be. For the present I am admitting only what is necessarily true; so 'I am' precisely taken refers only to a conscious being; that is a mind, a soul (*animus*), an intellect, a reason — words whose meaning I did not previously know. I am a real being, and really exist; but what sort of being? As I said, a conscious being (*cogitans*).

What now? I will use my imagination. I am not that set of limbs called the human body; I am not some rarefied gas infused into those limbs — air or fire or vapour or exhalation or whatever I picture to myself; all these things I am supposing to be nonentitities. But I still have the assertion 'nevertheless *I* am something'. 'But perhaps it is the case that these very things which I suppose to be nonentities, and which are not properly known to me, are yet in reality not different from the "I" of which I am aware?' I do not know, and will not dispute the point; I can judge only about the things I am aware of. I am aware of my own existence; I want to know what is this 'I' of which I am aware. Assuredly, the conception of this 'I', precisely as such, does not depend on things of whose existence I am not yet aware; nor, therefore, on what I feign in my imagination. And this very word 'feign' shows me my mistake; it would indeed be a fiction to imagine myself to be anything, for imagination consists in contemplating the likeness or picture of a body. Now I know for certain that I am, and that at the same time it is possible that all these images, and in general everything of the nature of the body, are mere dreams. When I consider this, it seems as absurd to say 'I will use my imagination, so as to recognise more distinctly who I am', as though I were to say 'I am awake now, and discern some truth; but I do not yet see it clearly enough; so I will set about going to sleep, so that my dreams may give me a truer and clearer picture of the fact'. So I know that nothing I can comprehend by the help of imagination belongs to my conception of myself; the mind's attention must be carefully diverted from these things, so that she may discern her own nature as distinctly as possible.

What then am I? A conscious being (*res cogitans*). What is that? A being that doubts, understands, asserts, denies, is willing, is unwilling; further, that has sense and imagination. These are a good many properties — if only they all belong to me. But how can they fail to? Am *I* not the very person who is now 'doubting' almost everything; who 'understands' something and 'asserts' this one thing to be true, and 'denies' other things; who 'is willing' to know more, and 'is unwilling' to be deceived; who 'imagines' many things, even involuntarily, and perceives many things coming as it were from the 'senses'? Even if I am all the while asleep; even if my creator does all he can to deceive me; how can any of these things be less of a fact than my existence? Is any of these something distinct from my consciousness (*cogitatione*)? Can any of them be called a separate thing from myself? It is so clear that it is I who doubt, understand, will, that I cannot think how to explain it more clearly. Further, it is I who imagine; for even if, as I supposed, no imagined object is real, yet the power of imagination really exists and goes to make up my experience (*cogitationis*). Finally, it is I who have sensations, or who perceive corporeal objects as it were by the senses. Thus, I am now seeing light, hearing a noise, feeling heat. These objects are unreal, for I am asleep; but at least I seem to see, to hear, to be warmed. This cannot be unreal; and this is what is properly called my sensation; further, sensation, precisely so regarded, is nothing but an act of consciousness (*cogitare*).

From these considerations I begin to be a little better acquainted with myself. But it still appears, and I cannot help thinking, that corporeal objects, whose images are formed in consciousness (*cogitatione*), and which the senses actually examine, are known much more clearly than this 'I', this 'something I know not what', which does not fall under imagination. It is indeed surprising that I should comprehend more distinctly things that I can tell are doubtful, unknown, foreign to me, than what is real, what I am aware of — my very self. But I can see how it is; my mind takes pleasure in wandering, and is not yet willing to be restrained within the bounds of truth. So be it, then; just this once I will ride her on a loose rein, so that in good time I may pull her up and that thereafter she may more readily let me control her.

Let us consider the objects commonly thought to be the best known of all, the bodies we touch and see. I will take, not body in general, for these generic concepts (*perceptiones*) are often the more confused, but one particular body; say, this wax. It has just been extracted from the honeycomb; it has not completely lost the taste of the honey; it retains some of the smell of the flowers from which it was gathered; its colour, shape, size are manifest; it is hard, cold, and easily handled, and gives out a sound if you rap it with your knuckle; in fact it has all the properties that seem to be needed for our knowing a body with the utmost distinctness. But while I say this, the wax is put by the fire. It loses the remains of its flavour, the fragrance evaporates, the colour changes, the shape is lost, the size increases; it becomes fluid and hot, it can hardly be handled, and it will no longer give out a sound if you rap it. Is the same wax, then, still there? 'Of course it is; nobody denies it, nobody thinks otherwise.' Well, what was in this wax that was so distinctly known? Nothing that I got through the senses; for whatever fell under taste, smell, sight, touch, or hearing has now changed; yet the wax is still there.

'Perhaps what I distinctly knew was what I am now thinking of: namely, that the wax was not the sweetness, not the fragrance of the flowers, nor the whiteness, nor the shape, nor the sound, but body; manifested to me previously in those aspects, and now in others.' But what exactly am I thus imagining? Let us consider; let us remove what is not proper to the wax, and see what is left: simply something extended, flexible, and changeable. But what is its being 'flexible' and 'changeable'? Does it consist in my imagining the wax to be capable of changing from a round shape to a square one and from that again to a triangular one? By no means; for I comprehend its potentiality for an infinity of such changes, but I cannot run through an infinite number of them in imagination; so I do not comprehend them by my imaginative power. What again is its being 'extended'? It this likewise unknown? For extension grows greater when the wax melts, greater still when it boils, and greater still again with increase of heat; and I should mistake the nature of wax if I did not think this piece capable also of more changes, as regards extension, than my imagination has ever grasped. It remains then for me to admit that I know the nature even of this piece of wax not by imagination, but by purely mental perception. (I say this as regards a particular piece of wax; it is even clearer as regards wax in general.) What then is this wax, perceived only by the mind? It is the very same wax as I see, touch, and imagine — that whose existence I believed in originally. But it must be observed that perception of the wax is not sight, not touch, not imagination; nor was it ever so, though it formerly seemed to be; it is a purely mental contemplation (*inspectio*); which may be either imperfect or confused, as it originally was, or clear and distinct, as it not is, according to my degree of attention to what it consists in.

But it is surprising how prone my mind is to errors. Although I am considering these points within myself silently and without speaking, yet I stumble over words and am almost deceived by ordinary language. We say we see the wax itself, if it is there; not that we judge from its colour or shape that it is there. I might at once infer: I see the wax by ocular vision, not by merely mental contemplation. I chanced, however, to look out of the window, and see men walking in the street; now I say in ordinary language that I 'see' them, just as I 'see' the wax; but what can I 'see' besides hats and coats, which may cover automata? I judge that they are men; and similarly, the objects that I thought I saw with my eyes, I really comprehend only by my mental power of judgment.

It is disgraceful that a man seeking to know more than the mass of mankind should have sought occasions for doubt in popular modes of speech! Let us go on, and consider when I perceived the wax more perfectly and manifestly; was it when I first looked at it, and thought I was aware of it by my external senses, or at least by the so-called 'common' sense, i.e. the imaginative faculty? or is it rather now, after careful investigation of its nature and of the way that I am aware of it? It would be silly to doubt as to the matter; for what was there clear about my original perception? Surely any animal could have one just as good. But when I distinguish the wax from its outward form, and as it were unclothe it and consider it in its naked self, I get something which, mistaken as my judgment may still be, I need a human mind to perceive.

What then am I to say about this mind, that is, about myself? (So far, I allow of no other element in myself except mind.) What is the 'I' that seems to perceive this wax so distinctly? Surely I am aware of myself not only much more truly and certainly, but also much more distinctly and manifestly. For if I judge that wax exists from the fact that I see this wax, it is much clearer that I myself exist because of this same fact that I see it. Possibly what I see is not wax; possibly I have no eyes to see anything; but it is just not possible, when I see or (I make no distinction here) I think I see (*cogitem me videre*), that my conscious self (*ego ipse cogitans*) should not be something. Similarly, if I judge that wax exists from the fact that I touch this wax, the same result follows: I exist. If I judge from the fact that I imagine it, or for some other reason, it is just the same. These observations about the wax apply to all external objects. Further, if the perception of wax is more distinct when it has become known to me not merely by sight or by touch, but from a plurality of sources; how much more distinct than this must I admit my knowledge of myself to be! No considerations can help towards my perception of the wax or any other body, without at the same time all going towards establishing the nature of my mind. And the mind has such further resources within itself from which its self-knowledge may be made more distinct, that the information thus derived from the body appears negligible.

I have thus got back to where I wanted; I now know that even bodies are not really perceived by the senses or the imaginative faculty, but only by intellect; that they are perceived, not by being touched or seen, but by being understood; I thus clearly recognise that nothing is more easily or manifestly perceptible to me than my own mind. But because the habit of old opinion is not to be laid aside so quickly, I will stop here, so that by long meditation I may imprint this new knowledge deep in my memory.

SIXTH MEDITATION
The Existence of Material Things: the Real Distinction of Mind and Body

It remains for me to examine whether material things exist. I already know at least the possibility of their existence, in so far as they are the subject-matter of pure mathematics, since in this regard I clearly and distinctly perceive them. For God is undoubtedly able to effect whatever I am thus able to perceive; and I have never decided that anything could not be done by him, except on the ground that it would involve contradiction for me to perceive such a thing distinctly. Further, when I am occupied with material objects, I am aware of using the faculty of imagination; and this seems to imply that they exist. For when I consider carefully what imagination is, it seems to be a kind of application of the cognitive faculty to a body intimately present to it — a body, therefore, that exists.

To explain this, I begin by examining the difference between imagination and pure understanding. For instance, when I imagine a triangle, I do not just understand that it is a figure enclosed in three lines; I also at the same time see the three lines present before my mind's eye, and this is what I call imagining them. Now if I want to think of a chiliagon, I understand just as well that it is a figure of a thousand sides as I do that a triangle is a figure of three sides; but I do not in the same way imagine the thousand sides, or see them as presented to me. I am indeed accustomed always to imagine something when I am thinking of a corporeal object; so I may confusedly picture to myself some kind of figure; but obviously this picture is not a chiliagon, since it is in no way different from the one I should form if I were thinking of a myriagon, or any other figure with very many sides; and it in no way helps me to recognise the properties that distinguish a chiliagon from other polygons. If now it is a pentagon that is in question, I can understand its figure, as I can the figure of a chiliagon, without the aid of imagination; but I may also imagine this very figure, applying my mind's eye to its five sides and at the same time to the area contained by them; and here I clearly discern that I have to make some special effort of mind to imagine it that I do not make in just understanding it; this new mental effort plainly shows the difference between imagination and pure understanding.

I further consider that this power of imagination in me, taken as distinct from the power of understanding, is not essential to the nature of myself, that is, of my mind; for even if I lacked it, I should nevertheless undoubtedly still be the selfsame one that I am; it seems, therefore, that this power must depend on some object other than myself. And if there is a body to which the mind is so conjoined that it can at will apply itself, so to say, to contemplating it, then I can readily understand the possibility of my imagining corporeal objects by this means. The difference between this mode of consciousness and pure understanding would then be simply this: in the act of understanding the mind turns as it were towards itself, and contemplates one of the ideas contained in itself; in the act of imagining, it turns to the body, and contemplates something in its resembling an idea understood by the mind itself or perceived by sense. I can readily understand, I say, that imagination could be performed in this way, if a body exists; and since there does not occur to me any other equally convenient way of explaining it, I form from this the probable conjecture that the body exists. But this is only probable; and, in spite of a careful investigation of all points, I can as yet see no way of arguing conclusively from the fact that there is in my imagination a distinct idea of a corporeal nature to the existence of any body.

Besides that aspect of body which is the subject-matter of pure mathematics, there are many other things that I habitually imagine — colours, sounds, flavours, pain, and so on; but none of these are so distinctly imagined. In any case, I perceive them better by way of sensation, and it is from thence that they seem to have reached my imagination, by the help of memory. Thus it will be more convenient to treat of them by treating of sense at the same time; I must see whether I can get any certain argument in favour of the existence of material objects from the things perceived in the mode of consciousness that I call sensation.

I will first recall to myself what kinds of things I previously thought were real, as being perceived in sensation; then I will set out my reasons for having later on called them in question; finally I will consider what to hold now.

In the first place, then: I had sensations of having a head, hands, feet, and the other members that make up the body; and I regarded the body as part of myself, or even as my whole self. I had sensations of the commerce of this body with many other bodies, which were capable of being beneficial or injurious to it in various ways; I estimated the beneficial effects by a sensation of pleasure, and the injurious, by a sensation of pain. Besides pain and pleasure, I had internal sensations of hunger, thirst, and other such appetites; and also of physical inclinations towards gladness, sadness, anger, and other like emotions. I had external sensations not only of the extension, shapes, and movements of bodies, but also of their hardness, heat, and other tangible qualities; also, sensations of light, colours, odours, flavours, and sounds. By the varieties of these qualities I distinguished from one another the sky, the earth, the seas, and all other bodies.

I certainly had some reason, in view of the ideas of these qualities that presented themselves to my consciousness (*cogitationi*), and that were the only proper and immediate object of my sensations, to think that I was aware in sensation of objects quite different from my own consciousness: viz. bodies from which the ideas proceeded. For it was my experience (*experiebar*) that the ideas came to me without any consent of mine; so that I could neither have a sensation of any object, however I wished, if it were not present to the sense-organ, nor help having the sensation when the object was present. Moreover, the ideas perceived in sensation were much more vivid and prominent, and, in their own way, more distinct, than any that I myself deliberately produced in my meditations, or observed to have been impressed on my memory; and thus it seemed impossible for them to proceed from myself; and the only remaining possibility was that they came from some other objects. Now since I had no conception of these objects from any other source than the ideas themselves, it could not but occur to me that they were like the ideas. Further, I remembered that I had had the use of the senses before the use of reason; and I saw that the ideas I formed myself were less prominent than those I perceived in sensation, and mostly consisted of parts taken from sensation; I thus readily convinced myself that I had nothing in my intellect that I had not previously had in sensation.

Again, I had some reason for holding that the body I called '*my* body' by a special title really did belong to me more than any other body did. I could never separate myself entirely from it, as I could from other bodies. All the appetites and emotions I had, I felt in the body and on its account. I felt pain, and the titillations of pleasure, in parts of *this* body, not of other, external bodies. Why should a sadness of the mind follow upon a sensation of pain, and a kind of happiness upon the titillation of sense? Why should that twitching of the stomach which I call hunger tell me that I must eat; and a dryness of the throat, that I must drink; and so on? I could give no account of this except that nature taught me so; for there is no likeness at all, so far as I can see, between the twitching in the stomach and the volition to take food; or between the sensation of an object that gives me pain, and the experience (*cogitationem*) of sadness that arises from the sensation. My other judgments, too, as regards the objects of sensation seemed to have been lessons of nature; for I had convinced myself that things were so, before setting out any reasons to prove this.

Since then, however, I have had many experiences that have gradually sapped the faith I had in the senses. It sometimes happened that towers which had looked round at a distance looked square when close at hand; and that huge statues standing on the roof did not seem large to me looking up from the ground. And there were countless other cases like these, in which I found the external senses to be deceived in their judgment; and not only the external senses, but the internal senses as well. What [experience] can be more intimate than pain? Yet I had heard sometimes, from people who had had a leg or arm cut off, that they still seemed now and then to feel pain in the part of the body that they lacked; so it seemed in my own case not to be quite certain that a limb was in pain, even if I felt pain in it. And to these reasons for doubting I more recently added two more, of highly general application. First, there is no kind of sensation that I have ever thought I had in waking life, but I may also think I have some time when I am asleep; and since I do not believe that sensations I seem to have in sleep come from external objects, I did not see why I should believe this any the more about sensations I seem to have when I am awake. Secondly, I did not as yet know the Author of my being (or at least pretended I did not); so there seemed to be nothing against my being naturally so constituted as to be deceived even about what appeared to myself so true. As for the reasons of my former conviction that sensible objects are real, it was not difficult to answer them. I was, it seemed, naturally impelled to many courses from which reason dissuaded me; so I did not think I ought to put much reliance on what nature had taught me. And although sense-perceptions did not depend on my will, it must not be concluded, I thought, that they proceed from objects distinct from myself; there might perhaps be some faculty in myself, as yet unknown to me, that produced them.

But now that I am beginning to be better acquainted with myself and with the Author of my being, my view is that I must not rashly accept all the apparent data of sensation; nor, on the other hand, call them all in question.

In the first place, I know that whatever I clearly and distinctly understand can be made by God just as I understand it; so my ability to understand one thing clearly and distinctly apart from another is enough to assure me that they are distinct, because God at least can separate them. (It is irrelevant what faculty enables me to think of them as separate.) Now I know that I exist, and at the same time I observe absolutely nothing else as belonging to my nature or essence except the mere fact that I am a conscious being; and just from this I can validly infer that my essence consists simply in the fact that I am a conscious being. It is indeed possible (or rather, as I shall say later on, it is certain) that I have a body closely bound up with myself; but at the same time I have, on the one hand, a clear and distinct idea of myself taken simply as a conscious, not an extended, being; and, on the other hand, a distinct idea of body, taken simply as an extended, not a conscious, being; so it is certain that I am really distinct from my body, and could exist without it.

Further, I find in myself powers for special modes of consciousness, e.g. imagination and sensation; I can clearly and distinctly understand myself as a whole apart from these powers, but not the powers apart from myself — apart from an intellectual substance to inhere in; for the essential (*formali*) conception of them includes some kind of intellectual act; and I thus perceive that they are distinct from me in the way aspects (*modos*) are from the object to which they belong. I also recognise other powers — those of local motion, and change of shape, and so on; these, like the ones I mentioned before, cannot be understood apart from a substance to inhere in; nor, therefore, can they exist apart from it. Clearly these, if they exist, must inhere in a corporeal or extended, not an intellectual substance; for it is some form of extension, not any intellectual act, that is involved in a clear and distinct conception of them. Now I have a passive power of sensation — of getting and recognising the ideas of sensible objects. But I could never have the use of it if there were not also in existence an active power, either in myself or in something else, to produce or make the ideas. This power certainly cannot exist in me; for it presupposes no action of my intellect, and the ideas are produced without my co-operation, and often against my will. The only remaining possibility is that it inheres in some substance other than myself. This must contain all the reality that exists representatively in the ideas produced by this active power; and it must contain it (as I remarked previously) either just as it is represented, or in some higher form. So either this substance is a body — is of corporeal nature — and contains actually whatever is contained representatively in the ideas; or else it is God, or some creature nobler than bodies, and contains the same reality in a higher form. But since God is not deceitful, it is quite obvious that he neither implants the ideas in me by his own direct action, nor yet by means of some creature that contains the representative reality of the ideas not precisely as they represent it, but only in some higher form. For God has given me no faculty at all to discern their origin; on the other hand, he has given me a strong inclination to belive that these ideas proceed from corporeal objects; so I do not see how it would make sense to say God is not deceitful, if in fact they proceed from elsewhere, not from corporeal objects. Therefore corporeal objects must exist. It may be that not all bodies are such as my senses apprehend them, for this sensory apprehension is in many ways obscure and confused; but at any rate their nature must comprise whatever I clearly and distinctly understand — that is, whatever, generally considered, falls within the subject-matter of pure mathematics.

There remain some highly doubtful and uncertain points; either mere details, like the sun's having a certain size or shape, or things unclearly understood, like light, sound, pain, and so on. But since God is not deceitful, there cannot possibly occur any error in my opinions but I can correct by means of some faculty God has given me to that end; and this gives me some hope of arriving at the truth even on such matters. Indeed, all nature's lessons undoubtedly contain some truth; for by nature, as a general term, I now mean nothing other than either God himself, or the order of created things established by God; and by *my* nature in particular I mean the complex of all that God has given *me*.

Now there is no more explicit lesson of nature than that I have a body; that it is being injured when I feel pain; that it needs food, or drink, when I suffer from hunger, or thirst, and so on. So I must not doubt that there is some truth in this. Nature also teaches by these sensations of pain, hunger, thirst, etc., that I am not present in my body merely as a pilot is present in a ship; I am most tightly bound to it, and as it were mixed up with it, so that I and it form a unit. Otherwise, when the body is hurt, I, who am simply a conscious being, would not feel pain on that account, but would perceive the injury by a pure act of understanding, as the pilot perceives by sight any breakages there may be in the ship; and when the body needs food or drink, I should explicitly understand the fact, and not have confused sensations of hunger and thirst. For these sensations of thirst, hunger, pain, etc., are simply confused modes of consciousness that arise from the mind's being united to, and as it were mixed up with, the body.

Moreover, nature teaches me that my body has an environment of other bodies, some of which must be sought for and others shunned. And from the wide variety of colours, sounds, odours, flavours, degrees of hardness, and so on, of which I have sensations, I certainly have the right to infer that in the bodies from which these various sense-perceptions arise there is corresponding, though perhaps not similar, variety. Again, from the fact that some of these perceptions are pleasant to me and others unpleasant, it is quite certain that my body — or rather myself as a whole, who am made up of body and mind — can be variously affected for good or ill by bodies in its environment.

There are many other beliefs which may seem to be lessons of nature, but which I really derive not from nature but from a habit of inconsiderate judgment; e.g. that a region is empty if there is no occurrence in it that affects my senses; that if a body is (say) hot, it has some property just like my idea of heat; that in a white or green object there is the same whiteness or greenness as in my sensation, and in a sweet or bitter body the same flavour as I taste, and so on; that stars and towers and other distant bodies have just the size and shape they manifest to my senses; and the like. But to avoid an indistinct view of this matter, I must define here more accurately just what I mean by a lesson of nature. I am using 'nature' here in a more restricted sense than the complex of everything that God has given me. For this complex includes much that belongs only to the mind — e.g. my seeing that what is once done cannot be undone, and the rest of what I know by the light of nature; I am not speaking here about this. Again, it includes much that has regard only to the body, e.g. a downward tendency; this again I am not now discussing. I am concerned only with what God has given to me considered as a compound of mind and body. It is a lesson of my 'nature', in this sense, to avoid what gives me a sensation of pain, and pursue what gives me a sensation of pleasure, and so on. But it does not seem to be also a lesson of nature to draw any conclusion from sense-perception as regards external objects without a previous examination by the understanding; for knowledge of the truth about them seems to belong to the mind alone, not to the composite whole.

Thus, a star has no more effect on my eye than the flame of a small candle; but from this fact I have no real, positive inclination to believe it is no bigger; this is just an irrational judgment that I made in my earliest years. Again, I have a sensation of heat as I approach the fire; but when I approach the same fire too closely, I have a sensation of pain; so there is nothing to convince me that something in the fire resembles heat, any more than the pain; it is just that there must be something in it (whatever this may turn out to be) that produces the sensations of heat or pain. Again, even if in some region there is nothing to affect the senses, it does not follow that there is no body in it. I can see that on these and many other questions I habitually pervert the order of nature. My sense-perceptions were given me by nature properly for the sole purpose of indicating to the mind what is good or bad for the whole of which the mind is a part; and to this extent they are clear and distinct enough. But I use them as if they were sure criteria for a direct judgment as to the essense of external bodies; and here they give only very obscure and confused indications.

I have already examined sufficiently the reason why, in spite of God's goodness, my judgments are liable to be false. But a new problem arises here about the objects that nature shows me I ought to seek or shun; and also as regards the errors I seem to have observed in internal sensations. For instance, a man is deceived by the pleasant taste of some food, and swallows the poison concealed within it. But what his nature impels him to desire is what gives the food its pleasant taste; not the poison, of which his nature knows nothing. All that can be inferred from this is that his nature is not omniscient; and this is not surprising, for a man is a finite thing and his nature has only a finite degree of perfection.

But we quite often go wrong about the things that nature does impel us towards. For instance, sick men long for drink or food that would soon be harmful to them. It might be said that they go wrong because their nature is corrupted; but this does not seem to remove the problem. A sick man is no less God's creature than a healthy man; and it seems just as absurd that God should give him a nature that deceives him.

Now a clock built out of wheels and weights, obeys all the laws of 'nature' no less exactly when it is ill-made and does not show the right time, than when it satisfies its maker's wishes in every respect. And thus I may consider the human body as a machine fitted together and made up of bones, sinews, muscles, veins, blood, and skin in such a way that, even if there were no mind in it, it would still carry out all the operations that, as things are, do not depend on the command of the will, nor, therefore, on the mind. Now, if, for instance, the body is suffering from dropsy, it has the dryness of the throat that normally gives the mind the sensation of thirst; and this disposes its nerves and other parts to taking drink, so as to aggravate the disease. But I can easily recognise that this is just as 'natural' as it is for a body not so affected to be impelled by a similar dryness of the throat to take drink that will be beneficial to it.

Of course, if I consider my preconceived idea of the use of a clock, I may say that when it does not show the right time it is departing from its 'nature'. Similary, if I consider the machine of the human body in relation to its normal operations, I may think it goes astray from its 'nature' if its throat is dry at a time when drink does not help to sustain it. But I see well enough that this sense of 'nature' is very different from the other. In this sense, 'nature' is a term depending on my own way of thinking (*a cogitatione mea*), on my comparison of a sick man, or an ill-made clock, to a conception of a healthy man and a well-made clock; it is something extrinsic to the object it is ascribed to. In the other sense, 'nature' is something actually found in objects; so this conception has some degree of truth.

'It may be a merely extrinsic application of a term when, considering a body that suffers from dropsy, we call its nature corrupted because it has a dry throat and yet has no need of drink. But if we consider the compound, the mind united to the body, it is not just a matter of terms; there is a real fault in its nature, for it is thirsty at a time when drink would be hurtful to it. So the question remains: how is it that the divine goodness does not prevent "nature" (in this sense) from deceiving us?'

I must begin by observing the great difference between mind and body. Body is of its nature always divisible; mind is wholly indivisible. When I consider the mind — that is, myself, in so far as I am merely a conscious being — I can distinguish no parts within myself; I understand myself to be a single and complete thing. Although the whole mind seems to be united to the whole body, yet when a foot or an arm or any other part of the body is cut off I am not aware that any subtraction has been made from the mind. Nor can the faculties of will, feeling, understanding and so on be called its parts; for it is one and the same mind that wills, feels, and understands. On the other hand, I cannot think of any corporeal or extended object without being readily able to divide it in thought and therefore conceiving of it as divisible. This would be enough to show me the total difference between mind and body, even if I did not sufficiently know this already.

Next, I observe that my mind is not directly affected by all parts of the body; but only by the brain, and perhaps only by one small part of that — the alleged seat of common sensibility. Whenever this is disposed in a given way, it gives the same indication to the mind, even if the other parts of the body are differently disposed at the time; of this there are innumerable experimental proofs, of which I need not give an account here.

I observe further that, from the nature of body, in whatever way a part of it could be moved by another part at some distance, that same part could also be moved in the same way by intermediate parts, even if the more distant part did nothing. For example, if ABCD is a cord, there is no way of moving A by pulling the end D that could not be carried out equally well if B or C in the middle were pulled and the end D were not moved at all. Now, similarly, when I feel pain in my foot, I have learnt from the science of physic that this sensation is brought about by means of nerves scattered throughout the foot; these are stretched like cords from there to the brain, and when they are pulled in the foot they transmit the pull to the inmost part of the brain, to which they are attached, and produce there a kind of disturbance which nature has decreed should give the mind a sensation of pain, as it were in the foot. But in order to reach the brain, these nerves have to pass through the leg, the thigh, the back, and the neck; so it may happen that, although it is not the part in the foot that is touched, but only some intermediate part, there is just the same disturbance produced in the brain as when the foot is injured; and so necessarily the mind will have the same sensation of pain. And the same must be believed as regards any other sensation.

Finally, I observe that, since any given disturbance in the part of the brain that directly affects the mind can produce only one kind of sensation, nothing better could be devised than that it should produce that one among all the sensations it could produce which is most conducive, and most often conducive, to the welfare of a healthy man. Now experience shows that all the sensations nature has given us are of this kind; so nothing can be found in them but evidence of God's power and goodness. For example: when the nerves of the foot are strongly and unusually disturbed, this disturbance, by way of the spinal cord, arrived at the interior of the brain; there it gives the mind the signal for it to have a certain sensation, viz. pain, as it were in the foot; and this arouses the mind to do its best to remove the cause of the pain, as being injurious to the foot. Now God might have so made human nature that this very disturbance in the brain was a sign to the mind of something else; it might have been a sign of its own occurrence in the brain; or of the disturbance in the foot, or in some intermediate place; or, in fact, of anything else whatever. But there would be no alternative equally conducive to the welfare of the body. Similarly, when we need drink, there arises a dryness of the throat, which disturbs the nerves of the throat, and by means of them the interior of the brain; and this disturbance gives the mind the sensation of thirst, because the most useful thing for us to know in this whole process is that we then need drink to keep healthy. And so in other cases.

From all this it is clear that in spite of God's immeasurable goodness, man as a compound of body and mind cannot but be sometimes deceived by his own nature. For some cause that occurs, not in the foot, but in any other of the parts traversed by the nerves from the foot to the brain, or even in the brain itself, may arouse the same disturbance as is usually aroused by a hurt foot; and then pain will be felt as it were in the foot, and there will be a 'natural' illusion of sense. For the brain-disturbance in question cannot but produce always the same sensation in the mind; and it usually arises much more often from a cause that is hurting the foot than from another cause occurring somewhere else; so it is in accordance with reason that it should always give the mind the appearance of pain in the foot rather than some other part. Again, sometimes dryness of the throat arises not, as usual, from the fact that drink would be conducive to bodily health, but from some contrary cause, as in dropsy; but it is far better that it should deceive us in that case, than if it always deceived us when the body was in good condition. And so generally.

This consideration is of the greatest help to me, not only for noticing all the errors to which my nature is liable, but also for readily correcting or avoiding them. I know that all my sensations are much more often true than delusive signs in matters regarding the well-being of the body; I can almost always use several senses to examine the same object; above all, I have my memory, which connects the present to the past, and my understanding, which has now reviewed all the causes of error. So I ought not to be afraid any longer that all the senses show me daily may be an illusion; the exaggerated doubts of the last few days are to be dismissed as ridiculous. In particular, this is true of the chief reason for doubt — that sleep and waking life were indistinguishable to me; for I can now see a vast difference between them. Dreams are never connected by memory with all the other events of my life, like the things that happen when I am awake. If in waking life somebody suddenly appeared and directly afterwards disappeared, as happens in dreams, and I could not see where he had come from or where he went, I should justifiably decide he was a ghost, or a phantasm formed in my own brain, rather than a real man. But when I distinctly observe where an object comes from, where it is, and when this happens; and when I can connect the perception of it uninterruptedly with the whole of the rest of my life; then I am quite certain that while this is happening to me I am not asleep but awake. And I need not have the least doubt as to the reality of things, if after summoning all my senses, my memory, and my understanding to examine them I have no conflicting information from any of these sources. But since practical needs do not always leave time for such a careful examination, we must admit that in human life errors as regards particular things are always liable to happen; and we must recognise the infirmity of our nature.

SUBJECT-MATTER, METHOD AND PROBLEM OF PSYCHOLOGY

E.B. Titchener

§ **1. Science and Experience.** — A science consists of a large body of observed facts, which are related to one another, and are arranged under general laws. If, for instance, you open a text-book of physics, you find that it gives the results of numerous observations, or prescribes experiments in which you are to observe for yourself; and you find that these results or experiments are grouped under certain main headings (mechanics, heat, electricity) and are made to illustrate certain comprehensive laws (Newton's laws of motion, Kirchoff's law of radiation, Ohm's law of the strength of the electric current). All scientific text-books, whether the science is physics or chemistry, biology or psychology, philology or economics, are of the same pattern.

It is worth while, before we begin our special study of psychology, briefly to consider some of the questions which this definition of science suggests. How, we may ask, do the various sciences come into being? How are they differentiated, their several fields laid out and marked off? What do we mean when we say that the facts of any given science are related to one another? What is the nature of the relation? What precisely is a scientific law? Why is it important for the progress of science that laws should be established? An answer, even a rough answer, to these questions will help us to understand the scope and aim of psychology.

First of all, then, it is plain that all the sciences have the same sort of subject-matter; they all deal with some phase or aspect of the world of human experience. If we take a mere fragment of this world, — say, our own experience during a single day, — we find it a rather hopeless mixture. Our lawn-sprinkler obeys the third law of motion, while our pleasure in possessing it is a fact for psychology;

Titchener, E.B. 1913. "Subject-Matter, Method and Problem of Psychology" in *A Text-book of Psychology*, pp. 1-41. © 1913 Macmillan.

the preparation of our food is an applied chemistry, its adulteration depends upon economic conditions, and its effect upon health is a matter of physiology; our manner of speech is governed by phonetic laws, while the things we say reflect the moral standards of the time: in a word, one science seems to run into another science as chance may decide, without order or distinction. If, however, we look over the world as a whole, or examine historically any long period of human existence, the survey is less bewildering. The world of nature breaks up at once, as we inspect it, into living objects, the objects that change by growth, and non-living objects, the objects that change only by decay. And living objects divide, again, into objects that grow in one place, the plants, and objects that move about as they grow, the animals. Here, almost at the first glance, we have distinguished the raw materials of three different sciences: geology, botany, zoology. Now let us turn to some stage of human evolution: we may choose the social life of mankind before the dawn of civilisation. Primitive man was required, by the necessities of his case, to make himself weapons; to hunt animals for food; to protect himself by clothing and shelter, and to avoid eating or drinking from poisonous or tainted sources. If he ventured upon the water, he must steer his course by the stars; if he banded with his fellows, he must hold to the code of honour of the tribe. He dreamed, and told his dreams; when he was glad, or angry, or afraid, he showed his feelings in gesture or by the expression of his face. Doubtless, his daily experience, if he ever thought about it, seemed to him as chaotic as our own has just appeared to us. But we, who have a larger version of that experience, can see that it contained the natural germs of many sciences: mechanics, zoology and physiology, — astronomy, ethics and psychology.

We are thus led to the conclusion that the world of human experience is not altogether confused and disorderly. It shows lines of cleavage; to a certain extent, it arranges itself for us; so that the raw materials of the natural germs of what, in the higher forms of civilisation, become the separate sciences force themselves separately upon the attention. But we have not, as yet, anything more than raw materials. Science appears only when some man, taking the hint from nature, deliberately follows up a special line of enquiry throughout the whole of experience. Bridges and dwellings and weapons and furniture and tools and utensils were made long before there was a science of mechanics. The science begins when men begin to interpret the universe in mechanical terms, when the world at large is looked upon as a vast machine, working precisely as a tool or an engine works. Dreams, and the phenomena of trance, and the movements which express emotion were observed long before there was a science of psychology. The science begins when men begin to interpret the universe in psychological terms, when the world at large is looked upon as mind, as a body of experience subject to psychological laws. In a word, every science takes up a certain attitude towards the world of human experience, or regards it from a definite point of view, and it is the business of a science to describe the world as it appears after the attitude has been taken up or the point of view adopted. What differentiates the sciences is just this difference of human interest; and what holds a science together, and brings its observations into relation, is just the fact that all the work has been done under the guidance of the same principles and from the same point of view.

We have now answered some of our general questions. Experience, we have seen, presents itself under different aspects. The differences are roughly outlined, but are definite enough to serve as a starting-point. These different aspects engage the attention of different men. Division of labour is necessary, if the whole of experience is to be brought within the sphere of science; and men's interests are so various that every aspect of experience is sure, in the long run, to find a student. As scientific investigation proceeds, and as the number of scientific men increases, more and more aspects of experience are revealed, and the sciences multiply. They do not exist independently, side by side, as accounts of separate positions of the world or of separate regions of experience; they overlap and coincide, describing one and the same world of experience as it appears from their special standpoints. They are not like blocks of knowledge, which when cut to the proper size and properly fitted together will give us a map of the universe; they are rather like the successive chapters of a book which discusses a large topic from every possible point of view. Some chapters are long, and some are short; some are general, and some are special: this depends upon the sort of attitude which a given science takes towards experience. But all the chapters, or sciences, deal with the same world under its various aspects. —

We have still to enquire what science means by a law, and why it is that the advance of science depends upon the establishment of laws. The answer is simple. the longer scientific observations are continued, and the scientific methods are refined, the clearer does it become that experience is regular and orderly. If only the conditions of an occurrence remain the same, the occurrence will always take place in the same way. A scientific law thus expresses a regularity, an unbroken uniformity, of some aspect of experience. Go to a dictionary, and look up Charles' law, and Grimm's law, and Weber's law: you will find that in all three cases — physics, philology, psychology — the laws are of this sort.

The formulation of a scientific law, therefore, means the final writing of some paragraph in some chapter of that book of the world which contains all the different sciences. No science is as yet complete: but the formulation of a law means that the science of which it holds is complete up to a certain point. The law embraces, covers, summarises a large body of observations, and also serves as a point of departure for the making of fresh observations. This is why the important dates in the history of science are the years in which scientific laws were established, and why the most honoured names in science are the names of the men who established them. It would, perhaps, make the study of science easier for the beginner if all proper names were omitted, and we ceased to speak of the principle of Archimedes, and Euclidean geometry, and Newton's laws of motion. But these terms serve a good purpose: they show the importance of scientific laws, and they also reinforce a conclusion at which we have already arrived, — that what differentiates the sciences is the difference of human interests, and that what makes a science is some man's consistent adherence to a definite point of view.

§ 2. The Subject-matter of Psychology. — If it is true that all the sciences have the same sort of subject-matter, there can be no essential difference between the raw materials of physics and the raw materials of psychology. Matter and mind, as we call them, must be fundamentally the same thing. Let us find out, now, whether this statement is really as paradoxical as at first thought it appears.

All human knowledge is derived from human experience; there is no other source of knowledge. But human experience, as we have seen, may be considered from different points of view. Suppose that we take two points of view, as far as possible apart, and discover for ourselves what experience looks like in the two cases. First, we will regard experience as altogether independent of any particular person; we will assume that it goes on whether or not anyone is there to have it. Secondly, we will regard experience as altogether dependent upon the particular person; we will assume that it goes on only when someone is there to have it. We shall hardly find standpoints more diverse. What are the differences in experience, as viewed from them?

Take, to begin with, the three things that you first learn about in physics: space, time and mass. Physical space, which is the space of geometry and astronomy and geology, is constant, always and everywhere the same. Its unit is 1 cm., and the cm. has precisely the same value wherever and whenever it is applied. Physical time is similarly constant; and its constant unit is 1 sec. Physical mass is constant; its unit, the 1 gr., is always and everywhere the same. Here we have experience of space, time and mass considered as independent of the person who experiences them. Change, then, to the point of view which brings the experiencing person into account. The two vertical lines in Fig 1 are physically equal; they measure alike in units of 1 cm. To you, who see them, they are not equal. The hour that you spend in the waiting-room of a village station and the hour that you spend in watching an amusing play are physically equal; they measure alike in units

Figure 1

of 1 sec. To you, the one hour goes slowly, the other quickly; they are not equal. Take two circular cardboard boxers of different diameter (say, 2 cm. and 8 cm.), and pour sand into them until they both weigh, say, 50 gr. The two masses are physically equal, placed on the pans of a balance, they will hold the beam level. To you, as you lift them in your to hands, or raise them in turn by the same hand, the box of smaller diameter is considerably the heavier. Here we have experience of space, time and mass considered as dependent upon the experiencing person. It is the same experience that we were discussing just now. But our first point of view gives us facts and laws of physics; our second gives us facts and laws of psychology.

Now take three other topics that are discussed in the physical text-books; heat, sound and light. Heat proper, the physicists tell us, is the energy of molecular motion; that is to say, heat is a form of energy due to a movement of the particles of a body among themselves. Radiant heat belongs, with light, to what is called radiant energy, — energy that is propagated by wave-movements of the luminiferous ether with which space is filled. Sound is a form of energy due to the vibratory movements of bodies, and is propagated by wave-movements of some elastic medium, solid, liquid or gaseous. In brief, heat is a dance of molecules; light is a wave-motion of the ether; sound is a wave-motion of the air. The world of physics, in which these types of experience are considered as independent of the experiencing person, is neither warm nor cold, neither dark nor light, neither silent nor noisy. It is only when the experiences are considered as dependent upon some person what we have warmth and cold, blacks and whites and colours and greys, tones and hisses and thuds. And these things are subject-matter of psychology.

We find, then, a great difference in the aspect of experience, according as it is viewed from the one or the other of our different standpoints. It is the same experience all through; physics and psychology deal with the same stuff, the same material; the sciences are separated simply — and sufficiently — by their point of view. From the standpoint of physics, we get such sciences as physics (in the narrower sense), chemistry, geology, astronomy, meteorology. From the standpoint of psychology we get, in the same way, a special group of sciences: their names and provinces are given in § 7.

It must be clearly understood that we are not here attempting to give a strict definition of the subject-matter of psychology. We assume that everybody knows, at first hand, what human experience is, and we then seek to mark off the two aspects of this experience which are dealt with respectively by physics and psychology. Any further definition of the subject-matter of psychology is impossible. Unless one knows, by experience itself, what experience is, one can no more give a meaning to the term 'mind' than a stone can give a meaning to the term 'matter.'

§ 3. The Common-sense View of Mind. — If, before you read the two preceding sections, you had been asked to define psychology, you would probably have said, without hesitation, that it is the science of the mind. But you would have meant by mind something that, at all events in appearance, is very different from the meaning that these two sections have given it. Let us see how nearly we can reconcile the common-sense idea of mind with the view that it is the sum-total of human experience considered as dependent upon the experiencing person.

The common-sense idea of the world is roughly this. The world is made up of, or contains, two radically different things: matter and mind. Matter is found in the physical objects around us; it always fills space; it is governed by mechanical laws, laws of cause and effect. Mind is found in ourselves and, very likely, in some of the other animals; it is immaterial, not spatial; it is not bound by mechanical laws, but is free to act as it will; if it submits to laws at all (as, for instance, to the laws of thought in our processes of reasoning), these are laws peculiar to it, and are not the same as the laws of nature. Nevertheless, different as mind and matter are, they are joined together, in a very intimate way, both in ourselves and in such of the animals as possess minds; for our physical bodies are material. And when they are thus joined together, they act upon each other, mind affecting matter and matter affecting mind. We cry because we are grieved; we cannot think clearly because we have eaten too heavy a dinner.

Compare these statements, now, with the statements of §§ 1 and 2. Common sense declares that mind and matter are radically different. We have said that, in order to get the subject-matter of physics and of psychology, one must regard human experience from standpoints as diverse as can be found. So far there is a general agreement. Common sense declare that the laws of matter are different from the laws of mind. We have seen that, for instance, space, time and mass behave very differently, according as they are taken to be independent of, or dependent upon, the experiencing person. Again there is agreement. Common sense declares that we, and perhaps the animals, are made up of both matter and of mind. Here also, if we go beneath the difference of terms, there is agreement. The living body, as it is treated in the science of physiology, is treated from the physical point of view; it belongs to the independent aspect of experience. The same living body — that is to say, an organism, and organised individual — is, however, precisely the 'experiencing person' referred to in our definition of mind. It is when heat-waves strike the skin, and sound-waves strike the ear, and light-waves strike the eye, that we have experience in its dependent aspect, as warmth and tone and colour. On these three points, therefore, we have no serious quarrel with common sense.

On the other hand, common sense makes certain other statements that we cannot accept. These statements all point to a view of mind which is not often expressed outright, in so many words, but which is very generally held; the view, namely, that mind is a living being, with all the qualities and powers that are possessed by material living beings; an immaterial mind, so to say, that dwells within the material animal; an inward man, manifesting itself in the behaviour of the outward man. A mind so conceived cannot fill space, because it is not material; but it has all the other properties of a living creature. It is free to act as it pleases, just as you are free to come or to go, to do this or do that. It can influence the body, and be influenced by the body, just as you may influence or be influenced by your friend. This view of mind probably appears natural enough, although, as soon as you begin to ask questions, you will find that it is by no means clear. Natural or not, however, it is a view which we must here reject, for the following reasons.

(1) A statement that rests upon common sense is not likely to be argued; it is taken for granted, as something that needs no discussion. Yet, in theoretical matters, common sense is an unsafe guide. For the common sense of our own generation simply sums up so much of the advanced thought of former generations as the great body of mankind has found acceptable and intelligible. A brilliant speculation of one age may become the common sense of the next: but this does not make it any the less speculation, while in the course of becoming sense its logical structure has, inevitably, been more or less damaged. Common sense, in theoretical matters, is past philosophy; and the philosophy is the more vulgarised, the farther it has travelled from its source.

There is no dispute as to the philosophical source from which, in the present instance, our common-sense ideas are derived. The view of mind and matter which we are now criticising was set forth, in all essential points, by the French philosopher, René Descartes (1596-1650). No doubt, the common-sense version has certain crude elements which are indefinitely older than Descartes; no doubt, also, it has been tinged by later thought, notably by the doctrine of organic evolution. In the main, however, what is common sense to-day was high Cartesian philosophy two centuries and a half ago.[1]

Plainly, then, we cannot take common sense for granted. And we should not nowadays pin our philosophical faith to Descartes, so we cannot leave Cartesian doctrines unquestioned when they appear in the garb of common sense. We shall rather expect to find that Descartes, and with him our own common sense, are partly right and partly wrong.

(2) That some of the doctrines of common sense agree, in general, with the position of §§ 1 and 2 has already been shown. The remainder must be rejected, because the evidence is against them. We are told that mind is not spatial: yet, as Fig. 1 shows, mental experience takes on the spatial form as readily as physical experience. We are told that mind is free to act as it pleases: yet, as we shall see in this book, the more carefully mind is studied, the more plainly are the laws of mental experience revealed. We are told that mind influences body, and body mind. How an immaterial thing can influence and be influenced by a material thing we are not told, — for the very good reason that nobody knows: though, if this were the only view that did justice to the facts, we should nevertheless be bound to accept it. Since, as the following section shows, all the observed facts can be rationally explained from the standpoint of §§ 1 and 2, this standpoint must be preferred.

§4. Psychophysical Parallelism. — Common sense says that we cry because we are sorry, laugh because we are amused, run because we are frightened; that we feel gloomy and morose because we do not digest our food, go insane from softening of the brain, lose consciousness because we have inhaled ether. Mind influences body, and body influences mind. Our own position has been that mind and body, the subject-matter of psychology and the subject-matter of physiology, are simply two aspects of the same world of experience. They cannot influence each other, because they are not separate and independent things. For the same reason, however, wherever the two aspects appear, any change that occurs in the one will be accompanied by a corresponding change in the other. Your view of a town from the east cannot influence your view of the same town from the west; but as your view from the east differs in sunlight and moonlight, so correspondingly will your view from the west differ. This doctrine of the relation of mind and body is known as the doctrine of psychophysical parallelism: the common-sense doctrine is that of interaction.

From the point of view of psychophysical parallelism, then, it is not strictly true to say that we cry because we are sorry. If we look at the whole experience under its independent aspect, we find that certain physical events, certain stimuli, affect the body; they set up in the body, and especially in the nervous system, certain physical changes; these changes cause the secretion of tears. This is an exhaustive account of the experience, considered as independent of the experiencing person. If we look at the experience under its dependent aspect, we find that our consciousness has been invaded by grief or remorse or some kindred emotion. The two sets of events, physical and mental, are parallel, but they do not interfere with each other. And the same thing holds of all the other cases cited at the beginning of this section.

By accepting this doctrine of parallelism we gain a two-fold advantage. On the positive side, we are able to do justice to all the observed facts; we never come into contradiction with facts. On the negative side, we avoid perplexing questions, questions that lead nowhere because they are put from a wrong standpoint. The common-sense view of mind appears natural; but as soon as you ask questions, you find it obscure. Where, for instance, on that view, does the body end and the mind begin? Do the senses belong to mind or to body? Is the mind always active and the body always passive? Do body and mind ever act independently of each other? Questions such a these arise at once; but it is a hard matter to answer them. Parallelism has no logical pitfalls of this kind.

At the same time, we need not be pedantic, and change our manner of speech to accord with the strict letter of parallelism. The astronomer does not scruple to talk, with all the rest of us, about sunrise and sunset. It is not strictly true to say that we cry because we are sorry; our crying is the effect of certain nervous (that is, physical) changes, whose parallel on the mental side is the emotion of grief. But this parallel is constant and invariable. We should not cry, under the circumstances, unless we are sorry, because our sorrow is the mental aspect of the nervous changes that make us cry: we have only to shift our point of view, and what appeared as nervous change appears as emotion. So that, for all practical purposes, it is true to say that we cry because we are sorry, and run because we are frightened, and so forth. What we have to guard against is not the phrasing of these statements, but their popular interpretation. To suppose that the sorrow and the fear are literally the cause of tear and bodily movements would be on a par with supposing that the idea of watering the lawn can, literally and directly, turn the tap and start the sprinkler in motion.

§ 5. Mental Processes, Consciousness and Mind. — The most striking fact about the world of human experience is the fact of change. Nothing stands still; everything goes on. The sun will someday lose its heat; the eternal hills are, little by little, breaking up and wearing away. Whatever we observe, and from whatever standpoint we observe it, we find process, occurrence; nowhere is there permanence or stability. Mankind, it is true, has sought to arrest this flux, and give stability to the world of experience, by assuming two permanent substances, matter and mind: the occurrences of the physical world are then supposed to be manifestations of matter, and the occurrences of the mental world to be manifestations of mind. Such an hypothesis may be of value at a certain stage of human thought; but every hypothesis that does not accord with the facts must, sooner or later, be given up. Physicists are therefore giving up the hypothesis of an unchanging substantial matter, and psychologists are giving up the hypothesis of an unchanging, substantial mind. Stable objects and substantial things belong, not to the world of science, physical or psychological, but only to the world of common sense.

We have defined mind as the sum-total of human experience considered as dependent upon the experiencing person. We have said, further, that the phrase 'experiencing person' means the living body, the organised individual; and we have hinted that, for psychological purposes, the living body may be reduced to the nervous system and its attachments. Mind thus becomes the sum-total of human experience considered as dependent upon a nervous system. And since human experience is always process, occurrence, and the dependent aspect of human experience is its mental aspect, we may say, more shortly, that mind is the sum-total of mental processes. All these words are significant. 'Sum-total' implies that we are concerned with the whole world of experience, not with a limited portion of it; 'mental' implies that we are concerned with experience under its dependent aspect, as conditioned by a nervous system; and 'process' implies that our subject-matter is a stream, a perpetual flux, and not a collection of unchangeable objects.

It is not easy, even with the best will possible, to shift from the common-sense to the scientific view of mind; the change cannot be made all in a moment. We are to regard mind as a stream of processes? But mind is personal, my mind; and my personality continues throughout my life. The experiencing person is the only bodily organism? But, again, experience is personal, the experience of a permanent self. Mind is spatial, just as matter is? But mind is invisible, intangible; it is not here or there, square or round.

These objections cannot be finally met until we have gone some distance into psychology, and can see how the scientific view of mind works out. Even now, however, they will weaken as you look at them. Face the question of personality. Is your life, as a matter of fact, always personal? Do you not, time and again, forget yourself, lose yourself, disregard yourself, neglect yourself, contradict yourself, in a very literal sense? Surely, the mental life is only intermittently personal. And is your personality, when it is realised, unchanging? Are you the same self in childhood and manhood, in your working and in your playing moods, when you are on your best behaviour and when you are freed from restraint? Surely, the self-experience is not the only intermittent, but also composed, at different times, of very different factors. As to the other questions: mind is, of course, invisible, because sight is mind; and mind is intangible, because touch is mind. Sight-experience and touch-experience are dependent upon the experiencing person. But common sense itself bears witness, against its own belief, to the fact that mind is spatial; we speak, and speak correctly, of an idea in our head, a pain in our foot. And if the idea is the idea of a circle seen in the mind's eye, it is round; and it is the visual idea of a square, it is square.

Consciousness, as reference to any dictionary will show, is a term that has many meanings. Here it is, perhaps, enough to distinguish two principal uses of the word.

In its first sense, consciousness means the mind's awareness of its own processes. Just as, from the common-sense point of view, mind is that inner self which thinks, remembers, chooses, reasons, directs the movements of the body, so is consciousness the inner knowledge of this thought and government. You are conscious of the correctness of your answer to an examination question, of the awkwardness of your movements, of the purity of your motives. Consciousness is thus something more than mind; it is "the perception of what passes in a man's own mind";[2] it is "the immediate knowledge which the mind has of its sensations and thoughts."[3]

In its second sense, consciousness is identified with mind, and 'conscious' with 'mental.' So long as mental processes are going on, consciousness is present; as soon as mental processes are in abeyance, unconsciousness sets in. "To say I am conscious of a feeling, is merely to say that I feel it. To have a feeling is to be conscious; and to be conscious is to have a feeling. To be conscious of the prick of the pin, is merely to have the sensation. And though I have these various modes of naming my sensation, by saying, I feel the prick of a pin, I feel the pain of a prick, I have the sensation of a prick, I have the feeling of a prick, I am conscious of the feeling; the thing named in all these various ways is one and the same."[4]

The first of these definitions we must reject. It is not only unnecessary, but it is also misleading to speak of consciousness as the mind's awareness of itself. The usage is unnecessary, because, as we shall see later, this awareness is a matter of observation of the same general kind as observation of the external world; it is misleading, because it suggests that mind is a personal being, instead of a stream of processes. We shall therefore take mind and consciousness to mean the same thing. But as we have the two different words, and it is convenient to make some distinction between them, we shall speak of mind when we mean the sum-total of mental processes occurring in the life-time of an individual, and we shall speak of consciousness when we mean the sum-total of mental processes occurring *now*, at any given 'present' time. Consciousness thus will be a section, a division, of the mind-stream. This distinction is, indeed, already made in common speech: when we say that a man has 'lost consciousness,' we mean that the lapse is temporary, that the mental life will shortly be resumed; when we say that a man has 'lost his mind,' we mean — not, it is true, that mind has altogether disappeared, but certainly that the derangement is permanent and chronic.

While, therefore, the subject-matter of psychology is mind, the direct object of psychological study is always consciousness. In strictness, we can never observe the same consciousness twice over; the stream of mind flows on, never to return. Practically, we can observe a particular consciousness as often as we wish, since mental processes group themselves in the same way, show the same pattern of arrangement, whenever the organism is placed under the same circumstances. Yesterday's high tide will never recur; but we have a science of psychology, as we have a science of oceanography.

§ 6. The Method of Psychology. — Scientific method may be summed up in the single word 'observation'; the only way to work in science is to observe those phenomena which form the subject-matter of science. An observation implies two things: attention to the phenomena, and record of the phenomena; that is, clear and vivid experience, and an account of the experience in words or formulas.

In order to secure clear experience and accurate report, science has recourse to experiment. An experiment is an observation that can be repeated, isolated and varied. The more frequently you can *repeat* an observation, the more likely you are to see clearly what is there and to describe accurately what you have seen. The more strictly you can *isolate* an observation, the easier does your task of observation become, and the less danger there is of your being led astray by irrelevant circumstances, or of placing emphasis on the wrong point. The more widely you can *vary* an observation, the more clearly will the uniformity of experience stand out, and the better is your chance of discovering laws. All experimental appliances, all laboratories and instruments, are provided and devised with this one end in view: that the student shall be able to repeat, isolate and vary his observations. —

The method of psychology, then, is observation. To distinguish it from the observation of physical science, which is inspection, a looking-at, psychological observation has been termed introspection, a looking-within. But this difference of name must not blend us to the essential likeness of the methods. Let us take some typical instances.

We may begin with two very simple cases. (1) Suppose that you are shown two paper discs: the one of an uniform violet, the other composed half of red and half of blue. If this second disc is rapidly rotated, the red and blue will mix, as we say, and you will see a certain blue-red, that is a kind of violet. Your problem is, so to adjust the proportions of red and blue in the second disc that the resulting violet exactly matches the violet of the first disc. You may repeat this set of observations as often as you like; you may isolate the observations by working in a room that is free from the other, possibly disturbing colours; you may vary the observation by working to equality of the violets first from a two-colour disc that is distinctly too blue, and secondly from a disc that is distinctly too red. (2) Suppose, again, that the chord c-e-g is struck, and that you are asked to say how many tones it contains. You may repeat this observation; you may isolate it, by working in a quiet room; you may vary it, by having the chord struck at different parts of the scale, in different octaves.

It is clear that, in these instances, there is practically no difference between introspection and inspection. You are using the same method that you would use for counting the swings of a pendulum, or taking reading from a galvanometer scale, in the physical laboratory. There is a difference in subject-matter: the colours and the tones are dependent, not independent experiences: but the method is essentially the same.

Now let us take some cases in which the material of introspection is more complex. (1) Suppose that a word is called out to you, and that you are asked to observe the effect which this stimulus produces upon consciousness: how the word affects you, what ideas it calls up, and so forth. The observation may be repeated; it may be isolated, — you may be seated in a dark and silent room, free from disturbances; and it may be varied, — different words may be called out, the word may be flashed upon a screen instead of spoken, etc. Here, however, there seems to be a difference between introspection and inspection. The observer who is watching the course of a chemical reaction, or the movements of some microscopical creature, can jot down from moment to moment the different phases of the observed phenomenon. But if you try to report the changes in consciousness, while these changes are in progress, you interfere with consciousness; your translation of the mental experience into words introduces new factors into that experience itself. (2) Suppose, again, that you are observing a feeling or an emotion: a feeling of disappointment or annoyance, an emotion of anger or chagrin. Experimental control is still possible; situations may be arranged, in the psychological laboratory, such that these feelings may be repeated, isolated and varied. But your observation of them interferes, even more seriously than before, with the course of consciousness. Cool consideration of an emotion is fatal to its very existence; your anger disappears, your disappointment evaporates, as you examine it.

To overcome this difficulty of the introspective method, students of psychology are usually recommended to delay their observation until the process to be described has run its course, and then to call it back and describe it from memory. Introspection thus becomes retrospection; introspective examination becomes *post mortem* examination. The rule is, no doubt, a good one for the beginner; and there are cases in which the experienced psychologist will be wise to follow it. But it is by no means universal. For we must remember (*a*) that the observation in question may be repeated. There is, then, no reason why the observer to whom the word is called out, or in whom the emotion is set up, should not report at once upon the first stage of his experience: upon the immediate effect of the word, upon the beginnings of the emotive process.[5] It is true that this report interrupts the observation. But, after the first stage has been accurately described, further observations may be taken, and the second, third and following stages similarly described; so that presently a complete report upon the whole experience is obtained. There is, in theory, some danger that the stages become artificially separated; consciousness is a flow, a process, and if we divide it up we run the risk of missing certain intermediate links. In practice, however, this danger has proved to be very small; and we may always have recourse to retrospection, and compare our results with our memory of the unbroken experience. Moreover, (*b*) the practised observer gets into an introspective habit, has the introspective attitude ingrained in his system; so that it is possible for him, not only to take mental notes while the observation is in progress, without interfering with consciousness, but even to jot down written notes, as the histologist does while his eye is still held to the ocular of the microscope.

In principle, then, introspection is very like inspection. The objects of observation are different; they are objects of dependent, not of independent experience; they are likely to be transient, elusive, slippery. Sometimes they refuse to be observed while they are in passage; they must be preserved in memory, as a delicate tissue is preserved in hardening fluid, before they can be examined. And the standpoint of the observer is different; it is the standpoint of human life and of human interest, not of detachment and aloofness. But, in general, the method of psychology is much the same as the method of physics.

It must not be forgotten that, while the method of the physical and the psychological sciences is substantially the same, the subject-matter of these sciences is as different as is can well be. Ultimately, as we have seen, the subject-matter of all the sciences is the world of human experience; but we have also seen that the aspect of experience treated by physics is radically different from the aspect treated by psychology. The likeness of method may tempt us to slip from the one aspect to the other, as when a text-book of physics contains a chapter on vision and the sense of colour, or a text-book of physiology contains paragraphs on delusions of judgment; but this confusion of subject-matter must inevitably lead to confusion of thought. Since all the sciences are concerned with the one world of human experience, it is natural that scientific method, to whatever aspect of experience it is applied, should be in principle the same. On the other hand, when we have decided to examine some particular aspect of experience, it is necessary that we hold fast to that aspect, and do not shift our point of view as the enquiry proceeds. Hence it is a great advantage that we have the two terms, introspection and inspection, to denote observation taken from the different stand-points of psychology and of physics. The use of the word introspection is a constant reminder that are working in psychology, that we are observing the dependent aspect of the world of experience.

Observation, as we said above, implies two things: attention to the phenomena, and record of the phenomena. The attention must be held at the highest possible degree of concentration; the record must be photographically accurate. Observation is, therefore, both difficult and fatiguing; and introspection is, on the whole, more difficult and more fatiguing that inspection. To secure reliable results, we must be strictly impartial and unprejudiced, facing the facts as they come, ready to accept them as they are, not trying to fit them to any preconceived theory; and we must work only when our general disposition is favourable, when we are fresh and in good health, at ease in our surroundings, free from outside worry and anxiety. If these rules are not followed, no amount of experimenting will help us. The observer in the psychological laboratory is placed under the best possible external conditions; the room in which he works is fitted up and arranged in such a way that the observation may be repeated, that the process to be observed may stand out clearly upon the background of consciousness, and that the factors in the process may be separately varied. But all this care is of no avail, unless the observer himself comes to the work in an even frame of mind, gives it his full attention, and is able adequately to translate his experience into words.

§ 7. The Scope of Psychology. — If mind is the sum-total of human experience considered a dependent upon the experiencing person, it follows that each one of us can have direct acquaintance only with a single mind, namely, with his own. We are concerned in psychology with the whole world of human experience; but we concerned with it solely under its dependent aspect, as conditioned by a nervous system; and a nervous system is a particular thing, possessed by a particular individual. In strictness, therefore, it is only his own mind, the experience dependent upon his own nervous system, that each of us knows first-hand; it is only to this limited and individual subject-matter that the method of experimental introspection can be directly applied. How, then, is a scientific psychology possible? How can psychology be anything more than a body of personal beliefs and individual opinions?

The difficulty is more apparent that real. We have every reason to believe, not only in general that our neighbors have minds like our own, that is, are able like ourselves to view experience in its dependent aspect, but also in detail that human minds resemble one another precisely as human bodies do. Within a given race there is much apparent diversity of outward form: differences in height and figure, in colour of hair and eyes, in shape of nose and mouth. We notice these differences because we are obliged in everyday life to distinguish the persons with whom we come in contact. But the resemblances are more fundamental than differences. If we have recourse to exact measurements, we find that there is in every case a certain standard or type to which the individual more or less closely conforms and about which all the individuals are more or less closely grouped. And even without measurements we have evidence to the same effect: strangers see family likenesses which the members of the family cannot themselves detect, and the units in a crowd of aliens, Chinese or Negroes, look bewilderingly alike.

Now all of our main social institutions rest upon the assumption that the individuals of whom society is composed possess minds, and possess minds that are of the same sort. Language, religion, law and custom, — they one and all rest upon this assumption, and they one and all bear testimony that the assumption is well grounded. Would a man invent a language in order to talk to himself? Language implies that there are more minds than one. And would the use of a common speech be possible if minds were not essentially alike? Men differ in their command of language, as they differ in complexion, or in liability to disease; but the general use of language testifies to a fundamental likeness of mental constitution in us all.

Hence the psychologist is fully justified in believing that other men have minds of the same kind as his own, and in basing psychology upon the introspective reports furnished by a number of different observers. These reports show, in point of fact, just what we would expect them to show: a fundamental agreement, and a great variety of detail, — the mental differences grouping themselves, as we have seen that physical differences group themselves, about a central type or standard.

If, however, we attribute minds to other human beings, we have no right to deny them to the higher animals. These animals are provided with a nervous system of the same pattern as ours, and their conduct or behaviour, under circumstances that would arose certain feelings in us, often seems to express, quite definitely, similar feelings in them. Surely we must grant that the highest vertebrates, mammals and birds, have minds. But the lower vertebrates, fishes and reptiles and amphibia, possess a nervous system of the same order, although of simpler construction. And many of the invertebrates, insects and spiders and crustaceans, show a fairly high degree of nervous development. Indeed, it is difficult to limit mind to the animals that possess even a rudimentary nervous system, practically everything that their superiors do by its assistance. The range of mind thus appears to be as wide as the range of animal life.

The plants, on the other hand, appear to be mindless. Many of them are endowed with what we may term sense-organs, that is, organs differentiated to receive certain forms of stimulus, pressure, impact, light, etc. These organs are analogous in structure to the sense-organs of the lower animal organisms: thus, plant 'eyes' have been found, which closely resemble rudimentary animal eyes, and which — if they belonged to animals — might mediate the perception of light: so that the development of the plant-world has evidently been governed by the same general laws of adaptation to environment that have been at work in the animal kingdom. But we have no evidence of a plant-consciousness.

Just as the scope of psychology extends beyond man to the animals, so does it extend from the individual man to groups of men to societies. The subject-matter of psychology is human experience considered as dependent upon the individual. But since the individuals of the same race and epoch are organised in much the same way, and since they live together in a society where their conduct affects and is affected by the conduct of others, their view of experience under its dependent aspect naturally becomes, in certain main features, a common or general view; and this common view is embodied in those social institutions to which we have referred above, — in language, religion, law and custom. There is no such thing as a collective mind, if we mean by it the sum-total of human experience considered as dependent upon a social group of similar individuals. The study of the collective mind gives us a psychology of language, a psychology of myth, a psychology of custom, etc.; it also gives us a differential of psychology of the Latin mind, of the Anglo-Saxon mind, of the Oriental mind, etc.

And this is not all: the scope of psychology extends, still further, from the normal to the abnormal mind. Life, as we know, need not be either complete or completely healthy life. The living organism may show defect, the lack of a limb or of a sense-organ; and it may show disorder and disease, a temporary or a permanent lapse from health. So it is with mind. The consciousness of those who are born deaf or blind are defective; they lack certain sensations and images that are normally present. In dreaming and the hypnotic state, during intoxication, after prolonged sleeplessness or severe strain of any kind, we have illustrations of temporary mental derangement. And the various forms of insanity — mania, melancholia, dementia — are forms of permanent mental disorder.

Derangement of the social mind may be studied in the various panics, fads, epidemics of speculation, of false belief, etc., which occur from time to time even in the most highly civilised societies. The mob consciousness stands to a healthy social consciousness very much as dreaming to the waking life. Permanent disorder of the social mind means the downfall of society.

All these various field of psychology may be cultivated for their own sake, on account of their intrinsic interest and value; they must, indeed, be so cultivated, if psychology is to progress. At the same time, their facts and laws often throw light upon the problems of normal human psychology. Suppose, for instance, that a man, blind from birth, is rendered able to see by a surgical operation. He must learn to use his eyes, as a child learns to walk. And the gradual perfecting of his vision, the mistakes and confusions to which he is liable, all the details of his visual education, form a storehouse of facts upon which the psychologist can draw when he seeks to illustrate the development of the perception of space in the normal mind, — the manner in which we come to judge of the distance of objects from ourselves and from one another, of their direction, and of their size and shape. Instructive, also, are those forms of mental unsoundness which consist in the derangement of a single group of processes. The various types of morbid fear — agoraphobia, the fear of being alone in open spaces; neophobia, the fear of everything that is new; phobophobia, the nervous dread of being afraid — are only exaggerated forms of experiences that most of us have had. The sanest man will feel lost when he passes, suddenly, from a quiet country life to the bustle of a large town: we are all a little timid when we enter a strange community; we have all been afraid that on such-and-such an occasion we shall show our nervousness. Similarly, the self-importance of paranoia is merely an exaggeration of the pleased self-consciousness, the self-complacency, that we often observe in others and, if we are honest, must often detect in ourselves. In all these instances, the strong lines of the caricature may help us to a more correct picture of the normal consciousness.

§ 8. **The Use of Analogy in Psychology.** — We have agreed that the psychologist is not confined to a knowledge of his own mind. Although this is the only mind to which he can directly apply the method of experimental introspection, he can apply the method indirectly to any number of minds. Psychology is based upon the introspections of a large number of trained observers.

But we have gone much farther than this. We have spoken of an animal psychology, a social psychology, and a psychology of the abnormal mind. What, then, is the method to be employed in these branches of psychology? We cannot ask the animal or the society or the madman to introspect!

Yet, in a sense, this is just what we do. Observation, it will be remembered, implies two things: attention to the phenomena, and record of the phenomena. We ourselves record mental phenomena, for psychological purposes, in language. This form of record has great advantages: it is flexible, since we have a large vocabulary at our disposal; it is constant, since written or printed reports may be preserved for a long time; and it is easily intelligible, since we are accustomed to the use of words in everyday life. At the same time, language is not the only possible means of expression. Physically regarded, it is a complex bodily movement: spoken language is a movement of the larynx, written language a movement of the hand: and it belongs to the class of movements that we term gestures. We can express our ideas by a grimace or a shrug of the shoulders, as well as by spoken words or a written paragraph.

Now the psychologist argues, by analogy, that what holds of himself holds also, in principle, of the animal, of society, and of the insane. He argues that the movements of animals are, to a large extent, gestures; that they express or record the animal's mental processes. He therefore tries, so far as possible to put himself in the place of the animal, to find the conditions under which his own movements would be of the same general kind; and then, from the character of his human consciousness, he attempts — always bearing in mind the limit of development of the animal's nervous system — to reconstruct the animal consciousness. He calls experiment to his assistance, and places the animal in circumstances which permit of the repetition, isolation and variation of certain types of movement or behaviour. The animal is thus made, so to say, to observe, to introspect; it attends to certain stimuli, and registers its experience by gesture. Of course, this is not scientific observation: science, as we said in § 1, implies a definite attitude to the worlds of experience, and consists in a description of the world as viewed from a definite standpoint. None the less, it is observation, and as such furnishes raw material for science. The psychologist works the raw material into shape; he observes the gesture, and transcribes the animal consciousness in the light of his own introspection.

Roundabout as this method appears, it has nevertheless led, in the hands of skilled investigators, to perfectly definite results. And it is by way of detailed investigation, and by that way only, that the general questions of animal psychology can be finally answered. One of these questions is that of the 'criterion of mind.' How are we to decide whether the animal before us does or does not possess mind? How are we to decide whether it has attended to the stimulus, so that its movement is a gesture movement, or whether it has received the stimulus mindlessly and mechanically, so that the movement is a reflex? An answer now commonly given to this question is that we may assume the presence of mind whenever the animal rapidly adjusts itself to new conditions, quickly learns to get its bearings in a novel environment. The answer is, of course, based upon the analogy of human experience. It is, however, unwise to commit oneself to a criterion of this nature. What is needed is an exhaustive study of all the various modes in which animals do, as a matter of fact, adjust themselves to new conditions. Then the criterion of mind will appear, so to speak, of its own accord.

Another general question is that of the interpretation of the animal consciousness. Shall we assume that this consciousness is always as simple as possible? Or shall we give the animal the benefit of our doubt, take its different forms of behaviour at their face value, and ascribe to it processes of memory, of ideation, of reasoning, that differ from our own only in degree? On this question opinion is sharply divided. Both positions may be supported by the analogy of the human consciousness, since this may be, under very similar circumstances, either extremely complex or surprisingly simple. And so we find one authority laying it down that "in no case may we interpret an action as the outcome of the exercise of a higher physical faculty, if it can be interpreted as the outcome of the exercise of one which stands lower in the physiological scale';[6] while another authority declares that "we are too ready to adopt simple — unduly simple — explanations of the animals by which we are surrounded."[7] It is, again, unwise to commit oneself to either view. The animal must be subjected to experimental test, under conditions of gradually increasing complexity, and we must find out by actual trial how far it is able to cope with these conditions. Then our principles of interpretation will, also, emerge of their own accord.—

We do, then, make the animals attend to stimuli and report their experiences to us; we do, after a fashion, make them introspect. This would be impossible if introspection implied a reflective attitude towards mind, or a special kind of mental awareness of mental processes. But, as we have seen, introspection is simply observation of dependent experience: it is therefore precisely the sort of observation that an animal can make, if it has a mind at all. Our own task is to do what the animals cannot do: to systematise and interpret the observations in terms of human consciousness.

What holds of the study of the animal mind holds also of social psychology. The introspections made in common by the members of a social group are recorded for us in the forms of speech, in custom and law, in myth and religion. Society has introspected, and has recorded its introspections in these various institutions. It is, obviously, impossible for the psychologist to experiment upon the social mind in any direct way. It is therefore fortunate that nature has made experiments for him. By comparing the languages, customs, etc., of different types of human society at all the different levels of human evolution, he is able to repeat, isolate and vary his observations; history furnishes him with a laboratory of social psychology.

It is clear that the study of social psychology requires the use of analogy. It is we, the moderns, who study the myths and customs of primitive man, and we have to psychologise these myths and customs from our own modern standpoint. Hence it is natural to find, in works upon the subject, the same sort of disagreement on general principles that we have noted in the case of animal psychology. And the remedy is the same. We must not hastily adopt a particular view of human evolution, but must patiently examine all the available records; must seek to add to the records by researches among the lower races of mankind; and must then accept the general principles that an exhaustive survey of the facts suggests to us.

Since social psychology is thus a genetic study, a study of human development, it has become customary to speak of its method as a genetic method. In strictness, however, there is no such thing as a genetic method. There is a genetic point of view, as there is a static point of view. We may be interested in the sequence of mental processes, in tracing the course of mind from simple to complex; or we may be interested in the coexistence of mental processes, in unravelling the tangle of a special sort of consciousness. But the difference of interest does not mean a difference of method.

For the psychology of dreaming and of intoxication we have the advantage of direct introspective records. We may also have recourse to experiment. A sleeping person, for example, may be subjected to various kinds of stimulation, and may be aroused, after the stimuli have been applied, to give an account of the dream which they occasioned.

The psychological study of hypnosis is less direct, since the hypnotic subject usually forgets, on arousal, what has take place during the hypnotic state. We must therefore observe his behaviour during hypnosis, taking care to make our tests as simple and straightforward as possible, and must then seek to reconstruct the hypnotic consciousness on the analogy of the normal waking consciousness. It is, of course, possible to secure introspective reports from hypnotic subjects; but it is still a matter of dispute whether these reports are true records of observations, or do not rather reflect the ideas and opinions of those who are conducting the experiment. The hypnotic subject is extremely suggestible; that is to say, he is exceedingly liable to pick up a hint from the experimenter, and to report as he thinks the experimenter desires or expects him to report.

For the study of the insane mind, we have, in the first place, the utterance and behaviour of insane persons. We have also the opportunity to experiment; the inmates of hospitals may be subjected to systematic tests, the results of which will give us an insight into their mental processes. So far, this branch of psychology is in a backward condition, since we have been more concerned to shelter and, if possible, to cure the insane than to describe the insane consciousness. Certain forms of insanity are, however, of great psychological interest, and we may look confidently to a realisation of this interest in the near future. —

After all, therefore, it is not so absurd as at first thought it seems, to say that we require the animal and society and the madman to introspect. All three may attend; all three may report their experiences. The attention is likely to be partial, fitful, roving, and the report is likely to be transient, equivocal, imperfect; and so we are compelled, in all three cases, to fall back upon the analogy of our own consciousness. In other words, it is entirely possible to work out, by psychological method, a psychology of the animal, of the social, and of the unsound mind, but it is also very difficult: the psychologist is exposed, at every moment, to the danger of misinterpretation. However, here as elsewhere in science, the pursuit of knowledge furnishes its own corrective. Sooner or later the unfit hypothesis breaks down in face of newly discovered facts.

§ 9. The Problem of Psychology. — Science seeks always to answer three questions in regard to its subject-mater, the questions of what, how, and why. What precisely, stripped of all complications and reduced to its lowest terms, is this subject-matter? How, then, does it come to appear as it does; how are its elements combined and arranged? And, finally, why does it appear now in just this particular combination or arrangement? All three questions must be answered, if we are to have a science that shall satisfy the definition of § 1.

It is often said that the answers to the questions 'what' and 'how' give us a description, the answer to the question 'why' an explanation, of the facts with which science deals. The distinction is useful, if we do not make it to rigid. It would be a grave mistake to suppose, for instance, that we may first of all work out an exhaustive description of the world, and then proceed deliberately to explain what we have already described. On the contrary, knowledge grows by a constant give and take between description and explanation; we describe in terms of some theory, that is, in terms of some tentative explanation, and then we rectify our theory in the light of the observed facts; and so on, over and over again. The distinction is thus logical only; it does not point to two successive stages in the history of the special sciences.

To answer the question 'what' is the task of analysis. Physical science, for example, tries by analysis to reduce the world of independent experiences to its lowest terms, and so arrives at the various chemical elements. To answer the question 'how' is the task of synthesis. Physical science traces the behavior of the elements in their various combinations, and presently succeeds in formulating the laws of nature. When these two questions have been answered, we have a description of physical phenomena. But science enquiries, further, why a given set of phenomena occurs in just this given way, and not otherwise; and it answers the question 'why' by laying bare the cause of which the observed phenomena are the effect. There was dew on the ground last night because the surface of the earth was colder than the layer of air above it; dew forms on glass and not on metal because the radiating power of the one is great and of the other is small. When the cause of a physical phenomenon has thus been assigned, the phenomenon is said to be explained.

So far, now, as description is concerned, the problem of psychology closely resembles the problem of physics. The psychologist seeks, first of all, to analyse mental experience into its simplest components. He takes a particular consciousness and works over it again and again, phase by phase and process by process, until his analysis can go no further. He is left with certain mental processes which resist analysis, which are absolutely simple in nature, which cannot be reduced, even in part, to their processes. The work is continued, with other consciousness, until he is able to pronounce with some confidence upon the nature and number of the elementary mental processes. Then he proceeds to the task of synthesis. He puts the elements together, under experimental conditions: first, perhaps, two elements of the same kind, then more of that kind, then elementary processes of diverse kinds: and he presently discerns that regularity and uniformity of occurrence which we have seen to be characteristic of all human experience. He thus learns to formulate the laws of connection of the elementary processes. If sensations of tone occur together, they blend or fuse; if sensation of colour occur side by side, they enhance one another: and all this takes place in a perfectly regular way, so that we can write out laws of tonal fusion and laws of colour contrast.

If, however, we attempted to work out a merely descriptive psychology, we should find that there was not hope in it of a true science of mind. A descriptive psychology would stand to scientific psychology very much as the old-fashioned natural histories stand to modern text-books of biology, or as the view of the world which a boy gets from his cabinet of physical experiments stands to the trained physicist's view. It would tell us a good deal about mind; it would include a large body of observed facts, which we might classify and, in large measure, bring under general laws. But there would be no unity or coherence in it; it would lack that single guiding principle which biology has, for instance, in the law of evolution, or physics in the law of conservation of energy. In order to make psychology scientific we must not only describe, we must also explain mind. We must answer the question 'why.'

But here is a difficulty. It is clear that we cannot regard one mental process as the cause of another mental process, if only for the reason that, with change of our surroundings, entirely new consciousnesses may be set up. When I visit Athens or Rome for the first time, I have experiences which are due, not to past consciousnesses, but to present stimuli. Nor can we, on the other hand, regard nervous processes as the cause of mental processes. The principle of psychophysical parallelism lays it down that the two sets of events, processes in the nervous system and mental processes, run their course side by side, in exact correspondence but without interference: they are, in ultimate fact, two different aspects of the same experience. The one cannot be the cause of the other.

Nevertheless, it is by reference to the body, to the nervous system and the organs attached to it, that we explain mental phenomena. The nervous system does not cause, but it does explain mind. It explains mind as the map of a country explains the fragmentary glimpses of hills and rivers and towns that we catch on our journey through it. In a word, reference to the nervous system introduces into psychology just that unity and coherence which a strictly descriptive psychology cannot achieve.

It is worth while, for the sake of clearness, to dwell on this point in more detail. The physical world, the world of independent experience, just because it is independent of the individual man, is complete and self-contained. All of the processes that make it up are bound together as cause and effect; nowhere is there a gap or break in their connection. Now, among the processes that make up this independent world are the processes of the nervous system. These are linked, as cause and effect, both to one another and also to physical process, outside the body, which precede and follow them; they have their fixed place in the unbroken chain of physical events; they may themselves be explained, exactly as the occurrence of dew is explained. Mental processes, on the other hand, correspond, not to the whole series of physical events, but only to a small part of them, namely, to certain events within the nervous system. It is natural, then, that mental phenomena should appear scrappy, disconnected, unsystematic. It is also natural that we should seek their explanation in the nervous processes which run parallel to them, and whose causal connection with all other processes of the independent world ensures the continuity that they so conspicuously lack. Mind lapses every night, and reforms every morning; but the bodily processes go on, in sleep and in waking. An idea drops out of memory, to recur, perhaps quite unexpectedly, many years later; but the bodily processes have been going on without interruption. Reference to the body does not add one iota to the data of psychology, to the sum of introspections. It does furnish us with an explanatory principle for psychology; it does enable us to systematise our introspective data. Indeed, if we refuse to explain mind by body, we must accept the one or the other of two, equally unsatisfactory alternatives: we must either rest content with a simple description of mental experience, or must invent an unconscious mind to give coherence and continuity to the conscious. Both courses have been tried. But, if we take the first, we never arrive at a science of psychology; and if we take the second, we voluntarily leave the sphere of fact for the sphere of fiction.

These are scientific alternatives. Common sense, also, has in its own fashion realised the situation, and has found its own way out. It is precisely because of the incompleteness and disconnectedness of mental experience that common sense constructs a hybrid world, travelling easily from mental to physical and back again, filling up the breaks in the mental by material borrowed from the physical. — That way, we may be sure, lies confusion of thought. The truth underlying the confusion is, however, the implicit knowledge that the explanatory principle for psychology must be looked for beyond, and not within, the world of dependent experience. —

Physical science, then, explains by assigning a cause; mental science explains by reference to those nervous processes that are under observation. We may bring these two modes of explanation together, if we define explanation itself as the statement of the proximate circumstances or conditions under which the described phenomenon occurs. Dew is formed under the condition of a difference of temperature between the air and the ground; ideas are formed under the condition of certain processes in the nervous system. Fundamentally, the object and the manner of explanation, in the two cases, are one and the same.

In fine, just as the method of psychology is, on all essential points, the method of the natural sciences, so is the problem of psychology essentially of the same sort as the problem of physics. The psychologist answers the question 'what' by analysing mental experience into its elements. He answers the question 'how' by formulating the laws of connection of these elements. And he answers the question 'why' by explaining mental processes in terms of their parallel processes in the nervous system. His programme need not be carried out in this order: he may get the hint of a law before his analysis is completed, and the discovery of a sense-organ may suggest the occurrence of certain elementary processes before he has found these processes by introspection. The three question are intimately related, and an answer to any one helps towards the answers to the other two. The measure of our progress in scientific psychology is our ability to return satisfactory answers to all three.

Notes

1 You will find that this statement is borne out by the histories of philosophy. Turn, for instance, to A. K. Rogers, *A Student's History of Philosophy*, 1901, pp. 269-289, especially 284-287. The passage is not easy reading; but you will understand it well enough to see that what is said in the text is historically correct.

2 John Locke, *An Essay Concerning Human Understanding*, [1690] Bk. II, Ch i., §19.

3 Dugald Stewart, *Outlines of Moral Philosophy*, [1793]. Pt. I., Section i., §7.

4 James Mill, *Analysis of the Phenomena of the Human Mind*, [1829] Vol. I., Ch. v. Mill uses the word 'feeling' to denote what we have called 'mental process.'

5 We discuss in § 69, where we are dealing with the elementary processes in emotion, the special difficulty mentioned above: that, if you concentrate your attention, say, upon your anger, the

anger disappears. This difficulty makes it necessary to lay down special rules for the observation of emotion. But it does not makes it necessary — and that is the point here — to observe emotion retrospectively.

[6]   C.L. Morgan, *An Introduction to Comparative Psychology*, 1894, 53.

[7]   W. Mills, *The Nature and Development of Animal Intelligence*, 1898, 12.

4

A CRITICISM OF INTROSPECTION

W. Köhler

> Round about the accredited and orderly facts of every science there ever floats a sort of dust-cloud of exceptional observations.
> W. James, *The Will to Believe*

William James has well described how a sudden interest in certain "irregular" phenomena often marks the beginning of a new era in science. At such times, what has been exceptional often becomes the very center of scientific work. We shall now become acquainted with introspection as a procedure by which an artificial system of psychology is protected against a similar revolution. The protection is achieved by a technique which serves to discard particularly interesting observations. In discussing introspection, I do not intend to consider a particular school. What I have to say refers to all psychologists who treat experience in the manner which will be discussed in the following paragraphs.

For the most part, Introspectionists are likely to agree with my criticism of Behaviorism. In fact, some may have recognized their own arguments in the preceding chapters. What, then, is the difference between Introspectionism and the point of view of Gestalt Psychology? This difference will become obvious as soon as we consider how experience is to be observed. First of all, I propose to examine the way in which Introspectionists deal with objective experience, the field in which they have been particularly active. Surprisingly enough, the premises of their work will prove to be quite similar to those of Behaviorism.

The very moment we try to observe experience in an impartial fashion we are bound to hear objections from the Introspectionists. If I say that before me on my

Köhler, W. 1947. "A Criticism of Introspection," in *Gestalt Psychology: An Introduction to New Concepts in Modern Psychology*, pp. 67-99. © 1947 W. W. Norton & Company.

desk I see a book, the criticism will be raised that nobody can see a book. If I lift the book, I shall be inclined to say that I feel its weight as something external to my fingers and roughly in the place in which the book is also seen. These statements, my critic would remark, are typical of the language of untrained observers. He would add that for the practical purposes of common life such statements may be entirely satisfactory, but that none the less they differ widely from the descriptions which a trained psychologist would have to give. For instance, the statements imply that the terms "book" and "desk" refer to objects or things. In correct psychological discussion terms are not admissible according to the Introspectionist. For if observation is to give us the simple and primary data of experience, we must learn to make the all-important distinction between *sensations* and *perceptions*, between the bare sensory material as such and the host of other ingredients with which this material has been imbued by processes of learning. One cannot see a book, the Introspectionist tells us, since this term involves knowledge about a certain class of objects to which the present specimen belongs, about the use of such objects, and so forth. Pure seeing has nothing to do with such knowledge. As psychologists, we have the task of separating all these acquired meanings from the seen material *per se*, which consists of simple sensations. It may be difficult actually to effect the separation, and to concentrate on the sensations with which alone we ought to be concerned; but the ability to do so is precisely what distinguishes the psychologist from the layman. Everybody must admit that originally the lifting of a book cannot have given the experience of a weight which is external to the lifting fingers. In the beginning there can have been only sensations of touch, and perhaps strain, within the fingers. It follows that the weight outside must be the product of a long development in which the pure sensations in our hand have gradually been connected with other factors. A similar consideration shows at once that among the genuine sensory data there can be nothing like objects. Objects exist for us only when sensory experience has become thoroughly imbued with meaning. Who can deny that in adult life meaning pervades all experience? Eventually it even leads to a kind of illusion. To Germans the German noun "*Igel*" sounds as though no animal but a hedgehog could have this name. The word "eagle," however, which in English has the same sound as "*Igel*" in German, sounds to an American or an Englishman as though only an "*Adler*" could be called by this name.[1] In this instance it will be admitted that we must discriminate between the auditory experience as such, which is the same in both languages, and the attached meanings, which vary from one country to the other. Again, the sign + fairly looks its meaning of the operation of adding, especially if it is seen between numbers; and yet it might as well have been chosen as a symbol for the operation of dividing. If for a moment we hesitate to accept this last statement, we do so only because the connection of a particular meaning with this simple figure has been impressed upon us ever since we went to school. But once the enormous strength of the connection has been realized in the present situation, we shall be ready to admit that probably nothing in the naïve experience of an adult can be devoid of similar influences. Even the most imposing characteristics of given experiences may derive from this source.

Now, meaning in this sense depends upon personal biography. It represents a somewhat accidental trait of our experience. In psychology, we must therefore try to ignore it and to focus only on the actual sensations. The procedure by which this is achieved is call *introspection.*

When I was a student, all young psychologists learned this lesson most thoroughly, although in some cases the doctrine was transmitted implicitly rather that in a clear formulation. Unfortunately, if Introspectionism is right about this, direct experience as such has only limited value. Of all objective experience only selected parts are likely to survive when the great house-cleaning has been completed.

The main question is, of course, according to what criteria some experiences are to be selected as genuine sensory facts while all others are discarded as mere products of learning. Whatever the answer may be, we will now consider a few examples which in essential respects differ from those discussed in the preceding paragraphs.

Suppose, while standing at a street corner, we see a man approaching us. Now he is ten yards away, and presently five. What are we to say about his size at the two distances? We shall be inclined to say that at both distances his visual size was approximately the same. But such a statement, we are told, is utterly unacceptable. A simple consideration in geometrical optics shows that during the man's approach his visual height must have doubled, and that the same holds for his width. His total size must therefore have become four times the area which it was at ten yards. If this is to become entirely clear, we must repeat the observation in the laboratory. Here we replace the man by two cardboard rectangles. The sides of the first are two and three inches long; those of the second, six and nine. If now the first is held before our eyes at a distance of one yard and the second at three yards, they must have the same size from the point of view of optics; for their linear dimensions vary exactly as do their distances. It is quite true, the rectangle at the greater distance appears much larger than the nearer one. But this is precisely what the Introspectionist does not accept as a true statement about the sensory facts. Such a statement, he will say, cannot refer to actual sensory experience. He will also offer a proof that his opinion is right. He will invite us to look through a hole in a screen which he holds before our eyes. The two rectangles now appear on a homogenous background, because the screen hides all other objects. Under these conditions the difference between the sizes of the rectangles will probably be somewhat reduced. If it does not entirely disappear, the experimenter may go further in helping us to see the sizes as they actually are according to his conviction. He may darken the room, and turn the light on only for a fraction of a second. This serves to exclude movements of the eyes and of the head. It is quite possible that now the rectangles have the same size. The Introspectionist may also invite us to practice in a certain fashion which I cannot here describe, and after some training the rectangles may indeed assume the same size, even if the screen with its hole and any other devices are omitted. Once this has been achieved, the Introspectionist will be satisfied. Now, he will say, you know what introspection means. After all, he will add, trained observers are bound to find the rectangles equal. Otherwise, people might go so far as to believe that the after-image of an object changes its size according to the distance from which they see it upon a screen, because in untrained observation the size of the after-image does seem to change when the distance of the fixation point from the eye is varied. Of course, according to the Introspectionist, it cannot actually change, since under these circumstances the area of the retinal after-effect remains strictly constant.

My next example may be regarded as a natural consequence of the first. When dining with friends, in what shapes do we see the plates on the table, to the left, to the right and opposite us? We shall be inclined to say that they are circular, just as our own plate. But this again is a statement which the Introspectionist will not accept. According to him, they must be elliptical; and he will add that once we have thought about their projection upon our retina we shall have to admit that this is true. In fact, some of the plates must be very flat ellipses, and even our own plate will become an ellipse as soon as our eyes do not look down upon it vertically. To this case a similar procedure may be applied as has been used in the preceding example. On a screen which is oblique to the direction of the eye is shown a circle; on another place, at right angles to the direction of the eye, an ellipse is presented. The shape of the latter figure is chosen in such a manner that its projection upon the retina has the same shape as the projection of the circle from its oblique plane. An untrained observer will maintain that he sees the circle as a circle and the ellipse as an ellipse. But the Introspectionist maintains that in actual sensory experience there are two vertically identical ellipses. He will offer us a screen with two holes in it, through which we can see both forms, but which excludes the data by which the angles of the planes could at first be recognized. Now both shapes do look alike; both look like ellipses. Thus the Introspectionist seems to have made his point. With some training, he will again remark, anybody can see these real sensory facts, even without the screen, provided he assumes the right attitude, the attitude of introspection. As a further elucidation, he will remark that if an after-image is projected on planes of different angles in relation to the eye, the image will seem to change its shape as we project it on one plane or another. Since during these observations the retinal after-effect does not change at all, only uninformed people will trust what they seem to be seeing under these circumstances. Thus the importance of observing given sensory experiences by way of trained introspection appears to be convincingly demonstrated.

Another paradoxical experience has been widely discussed ever since Helmholtz wrote his *Physiologische Optik*. An untrained observer sees not only sizes and shapes of objects more constant than corresponds to the variations of retinal sizes and retinal shapes; the same holds true for the way in which he seems to see brightnesses in their relation to the varying intensities of retinal projection. Suppose that a vertical screen is placed on a table, near a window and parallel to it. On the window side of the screen a black paper is laid on the table, and symmetrically on the other side of the screen, a white paper. The papers are selected in a special manner: the dark one, which is exposed to the direct illumination from the window, reflects the same absolute amount of light as the white paper, which receives so much less light. In spite of this fact, the former paper appears black and the latter white. This again is an observation which the Introspectionist refuses to accept, because under the given circumstances the images projected upon the retina of the observer are both equally intense. He assumes that the sensations, i.e. the brightnesses of the papers, must therefore be the same. He also believes that this equality can actually be demonstrated. Once more he will take a piece of cardboard with two small holes in it, and will hold it so that one of them is filled by a section of the black, and the other by a section of the white paper. Now the surroundings of the papers, the vertical screen, and so forth, are excluded from the visions. And under these conditions the same nuance of gray appears in both openings. Clearly, he tells us, these are the true sensations. He is also likely to point out that after some practice most people can recognize the equality of the two brightnesses without the help of any special device. When this is the case, they have learned to observe in the attitude of introspection. At the time when painters were still interested in the representation of objects, they generally assumed this attitude in order to see the right brightness of things.

All these facts, the so-called constancies of size, shape and brightness, are from this point of view mere illusions, which must be destroyed if the true sensory phenomena are to appear. In this and in other respects they are comparable to a great many other "optical illusions," the diagrams of which fill pages in the textbooks of psychology. There is, for instance, the famous Müller-Lyer pattern, the figure with the arrow-heads, between which two equal lines seem to have strikingly different length. When this pattern is repeatedly inspected, and if the subject makes an effort to detach the objectively equal lines from their surroundings, he will soon find that the illusion becomes less striking, until eventually it may entirely disappear. It seems to follow that the inequality of the lines as first seen has not been a sensory fact. If we believe what the Introspectionists say, the same. can also be demonstrated as follows: The two figures are drawn precisely one above the other. If now the observer focuses his attention upon the two left ends of the equal lines, he will find that an imaginary connection of these ends is vertical. If he makes the same test with the right ends, he will find the same result. If we have any knowledge of geometry, we seem thus forced to admit that both lines have the same length. Similarly, it can be shown that most other illusions disappear, if the observer is careful to assume the right analytical attitude. How, then, can these illusions be regarded as genuine sensory fact?

Here is a further example. During the past thirty years stroboscopic movement has been thoroughly investigated by German and American psychologists. Under appropriate conditions successive presentation of two lights at two points not too distant from each other results in an experience of movement from the first to the second. But if the observer adopts the attitude of introspection, he finds nothing but a "gray flash." Consequently, the Introspectionists say, any reports about actual movements in such a situation must be received with suspicion. Did not Benussi's subjects describe similar experiences when two points of their skin were touched in rapid succession? In their description the experienced movement did not for the most part occur along the surface of the skin; rather, it formed an arc through empty space and touched the skin only at the points of actual stimulation. As the Introspectionists see it, such an experience cannot possibly belong to the world of touch alone. All tactual experiences stay, of course, on the skin.

If all observations of this kind are illusions which deceive us not only as to the nature of given physical conditions but also about our own sensory data, then some powerful factor must be at work which obscures these data so long as they are not revealed by introspection. We already know what the nature of the distorting influence is. At least the Introspectionist is quite convinced that, just as in previous instances, it can only be *learning*. He argues as follows: The man who approaches us on the street does not seem to grow larger as for simple optical reasons he should. The circle which lies in an oblique place does not appear as an ellipse; it seems to remain a circle even though its retinal image may be a very flat ellipse. The white object with the shadow across it remains white, the black paper in full light remains black, although the former may reflect much less light than the latter. Obviously, these three phenomena have something in common. The physical object as such always remains the same, while the stimulation of our eyes varies, as the distance, the orientation or the illumination of that constant object are changed. Now, what we seem to experience agrees with the actual invariance of the physical object much better than it does with the varying stimulations. Hence the terms constancy of size, constancy of shape and constancy of brightness. Clearly, this is just what we have to expect if such constancies spring from our knowledge of the physical situation, in other words, if they develop in some form of learning. Day after day, since early childhood, we have found that when we approach a distant object it proves to be much bigger than it seemed to be from a greater distance. In the same way we have learned that objects in oblique orientations do not exhibit those real shapes which they show when inspected from in front. Again in the same fashion we have become thoroughly acquainted with the fact that objects seen under abnormal conditions of illumination show wrong brightness or darkness which are replaced by the right ones when conditions become normal. Such observations have been repeated so many times, and we have so fully learned what the real sizes, the real shapes and the real brightnesses are in each case, that gradually we have become unable to distinguish between our acquired knowledge and actual sensory facts. As a result, we now seem to *see* the constant real characteristics while the sensory facts as such which, of course, depend upon distance, orientation and illumination, are no longer recognizable. Thus meaning, knowledge or learning are just as effective in the present examples as they are when we seem to be aware of "things," of "weights" outside in space, and so forth.

We can accept the Introspectionist's claim that probably few experiences remain entirely uninfluenced by learning. After all, this is not a novel assumption. Moreover, he can point out that if untrained people seem to *see* what from this point of view is merely an effect of learning, this is merely an illusion which also occurs in other instances: we remember the symbol +, which *looks* like the sign for addition. But the Introspectionist has further arguments which seem to support his interpretation. All effects of past learning can be effective only to the degree to which they are recalled. Now, recall presupposes that some parts of the present situation can evoke what has been learned in the past. In the case of the constancies, such parts are, among others, the distances, the oblique orientations, and the various illuminations, as seen in each case. Obviously, then, if distances, oblique orientations and varying illuminations are no longer visible, the normal sizes, shapes and brightnesses cannot be reactivated. But precisely this happens when the situations here under discussion are observed though holes in a screen. Under these conditions, the surroundings of the crucial surfaces and, with the surroundings, the distances, orientations and illuminations of the surfaces are excluded from vision. Consequently, there can be no recall of what we have learned about the situations; the constancies must disappear; and the surfaces must for once exhibit their true sensory characteristics. The same follows from the fact that the constancies can be destroyed by introspection. Obviously, in this procedure the sizes, shapes and brightnesses of surface are to a degree separated from their contexts. But, as we have just seen, this means separation from the factors which would otherwise cause recall of previously acquired knowledge. It is therefore only natural that under these conditions the pure sensory facts come to the fore.

If the size and the shape of after-images prove to be surprisingly variable when the distance and the orientation of the background are changed, this also appears as a direct consequence of the Introspectionist's explanation. After-images are localized upon the background. If the distance and the orientation of this background again operate as factors of recall, a given after-image must seem to assume different sizes and shapes when the distance or the orientation of the background are varied.

The same explanation helps us to understand why the constancies do not survive under extreme conditions. Ten yards away a man appears to be scarcely smaller that at a distance of five yards; but fifty yards off he does look smaller, and a thousand yards away he is likely to become a tiny object indeed. Most of the time we are, of course, interested in objects in our neighborhood. Thus we learn little about things far off, and the result is that with increasing distance true sensory experience is less and less obscured by acquired knowledge.

It must be admitted that in all these arguments there is a great persuasive force. Many psychologists do not for a moment doubt the truth of the explanation in terms of acquired knowledge. This explanation seems to satisfy a very natural tendency in human thinking. Physicists who have never studied psychology will give this explanation as soon as they become acquainted with the facts we are here considering. If you demonstrate the phenomena to a freshman, he will at once suggest similar interpretations.

The theory applies to countless facts. There is practically no visual situation which does not exhibit some of the experiences in question. When we open our eyes, we behold sizes, shapes and brightnesses all the time, and of these only a few will escape the verdict which is imposed on them by the Introspectionist. It is not the facts themselves which are exceptional; only the demonstration of their surprising deviation from what one should expect them to be is something unusual. This demonstrating is a matter of psychological sophistication; the facts themselves are affairs of every moment and of everybody.

Even so the extent of objective experience which is not to be trusted has not yet been exhausted is these paragraphs. The location of objects is open to similar criticism. When fixating a point before me, I see objects around it in various places which correspond to the different positions of their images on my retina. If I now fixate another point, the same objects ought to appear in changed places since their images now occupy new positions on the retina. But actually the objects do not seem to have moved. When the eye moves, their location in space proves to be virtually independent of retinal position. Or take the speed of seen movement. The same physical movement may be seen from many different distances. When I am ten yards away from the moving object, retinal speed will be one half of what it is at a distance of five yards. And yet, in my experience the speed seems to be about the same in both cases. Clearly, the explanation which has been given to the constancies of size, shape and brightness also applies to this constancy of visual speed. Thus, of the objective experiences around us little is left that would be called a true sensory fact by the Introspectionist.

None the less, this is not yet the most serious consequence of the view held by the Introspectionists. Apparently, the phases of experience which are interpreted as products of learning will not only be excluded from the sensory world; they will also be excluded from investigation in general. Most Introspectionists, it is true, would hesitate to acknowledge this as an explicit principle; but in their research they actually proceed as though they had adopted it. Once an experience has had the misfortune of being so interpreted, they seem to take no more interest in its existence than they would take in the subject matter of astronomy. This means that most objective experience plays virtually no part in the Introspectionist's psychology. In fact, wherever observation touches upon a somewhat unusual and therefore particularly interesting phenomenon, the Introspectionist is ready to offer his monotonous explanation, and henceforth he is extremely unlikely ever to give that phenomenon the slightest attention. Now, this is a serious situation. Whether the *empiristic explanation*, as the explanation by previous learning has been called, is right or wrong, in common like we are dealing almost exclusively with the first-hand objective experience which is discarded by the Introspectionist. Toward this common experience all our interests are directed. Millions of people will never transform the objects of their environments into true sensation, will always react to sizes, shapes, brightnesses and speeds as they find them, will like and dislike forms as they appear to them without recourse to introspection, and will therefore have no commerce with the particular sensory facts of which the Introspectionist is so fond. Thus, if his attitude were to prevail, such experiences as form the matrix of our whole life would never be seriously studied. Psychology would observe and discuss only such experiences as are, to most of us, forever hidden under the cover of merely acquired characteristics. Even the best Introspectionist is not aware of his true sensory facts unless he assumes his special attitude, which — fortunately for him — he drops when leaving the psychological laboratory. So far removed from common experience is his true sensory world that, if we should ever learn its laws, all of them together would not lead us back to the world we actually live in. This being the case, the Introspectionist cannot complain about his own fate. His psychology is quite unable to satisfy people for long. Since he ignores the experiences of daily life, and concentrates on rare facts which only an artificial procedure can reveal, both his professional and his lay audience will sooner or later lose patience. And something else will happen. There will be psychologists who will take him at his word when he says that this is the only right way of dealing with experience. If this is true, they will say, the study of experience can surely not interest us. We will do more lively things. We will study natural behavior. At the present time we know that what has just been described as a consequence of the Introspectionist's views is no longer a possibility but a fact. Behaviorism has come into existence very much in a reaction against Introspectionism.

Let us return to our discussion of Introspectionism as such. One would not be justified in calling its findings "unreal." When I apply the Introspectionist's methods I often find the same experiences as he does. But I am far from attributing to such facts a rare value as though they were more "true" than the facts of everyday experience. If common experience involves acquired knowledge, the experiences revealed by introspection depend upon the attitude of introspecting. One cannot show that they also exist in the absence of this attitude. Moreover, if for a moment we take it for granted that all the phenomena we have been discussing are actually products of previously acquired knowledge, does it follow that these phenomena are not actual facts, and therefore devoid of psychological significance? Is a certain amount of H_2O which I have before me no real chemical substance because I know that it has been formed by the oxidation of hydrogen? Would the hydrogen be a "true" chemical substance, but not the water? Is water not to be investigated by the chemist? I do not see why an experience which is imbued with acquired knowledge is to be regarded as less important than experiences which are not so influenced. Take the case of the symbol +, the appearance of which is surely affected by our knowledge of a mathematical operation. When seen between numbers it looks like "plus," i.e., its acquired meaning appears localized in the visual field. Clearly, this is a strange fact which immediately raises fascinating questions. Why are we not to investigate such problems? The situation is precisely the same with regard to all other experiences to which, correctly or incorrectly, the empiristic explanation is being applied. Why should we ignore the problems which they involve, when such labels as learning, meaning and previously acquired knowledge have been attached to them.

As a matter of fact, problems of this kind deserve special attention. Among the examples which have here been considered there are two kinds of phenomena. One, to which the symbol + belongs, is clearly defined by the fact that we actually know how during childhood a certain meaning creeps into a given experience. For the second type, which is represented by the majority of our examples, such an account has not been given. By no means has it been demonstrated that the objectivity of things, the localization of weights outside our hand, the constancies of size, shape, speed, location and brightness, and so forth, are really products of learning. To most of us it may seem extremely plausible that this is actually the case; but none of the observations and arguments which I have mentioned in this connection can be regarded as convincing proof of the empiricist thesis. Thus it is merely an hypothesis that facts of the second class are not essentially different from those of the first, and as an hypothesis it ought therefore to be clearly recognized.

The customary thing to do with an hypothesis is to subject it to tests. Does Introspectionism test its empiristic assumptions? We see no evidence that it does, or intends to do so, since once the assumption is made the Introspectionist is no longer interested in the facts. Consequently, if all psychologists were Introspectionists, such assumptions would never be examined. This is the more disturbing since many psychologists tend to lose their temper when their empiristic convictions are called hypotheses. If these convictions are no more than assumptions, what other explanations will the Gestalt Psychologist offer? Quite probably our criticism of the empiristic thesis is only the beginning, and more or less fantastic new notions about sensory function are to follow.

When a scientific discussion tends to assume this direction, it is always touched upon some particularly deep-rooted presupposition which one does not want to see regarded as an open issue. This makes it only the more obvious that the Introspectionist's attitude constitutes a danger to the advance of psychology. For a moment let us suppose that the constancies of size, shape, speed, localization, brightness and so on are actually *not* products of learning. The consequence would be that all these phenomena belong to sensory experience. But if so, sensory experience would be something fundamentally different from the aggregate of sensations which constitutes the Introspectionist's sensory world. It would follow that his conception of sensory function must be discarded. Of course, whether or not we have to draw this conclusion depends entirely upon the validity of the empiristic thesis. But precisely this thesis is apparently not to be freely discussed and tested. This is an extraordinary situation: as used by the Introspectionist, the empiristic explanation serve as a bulwark which protects his particular views about sensory function. It seems that Introspectionists adhere to the empiristic thesis not so much because it is as such attractive as because their firm belief about a certain nature of sensory facts does not permit them to acknowledge certain experiences. These "irregular" experiences are constantly being explained away by the empiristic assumption, and therefore this assumption must be right. That this is the correct interpretation of the Introspectionst's attitude will be seen as soon as his arguments in favor of the empiristic hypothesis are closely examined. These arguments have little to do with learning, but very much with convictions about the world of pure sensory experience.

Take the constancy of brightness as an example. A white paper on which a shadow lies appears as white, a black one in bright illumination remains black, even if under these conditions the white paper may reflect less light that the black one does. In this experience, do the white and the black *per se* tell the Introspectionist that they are products of previous learning? By no means. His argument is entirely indirect: since the observation is incompatible with his beliefs about the nature of true sensations, it cannot be accepted. What can he do with it? The Introspectionist is not at all embarrassed. Interpreted as a mere product of learning, the constancy of brightness becomes at once quite harmless.

Let us follow his argument in more detail. In the present observation one can change the brightness of the papers by looking at them in a special fashion. Therefore, the Introspectionist says, the brightnesses as first seen can not have been genuine sensory experiences. This statement obviously implies a presupposition about the nature of sensory facts. Such facts, the Introspectionist assumes, must be independent of changes in the attitude of the observer. But at this point his reasoning is not entirely consistent. If in the attitude of introspection an apparent white can be transformed into a dark nuance, and an apparent black into a relatively bright one, the opposite change occurs spontaneously as soon as that attitude is discontinued. Thus the true brightnesses which are said to be revealed during introspection are just as changeable as the brightnesses which are seen before, and are now seen again. From a purely logical point of view, the experience found during introspection might therefore just as well be rejected, since they disappear when the observer returns to his everyday attitude. The Introspectionist, however, is far from treating both experiences with the same measure. He holds that what he experiences during introspection is true experience, and that it persists when he falls back into a more naïve attitude, although now it is obscured by the effects of knowledge. Hence, there must be a further belief which makes him prefer his special sensory experiences.

This other belief is easy to find. Why is the Introspectionist surprised by the constancies of size, shape, localization, speed, and brightness? Why does he not take these facts at their face value? Obviously, because under the given conditions of stimulation he expects to have experiences quite different from those which he actually has. Visual size, he would say, should be proportional to retinal size; changes in retinal shape should be followed by changes in seen shape; localization in the visual field should vary with retinal position; visual speed with retinal speed; and visual brightness with retinal intensity. Now, while the everyday experience of the layman contradicts these expectations all the time, the special attitude cultivated by Introspectionism succeeds in obtaining those other experiences which we always ought to have. This is the fact which makes the Introspectionist prefer his particular findings, and which also makes him believe in a permanent, though hidden, existence of such "pure sensations." Thus it becomes apparent that the procedure and the results of introspection are sanctioned by their agreement with certain premises about the relation between stimulation and sensory experience. The same premises lead, of course, to the condemnation of many phenomena such as the constancies. Nobody can understand the ways of Introspectionism who is not aware of this decisive point. As a young student, how many times have I read that the Müller-Lyer illusion does not represent a true sensory fact because it can be destroyed by analytical observation and corresponding practice. If this is to be taken as a proof, one kind of experience is obviously given a higher value than another. Why should this be the case? The answer is that one experience agrees with what peripheral stimulation makes one expect, while the other does not. The one that does not agree is discarded with the aid of empiristic assumptions or other devices of a similar kind. A second fundamental conviction, then, which underlies the scientific decisions of Introspectionism is this: the characteristics of true sensory experiences depend only upon corresponding characteristics of peripheral stimuli.

The Introspectionist's belief takes a still more extreme form. How does he proceed in order to find the true sensory facts, say, in the case of brightness constancy? He tries to isolate parts of the white and of the black paper so that they are no longer related to their specific environments. Isolation, it seems, is also the procedure by which the Müller-Lyer illusion can be destroyed, and similarly in all the other cases. Such an analytical attitude will have effects similar to those of a screen with a hole, which conceals the specific surroundings of objects and gives them instead a new homogenous environment. If now the disturbing facts disappear, this effect of isolation is explained by the exclusion of all factors which otherwise distort the true sensory situation. How do these factors operate? According to the Introspectionist, they act as clues for the processes of recall which import previously acquired knowledge. We have to realize that at this point the Introspectionist's interpretation is once more one-sided. Without any doubt, isolation of facts in the sensory field affect these facts. Under these circumstances they tend to be more strictly related to local stimulating conditions. But for this two entirely different explanations may be given: (1) Either true sensory experience always depends upon local stimulation alone, and it is only the recall of previously acquired knowledge which depends upon factors in the environment. This is the Introspectionist's view. (2) Or sensory experience in a given place depends not only on the stimuli corresponding to this place, but also on the stimulating conditions in the environment. I will at once remark that this is the view held by Gestalt Psychology. With the second interpretation as with the first, isolation and the introduction of a homogenous environment will tend to make local experience correspond better to local stimulation. The Introspectionist, however, considers only the alternative. He prefers the thesis which allows him to believe that local sensory facts are strictly determined by local stimulation. His partiality in this respect is also obvious when it is not empiristic assumptions but other hypotheses by which he protects his picture of a simple sensory world. In a well-known example, when subjects make eye movements along the main lines of the Müller-Lyer pattern, which are objectively equal, these movements prove to have different amplitudes for the two parts of the pattern, and the difference corresponds to the difference of their appearance, i.e., to the illusion. From this it has been concluded that the illusion is not a visual fact; that, rather, it is caused by such asymmetrical eye movements, or at least by corresponding innervation tendencies. This statement is biased because, in case the two lines actually have different visual length in the first place, the eye movements or innervation tendencies will, of course, be similarly asymmetrical. Only a prejudiced person can draw the conclusion that such observations prove the indirect genesis of the Müller-Lyer effect. And what is the prejudice of such a person? He will under no circumstances admit that the length of a line depends upon more conditions than the length of its retinal image. The most fundamental assumption of Introspectionism is therefore this: true sensory facts are local phenomena which depend upon local stimulation, but not at all upon stimulating conditions in their environment.[2] Only if we know this rule can we understand on what occasions the Introspectionist begins to introspect. Very seldom do we find him introspecting when simple relations between local stimulation and sensory facts obtain without a special effort. But where *prima facie* such relations do not obtain he will always take recourse both to his introspective procedure and to the assumptions which serve to protect his main thesis.

Our inquiry has led to a remarkable result. At first the tenets of Introspectionism appear to be sharply contrasted with the views of Behaviorism. If the Introspectionist is not the advocate of direct experience, who else should be able to play this rôle? In actual fact, however, his enthusiasm for direct experience is obviously limited. Introspectionism follows the orders of an authority to whom the testimony of experience as such means little. This authority subjects direct experience to a screening process, finds most of its defective, and condemns it to corrective measures. The authority is commonly called physiology of the sense organs. This branch of physiology has very definite ideas about the sensory functions of the nervous system. When the Introspectionist mentions physiology, he seems to talk about a helpful servant. But when we look at the facts, the servant is the Introspectionist's master.

This being the case, does Introspectionism differ quite as much from Behaviorism as was our first impression? If we compare the physiological premises of Introspectionism with those of Behaviorism, we shall soon realize that, on the contrary, in this respect the two schools have much in common.

The main concepts of Behaviorism are those of the reflex and the conditioned reflex. The principal characteristic of reflex action consists in the fact that nerve impulses travel from a receptor along prescribed paths to prescribed centers, and from these along further prescribed paths toward an effector organ. This conception explains the order of organic reactions in their dependence upon a given stimuli: the order is enforced by a particular arrangement of the conductors. It is true, Behaviorists do not suppose that such anatomical arrangements are entirely rigid and constant. But although a certain diffusion of excitation is admitted, the only biological value of this "tolerance" is seen in the fact that other conditions, which can make the connections quite rigid, have thus a certain range of possibilities to work upon. In this fashion, order of function is to a degree prescribed by the reflex arc; but, at a higher level of the nervous system, connections may be built (or blocked) by another factor. This other factor is conditioning.

With this picture we can now compare the ideas which underlie the Introspectionist's criteria for true sensory experience. First, local sensation depends upon local stimulation. It does not depend upon other processes in the nervous system, not even upon those which issue from adjacent parts of the same sense organ. The only assumption which can explain this independence of local sensation is conduction of processes along insulated pathways from one point of the sense organ to one point in the brain, where activity is accompanied by sensory experience. But this is only the first half of a reflex arc, so that in this respect Introspectionism entirely agrees with Behaviorism. Now, if often experience does not seem to obey this principle, the reason lies in a second principle. At a higher level of the nervous system, connections which did not exist originally may still be formed in individual development. As a consequence, certain experiences will regularly be followed and accompanied by others, particularly in the form of recall which adds its material to those experiences. Essentially, this principle is the same as that of conditioning, inasmuch as in both cases the formation of new connections is the main point. Hence, here again we find no real difference between Introspectionism and Behaviorism.

During their lively dispute as to whether introspection of the objective observation of behavior is the right procedure in psychology, it does not occur to either party that another question might be much more urgent, namely, whether their common assumptions about the functions of the nervous system are adequate. Both seem to regard these assumptions as self-evident. And since their essential premises are taken for granted by both, we cannot be surprised to find the same conservatism in Introspectionism as disturbed us in Behaviorism.

Most Introspectionists do not seem to realize that psychology is a very young science, and that therefore its future must depend upon discoveries which are unsuspected at the present time. At least in sensory experience, the essentials of all possible observations are finally given to them before they begin to observe. Accordingly, they show a negativistic attitude whenever observations do not agree with the established truth; and their experimentation tends to become a merely defensive procedure. If others point to new facts which do not fit, they are eager to remove the disturbance by introspection and auxiliary assumptions. Criticism of new observations is a healthy procedure in science; but I have known Introspectionists who spent their scientific lives in bitter defence of their dogma.

Under these circumstances, I do not see why Introspectionism should be preferred to Behaviorism. In their fundamental concepts the two schools are so much alike that all their disputes remind me of unnecessary quarrels in the family. At any rate, the principal questions of Gestalt Psychology refer to an issue which is never mentioned in their discussions, because for these schools it does not yet exist: Is it true that the processes underlying experience and behavior depend upon the connections of nerve paths, and that changes in the conductivity of these connections constitute an individual's development?

NOTES

1   "*Adler*" is the German word for "eagle."

2   This is the famous mosaic hypothesis. Some Introspectionists have said that Gestalt Psychology must also acknowledge certain relations between stimulation conditions and sensory facts. Quite! We do not argue against relations between such conditioned and sensory facts in general, but only against a rigid relation between *local* stimulation and *local* experience.

BIBLIOGRAPHY

M. Bentley: *The Field of Psychology.* 1924.

D. Katz: *The World of Color.* 1935.

K. Koffka: "Gestalt Psychology." *Psychol. Bull., 19,* 1922.

K. Koffka: *The Growth of the Mind,* 1928.

K. Koffka: *Principles of Gestalt Psychology.* 1935.

W. Köhler: "A Kustische Untersuchungen III." *Zeitschr. f. Psychol., 72,* 1915.

W. Köhler: "Uber unbemerkte Empfindungen und Urteilstäuschungen." *Zeitschr. f. Psychol., 63,* 1913.

5

THE QUESTION OF LAY-ANALYSIS

Sigmund Freud

II

If I am to say anything intelligible to you, I shall no doubt have to tell you something of a psychological theory which is not known or not appreciated outside analytic circles. It will be easy to deduce from this theory what we want from our patients and how we obtain it. I shall expound it to you dogmatically, as though it were a complete theoretical structure. But do not suppose that it came into being as such a structure, like a philosophical system. We have developed it very slowly, we have wrestled over every small detail of it, we have unceasingly modified it, keeping a continuous contact with observation, till it has finally taken a shape in which it seems to suffice for our purposes. Only a few years ago I should have had to clothe this theory in other terms. Nor, of course, can I guarantee to you that the form in which it is expressed today will remain the final one. Science, as you know, is not a revelation; long after its beginnings it still lacks the attributes of definiteness, immutability, and infallibility for which human thought so deeply longs. But such as it is, it is all that we can have. If you will further bear in mind that our science is very young, scarcely as old as the century, and that it is concerned with what is perhaps the most difficult material that can be the subject of human research, you will easily be able to adopt the correct attitude towards my exposition. But interrupt me whenever you feel inclined, if you cannot follow me or if you want further explanations.

'I will interrupt you before you have even begun. You say that you intend to expound a new psychology to me; but I should have thought that psychology was

Freud, S. *Two Short Accounts of Psycho-Analysis*. Pp. 100-144 in "The Question of Lay Analysis," translated and edited by James Strachey. London: Penguin.

no new science. There have been psychologies and psychologists enough; and I heard of great achievements in that field while I was at college.'

I should not dream of disputing them. But if you look into the matter more closely you will have to class these great achievements as belonging rather to the physiology of the sense organs. The theory of mental life could not be developed, because it was inhibited by a single essential misunderstanding. What does it comprise today, as it is taught at college? Apart from those valuable discoveries in the physiology of the senses, a number of classifications and definitions of our mental processes which, thanks to linguistic usage, have become the common property of every educated person. That is clearly not enough to give a view of our mental life. Have you not noticed that every philosopher, every imaginative writer, every historian, and every biographer makes up his own psychology for himself, brings forward his own particular hypotheses concerning the interconnexions and aims of mental acts — all more or less plausible and all equally untrustworthy? There is an evident lack of any common foundation. And it is for that reason too that in the field of psychology there is, so to speak, no respect and no authority. In that field everyone can 'run wild' as he chooses. If you raise a question in physics or chemistry, anyone who knows he possesses no 'technical knowledge' will hold his tongue. But if you venture upon a psychological assertion you must be prepared to meet judgements and contradictions from every quarter. In this field, apparently, there is no 'technical knowledge'. Everyone has a mental life, so everyone regards himself as a psychologist. But that strikes me as an inadequate legal title. The story is told of how someone who applied for a post as a children's nurse was asked if she knew how to look after babies. 'Of course,' she replied, 'why, after all, I was a baby once myself.'

'And you claim that you have discovered this "common foundation" of mental life, which has been overlooked by every psychologist, from observations on *sick people*?'

The source of our findings does not seem to me to deprive them of their value. Embryology, to take an example, would not deserve to be trusted if it could not give a plain explanation of the origin of innate malformations. I have told you of people whose thoughts go their own way, so that they are obliged to worry over problems to which they are perfectly indifferent. Do you think that academic psychology could ever make the smallest contribution towards explaining an abnormality such as that? And, after all, we all of us have the experience at night-time of our thoughts going their own way and creating things which we do not understand, which puzzle us, and which are suspiciously reminiscent of pathological products. Our dreams, I mean. The common people have always firmly believed that dreams have a sense and a value — that they mean something. Academic psychology has never been able to inform us what this meaning is. It could make nothing of dreams. If it attempted to produce explanations, they were non-psychological — such as tracing them to sensory stimuli, or to an unequal depth of sleep in different portions of the brain, and so on. But it is fair to say that a psychology which cannot explain dreams is also useless for an understanding of normal mental life, that it has no claim to be called a science.

'You are becoming aggressive; so you have evidently got on to a sensitive spot. I have heard, it is true, that in analysis great value is attached to dreams, that they are interpreted, and that memories of real events are looked for behind them, and so on. But I have heard as well that the interpretation of dreams is left to the caprice of analysts, and that they themselves have never ceased disputing over the way of interpreting dreams and the justification for drawing conclusions from them. If that is so, you ought not to underline so heavily the advantage that analysis has won over academic psychology.'

There is really a great deal of truth in what you say. It is true that the interpretation of dreams has come to have unequalled importance both for the theory and the practice of analysis. If I seem to be aggressive, that is only a way of defending myself. And when I think of all the mischief some analysts have done with the interpretation of dreams I might lose heart and echo the pessimistic pronouncement of our great satirist Nestroy[1] when he says that every step forward is only half as big as it looks at first. But have you ever found that men do anything but confuse and distort what they get hold of? By the help of a little foresight and self-discipline most of the dangers of dream-interpretation can be avoided with certainty. But you will agree that I shall never come to my exposition if we let ourselves be led aside like this.

'Yes. If I understood rightly, you wanted to tell me about the fundamental postulate of the new psychology.'

That was not what I wanted to begin with. My purpose is to let you hear what pictures we have formed of the structure of the mental apparatus in the course of our analytic studies.

'What do you mean by the "mental apparatus"? and what, may I ask, is it constructed of?'

It will soon be clear what the mental apparatus is; but I must beg you not to ask what material it is constructed of. That is not a subject of psychological interest. Psychology can be as indifferent to it as, for instance, optics can be to the question of whether the walls of a telescope are made of metal or cardboard. We shall leave entirely on one side the *material* line of approach,[2] but not so the *spatial* one. For we picture the unknown apparatus which serves the activities of the mind as being really like an instrument constructed of several parts (which we speak of as 'agencies'), each of which performs a particular function and which have a fixed spatial relation to one another: it being understood that by spatial relation — 'in front of' and 'behind', 'superficial' and 'deep' — we merely mean in the first instance a representation of the regular succession of the functions. Have I made myself clear?

'Scarcely. Perhaps I shall understand it later. But, in any case, here is a strange anatomy of the soul — a thing which, after all, no longer exists at all for the scientists.'

What do you expect? It is a hypothesis like so many others in the sciences: the very earliest ones have always been rather rough. 'Open to revision' we can say in such cases. It seems to me unnecessary for me to appeal here to the 'as if' which has become so popular. The value of a 'fiction' of this kind (as the philosopher Vaihinger[3] would call it) depends on how much one can achieve with its help.

But to proceed. Putting ourselves on the footing of everyday knowledge, we recognize in human beings a mental organization which is interpolated between their sensory stimuli and the perception of their somatic needs on the one hand and their motor acts on the other, and which mediates between them for a particular purpose. We call this organization their *'Ich'* ['ego'; literally, 'I']. Now there is nothing new in this. Each one of us makes this assumption without being a philosopher, and some people even in spite of being philosophers. But this does not, in our opinion, exhaust the description of the mental apparatus. Besides this 'I', we recognize another mental region, more extensive, more imposing, and more obscure than the 'I', and this we call the *'Es'* ['id'; literally, 'it']. The relation between the two must be our immediate concern.

You will probably protest at our having chosen simple pronouns to describe our two agencies or provinces instead of giving them orotund Greek names. In psycho-analysis, however, we like to keep in contact with the popular mode of thinking and prefer to make its concepts scientifically serviceable rather than to reject them. There is no merit in this; we are obliged to take this line; for our theories must be understood by our patients, who are often very intelligent, but not always learned. The impersonal 'it' is immediately connected with certain forms of expression used by normal people. 'It shot through me,' people say; 'there was something in me at that moment that was stronger than me.' *'C'était plus fort que moi.'*

In psychology we can only describe things by the help of analogies. There is nothing peculiar in this; it is the case elsewhere as well. But we have constantly to keep changing these analogies, for none of them lasts long enough. Accordingly, in trying to make the relation between the ego and the id clear, I must ask you to picture the ego as a kind of façade of the id, as a frontage, like an external, cortical, layer of it. We can hold on to this last analogy. We know that cortical layers owe their peculiar characteristics to the modifying influence of the external medium on which they abut. Thus we suppose that the ego is the layer of the mental apparatus (of the id) which has been modified by the influence of the external world (of reality). This will show you how in psycho-analysis we take spatial ways of looking at things seriously. For us the ego is really something superficial and the id something deeper — looked at from outside, of course. The ego lies between reality and the id, which is what is truly mental.

'I will not ask any question yet as to how all this can be known. But tell me first what you gain from this distinction between an ego and an id? What leads you to make it?'

Your question shows me the right way to proceed. For the important and valuable thing is to know that the ego and the id differ greatly from each other in several respects. The rules governing the course of mental acts are different in the ego and id; the ego pursues different purposes and by other methods. A great deal could be said about this; but perhaps you will be content with a fresh analogy and an example. Think of the difference between 'the front' and 'behind the lines', as things were during the war. We were not surprised then that some things were different at the front from what they were behind the lines, and that many things were permitted behind the lines which had to be forbidden at the front. The determining influence was, of course, the proximity of the enemy; in the case of mental life it is the proximity of the external world. There was a time when 'outside', strange', and 'hostile' were identical concepts. And now we come to the example. In the id there are no conflicts; contradictions and antitheses persist side by side in it unconcernedly, and are often adjusted by the formation of compromises. In similar circumstances the ego feels a conflict which must be decided; and the decision lies in one urge being abandoned in favour of the other. The ego is an organization characterized by a very remarkable trend towards unification, towards synthesis. This characteristic is lacking in the id; it is, as we might say, 'all to pieces'; its different urges pursue their own purposes independently and regardless of one another.

'And if such an important mental region "behind the lines" exists, how can you explain its having been overlooked till the time of analysis?'

That brings us back to one of your earlier questions. Psychology had barred its own access to the region of the id by insisting on a postulate which is plausible enough but untenable: namely, that all mental acts are conscious[4] to us — that being conscious is the criterion of what is mental, and that, if there are processes in our brain which are not conscious, they do not deserve to be called mental acts and are no concern of psychology.

'But I should have thought that was obvious.'

Yes, and that is what psychologists think. Nevertheless it can easily be shown to be false — that is, to be a quite inexpedient distinction. The idlest self-observation shows that ideas may occur to us which cannot have come about without preparation. But you experience nothing of these preliminaries of your thought, though they too must certainly have been of a mental nature; all that enters your consciousness is the ready-made result. Occasionally you can make these preparatory thought-structures conscious *in retrospect*, as though in a reconstruction.

'Probably one's attention was distracted, so that one failed to notice the preparations.'

Evasions! You cannot in that way get around the fact that acts of a mental nature, and often very complicated ones, can take place in you, of which your consciousness learns nothing and of which you know nothing. Or are you prepared to suppose that a greater or smaller amount of your 'attention' is enough to transform a non-mental act into a mental one? But what is the use of disputing? There are hypnotic experiments in which the existence of such non-conscious thoughts are irrefutably demonstrated to anyone who cares to learn.

'I shall not retract; but I believe I understand you at last. What you call "ego" is consciousness; and your "id" is the so-called subconscious that people talk about so much nowadays. But why the masquerading with the new names?'

It is not masquerading. The other names are of no use. And do not try to give me literature instead of science. If someone talks of subconsciousness, I cannot tell whether he means the term topographically — to indicate something lying in the mind beneath consciousness — or qualitatively — to indicate another consciousness, a subterranean one, as it were. He is probably not clear about any of it. The only trustworthy antithesis is between conscious and unconscious. But it would be a serious mistake to think that this antithesis coincides with the distinction between ego and id. Of course it would be delightful if it were as simple as that: our theory would have a smooth passage. But things are not so simple. All that is true is that everything that happens in the id is and remains unconscious, and that processes in the ego, and they alone, *can* become conscious. But not all of them are, nor always, nor necessarily; and large portions of the ego can remain permanently unconscious.

The becoming conscious of a mental process is a complicated affair. I cannot resist telling you — once again, dogmatically — our hypothesis about it. The ego, as you will remember, is the external, peripheral layer of the id. Now, we believe that on the outermost surface of this ego there is a special agency directed immediately to the external world, a system, an organ, through the excitation of which alone the phenomenon that we call consciousness comes about. This organ can be equally well excited from outside — thus receiving (with the help of the sense-organs) the stimuli from the external world — and from inside — thus becoming aware, first, of the sensations in the id, and then also of the processes in the ego.

'This is getting worse and worse and I can understand it less and less. After all, what you invited me to was a discussion of the question whether laymen (= non-doctors) ought to undertake analytic treatments. What is the point, then, of all these disquisitions on daring and obscure theories which you cannot convince me are justified?'

I know I cannot convince you. That is beyond any possibility and for that reason beyond my purpose. When we give our pupils theoretical instruction in psycho-analysis, we can see how little impression we are making on them to begin with. They take in the theories of analysis as coolly as other abstractions with which they are nourished. A few of them may perhaps *wish* to be convinced, but there is not a trace of their being so. But we also require that everyone who wants to practise analysis on other people shall first himself submit to an analysis. It is only in the course of this 'self-analysis' (as it is misleadingly termed),[5] when they actually experience as affecting their own person — or rather, their own mind — the processes asserted by analysis, that they acquire the convictions by which they are later guided as analysts. How then could I expect to convince you, the Impartial Person, of the correctness of our theories, when I can only put before you an abbreviated and therefore unintelligible account of them, without confirming them from your own experiences?

I am acting with a different purpose. The question at issue between us is not in the least whether analysis is sensible or nonsensical, whether it is right in its hypothesis or has fallen into gross errors. I am unrolling our theories before you since that is the best way of making clear to you what the range of ideas is that analysis embraces, on the basis of what hypothesis it approaches a patient and what it does with him. In this way a quite definite light will be thrown on the question of lay analysis. And do not be alarmed. If you have followed me so far you have got over the worst. Everything that follows will be easier for you. But now, with your leave, I will pause to take breath.

III

'I expect you will want to tell me how, on the basis of the theories of psycho-analysis, the origin of a neurotic illness can be pictured.'

I will try to. But for that purpose we must study our ego and our id from a fresh angle, from the *dynamic* one — that is to say, having regard to the forces at work in them and between them. Hitherto we have been content with a *description* of the mental apparatus.

'My only fear is that it may become unintelligible again!'

I hope not. You will soon find your way about in it. Well then, we assume that the forces which drive the mental apparatus into activity are produced in the bodily organs as an expression of the major somatic needs. You will recollect the words of our poet philosopher: 'Hunger and love [are what moves the world]'.[1] Incidentally, quite a formidable pair of forces! We give these bodily needs, in so far as they represent an instigation to mental activity, the name of *'Triebe'* [instincts], a word for which we are envied by many modern languages.[2] Well, these instincts fill the id: all the energy in the id, as we may put it briefly, originates from them. Nor have the forces in the ego any other origin; they are derived from those in the id. What, then, do these instincts want? Satisfaction — that is, the establishment of situations in which the bodily needs can be extinguished. A lowering of the tension of need is felt by our organ of consciousness as pleasurable; an increase of it is soon felt as unpleasure. From these oscillations arises the series of feelings of pleasure-unpleasure, in accordance with which the whole mental apparatus regulates its activity. In this connexion we speak of a 'dominance of the pleasure principle'.

If the id's instinctual demands meet with no satisfaction, intolerable conditions arise. Experience soon shows that these situations of satisfaction can only be established with the help of the external world. At that point the portion of the id which is directed towards the external world — the ego — begins to function. If all the driving force that sets the vehicle in motion is derived from the id, the ego, as it were, undertakes the steering, without which no goal can be reached. The instincts in the id press for immediate satisfaction at all costs, and in that way they achieve nothing or even bring about appreciable damage. It is the task of the ego to guard against such mishaps, to mediate between the claims of the id and the objections of the external world. It carries on its activity in two directions. On the one hand, it observes the external world with the help of its sense-organ, the system of consciousness, so as to catch the favourable moment for harmless satisfaction; and on the other hand it influences the id, bridles its 'passions', induces its instincts to postpone their satisfaction and, indeed, if the necessity is recognized, to modify its aims, or, in return for some compensation, to give them up. In so far as it tames the id's impulses in this way, it replaces the pleasure principle, which was formerly alone decisive, by what is known as the 'reality principle', which, though it pursues the same ultimate aims, takes into account the conditions imposed by the real external world. Later, the ego learns that there is yet another way of securing satisfaction besides the *adaptation* to the external world which I have described. It is also possible to intervene in the external world by *changing* it, and to establish in it intentionally the conditions which make satisfaction possible. This activity then becomes the ego's highest function; decisions as to when it is more expedient to control one's passions and bow before reality, and when it is more expedient to side with them and to take arms against the external world — such decisions make up the whole essence of worldly wisdom.

'And does the id put up with being dominated like this by the ego, in spite of being, if I understand you aright, the stronger party?'

Yes, all will be well if the ego is in possession of its whole organization and efficiency, if it has access to all parts of the id and can exercise its influence on them. For there is no natural opposition between ego and id; they belong together, and under healthy conditions cannot in practice be distinguished from each other.

'That sounds very pretty; but I cannot see how in such an ideal relation there can be the smallest room for a pathological disturbance.'

You are right. So long as the ego and its relations to the id fulfil these ideal conditions there will be no neurotic disturbance. The point at which the illness makes its breach is an unexpected one, though no one acquainted with general pathology will be surprised to find a confirmation of the principle that it is precisely the most important developments and differentiations that carry in them the seeds of illness, of failure of function.

'You are becoming too learned. I cannot follow you.'

I must go back a little bit further. A small living organism is a truly miserable, powerless thing, is it not? compared with the immensely powerful external world, full as it is of destructive influences. A primitive organism, which has not developed any adequate ego-organization, is at the mercy of all these 'traumas'. It lives by the 'blind' satisfaction of its instinctual wishes and often perishes in consequence. The differentiation of an ego is above all a step towards self-preservation. Nothing, it is true, can be learnt from being destroyed; but if one has luckily survived a trauma one takes notice of the approach of similar situations and signalizes the danger by an abbreviated repetition of the impressions one has experienced in connexion with the trauma — by an *affect of anxiety*. This reaction to the perception of the danger now introduces an attempt at flight, which can have a life-saving effect till one has grown strong enough to meet the dangers of the external world in a more active fashion — even aggressively, perhaps.

'All this is very far away from what you promised to tell me.'

You have no notion how close I am to fulfilling my promise. Even in organisms which later develop an efficient ego-organization, their ego is feeble and little differentiated from their id to begin with, during their first years of childhood. Imagine now what will happen if this powerless ego experiences an instinctual demand from the id which it would already like to resist (because it senses that to satisfy it is dangerous and would conjure up a traumatic situation, a collision with the external world) but which it cannot control, because it does not yet possess enough strength to do so. In such a case the ego treats the instinctual danger as if it was an external one; it makes an attempt at flight, draws back from this portion of the id, and leaves it to its fate, after withholding from it all the contributions which it usually makes to instinctual impulses. The ego, as we put it, institutes a *repression* of these instinctual impulses. For the moment this has the effect of fending off the danger; but one cannot confuse the inside and the outside with impunity. One cannot run away from oneself. In repression the ego is following the pleasure principle, which it is usually in the habit of correcting; and it is bound to suffer damage in revenge. This lies in the ego's having permanently narrowed its sphere of influence. The repressed instinctual impulse is now isolated, left to itself, inaccessible, but also uninfluenceable. It goes its own way. Even later, as a rule, when the ego has grown stronger, it still cannot lift the repression; its synthesis is impaired, a part of the id remains forbidden ground to the ego. Nor does the isolated instinctual impulse remain idle; it understands how to make up for being denied normal satisfaction; it produces psychical derivatives which take its place; it links itself to other processes which by its influence it likewise tears away from the ego; and finally it breaks through into the ego and into consciousness in the form of an unrecognizably distorted substitute, and creates what we call a symptom. All at once the nature of a neurotic disorder becomes clear to us: on the one hand an ego which is inhibited in its synthesis, which has no influence on parts of the id, which must renounce some of its activities in order to avoid a fresh collision with what has been repressed, and which exhausts itself in what are for the most part vain acts of defence against the symptoms, the derivatives of the repressed impulses; and on the other hand an id in which individual instincts have made themselves independent, pursue their aims regardless of the interests of the person as a whole, and henceforth obey the laws only of the primitive psychology that rules in the depths of the id. If we survey the whole situation we arrive at a simple formula for the origin of a neurosis: the ego has make an attempt to suppress certain portions of the id in an *inappropriate manner*, this attempt has failed, and the id has taken its revenge. A neurosis is thus the result of a conflict between the ego and the id, upon which the ego has embarked because, as careful investigation shows, it wishes at all costs to retain its adaptability in relation to the real external world. The disagreement is between the external world and the id; and it is because the ego, loyal to its inmost nature, takes sides with the external world that it becomes involved in a conflict with its id. But please observe that what creates the determinant for the illness is not the fact of this conflict — for disagreements of this kind between reality and the id are unavoidable and it is one of the ego's standing tasks to mediate in them — but the circumstance that the ego has made use of the inefficient instrument of repression for dealing with the conflict. But this in turn is due to the fact that the ego, at the time at which it was set the task, was undeveloped and powerless. The decisive repressions all take place in early childhood.

'What a remarkable business! I shall follow your advice and not make criticisms, since you only want to show me what psycho-analysis believes about the origin of neurosis so that you can go on to say how it sets about combating it. I should have various questions to ask and later on I shall raise some of them. But at the moment I myself feel tempted for once to carry your train of thought further and to venture upon a theory of my own. You have expounded the relation between external world, ego, and id, and you have laid it down as the determinant of a neurosis that the ego in its dependence on the external world struggles against the id. Is not the opposite case conceivable of the ego in a conflict of this kind allowing itself to be dragged away by the id and disavowing its regard for the external world? What happens in a case like that? From my lay notions of the nature of insanity I should say that such a decision on the part of the ego might be the determinant of insanity. After all, a turning away of that kind from reality seems to be the essence of insanity.'

Yes. I myself have thought of that possibility, and indeed I believe it meets the facts — though to prove the suspicion true would call for a discussion of some highly complicated considerations. Neuroses and psychoses are evidently intimately related, but they must nevertheless differ in some decisive respect. That might well be the side taken by the ego in a conflict of this kind. In both cases the id would retain its characteristic of blind inflexibility.

'Well, go on! What hints on the treatment of neurotic illnesses does your theory give?'

It is easy now to describe our therapeutic aim. We try to restore the ego, to free it from its restrictions, and to give it back the command over the id which it has lost owing to its early repressions. It is for this one purpose that we carry out analysis, our whole technique is directed to this aim. We have to seek out the repressions which have been set up and to urge the ego to correct them with our help and to deal with conflicts better than by an attempt at flight. Since these repressions belong to the very early years of childhood, the work of analysis leads us, too, back to that period. Our path to these situations of conflict, which have for the most part been forgotten and which we try to revive in the patient's memory, is pointed out to us by his symptoms, dreams, and free associations. These must, however, first be interpreted — translated — for, under the influence of the psychology of the id, they have assumed forms of expression that are strange to our comprehension. We may assume that whatever associations, thoughts, and memories the patient is unable to communicate to us without internal struggles are in some way connected with the repressed material or are its derivatives. By encouraging the patient to disregard his resistances to telling us these things, we are educating his ego to overcome its inclination towards attempts at flight and to tolerate an approach to what is repressed. In the end, if the situation of the repression can be successfully reproduced in his memory, his compliance will be brilliantly rewarded. The whole difference between his age then and now works in his favour; and the thing from which his childish ego fled in terror will often seem to his adult and strengthened ego no more than child's play.

IV

'Everything you have told me so far has been psychology. It has often sounded strange, difficult, or obscure; but it has always been — if I may put it so— "pure". I have known very little hitherto, no doubt, about your psycho-analysis; but the rumour has nevertheless reached my ears that you are principally occupied with things that have no claim to that predicate. The fact that you have not yet touched on anything of the kind makes me feel that you are deliberately keeping something back. And there is another doubt that I cannot suppress. After all, as you yourself say, neuroses are disturbances of mental life. Is it possible, then, that such important things as our ethics, our conscience, our ideals, play no part at all in these profound disturbances?'

So you feel that a consideration both of what is lowest and of what is highest has been missing from our discussions up till now? The reason for that is that we have not yet considered the *contents* of mental life at all. But allow me now for once myself to play the part of an interrupter who holds up the progress of the conversation. I have talked so much psychology to you because I wanted you to get the impression that the work of analysis is a part of applied psychology — and, moreover, of a psychology that is unknown outside analysis. An analyst must therefore first and foremost have learnt this psychology, this depth-psychology or psychology of the unconscious, or as much of it at least as is known today. We shall need this as a basis for our later conclusions. But now, what was it you meant by your allusion to 'purity'?

'Well, it is generally reported that in analyses the most intimate — and the nastiest — events in sexual life come up for discussion in every detail. If that is so — I have not been able to gather from your psychological discussions that it is necessarily so — it would be a strong argument in favour of restricting these treatments to doctors. How could one dream of allowing such dangerous liberties to people of whose discretion one was not sure and of whose character one had no guarantee?'

It is true that doctors enjoy certain privileges in the sphere of sex: they are even allowed to inspect people's genitals — though they were not allowed to in the East and though some idealistic reformers (you know whom I have in mind)[1] have disputed this privilege. But you want to know in the first place whether it is so in analysis and why it must be so. Yes, it is so.

And it must be so, firstly because analysis is entirely founded on complete candour. Financial circumstances, for instance, are discussed with equal detail and openness: things are said that are kept back from every fellow-citizen, even if he is not a competitor or a tax-collector. I will not dispute — indeed, I will myself insist with energy — that this obligation to candour puts a grave moral responsibility on the analyst as well. And it must be so, secondly, because factors from sexual life play an extremely important, a dominating, perhaps even a *specific*, part among the causes and precipitating factors of neurotic illnesses. What else can analysis do but keep close to its subject-matter, to the material brought up by the patient? The analyst never entices his patient on to the ground of sex. He does not say to him in advance: 'We shall be dealing with the intimacies of your sexual life!' He allows him to begin what he has to say wherever he pleases, and quietly waits until the patient himself touches on sexual things. I used always to warn my pupils: 'Our opponents have told us that we shall come upon cases in which the factor of sex plays no part. Let us be careful not to introduce it into our analyses and so spoil our chance of finding such a case.' But so far none of us has had that good fortune.

I am aware, of course, that our recognition of sexuality has become — whether admittedly or not — the strongest motive for other people's hostility to analysis. Can that shake our confidence? It merely shows us how neurotic our whole civilized life is, since ostensibly normal people do not behave very differently from neurotics. At a time when psycho-analysis was solemnly put on its trial before the learned societies of Germany — today things have grown altogether quieter — one of the speakers claimed to possess peculiar authority because, so he said, he even allowed his patients to talk: for diagnostic purposes, clearly, and to test the assertions of analysts. 'But', he added, 'if they begin to talk about sexual matters I shut their mouths.' What do you think of that as a method of demonstration? The learned society applauded the speaker to the echo instead of feeling suitably ashamed on his account. Only the triumphant certainty afforded by the consciousness of prejudices held in common can explain this speaker's want of logical thought. Years later a few of those who had at that time been my followers gave in to the need to free human society from the yoke of sexuality which psycho-analysis was seeking to impose on it. One of them explained that what is sexual does not mean sexuality at all, but something else, something abstract and mystical. And another actually declared that sexual life is merely one of the spheres in which human beings seek to put in action their driving need for power and domination. They have met with much applause, for the moment at least.

'I shall venture, for once in a way, to take sides on that point. It strikes me as extremely bold to assert that sexuality is not a natural, primitive need of living organisms, but an expression of something else. One need only take the example of animals.'

That makes no difference. There is no mixture, however absurd, that society will not willingly swallow down if it is advertised as an antidote to the dreaded predominance of sexuality.

I confess, moreover, that the dislike that you yourself have betrayed of assigning to the factor of sexuality so great a part in the causation of neurosis — I confess that this scarcely seems to me consistent with your task as an Impartial Person. Are you not afraid that this antipathy may interfere with your passing judgement?

'I'm sorry to hear you say that. Your reliance on me seems to be shaken. But in that case why not have chosen someone else as your Impartial Person?'

Because that someone else would not have thought any differently from you. But if he had been prepared from the first to recognize the importance of sexual life, everyone would have exclaimed: 'Why, that is no Impartial Person, he is one of your supporters!' No, I am far from abandoning the expectation of being able to influence your opinions. I must admit, however, that from my point of view this situation is different from the one we dealt with earlier. As regards our psychological discussions it is a matter of indifference to me whether you believe me or not, provided only that you get an impression that what we are concerned with are purely psychological problems. But here, as regards the question of sexuality, I should nevertheless be glad if you were accessible to the realization that your strongest motive for contradiction is precisely the ingrained hostility which you share with so many other people.

'But after all I am without the experience that has given you your unshakeable certainty.'

Very well. I can now proceed with my exposition. Sexual life is not simply something spicy; it is also a serious scientific problem. There was much that was novel to be learnt about it, many strange things to be explained. I told you just now that analysis has to go back into the early years of the patient's childhood, because the decisive repressions have taken place then, while his ego was feeble. But surely in childhood there is no sexual life? surely it only starts a puberty? On the contrary. We have to learn that sexual instinctual impulses accompany life from birth onwards, and that it is precisely in order to fend off those instincts that the infantile ego institutes repressions. A remarkable coincidence, is it not? that small children should already be struggling against the power of sexuality, just as the speaker in the learned society was to do later, and later still my followers who have set up their own theories. How does that come about? The most general explanation would be that our civilization is built up entirely at the expense of sexuality; but there is much more to be said on the subject.

The discovery of infantile sexuality is one of those of which we have reason to feel ashamed [because of its obviousness]. A few paediatricians have, it seems, always known about it, and a few children's nurses. Clever men, who call themselves child psychologists, have thereupon spoken in tones of reproach of a 'desecration of the innocence of childhood'. Once again, sentiment instead of argument! Events of that kind are of daily occurrence in political bodies. A member of the Opposition rises and denounces some piece of maladministration in the Civil Service, in the Army, in the Judiciary, and so on. Upon this another member, preferably one of the Government, declares that such statements are an affront to the sense of honour of the body politic, of the army, of the dynasty, or even of the nation. So they are as good as untrue. Feelings such as these can tolerate no affronts.

The sexual life of children is of course different from that of adults. The sexual function, from its beginnings to the definitive form in which it is so familiar to us, undergoes a complicated process of development. It grows together from numerous component instincts with different aims and passes through several phases of organization till at last it comes into the service of reproduction. Not all the component instincts are equally serviceable for the final outcome; they must be diverted, remodelled, and in part suppressed. Such a far-reaching course of development is not always passed through without a flaw; inhibitions in development take place, partial fixations at early stages of development. If obstacles arise later on to the exercise of the sexual function, the sexual urge — the libido, as we call it — is apt to hark back to these earlier points of fixation. The study of the sexuality of children and its transformations up to maturity has also given us the key to an understanding of what are known as the sexual perversions, which people used always to describe with all the requisite indications of disgust but whose origin they were never able to explain. The whole topic is of uncommon interest, but for the purposes of our conversation there is not much sense in telling you more about it. To find one's way about in it one of course needs anatomical and physiological knowledge, all of which is unfortunately not to be acquired in medical schools. But a familiarity with the history of civilization and with mythology is equally indispensable.

'After all that, I still cannot form any picture of the sexual life of children.'

Then I will pursue the subject further; in any case it is not easy for me to get away from it. I will tell you, then, that the most remarkable thing about the sexual life of children seems to me that it passes through the whole of its very far-reaching development in the first five years of life. From then onwards until puberty there stretches what is known as the period of latency. During it sexuality normally advances no further; on the contrary, the sexual urges diminish in strength and many things are given up and forgotten which the child did and knew. During that period of life, after the early efflorescence of sexuality has withered, such attitudes of the ego as shame, disgust, and morality arise, which are destined to stand up against the later tempest of puberty and to lay down the path of the freshly awakening sexual desires. This 'diphasic onset',[2] as it is named, of sexual life has a great deal to do with the genesis of neurotic illnesses. It seems to occur only in human beings, and it is perhaps one of the determinants of the human privilege of becoming neurotic. The prehistory of sexual life was just as much overlooked before psycho-analysis as, in another department, the background to conscious mental life. You will rightly suspect that the two are intimately connected.

There is much to be told, for which our expectations have not prepared us, about the contents, manifestations, and achievements of this early period of sexuality. For instance, you will no doubt be surprised to hear how often little boys are afraid of being eaten up by their father. (And you may also be surprised at my including this fear among the phenomena of sexual life.) But I may remind you of the mythological tale which you may still recall from your schooldays of how the god Kronos swallowed his children. How strange this must have sounded to you when you first heard it! But I suppose none of us thought about it at the time. Today we can also call to mind a number of fairy tales in which some ravenous animal like a wolf appears, and we shall recognize it as a disguise of the father. And this is an opportunity of assuring you that it was only through the knowledge of infantile sexuality that it became possible to understand mythology and the world of fairy tales. Here then something has been gained as a by-product of analytic studies.

You will be no less surprised to hear that male children suffer from a fear of being robbed of their sexual organ by their father, so that this fear of being castrated has a most powerful influence on the development of their character and in deciding the direction to be followed by their sexuality. And here again mythology may give you the courage to believe psycho-analysis. The same Kronos who swallowed his children also emasculated his father Uranus, and was afterwards himself emasculated in revenge by his son Zeus, who had been rescued through his mother's cunning. If you have felt inclined to suppose that all that psycho-analysis reports about the early sexuality of children is derived from the disordered imagination of the analysts, you must at least admit that their imagination has created the same product as the imaginative activities of primitive man, of which myths and fairy tales are the precipitate. The alternative friendlier, and probably also the more pertinent, view would be that in the mental life of children today we can still detect the same archaic factors which were once dominant generally in the primeval days of human civilization. In his mental development the child would be repeating the history of his race in an abbreviated form, just as embryology long since recognized was the case with somatic development.

Another characteristic of early infantile sexuality is that the female sexual organ proper as yet plays no part in it: the child has not yet discovered it. Stress falls entirely on the male organ, all the child's interest is directed towards the question of whether it is present or not. We know less about the sexual life of little girls than of boys. But we need not feel ashamed of this distinction; after all, the sexual life of adult women is a 'dark continent' for psychology. But we have learnt that girls feel deeply their lack of a sexual organ that is equal in value to the male one; they regard themselves on that account as inferior, and this 'envy for the penis' is the origin of a whole number of characteristic feminine reactions.

It is also characteristic of children that their two excretory needs are cathected [charged] with sexual interest. Later on, education draws a sharp distinction here, which is once more obliterated in the practice of joking. It may seem to us an unsavoury fact, but it takes quite a long time for children to develop feelings of disgust. This is not disputed even by people who insist otherwise on the seraphic purity of the child's mind.

Nothing, however, deserves more notice than the fact that children regularly direct their sexual wishes towards their nearest relatives — in the first place, therefore, towards their father and mother, and afterwards towards their brothers and sisters. The first object of a boy's love is his mother, and of a girl's her father (except in so far as an innate bisexual disposition favours the simultaneous presence of the contrary attitude). The other parent is felt as a disturbing rival and not infrequently viewed with strong hostility. You must understand me aright. What I mean to say is not that the child wants to be treated by its favourite parent merely with the kind of affection which we adults life to regard as the essence of the parent-child relation. No, analysis leaves us in no doubt that the child's wishes extend beyond such affection to all that we understand by sensual satisfaction — so far, that is, as the child's powers of imagination allow. It is easy to see that the child never guesses the actual facts of sexual intercourse; her replaces them by other notions derived from his own experience and feelings. As a rule his wishes culminate in the intention to bear, or in some indefinable way to procreate, a baby. Boys, too, in their ignorance, do not exclude themselves from the wish to bear a baby. We give the whole of this mental structure the name of 'Oedipus complex', after the familiar Greek legend. With the end of the early sexual period it should normally be given up, should radically disintegrate and become transformed; and the products of this transformation are destined for important functions in later mental life. But as a rule this is not effected radically enough, in which case puberty brings about a revival of the complex, which may have serious consequences.

I am surprised that you are still silent. That can scarcely mean consent. In asserting that a child's first choice of an object is, to use the technical term, an incestuous one, analysis no doubt once more hurt the most sacred feelings of humanity, and might well be prepared for a corresponding amount of disbelief, contradiction, and attack. And these it has received in abundance. Nothing has damaged it more in the good opinion of its contemporaries than its hypothesis of the Oedipus complex as a structure universally bound to human destiny. The Greek myth, incidentally, must have had the same meaning; but the majority of men today, learned and unlearned alike, prefer to believe that Nature has laid down an innate abhorrence in us as a guard against the possibility of incest.

But let us first summon history to our aid. When Caius Julius Caesar landed in Egypt, he found the young Queen Cleopatra (who was soon to become so important to him) married to her still younger brother Ptolemy. In an Egyptian dynasty there was nothing peculiar in this; the Ptolemies, who were of Greek origin, had merely carried on the custom which had been practised by their predecessors, the ancient Pharaohs, for a few thousand years. This, however, was merely brother-and-sister incest, which even at the present time is not judged so harshly. So let us turn to our chief witness in matters concerning primeval times — mythology. It informs us that the myths of every people, and not only of the Greeks, are filled with examples of love affairs between fathers and daughters and even between mothers and sons. Cosmology, no less than the genealogy of royal races, is founded upon incest. For what purpose do you suppose these legends were created? To brand gods and kings as criminals? to fasten on them the abhorrence of the human race? Rather, surely, because incestuous wishes are a primordial human heritage and have never been fully overcome, so that their fulfilment was still granted to gods and their descendants when the majority of common humans were already obliged to renounce them. It is in complete harmony with these lessons of history and mythology that we find incestuous wishes still present and operative in the childhood of the individual.

'I might take it amiss that you tried to keep back all this about infantile sexuality from me. It seems to me most interesting, particularly on account of its connexion with human pre-history.'

I was afraid it might take us too far from our purpose. But perhaps after all it will be of use.

'Now tell me, though, what certainty can you offer for your analytic findings on the sexual life of children? Is your conviction based solely on points of agreement with mythology and history?'

Oh, by no means. It is based on direct observation. What happened was this. We had begun by inferring the content of sexual childhood from the analysis of adults — that is to say, some twenty or forty years later. Afterwards, we undertook analysis on children themselves, and it was no small triumph when we were thus able to confirm in them everything that we had been able to divine, in spite of the amount to which it had been overlaid and distorted in the interval.

'What?' You have had small children in analysis? children of less than six years? *Can* that be done? And is it not most risky for the children?'

It can be done very well. It is hardly to be believed what goes on in a child of four or five years old. Children are very active-minded at that age; their early sexual period is also a period of intellectual flowering. I have an impression that with the onset of the latency period they become mentally inhibited as well, stupidier. From that time on, too, many children lose their physical charm. And, as regards the damage done by early analysis, I may inform you that the first child on whom the experiment was ventured, nearly twenty years ago, has since then grown into a healthy and capable young man, who has passed through his puberty irreproachably, in spite of some severe psychical traumas. It may be hoped that things will turn out no worse for the other 'victims' of early analysis. Much that is of interest attaches to these child analyses; it is possible that in the future they will become still more important. From the point of view of theory, their value is beyond question. They give unambiguous information on problems which remain unsolved in the analyses of adults; and they thus protect the analyst from errors that might have momentous consequences for him. One surprises the factors that lead to the formation of a neurosis while they are actually at work and one cannot then mistake them. In the child's interest, it is true, analytic influence must be combined with educational measures. The technique has still to receive its shaping. But practical interest is aroused by the observation that a very large number of our children pass through a plainly neurotic phase in the course of their development. Since we have learnt how to look more sharply, we are tempted to say that neurosis in children is not the exception but the rule, as though it could scarcely be avoided on the path from the innate disposition of infancy to civilized society. In most cases this neurotic phase in childhood is overcome spontaneously. But may it not also regularly leave its traces in the average healthy adult? On the other hand in those who are neurotics in later life we never fail to find links with the illness in childhood, though at the time it need not have been very noticeable. In a precisely analogous way physicians today, I believe, hold the view that each one of us has gone through an attack of tuberculosis in his childhood. It is true that in the case of the neurosis the factor of immunization does not operate, but only the factor of predisposition.

Let me return to your question about certainty. We have become quite generally convinced from the direct analytic examination of children that we were right in our interpretation of what adults told us about their childhood. In a number of cases, however, another sort of confirmation has become possible. The material of the analysis of some patients has enabled us to reconstruct certain external happenings, certain impressive events of their childhood years, of which they have preserved no conscious memory. Lucky accidents, information from parents or nurses, have afterwards provided irrefutable evidence that these occurrences which we had inferred really did take place. This, of course, has not happened often, but when it has it has made an overwhelming impression. The correct reconstruction, you must know, of such forgotten experiences of childhood always has a great therapeutic effect, whether they permit of objective confirmation or not. These events owe their importance, of course, to their having occurred at such an early age, at a time when they could still produce a traumatic effect on the feeble ego.

'And what sort of events can these be, that have to be discovered by analysis?'

Various sorts. In the first place, impressions capable of permanently influencing the child's budding sexual life — such as observations of sexual activities between adults, or sexual experiences of his own with an adult or another child (no rare events); or, again, overhearing conversations, understood either at the time or retrospectively, from which the child thought it could draw conclusions about mysterious or uncanny matters; or again, remarks or actions by the child himself which give evidence of significant attitudes of affection or enmity towards other people. It is of special importance in an analysis to induce a memory of the patient's own forgotten sexual activity as a child and also of the intervention by the adults which brought it to an end.

'That gives me an opportunity to bring up a question that I have long wanted to ask. What, then, is the nature of this "sexual activity" of children at an early age, which, as you say, was overlooked before the days of analysis?'

It is an odd thing that the regular and essential part of this sexual activity was *not* overlooked. Or rather, it is by no means odd; for it was impossible to overlook it. Children's sexual impulses find their main expressions in self-gratification by friction of their own genitals, or, more precisely, of the male portion of them. The extraordinarily wide distribution of this form of childish 'naughtiness' was always known to adults, and it was regarded as a grave sin and severely punished. But please do not ask me how people could reconcile these observations of the immoral inclinations of children — for children do it, as they themselves say, because it gives them pleasure — with the theory of their innate purity and non-sensuality. You must get our opponents to solve this riddle. *We* have a more important problem before us. What attitude should we adopt towards the sexual activity of early childhood? We know the responsibility we are incurring if we suppress it; but we do not venture to let it take its course without restriction. Among races at a low level of civilization, and among the lower strata of civilized races, the sexuality of children seems to be given free rein. This probably provides a powerful protection against the subsequent development of neuroses in the individual. But does it not at the same time involve an extraordinary loss of the aptitude for cultural achievements? There is a good deal to suggest that here we are faced by a new Scylla and Charybdis.

But whether the interests which are stimulated by the study of the sexual life of neurotics create an atmosphere favourable to the encouragement of lasciviousness — *that* is a question which I venture to leave to your own judgement.

V

'I believe I understand your purpose. You want to show me what kind of knowledge is needed in order to practise analysis, so that I may be able to judge whether only doctors should have a right to do so. Well, so far very little to do with medicine has turned up: a great deal of psychology and a little biology or sexual science. But perhaps we have not got to the end?'

Decidedly not. There are still gaps to be filled. May I make a request? Will you describe how you now picture an analytic treatment? — just as though you had to undertake one yourself.

'A fine idea, to be sure! No, I have not the least intention of settling our controversy by an experiment of that sort. But just to oblige, I will do what you ask — the responsibility will be yours. Very well. I will suppose that the patient comes to me and complains of his troubles. I promise him recovery or improvement if he will follow my directions. I call on him to tell me with perfect candour everything that he knows and that occurs to him, and not to be deterred from that intention even if some things are disagreeable to say. Have I taken in the rule properly?'

Yes. You should add: 'even if what occurs to him seems unimportant or senseless.'

'I will add that. Thereupon he begins to talk and I listen. And what then? I infer from what he tells me the kind of impressions, experiences, and wishes which he has repressed because he came across them at a time when his ego was still feeble and was afraid of them instead of dealing with them. When he has learnt this from me, he puts himself back in the old situations and with my help he manages better. The limitations to which his ego was tied then disappear, and he is cured. Is that right?'

Bravo! bravo! I see that once again people will be able to accuse me of having made an analyst of someone who is not a doctor. You have mastered it all admirably.

'I have done no more than repeat what I have heard from you — as though it was something I had learnt by heart. All the same, I cannot form any picture of how I should do it, and I am at quite a loss to understand why a job like that should take an hour a day for so many months. After all, an ordinary person has not as a rule experienced such a lot, and what was repressed in childhood is probably in every case the same.'

When one really practises analysis one learns all kinds of things besides. For instance: you would not find it at all such a simple matter to deduce from what the patient tells you the experiences he has forgotten and the instinctual impulses he has repressed. He says something to you which at first means as little to you as it does to him. You will have to make up your mind to look at the material which he delivers to you in obedience to the rule in a quite special way: as though it were ore, perhaps, from which its content of precious metal has to be extracted by a particular process. You will be prepared, too, to work over many tons of ore which may contain but little of the valuable material you are in search of. Here we should have a first reason for the prolonged character of the treatment.

'But how does one work over this raw material — to keep to your simile?'

By assuming that the patient's remarks and associations are only distortions of what you are looking for — allusions, as it were, from which you have to guess what is hidden behind them. In a word, this material, whether it consists of memories, associations, or dreams, has first to be *interpreted*. You will do this, of course, with an eye to the expectations you have formed as you listened, thanks to your special knowledge.

'"Interpret!" A nasty word! I dislike the sound of it; it robs me of all certainty. If everything depends on my interpretation who can guarantee that I interpret right? So after all everything *is* left to my caprice.'

Just a moment! Things are not quite as bad as that. Why do you choose to except your own mental processes from the rule of law which you recognize in other people's? When you have attained some degree of self-discipline and have certain knowledge at your disposal, your interpretations will be independent of your personal characteristics and will hit the mark. I am not saying that the analyst's personality is a matter of indifference for this portion of his task. A kind of sharpness of hearing for what is unconscious and repressed, which is not possessed equally by everyone, has a part to play. And here, above all, we are brought to the analyst's obligation to make himself capable, by a deep-going analysis of his own, of the unprejudiced reception of the analytical material.

Something, it is true, still remains over: something comparable to the 'personal equation' in astronomical observations. This individual factor will always play a larger part in psycho-analysis than elsewhere. An abnormal person can become an accurate physicist; as an analyst he will be hampered by his own abnormality from seeing the pictures of mental life undistorted. Since it is impossible to demonstrate to anyone his own abnormality, general agreement in matters or depth-psychology will be particularly hard to reach. Some psychologists, indeed, think it is quite impossible and that every fool has an equal right to give out his folly as wisdom. I confess that I am more of an optimist about this. After all, our experiences show that fairly satisfactory agreements can be reached even in psychology. Every field of research has its particular difficulty which we must try to eliminate. And, moreover, even in the interpretive art of analysis there is much that can be learnt like any other material of study: for instance, in connexion with the peculiar method of indirect representation through symbols.

'Well, I no longer have any desire to undertake an analytic treatment even in my imagination. Who can say what other surprises I might meet with?'

You are quite right to give up the notion. You see how much more training and practice would be needed. When you have found the right interpretation, another task lies ahead. You must wait for the right moment at which you can communicate your interpretation to the patient with some prospect of success.

'How can one always tell the right moment?'

That is a question of tact, which can become more refined with experience. You will be making a bad mistake if, in an effort, perhaps, at shortening the analysis, you throw your interpretations at the patient's head as soon as you have found them. In that way you will draw expressions of resistance, rejection, and indignation from him; but you will not enable his ego to master his repressed material. The formula is: to wait till he has come so near to the repressed material that he has only a few more steps to take under the lead of the interpretation you propose.

'I believe I should never learn to do that. And if I carry out these precautions in making my interpretation, what next?'

It will then be your fate to make a discovery for which you were not prepared.

'And what may that be?'

That you have been deceived in your patient; that you cannot count in the slightest on his collaboration and compliance; that he is ready to place every possible difficulty in the way of your common work — in a word, that he has no wish whatever to be cured.

'Well! that is the craziest thing you have told me yet. And I do not believe it either. The patient who is suffering so much, who complains so movingly about his troubles, who is making so great a sacrifice for the treatment — you say he has no wish to be cured! But of course you do not mean what you say.'

Calm yourself! I *do* mean it. What I said was the truth — not the whole truth, no doubt, but a very noteworthy part of it. The patient wants to be cured — but he also wants not to be. His ego has lost its unity, and for that reason his will has no unity either. If that were not so, he would be no neurotic.

"'Were I sagacious, I should not be Tell'"[1]

The derivatives of what is repressed have broken into his ego and established themselves there; and the ego has as little control over trends from that source as it has over what is actually repressed, and as a rule it knows nothing about them. These patients, indeed, are of a peculiar nature and raise difficulties with which we are not accustomed to reckon. All our social institutions are framed for people with a united and normal ego, which one can classify as good or bad, which either fulfills its function or is altogether eliminated by an overpowering influence. Hence the juridical alternative: responsible or irresponsible. None of these distinctions apply to neurotics. It must be admitted that there is difficulty in adapting social demands to their psychological condition. This was experienced on a large scale during the last war. Were the neurotics who evaded service malingerers or not? They were both. If they were treated as malingerers and if their illness was made highly uncomfortable, they recovered; if after being ostensibly restored they were sent back into service, they promptly took flight once more into illness. Nothing could be done with them. And the same is true of neurotics in civil life. They complain of their illness but exploit it with all their strength; and if someone tries to take it away from them they defend it like the proverbial lioness with her young. Yet there would be no sense in reproaching them for this contradiction.

'But would not the best plan be not to give these difficult people any treatment at all, but to leave them to themselves? I cannot think it is worth while to expend such great efforts over each of them as you lead me to suppose that you make.'

I cannot approve of your suggestion. It is undoubtedly a more proper line to accept the complications of life rather than struggle against them. It may be true that not every neurotic whom we treat is worth the expenditure of an analysis; but there are some very valuable individuals among them as well. We must set ourselves the goal of bringing it about that as few human beings as possible enter civilized life with such a defective mental equipment. And for that purpose we must collect much experience and learn to understand many things. Every analysis can be instructive and bring us a yield of new understanding quite apart from the personal value of the individual patient.

'But if a volitional impulse has been formed in the patient's ego which wishes to retain the illness, it too must have its reasons and motives and be able in some ways to justify itself. But it is impossible to see why anyone should want to be ill or what he can get out of it.'

Oh, that is not so hard to understand. Think of the war neurotics, who do not have to serve, precisely because they are ill. In civil life illness can be used as a screen to gloss over incompetence in one's profession or in competition with other people; while in the family it can serve as a means for sacrificing the other members and extorting proofs of their love or for imposing one's will upon them. All of this lies fairly near the surface; we sum it up in the term 'gain from illness'. It is curious, however, that the patient — that is, his ego — nevertheless knows nothing of the whole concatenation of these motives and the actions which they involve. One combats the influence of these trends by compelling the ego to take cognizance of them. But there are other motives, that lie still deeper, for holding on to being ill, which are not so easily dealt with. But these cannot be understood without a fresh journey into psychological theory.

'Please go on. A little more theory will make no odds now.'

When I described the relation between the ego and the id to you, I suppressed an important part of the theory of the mental apparatus. For we have been obliged to assume that within the ego itself a particular agency has become differentiated, which we name the super-ego. This super-ego occupies a special position between the ego and the id. It belongs to the ego and shares its high degree of psychological organization; but it has a particularly intimate connexion with the id. It is in fact a precipitate of the first object-cathexes of the id and is the heir to the Oedipus complex after its demise.[2] This super-ego can confront the ego and treat it like an object; and it often treats it very harshly. It is as important for the ego to remain on good terms with the super-ego as with the id. Estrangement between the ego and the super-ego are of great significance in mental life. You will already have guessed that the super-ego is the vehicle of the phenomenon that we call conscience. Mental health very much depends on the super-ego's being normally developed — that is, on its having become sufficiently impersonal. And that is precisely what it is not in neurotics, whose Oedipus complex has not passed through the correct process of transformation. Their super-ego still confronts their ego as a strict father confronts a child; and their morality operates in a primitive fashion in that the ego gets itself punished by the super-ego. Illness is employed as an instrument for this 'self-punishment', and neurotics have to behave as though they were governed by a sense of guilt which, in order to be satisfied, needs to be punished by illness.

'That really sounds most mysterious. The strangest thing about it is that apparently even this mighty force of the patient's conscience does not reach his consciousness.'

Yes, we are only beginning to appreciate the significance of all these important circumstances. That is why my description was bound to turn out so obscure. But now I can proceed. We describe all the forces that oppose the work of recovery as the patient's 'resistances'. The gain from illness is one such resistance. The 'unconscious sense of guilt' represents the super-ego's resistance; it is the most powerful factor, and the one most dreaded by us. We meet with still other resistances during the treatment. If the ego during the early period has set up a repression out of fear, then the fear still persists and manifests itself as a resistance if the ego approaches the repressed material. And finally, as you can imagine, there are likely to be difficulties if an instinctual process which has been going along a particular path for whole decades is suddenly expected to take a new path that has just been made open for it. That might be called the id's resistance. The struggle against all these resistances is our main work during an analytic treatment; the task of making interpretations is nothing compared to it. But as a result of this struggle and of the overcoming of the resistances, the patient's ego is so much altered and strengthened that we can look forward calmly to his future behaviour when the treatment is over. On the other hand, you can understand now why we need such long treatments. The length of the path of development and the wealth of the material are not the decisive factors. It is more a question of whether the path is clear. An army can be held up for weeks on a stretch of a country which in peace time an express crosses in a couple of hours — if the army has to overcome the enemy's resistance there. Such battles call for time in mental life too. I am unfortunately obliged to tell you that every effort to hasten analytic treatment appreciably has hitherto failed. The best way of shortening it seems to be to carry it out according to the rules.

'If I ever felt any desire to poach on your preserves and try my hand at analysing someone else, what you tell me about the resistances would have cured me of it. But how about the special personal influence that you yourself have after all admitted? Does not that come into action against the resistances?'

It is a good thing you have asked me about that. This personal influence is our most powerful dynamic weapon. It is the new element which we introduce into the situation and by means of which we make it fluid. The intellectual content of our explanations cannot do it, for the patient, who shares all the prejudices of the world around him, need believe us as little as our scientific critics do. The neurotic sets to work because he has faith in the analyst, and he believes him because he acquires a special emotional attitude towards the figure of the analyst. Children, too, only believe people they are attached to. I have already told you what use we make of this particularly large 'suggestive' influence. Not for suppressing the symptoms — that distinguishes the analytic method from other psychotherapeutic procedures — but as a motive force to induce the patient to overcome his resistances.

'Well, and if that succeeds, does not everything then go smoothly?'

Yes, it ought to. But there turns out to be an unexpected complication. It was perhaps the greatest of the analyst's surprises to find that the emotional relation which the patient adopts towards him is of a quite peculiar nature. The very first doctor who attempted an analysis — it was not myself — came up against this phenomenon and did not know what to make of it. For this emotional relation is, to put it plainly, in the nature of falling in love. Strange, is it not? Especially when you take into account that the analyst does nothing to provoke it but on the contrary rather keeps at a distance from the patient, speaking humanly, and surrounds himself with some degree of reserve — when you learn besides that this odd love-relationship disregards anything else that is really propitious and every variation in personal attraction, age, sex, or class. This love is of a positively compulsive kind. Not that that characteristic need be absent from spontaneous falling in love. As you know, the contrary is often the case. But in the analytic situation it makes its appearance with complete regularity without there being any rational explanation for it. One would have thought that the patient's relation to the analyst called for no more than a certain amount of respect, trust, gratitude, and human sympathy. Instead, there is this falling in love, which itself gives the impression of being a pathological phenomenon.

'I should have thought all the same that it would be favourable for your analytic purposes. If someone is in love, he is amenable, and he will do anything in the world for the sake of the other person.'

Yes. It *is* favourable to start with. But when this falling in love has grown deeper, its whole nature comes to light, much of which is incompatible with the task of analysis. The patient's love is not satisfied with being obedient; it grows exacting, calls for affectionate and sensual satisfactions, it demands exclusiveness, it develops jealousy, and it shows more and more clearly its reverse side, its readiness to become hostile and revengeful if it cannot obtain its ends. At the same time, like all falling in love, it drives away all other mental material; it extinguishes interest in the treatment and in recovery — in short, there can be no doubt that it has taken the place of the neurosis and that our work has had the result of driving out one form of illness with another.

'That does sound hopeless! What can be done about it? The analysis would have to be given up. But if, as you say, the same thing happens in every case, it would be impossible to carry through any analyses at all.'

We will begin by using the situation in order to learn something from it. What we learn may then perhaps help us to master it. Is it not an extremely noteworthy fact that we succeed in transforming every neurosis, whatever its content, into a condition of pathological love?

Our conviction that a portion of erotic life that has been abnormally employed lies at the basis of neuroses must be unshakeably strengthened by this experience. With this discovery we are once more on a firm footing and can venture to make this love itself the object of analysis. And we can make another observation. Analytic love is not manifested in every case as clearly and blatantly as I have tried to depict it. Why not? We can soon see. In proportion as the purely sensual and the hostile sides of his love try to show themselves the patient's opposition to them is aroused. He struggles against them and tries to repress them before our very eyes. And now we understand what is happening. The patient is *repeating* in the form of falling in love with the analyst mental experiences which he has already been through once before; he has *transferred* on to the analyst mental attitudes that were lying ready in him and were intimately connected with his neurosis. He is also repeating before our eyes his old defensive actions; he would like best to repeat in his relation to the analyst *all* the history of that forgotten period of his life. So what he is showing us is the kernel of his intimate life history: *he is reproducing it tangibly, as though it were actually happening, instead of remembering it.* In this way the riddle of the transference-love is solved and the analysis can proceed on its way — with the *help* of the new situation which had seemed such a menace to it.

'That is very cunning. And is the patient so easy to convince that he is not in love but only obliged to stage a revival of an old piece?'

Everything now depends on that. And the whole skill in handling the 'transference' is devoted to bringing it about. As you see, the requirements of analytic technique reach their maximum at this point. Here the gravest mistakes can be made or the greatest successes be registered. It would be folly to attempt to evade the difficulties by suppressing or neglecting the transference: whatever else had been done in the treatment, it would not deserve the name if an analysis. To send the patient away as soon as the inconveniences of his transference-neurosis make their appearance would be no more sensible, and would moreover be cowardly. It would be as though one had conjured up spirits and run away from them as soon as they appeared. Sometimes, it is true, nothing else is possible. There are cases in which one cannot master the unleashed transference and the analysis has to be broken off; but one must at least have struggled with the evil spirits to the best of one's strength. To yield to the demands of the transference, to fulfil the patient's wishes for affectionate and sensual satisfaction, is not only justly forbidden by moral considerations but is also completely ineffective as a technical method for attaining the purpose of the analysis. A neurotic cannot be cured by being enabled to reproduce uncorrected an unconscious stereotype plate that is ready to hand in him. If one engages in compromises with him by offering him partial satisfactions in exchange for this further collaboration in the analysis, one must beware of falling into the ridiculous situation of the cleric who was supposed to convert a sick insurance agent. The sick man remained unconverted but the cleric took his leave insured. The only possible way out of the transference situation is to trace it back to the patient's past, as he really experienced it or as he pictured it through the wish-fulfilling activity of his imagination. And this demands from the analyst much skill, patience, calm, and self-abnegation.

'And where do you suppose the neurotic experienced the prototype of his transference-love?'

In his childhood: as a rule in his relation with one of his parents. You will remember what importance we had to attribute to these earliest emotional ties. So here the circle closes.

'Have you finished at last? I am feeling just a little bewildered with all I have heard from you. Only tell me one thing more: how and where can one learn what is necessary for practising analysis?'

There are at the moment two Institutes at which instruction in psycho-analysis is given. The first has been founded in Berlin by Dr Max Eitingon, who is a member of the Society there. The second is maintained by the Vienna Psycho-Analytical Society at its own expense and at considerable sacrifice. The part played by the authorities is at present limited to the many difficulties which they put in the way of the young undertaking. A third training Institute is at this moment being opened in London by the Society there, under the direction of Dr Ernest Jones. At these Institutes the candidates themselves are taken into analysis, receive theoretical instruction by lectures on all the subjects that are important for them, and enjoy the supervision of older and more experienced analysts when they are allowed to make their first trials with comparatively slight cases. A period of some two years is calculated for this training. Even after this period, of course, the candidate is only a beginner and not yet a master. What is still needed must be acquired by practice and by an exchange of ideas in the psycho-analytical societies in which young and old members meet together. Preparation for analytic activity is by no means so easy and simple. The work is hard, the responsibility great. But anyone who has passed through such a course of instruction, who has been analyzed himself, who has mastered what can be taught today of the psychology of the unconscious, who is at home in the science of sexual life, who has learnt the delicate technique of psycho-analysis, the art of interpretation, of fighting resistances, and of handling the transference — anyone who has accomplished all this *is no longer a layman in the field of psycho-analysis*. He is capable of undertaking the treatment of neurotic disorders, and will be able in time to achieve in that field whatever can be required from this form of therapy.

NOTES

II

1   Johann Nestroy (1801-62), famous in Vienna as a writer of comedies and farces.

2   The question of what *material* the mental apparatus is constructed of.

3   Hans Vaihinger (1852-1933). His philosophical system was enunciated in *Die Philosophie des Als Ob*, 1911. An English translation by C. K. Ogden appeared in 1924 under the title T*he Philosophy of 'As if'*. The work had a considerable vogue in German-speaking countries, especially after the First World War.

4   It should be remarked that the German word for 'conscious' — *bewusst* — has a passive form and is regularly used by Freud in a passive sense. Thus he would not as a rule speak of a person being conscious of a sensation but of a sensation being conscious to a person.

5   This is now usually described as a 'training analysis'.

III

1   Schiller, 'Die Weltweisen'.

2   Various translations have been adopted for the word *Trieb*, the most literal being 'drive'.

IV

1   No doubt Tolstoy and his followers.

2   Onset in two waves.

V

1   Schiller, *Wilhelm Tell*, Act III, Scene 3.

2   The changes of energy (cathexes) directed from the id on to its first external objects (the parents) are transformed into identifications and the objects are introduced into the ego and there take the form of a super-ego.

6

INTRODUCTORY LECTURES ON PSYCHOANALYSIS (LECTURES 6, 7, 8 and 9)

Sigmund Freud

LECTURE 6
The Premisses and Technique of Interpretation

Ladies and Gentlemen, — What we need, then, is a new path, a method which will enable us to make a start in the investigation of dreams. I will put a suggestion to you which presents itself. Let us take it as a premiss from this point onwards that *dreams are not somatic by psychical phenomena.* You know what that means, but what justifies our making the assumption? Nothing: but there is nothing either to prevent our making it. Here is the position: if dreams are somatic phenomena they are no concern of ours, they can only interest us on the assumption that they are mental phenomena. We will therefore work on the assumption that they really are, to see what comes of it. The outcome of our work will decide whether we are to hold to this assumption and whether we may then go on to treat it in turn as a proved finding. But what is it actually that we want to arrive at? What is our work aiming at? We want something that is sought for in all scientific work — to understand the phenomena, to establish a correlation between them and, in the latter end, if it is possible, to enlarge our power over them.

We proceed with our work, accordingly, on the supposition that dreams are psychical phenomena. In that case they are products and utterances of the dreamer's, but utterances which tell us nothing, which we do not understand. Well, what do you do if I make an unintelligible utterance to you? You question me, is that not so? Why should we not do the same thing to the dreamer — *question him as to what his dream means?*

Freud, S. *Introductory Lectures on Psychoanalysis*, vol. 1. Translated by James Strachey, edited by James Strachey and Angela Richards, pp. 129-181. London: Penguin, 1973.

As you will remember, we found ourselves in this situation once before. It was while we were investigating certain parapraxes — a case of a slip of the tongue. Someone had said: 'Then facts came to *Vorschwein*' and we thereupon asked him — no, it was luckily not we but some other people who had no connection at all with psychoanalysis — these other people, then, asked him what he meant by this unintelligible remark. And he replied at once that he had intended to say 'these facts were *Schweinereien* [disgusting]', but had forced this intention back in favour of the milder version 'then facts came to *Vorschein* [light]'. I pointed out to you at the time that this piece of information was the model for every psychoanalytic investigation, and you will understand now that psychoanalysis follows the technique of getting the people under examination so far as possible themselves to produce the solution of their riddles. Thus, too, it is the dreamer himself who should tell us what his dream means.

But, as we know, things are not so simple with dreams. With parapraxes it worked all right in a number of cases; but then others came along in which the person who was questioned would say nothing, and even indignantly rejected the answer we proposed to him. With dreams cases of the first sort are entirely lacking; the dreamer always says he knows nothing. He cannot reject our interpretation as we have none to offer him. Are we to give up our attempt then? Since he knows nothing and we know nothing and a third person could know even less, there seems to be no prospect of finding out. If you feel inclined, then, give up the attempt! But if you feel otherwise, you can accompany me further. For I can assure you that it is quite possible, and highly probable indeed, that the dreamer *does* know what his dream means: *only he does not know that he knows it and for that reason thinks he does not know it.*

You will point out to me that I am once more introducing an assumption, the second already in this short argument, and that in doing so I am enormously reducing my procedure's claim to credibility: 'Subject to the premiss that dreams are psychical phenomena, and subject to the further premiss that there are mental things in a man which he knows without knowing that he knows them ...' and so on. If so, one has only to consider the internal improbability of each of these two premisses, and one can quietly divert one's interest from any conclusions that may be based on them.

I have not brought you here, Ladies and Gentlemen, to delude you or to conceal things from you. In my prospectus, it is true, I announced a course of 'Elementary Lectures to Serve as an Introduction to Psychoanalysis', but what I had in mind was nothing in the nature of a presentation *in usum Delphini*, which would give you a smooth account with all the difficulties carefully concealed, with the gaps filled in and the doubts glossed over, so that you might believe with an easy mind that you had learnt something new. No, for the very reason of your being beginners, I wanted to show you our science as it is, with its unevennesses and roughnesses, its demands and hesitations. For I know that it is the same in all sciences and cannot possibly be otherwise, especially in their beginnings. I know also that ordinarily instruction is at pains to start out by concealing such difficulties and incompletenesses from the learner. But that will not do for psychoanalysis. So I have in fact laid down two premises, one within the other; and if anyone finds the whole thing too laborious and too insecure, or if anyone is accustomed to higher certainties and more elegant deductions, he need go no further with us. I think, however, that he should leave psychological problems entirely alone, for it is to be feared that in this quarter he will find impassable the precise and secure paths which he is prepared to follow. And, for a science which has something to offer, there is no necessity to sue for a hearing and for followers. Its findings are bound to canvass on its behalf and it can wait until these have compelled attention to it.

But for those who would like to persist in the subject, I can point out that my two assumptions are not on a par. The first, that dreams are psychical phenomena, is the premiss which we seek to prove by the outcome of our work; the second one has already been proved in another field, and I am merely venturing to bring it over from there to our own problems.

Where, then, in what field, can it be that proof has been found that there is knowledge of which the person concerned nevertheless knows nothing, as we are proposing to assume of dreamers? After all, this would be a strange, surprising fact and one which would alter our view of mental life and which would have no need to hide itself: a fact, incidentally, which cancels itself in its very naming and which nevertheless claims to be something real — a contradiction in terms. Well, it does not hide itself. It is not its fault if people know nothing about it or do not pay enough attention to it. Any more than we are to blame because judgement is passed on all these psychological problems by people who have kept at a distance from all the observations and experiences which are decisive on the matter.

The proof was found in the field of hypnotic phenomena. When, in 1889, I took part in the extraordinarily impressive demonstrations by Liébeault and Bernheim at Nancy, I witnessed the following experiment among others. If a man was put into a state of somnambulism, was made to experience all kinds of things in a hallucinatory manner, and was then woken up, he appeared at first to know nothing of what has happened during his hypnotic sleep. Bernheim then asked him straight out to report what had happened to him under hypnosis. The man maintained that he could remember nothing. But Bernheim held out against this, brought urgent pressure to bear on him, insisted that he knew it and must remember it. And, lo and behold! the man grew uncertain, began to reflect, and recalled in a shadowy way one of the experiences that had been suggested to him, and then another piece, and the memory became clearer and clearer and more and more complete, and finally came to light without a break. Since, however, he knew afterwards what had happened and had learnt nothing about it from anyone else in the interval, we are justified in concluding that he had known it earlier as well. It was merely inaccessible to him; he did not know that he knew it and thought he did not know it. That is to say, the position was exactly the same as what we suspected in our dreamer.

I hope you will be surprised that this fact has been established and will ask me: 'Why did you omit to bring this proof forward earlier, in connection with the parapraxes, when we came to the point of attributing to a man who had made a slip of the tongue an intention to say things of which he knew nothing and which he denied? If a person thinks he knows nothing of the experiences the memory of which he nevertheless has within him, it is no longer so improbable that he knows nothing of other mental processes within him. This argument would certainly have impressed us, and helped us to understand parapraxes.' Of course I could have brought it forward then, but I reserved it for another place, where it was more needed. The parapraxes explained themselves in part, and in part left us with a suggestion that, in order to preserve the continuity of the phenomena concerned, it would be wise to assume the existence of mental processes of which the subject knows nothing. In the case of dreams we are compelled to bring in explanations from elsewhere and moreover I expect that in their case you will find it easier to accept my carrying over of the explanations from hypnosis. The state in which a parapraxis occurs is bound to strike you as being the normal one; it has no similarity with the hypnotic state. On the other hand there is an obvious kinship between the hypnotic state and the state of sleep, which is a necessary condition of dreaming. Hypnosis, indeed, is described as an artificial sleep. We tell the person we are hypnotizing to sleep, and the suggestions we make are comparable to the dreams of natural sleep. The psychical situations in the two cases are really analogous. In natural sleep we withdraw our interest from the whole external world; and in hypnotic sleep we also withdraw it from the whole world, but with the single exception of the person who has hypnotized us and with whom we remain in rapport. Incidentally, the sleep of a nursing mother, who remains in rapport with her child and can be woken only by him, is a normal counterpart of hypnotic sleep. So it scarcely seems a very bold venture to transpose a situation from hypnosis to natural sleep. The assumption that in a dreamer too a knowledge about his dreams is present, though it is inaccessible to him so that he does not believe it, is not something entirely out of the blue. It should be noticed, moreover, that a third line of approach to the study of dreams is opened at this point: from the stimuli which disturb sleep, from day-dreams, and now in addition from the suggested dreams of the hypnotic state.

We may now go back to our task with increased confidence perhaps. It is very probable, then, that the dreamer knows about his dream; the only question is how to make it possible for him to discover his knowledge and communicate it to us. We do not require him to tell us straight away the sense of his dream, but he will be able to find its origin, the circle of thoughts and interests from which it sprang.

You will recall that in the case of the parapraxis the man was asked how he had arrived at the wrong word '*Vorschwein*' and the first thing that occurred to him gave as the explanation. Our technique with dreams, then, is a very simple one, copied from this example. We shall once more ask the dreamer how he arrived at the dream, and once more his first remark is to be looked on as an explanation. Thus we disregard the distinction between his thinking or not thinking that he knows something, and we treat both cases as one and the same.

This technique is certainly very simple, but I fear it will rouse your liveliest opposition. You will say: 'A fresh assumption! the third! And the most unlikely of all! If I ask the dreamer what occurs to him in connection with the dream, is precisely the first thing that occurs to him going to bring the explanation we are hoping for? But nothing at all may occur to him, or heaven knows what may occur to him. I cannot see what an expectation of that kind is based on. That is really showing too much trust in Providence at a point where rather more exercise of the critical faculty would be appropriate. Besides, a dream is not a single wrong word; it consists of a number of elements. So which association are we to take up?'

You are correct on all your minor points. A dream differs from a slip of the tongue, among other things, in the multiplicity of its elements. Our technique must take this into account. I therefore suggest to you that we should divide the dream into its elements and start a separate inquiry into each element; if we do this, the analogy with a slip of the tongue is re-established. You are also right in thinking that when the dreamer is questioned about the separate elements of the dream he may reply that nothing occurs to him. There are some instances in which we let this reply pass, and you will later hear which these are; strangely enough, they are instances in which definite ideas may occur to us ourselves. But in general if the dreamer asserts that nothing occurs to him we contradict him; we bring urgent pressure to bear on him, we insist that something must occur to him — and we turn out to be right. He will produce an idea — some idea, it is a matter of indifference to us which. He will give us certain pieces of information, which may be described as 'historical', with particular ease. He may say: 'That's something that happened yesterday' (as was the case in our two 'matter-of-fact' dreams), or : 'That reminds me of something that happened a short time ago' — and we shall discover in this way that dreams are connected with impressions of the last day or two much more often than we thought to begin with [loc. cit.]. And finally he will also recall, starting from the dream, events from further back and even perhaps from the far distant past.

But on your main point you are wrong. If you think it is arbitrary to assume that the first thing that occurs to the dreamer is bound to bring what we are looking for or to lead us to it, if you think that what occurs to him might be anything in the world and might have no connection with what we are looking for, and that it is only exhibiting my trust in Providence if I expect something different — then you are making a great mistake. Once before I ventured to tell you that you nourish a deeply rooted faith in undetermined psychical events and in free will, but that this is quite unscientific and must yield to the demand of a determinism whose rule extends over mental life. I beg you to respect it as a fact that *that* is what occurred to the man when he was questioned and nothing else. But I am not opposing one faith with another. It can be proved that the idea produced by the man was not arbitrary nor indeterminable nor unconnected with what we were looking for. Indeed, not long ago I learnt — without, I may say, attaching too much importance to the fact — that experimental psychology too had brought up evidence to that effect.

In view of the importance of the matter, I will ask for your special attention. If I ask someone to tell me what occurs to him in response to a particular element of a dream, I am asking him to surrender himself to free association *while keeping an idea in mind as a starting-point*. This calls for a special attitude of the attention which is quite different from reflection and which excludes reflection. Some people achieve this attitude with ease; others show an incredibly high degree of clumsiness when they attempt it. There is, however, a higher degree of freedom of association: that is to say, I may drop the insistence on keeping an initial idea in mind and only lay down the sort or kind of association I want — I may, for instance, require the experimenter to allow a proper name or a number to occur to him freely. What then occurs to him would presumably be even more arbitrary and more indeterminable than with our own technique. It can be shown, however, that it is always strictly determined by important internal attitudes of mind which are not known to us at the moment at which they operate — which are as little known to us as the disturbing purposes of parapraxes and the provoking ones of chance actions.

I and many others after me have repeatedly made such experiments with names and numbers thought of at random, and a few of these have been published. Here the procedure is to produce a series of associations to the name which has emerged; these latter associations are accordingly no longer completely free but have a link, like the associations to the elements of dreams. One continues doing this until one finds the impulse exhausted. But by then light will have been thrown both on the motive and the meaning of the random choice of the name. These experiments always lead to the same result; reports on them often cover a wealth of material and call for extensive expositions. The associations to *numbers* chosen at random are perhaps the most convincing; they run off so quickly and proceed with such incredible certainty to a hidden goal that the effect is really staggering. I will give you only one example of an analysis like this of a name, since dealing with it calls for a conveniently small amount of material.

In the course of treating a young man I had occasion to discuss this topic, and mentioned the thesis that, in spite of an apparently arbitrary choice, it is impossible to think of a name at random which does not turn out to be closely determined by the immediate circumstances, the characteristics of the subject of the experiment and his situation at the moment. Since he was sceptical, I suggested that he should make an experiment of the kind himself on the spot. I knew that he carried on particularly numerous relationships of every kind with married women and girls, so I thought he would have a specially large choice open to him if it were to be a woman's name that he was asked to choose. He agreed to his. To my astonishment, or rather, perhaps, to his, no avalanche of women's names broke over me; he remained silent for a moment and then admitted that only a single name had come into his head and none other besides: 'Albine'. — How curious ! But what does that name mean to you? How many 'Albines' do you know? — Strange to say, he knew no one called 'Albine' and nothing further occurred to him in response to the name. So it might be thought that the analysis had failed. But not at all: it was already complete, and no further associations were needed. The man had an unusually fair complexion and in conversation during the treatment I had often jokingly called him an albino. We were engaged at the time in determining the feminine part of his constitution. So it was he himself who was this 'Albine', the woman who was the most interesting to him at the moment.

In the same way tunes that come into one's head without warning turn out to be determined by and to belong to a train of thought which has a right to occupy one's mind though without one's being aware of its activity. It is easy to show then that the relation to the tune is based on its text or its origin. But I must be careful not to extend this assertion to really musical people, of whom, as it happens, I have had no experience. It may be that for such people the musical content of the tune is what decides its emergence. The earlier case is certainly the commoner one. I know of a young man, for instance, who was positively persecuted for a time by the tune (incidentally a charming one) of Paris's song in [Offenbach's] *La belle Hélène*, till his analysis drew his attention to a contemporary competition in his interest between an 'Ida' and a 'Helen'.

If then things that occur to one quite freely are determined in this way and form parts of a connected whole, we shall no doubt be justified in concluding that things that occur to one with a single link — namely their link with the idea which serves as their starting-point — cannot be any less determined. Investigation shows, in fact, that, apart from the link we have given them with the initial idea, they are found to be dependent as well on groups of strongly emotional thoughts and interests, 'complexes', whose participation is not known at the moment — that is to say, is unconscious.

The occurrence of ideas with links of this kind has been the subject of very instructive experimental researches, which have played a notable part in the history of psychoanalysis. The school of Wundt had introduced what are known as association-experiments, in which a *stimulus word* is called out to the subject and he has the task of replying to it as quickly as possible with any *reaction* that occurs to him. It is then possible to study the interval that passes between the stimulus and the reaction, the nature of the answer given as a reaction, possible errors when the same experiment is repeated later, and so on. The Zurich school, led by Bleuler and Jung, found the explanation of the reactions that followed in the association-experiment by getting the subjects to throw light on their reactions by means of subsequent associations, if those reactions had shown striking features. It then turned out that these striking reactions were determined in the most definite fashion by the subject's complexes. In this manner Bleuler and Jung built the first bridge from experimental psychology to psychoanalysis.

Having learnt thus much, you will be able to say: 'We acknowledge now that thoughts that occur to one freely are determined and not arbitrary as we supposed. We admit that this is also true of thought occurring in response to the elements of dreams. But that is not what we are concerned with. You assert that what occurs to the dreamer in response to the dream-element will be determined by the psychical background (unknown to us) of that particular element. This does not seem to us to be proved. We quite expect that what occurs to the dreamer in response to the dream-element will turn out to be determined by one of the dreamer's complexes, but what good does that do us? This does not lead us to an understanding of dreams but, like the association-experiment, to a knowledge of these so-called complexes. But what have they got to do with dreams?'

You are right, but you are overlooking one factor. Moreover it is precisely the factor on account of which I did not choose the association-experiment as the starting-point of this exposition. In that experiment the single determinant of the reaction — that is, the stimulus-word — is arbitrarily chosen by us. The reaction is in that case an intermediary between the stimulus-word and the complex which has been aroused in the subject. In dreams the stimulus-word is replaced by something that is itself derived from the dreamer's mental life, from sources unknown to him, and may therefore very easily itself be a 'derivative of a complex'. It is therefore not precisely fantastic to suppose that the further associations linked to the dream-elements will be determined by the same complex as that of the element itself and will lead to its discovery.

Let me show you from another instance that the facts are as we expect. The forgetting of proper names is actually an excellent model of what happens in dream-analysis; the difference is only that events that are shared between two people in dream-analysis are combined in a single person in the parapraxis. If I forget a name temporarily, I nevertheless feel in myself a certainty that I know it — a certainty which in the case of the dreamer we only arrived at by the round-about path of the Bernheim experiment. The name which I have forgotten but which I know is, however, not accessible to me. Experience soon teaches me that thinking about it, with however much effort, is of no help. But in place of the forgotten name I can always call up one or several substitute names. It is only after a substitute name of this kind has occurred to me spontaneously that the conformity of this situation with that of dream-interpretation becomes obvious. Like this substitute name, the dream-element is not the right thing which I do not know and which I am to discover by means of the dream-analysis. The difference is once more only that in the case of forgetting the name, I recognize the substitute unhesitatingly as something ungenuine, whereas we had to acquire this view labouriously in the case of the dream-element. Now in the case of forgetting a name there is also a method by which we can start from the substitute and arrive at the unconscious genuine thing, the forgotten name. If I direct my attention to the substitute names and allow further ideas in response to them to occur to me, I arrive by shorter or longer détours at the forgotten name, and I find when this happens that both the spontaneous substitute name and the ones that I have called up are connected with the forgotten one and were determined by it.

I will describe an analysis of this kind to you. I noticed one day that I could not recall the name of the small country on the Riviera, of which Monte Carlo is the chief town. It was very tiresome, but so it was. I summoned up all that I knew about that country. I thought of Prince Albert of the House of Lusignan, of his marriages, of his devotion to deep-sea researches, and everything else I could bring together, but it was of no avail. So I gave up reflection and allowed substitute names to occur to me instead of the lost one. They came rapidly: Monte Carlo itself, then Piedmont, Albania, Montevideo, Colico. Of this series I was struck first by Albania, which was at once replaced by Montenegro, no doubt because of the contrast between white and black. I then saw that four of these substitute names contained the same syllable 'mon', then suddenly I had the forgotten word and exclaimed aloud: 'Monaco!' So the substitute names had in fact arisen from the forgotten one: the first four came from its first syllable while the last reproduced its syllabic structure and its whole last syllable. Moreover I was able to discover quite easily what it was that had temporarily deprived me of the name. Monaco is also the Italian name for Munich; and it was that town which exerted the inhibitory influence.

No doubt this example is a good one, but it is too simple. In other cases it would have been necessary to call up a longer string of ideas in response to the first substitute name, and then the analogy with dream-analysis would have been clearer. I have had experiences of that sort too. On one occasion a stranger had invited me to drink some Italian wine with him, but when we were in the inn it turned out that he had forgotten the name of the wine which he intended to order because of his very agreeable recollections of it. From a quantity of substitute ideas of different kinds which came into his head in place of the forgotten name, I was able to infer that thoughts about someone called Hedwig had made him forget the name. And he not only confirmed the fact that he had first tasted this wine when he was with someone of that name, but with the help of this discovery he recalled the name of the wine. He was happily married at the present time and this Hedwig belonged to earlier days which he had no wish to remember.

But if it is possible in the case of forgetting a name, it must also be possible in interpreting dreams to proceed from the substitute along the chain of associations attached to it and so to obtain access to the genuine thing which is being held back. From the example of the forgotten name we may conclude that the associations to the dream-element will be determined both by the dream-element and also by the unconscious genuine thing behind it. In this way, then, we seem to have produced some justification of our technique.

Lecture 7

The Manifest Content of Dreams and the Latent Dream-Thoughts

Ladies and Gentlemen, — As you see, our study of parapraxes has not been unprofitable. Thanks to our labours over them we have, subject to the premises I have explained to you, achieved two things: a conception of the nature of dream-elements and a technique for interpreting dreams. The conception of dream-elements tells us that they are ungenuine things, substitutes for something else that is unknown to the dreamer (like the purpose of a parapraxis), substitutes for something the knowledge of which is present in the dreamer but which is inaccessible to him. We are in hopes that it will be possible to carry over the same conception to whole dreams, which are made up of such elements. Our technique lies in employing a free association to these elements in order to bring about the emergence of other substitutive structures, which will enable us to arrive at what is concealed from view.

I now propose that we should introduce a change into our nomenclature which will give us more freedom of movement. Instead of speaking of 'concealed', 'inaccessible', or 'ungenuine', let us adopt the correct description and say 'inaccessible to the dreamer's consciousness' or *'unconscious'*. I mean nothing else by this than what may be suggested to you when you think of a word that has escaped you or the disturbing purpose in a parapraxis — that is to say, I mean nothing else than *'unconscious at the moment'*. In contrast to this, we can of course speak of the dream-elements themselves, and the substitutive ideas that have been newly arrived at from them by association, as *'conscious'*. This nomenclature so far involves no theoretical construction. No objection can be made to using the word 'unconscious' as an apt and easily understandable description.

If we carry over our conception of the separate elements to the whole dream, it follows that the dream as a whole is a distorted substitute for something else, something unconscious, and that the task of interpreting a dream is to discover this unconscious material. From this, however, there at once follow three important rules, which we must obey during the work of interpreting dreams.

(1) We must not concern ourselves with what the dream *appears* to tell us, whether it is intelligible or absurd, clear or confused, since it cannot possibly be the unconscious material we are in search of . (An obvious limitation to this rule will force itself on our notice later.) (2) We must restrict our work to calling up the substitutive ideas for each element, we must not reflect about them, or consider whether they contain anything relevant, and we must not trouble ourselves with how far they diverge from the dream-element. (3) We must wait till the concealed unconscious material we are in search of emerges of its own accord, exactly as the forgotten word 'Monaco' did in the experiment I have described.

Now, too, we can understand to what extent it is a matter of indifference how much or how little the dream is remembered and, above all, how accurately or how uncertainly. For the remembered dream is not the genuine material but a distorted substitute for it, which should assist us, by calling up other substitutive images, to come nearer to the genuine material, to make what is unconscious in the dream conscious. If our memory has been inaccurate, therefore, it has merely made a further distortion of this substitute — a distortion, moreover, which cannot have been without a reason.

The work of interpreting can be performed on one's own dreams just as on other people's. In fact one learns more from one's own: the process carries more conviction. If, then, we make the attempt, we notice that something is opposing our work. It is true that ideas occur to us, but we do not allow all of them to count; testing and selecting influences make themselves felt. In the case of one idea we may say to ourselves: 'No, this is not relevant, it does not belong here'; in the case of another: 'this is too senseless' and of a third: 'this is totally unimportant'. And we can further observe how with objections of this sort we may smother ideas and finally expel them altogether, even before they have become quite clear. Thus on the one hand we keep too close to the idea which was our starting-point, the dream-element itself; and on the other hand we interfere with the outcome of the free associations by making a selection. If we are not by ourselves while interpreting the dream, if we get someone else to interpret it, we become very clearly aware of yet another motive which we employ in making this illicit selection, for sometimes we say to ourselves: 'No, this idea is too disagreeable; I will not or cannot report it.'

These objections are obviously a threat to the success of our work. We must guard against them, and in our own case we do so by firmly resolving not to give way to them. If we are analysing someone else's dream, we do so by laying it down as an inviolable rule that he must not hold back any idea from us, even if it gives rise to one of the four objections — of being too unimportant or too senseless or of being irrelevant or too distressing to be reported. The dreamer promises to obey the rule, and we may be annoyed afterwards to find how badly he keeps his promise when the occasion arises. We may explain this to ourselves to begin with by supposing that, in spite of our authoritative assurance, he has not yet realized the justification for free association, and we may perhaps have the notion of first convincing him theoretically by giving him books to read or by sending him to lectures which may convert him into a supporter of our views on free association. But we shall be held back from blunders like this when we consider that in the case of ourselves, as to the strength of whose convictions we can, after all, hardly be in doubt, the same objections arise to certain ideas and are only set aside subsequently — by a court of appeal, as it were.

Instead of being annoyed by the dreamer's disobedience, we may take advantage of these experiences by learning something new from them — something which is all the more important the less we are expecting it. We perceive that the work of interpreting dreams is carried out in the face of a *resistance*, which opposes it and of which the critical objections are manifestations. This resistance is independent of the dreamer's theoretical conviction. We learn still more, indeed. We discover that a critical objection of this kind never turns out to be justified. On the contrary, the ideas which people try to suppress in this way turn out *invariably* to be the most important ones and those which are decisive in our search for the unconscious material. It amounts, in fact, to a special distinguishing mark, if an idea is accompanied by an objection like this.

This resistance is something entirely new: a phenomenon which we have come upon in connection with our premises, but one which was not included among them. The appearance of this new factor in our reckoning comes to us as a not altogether pleasant surprise. We suspect at once that it is not going to make our work any easier. It might mislead us into abandoning our whole concern with dreams: something so unimportant as a dream and, on top of that, all these difficulties instead of a simple straightforward technique! But, on the other hand, the difficulties might act precisely as a stimulus and make us suspect that the work will be worth the trouble. We regularly come up against resistance when we try to make our way forward from the substitute which is the dream-element to the unconscious material hidden behind it. So we may conclude that there must be something of importance concealed behind the substitute. Otherwise, what is the point of the difficulties that are trying to keep the concealment going? If a child refuses to open his clenched fist to show what he has in it, we may feel sure that it is something wrong — something he ought not to have.

The moment we introduce the dynamic idea of a resistance into the facts of the case, we must simultaneously reflect that this factor is something variable in quantity. There may be greater and smaller resistances, and we are prepared to find these differences showing themselves during our work as well. We may perhaps be able to link with this another experience we also meet with during the work of interpreting dreams: sometimes it requires only a single response, or no more than a few, to lead us from a dream-element to the unconscious material behind it, while on other occasions long chains of associations and the overcoming of many critical objections are required for bringing this about. We shall conclude that these differences relate to the changing magnitude of the resistance, and we shall probably turn out to be right. If the resistance is small, the substitute cannot be far distant from the unconscious material; but a greater resistance means that the unconscious material will be greatly distorted and that the path will be a long one from the substitute back to the unconscious material.

And now perhaps it is time to take a dream and try our technique upon it and see whether our expectations are confirmed. Yes, but what dream are we to choose for the purpose? You cannot imagine how hard I find it to decide; nor can I yet make the nature of my difficulties plain to you. There must obviously be dreams which have on the whole been subjected to only a little distortion, and the best plan would be to begin with them. But what dreams have been least distorted? The ones that are intelligible and not confused, two examples of which I have already put before you? That would be leading us quite astray. Investigation shows that such dreams have been subjected to an extraordinarily high degree of distortion. If, however, I were to disregard particular requirements and were to select a dream at haphazard, you would probably be greatly disappointed. We might have to notice or record such a profusion of ideas in response to the separate dream-elements that we should be unable to make head or tail of the work. If we write down a dream and then make a note of all the ideas that emerge in response to it, these may prove to be many times longer than the text of the dream. The best plan would therefore seem to be to choose out a number of short dreams for analysis, each of which will at least tell us something or confirm some point. So we will make up our minds to take that course, unless experience may perhaps show us where we can really find dreams that have been only slightly distorted.

I can however think of something else that will make things easier for us — something, moreover, which lies along our path. Instead of starting on the interpretation of *whole* dreams, we will restrict ourselves to a few dream-elements, and we will trace out in a number of examples how these can be explained by applying our technique to them.

(*a*) A lady reported that she very often dreamt when she was a child that *God wore a paper cocked-hat on his head.* What can you make of that without the dreamer's help? It sounds completely nonsensical. But it ceases to be nonsense when we hear from the lady that she used to have a hat of that sort put on her head at meals when she was a child, because she could never resist taking furtive glances at her brothers' and sisters' plates to see whether they had been given larger helpings than she had. So the hat was intended to act like a pair of blinkers. This, incidentally, was a piece of historical information and was given without any difficulty. The interpretation of this element and at the same time of the whole short dream was easily made with the help of a further idea that occurred to the dreamer: 'As I had heard that God was omniscient and saw everything', she said, 'the dream can only mean that I knew everything and saw everything, even though they tried to prevent me.' Perhaps this example is too simple.

(b) A sceptical woman patient had a longish dream in the course of which some people told her about my book on jokes [1905c] and praised it highly. Something came in then about *a 'channel', perhaps it was another book that mentioned a channel, or something else about a channel ... she didn't know ... it was all so indistinct.*

No doubt you will be inclined to expect that the element 'channel', since it was so indistinct, would be inaccessible to interpretation. You are right in suspecting a difficulty; but the difficulty did not arise from the indistinctness: both the difficulty and the indistinctness arose from another cause. Nothing occurred to the dreamer in connection with 'channel', and *I* could of course throw no light on it. A little later — it was the next day, in point of fact — she told me that she had thought of something that *might* have something to do with it. It was a joke, too, — a joke she had heard. On the steamer between Dover and Calais a well-known author fell into conversation with an Englishman. The latter had occasion to quote the phrase: 'Du sublime au ridicule il n'y a qu'un pas. [It is only a step from the sublime to the ridiculous.]' 'Yes,' replied the author, '*le Pas de Calais*' — meaning that he thought France sublime and England ridiculous. But the *Pas de Calais* is a channel — the English Channel. You will ask whether I think this had anything to do with the dream. Certainly I think so; and it provides the solution of the puzzling element of the dream. Can you doubt that this joke was already present before the dream occurred, as the unconscious thought behind the element 'channel'? Can you suppose that it was introduced as a subsequent invention? The association betrayed the scepticism which lay concealed behind the patient's ostensible admiration; and her resistance against revealing this was no doubt the common cause both of her delay in producing the association and of the indistinctness of the dream-element concerned. Consider the relation of the dream-element to its unconscious background: it was, as it were, a fragment of the background, an allusion to it, but it was made quite incomprehensible by being isolated.

(c) As part of a longish dream a patient dreamt that *several members of his family were sitting round a table of a peculiar shape,* etc. It occurred to him in connection with the table that he had seen a piece of furniture of the kind when he was on a visit to a particular family. His thoughts then went on to say that there was a peculiar relationship between the father and son in this family; and he soon added that the same thing was true of the relationship between himself and his own father. So the table had been taken into the dream in order to point out this parallel.

This dreamer had been long familiar with the requirement of dream-interpretation. Another person might perhaps have taken objection to such a trivial detail as the shape of a table being made the subject of investigation. But in fact we regard nothing in a dream as accidental or indifferent, and we expect to obtain information precisely from the explanation of such trivial and pointless details. You may perhaps also feel surprised that the thought that 'the same thing was true of us and of them' should have been expressed by, in particular, the choice of a table [*Tisch*]. But this too becomes clear when you learn that the name of the family in question was *Tischler* [literally, 'carpenter']. By making his relations sit at this *Tisch*, he was saying that they too were *Tischlers*. Incidentally, you will notice how inevitably one is led into being indiscreet when one reports these dream-interpretations. And you will guess that this is one of the difficulties I have hinted at over the choice of examples. I could easily have taken another example in place of this one, but I should probably merely have avoided this indiscretion at the price of committing another.

The moment seems to me to have arrived for introducing two terms, which we could have made use of long ago. We will describe what the dream actually tells us as the *manifest dream-content*, and the concealed material, which we hope to reach by pursuing the ideas that occur to the dreamer, as the *latent dream-thoughts*. Thus we are here considering the relations between the manifest content of the dream and the latent dream-thoughts as shown in these examples. These relations may be of very many different kinds. In examples (*a*) and (*b*) the manifest element is also a constituent of the latent thoughts, though only a small fragment of them. A small piece of the large and complicated psychical structure of unconscious dream-thoughts has made its way into the manifest dream as well — a fragment of them, or, in other cases, an allusion to them, a caption, as it were, or an abbreviation in telegraphic style. It is the business of the work of interpretation to complete these fragments or this allusion into a whole — which was achieved particularly nicely in the case of example (*b*). Thus one form of the distortion which constitutes the dream-work is replacement by a fragment or an allusion. In example (*c*) another kind of relation is to be observed in addition; and we shall find this expressed in a purer and clearer form in the examples which follow.

(*d*) The dreamer *was pulling a lady* (a particular one, of his acquaintance) *out from behind a bed*. He himself found the meaning of this dream-element from the first idea that occurred to him. It meant that he was giving this lady preference.

(*e*) Another man dreamt that *his brother was in a box* [*Kasten*]. In his first response '*Kasten*' was replaced by '*Schrank* [cupboard]', and the second gave the interpretation: his brother was restricting himself ['*schränkt sich ein*'].

(*f*) The dreamer *climbed to the top of a mountain, which commanded an unusually extensive view*. This sounds quite rational and you might suppose that there is nothing to interpret in it and that all we have to do is to enquire what memory gave rise to the dream and the reason for its being stirred up. But you would be wrong. It turned out that this dream stood in need of interpreting just as much as any other, more confused one. For none of his own mountain climbs occurred to the dreamer, but he thought of the fact that an acquaintance of his was the editor of a 'Survey', dealing with our relations with the most remote parts of the earth. Thus the latent dream-thought was an identification of the dreamer with the 'surveyor'.

Here we have a new type of relation between the manifest and latent dream-elements. The former is not so much a distortion of the latter as a representation of it, a plastic, concrete, portrayal of it, taking its start from the wording. But precisely on that account it is once more a distortion, for we have long since forgotten from what concrete image the word originated and consequently fail to recognize it when it is replaced by the image. When you consider that the manifest dream is made up predominantly of visual images and more rarely of thoughts and words, you can imagine what importance attaches to this kind of relation in the construction of dreams. You will see, too, that in this way it becomes possible in regard to a large number of abstract thoughts to create pictures to act as substitutes for them in the manifest dream while at the same time serving the purpose of concealment. This is the technique of the familiar picture-puzzles. Why it is that these representations have an appearance of being jokes is a special problem into which we need not enter here.

There is a fourth kind of relation between the manifest and latent elements, which I must continue to hold back from you until we come upon its key-word in considering technique. Even so I shall not have given you a full list; but it will serve our purpose.

Do you feel bold enough now to venture upon the interpretation of a *whole* dream? Let us make the experiment, to see whether we are well enough equipped for the task. I shall of course not select one of the most obscure ones; nevertheless, it will be one that gives a well-marked picture of the attributes of a dream.

Very well then. A lady who, though she was still young, had been married for many years had the following dream: *She was at the theatre with her husband. One side of the stalls was completely empty. Her husband told her that Elise L. and her fiancé had wanted to go too, but had only been able to get bad seats — three for 1 florin 50 kreuzers — and of course they could not take those. She thought it would not really have done any harm if they had.*

The first thing the dreamer reported to us was that the precipitating cause of the dream was touched on in its manifest content. Her husband had in fact told her that Elise L., who was approximately her contemporary, had just become engaged. The dream was a reaction to this information. We know already that it is easy in the case of many dreams to point to a precipitating cause like this from the previous day, and that the dreamer is often able to trace this for us without any difficulty. The dreamer in the present case put similar information at our disposal for other elements of the manifest dream as well. — Where did the detail come from about one side of the stalls being empty? It was an allusion to a real event of the previous week. She had planned to go to a particular play and had therefore bought her tickets *early* — so early that she had had to pay a booking fee. When they got to the theatre it turned out that her anxiety was quite uncalled-for, since *one side of the stalls was almost empty.* It would have been early enough if she had bought the tickets on the actual day of the performance. Her husband had kept on teasing her for having been *in too much of a hurry*. — What was the origin of the 1 florin 50 kreuzers? It arose in quite another connection, which had nothing to do with the former one but also alluded to some information from the previous day. Her sister-in-law had been given a present of 150 florins by her husband and had been in a great hurry — the silly goose — to rush off to the jewellers' and exchange the money for a piece of jewellery. — Where did the 'three' come from? She could think of nothing in connection with that, unless we counted the idea that her newly-engaged friend, Elise L., was only three months her junior, though she herself had been a married woman for nearly ten years. — And the absurd notion of taking three tickets for only two people? She had nothing to say to that, and refused to report any further ideas or information.

But all the same, she had given us so much material in these few associations that it was possible to guess the latent dream-thoughts from them. We cannot help being struck by the fact that periods of time occur at several points in the information she gave us about the dream, and these provide a common factor between the different parts of the material. She took the theatre tickets *too early*, bought them *over-hurriedly* so that she had to pay more than was necessary; so too her sister-in-law had been *in a hurry* to take her money to the jewellers and buy some jewellery with it, as though otherwise she would *miss it*. If, in addition to the 'too early' and 'in a hurry' which we have stressed, we take into account the precipitating cause of the dream — the news that her friend, though only three months *her junior*, had nevertheless got an excellent husband — and the criticism of her sister-in-law expressed in the idea that it was *absurd* of her to be in such a hurry, then we find ourselves presented almost spontaneously with the following construction of the latent dream-thoughts, for which the manifest dream is a severely distorted substitute:

'Really it was *absurd* of me to be in such a hurry to get married! I can see from Elise's example that *I* could have got a husband later too.' (Being in too great a hurry was represented by her own behaviour in buying the tickets and by her sister-in-law's in buying the jewellery. Going to the play appeared as a substitute for getting married.) This would seem to be the main thought. We may perhaps proceed further, though with less certainty, since the analysis ought not to have been without the dreamer's comments at these points: 'And I could have got one a hundred times better with the money!' (150 florins is a hundred times more than 1 florin 50.) If we were to put her dowry in place of the money, it would mean that her husband was bought with her dowry: the jewellery, and the bad tickets as well, would be substitutes for her husband. It would be still more satisfactory if the actual element 'three tickets' had something to do with a husband. But we have not got so far as that in our understanding of the dream. We have only discovered that the dream expresses the *low value* assigned by her to her own husband and her regret at having *married so early*.

We shall, I fancy, be more surprised and confused than satisfied by the outcome of this first dream-interpretation. We have been given too much in one dose — more than we are yet able to cope with. We can already see that we shall not exhaust the lessons of this interpretation of a dream. Let us hasten to single out what we can recognize as established new discoveries.

In the first place, it is a remarkable thing that the main emphasis in the latent thoughts lies on the element of being in too great a hurry; nothing of the sort is to be found in the manifest dream. Without the analysis, we should have had no suspicion that that factor plays any part. It seems, therefore, to be possible for what is in fact the main thing, the centre of the unconscious thoughts, to be absent in the manifest dream. This means that the impression made by the whole dream must be fundamentally altered. In the second place, there is an absurd combination in the dream: three for 1 florin 50. We detected in the dream-thoughts the assertion that 'it was absurd (to marry so early)'. Can it be doubted that this thought, 'it was absurd', is represented by the inclusion of an absurd element in the manifest dream? And in the third place, a glance of comparison shows us that the relation between the manifest and latent elements is no simple one; it is far from being the case that one manifest element always takes the place of one latent one. It is rather that there is a group-relation between the two layers, within which one manifest element can replace several latent ones or one latent element can be replaced by several manifest ones.

As regards the meaning of the dream and the dreamer's attitude to it, we might point out much that is similarly surprising. She agreed to the interpretation indeed, but she was astonished at it. She was not aware that she assigned such a low value to her husband; nor did she know *why* she should set such a low value on him. So there is still much that is unintelligible about it. It really seems to me that we are not yet equipped for interpreting a dream and that we need first to be given some further instruction and preparation.

LECTURE 8
Children's Dreams

Ladies and Gentlemen, — I am under the impression that we have advanced too quickly. Let us go back a little. Before we made our last attempt at overcoming the difficulty of distortion in dreams by the help of our technique, we were saying that our best plan would be to get round the difficulty by keeping to dreams in which there was no distortion or only a very little — if such dreams exist. This will once more mean a divergence from the historical development of our discoveries; for actually it was only after the technique of interpretation had been consistently applied and distorted dreams had been completely analysed that the existence of dreams that are free from distortion came to our notice.

The dreams we are in search of occur in children. They are short, clear, coherent, easy to understand and unambiguous; but they are nevertheless undoubtedly dreams. You must not suppose, however, that all children's dreams are of this kind. Dream-distortion sets in very early in childhood, and dreams dreamt by children of between five and eight have been reported which bear all the characteristics of later ones. But if you limit yourselves to ages between the beginning of observable mental activity and the fourth and fifth year, you will come upon a number of dreams which possess the characteristics that can be described as 'infantile' and you will find a few of the same kind in later years of childhood. Indeed, under certain conditions even adults have dreams which are quite similar to the typically infantile ones.

From these children's dreams we can draw conclusions with great ease and certainty on the essential nature of dreams in general, and we can hope that those conclusions will prove decisive and universally valid.

(1) No analysis, no application of any technique is necessary in order to understand these dreams. There is no need to question a child who tells us his dream. One has, however, to add a piece of information to it from the events of the child's life. There is invariably some experience of the previous day which explains the dream to us. The dream is the reaction of the child's mental life in his sleep to this experience of the previous day.

We will take a few examples on which to base our further conclusions.

(*a*) A boy of 22 months was told to hand over a basket of cherries to someone as a birthday present. He was obviously very unwilling to do it, although he was promosed that he should have a few of them for himself. Next morning he reported having dreamt: '*Hermann eaten all the chewwies!*'

(*b*) A girl of 3 1/4 years was taken across the lake for the first time. At the landing-stage she did not want to leave the boat and wept bitterly. The crossing had been too short for her. Next morning she announced: '*Last night I went on the lake.*'

(*c*) A boy of 5 1/4 years was taken on an excursion up the Echerntal near Hallstatt. He had been told that Hallstatt was at the foot of the Dachstein. He had shown great interest in this mountain. There was a fine view of it from where he was staying at Aussee, and the Simony Hut on it could be made out through a telescope. The child had often tried to see it through the telescope — with what success was not known. The excursion began in an atmosphere of cheerful expectation. Whenever a fresh mountain came into view the boy asked: 'Is that the Dachstein?' and he became more and more depressed the more often he was told it was not. Finally he fell completely silent and refused to go with the rest of the party up the short ascent to the waterfall, and it was thought that he must be overtired. But next morning he said with a radiant face: 'Last night I dreamt *we were at the Simony Hut*.' So that had been what he expected to do on the excursion. He gave no further details except something he had heard before: 'You have to climb up steps for six hours.'

These three dreams will give us all the information we require.

(2) As we can see, these children's dreams are not senseless. They are *intelligible, completely valid mental acts*. You will recall what I told you of the medical view of dreams and of the analogy with unmusical fingers wandering over the keys of a piano. You cannot fail to observe how sharply these children's dreams contradict this view. It would really be too strange if *children* could perform complete mental functions in their sleep while *adults* were content under the same conditions with reactions which were no more than 'twitchings'. Moreover, we have every reason to think that children's sleep is sounder and deeper.

(3) These dreams are without any dream-distortion, and therefore call for no interpretative activity. Here the manifest and the latent dream coincide. *Thus dream-distortion is not part of the essential nature of dreams*. I expect this will be a weight off your minds. But when we examine these dreams more closely, we shall recognize a small piece of dream-distortion even in them, a certain distinction between the manifest content of the dream and the latent dream-thoughts.

(4) A child's dream is a reaction to an experience of the previous day, which has left behind it a regret, a longing, a wish that has not been dealt with. *The dream produces a direct, undisguised fulfilment of that wish*. Let us recall now our discussions on the part played by somatic stimuli from outside and from within as disturbers of sleep and instigators of dreams. In that connection we came to know some quite undoubted facts, but by their means we were only able to explain a small number of dreams. In these children's dreams, however, there is nothing that points to the operation of somatic stimuli of that kind; we could not be mistaken in this, for the dreams are completely intelligible and easy to grasp. But this does not mean that we need abandon the stimulus aetiology of dreams. We can only ask how it has happened that from the first we have forgotten that besides somatic stimuli there are *mental* stimuli that disturb sleep. We know, after all, that it is

excitations of this kind that are chiefly responsible for disturbing the sleep of an adult by preventing him from establishing the mood required for falling asleep — the withdrawing of interest from the world. He does not want to interrupt his life but would rather continue his work on the things he is concerned with, and for that reason he does not fall asleep. In the case of children, therefore, the stimulus that disturbs sleep is a mental one — the wish that has not been dealt with — and it is to this that they react with the dream.

(5) This gives us the most direct approach to understanding the function of dreams. In so far as a dream is a reaction to a psychical stimulus, it must be equivalent to dealing with the stimulus in such a way that it is got rid of and that the sleep can continue. We do not yet know how this dealing with the stimulus by the dream is made possible dynamically, but we see already that *dreams are not disturbers of sleep*, as they are abusively called, but *guardians of sleep which get rid of disturbances of sleep*. We think we should have slept more soundly if there had been no dream, but we are wrong; in fact, without the help of the dream we should not have slept at all. It is due to it that we have slept as soundly as we have. It could not avoid disturbing us a little, just as the night-watchman often cannot help making a little noise while he chases away the disturbers of the peace who seek to waken us with their noise.

(6) What instigates a dream is a wish, and the fulfilment of that wish is the content of the dream — this is one of the chief characteristics of dreams. The other, equally constant one, is that a dream does not simply give expression to a thought, but represents the wish fulfilled as a hallucinatory experience. '*I should like to go on the lake*' is the wish that instigates the dream. The content of the dream itself is: '*I am going on the lake.*' Thus even in these simple children's dreams a difference remains between the latent and the manifest dream, there is a distortion of the latent dream-thought: *the transformation of a thought into an experience.* In the process of interpreting a dream this alteration must first be undone. If this turns out to be the most universal characteristic of dreams, the fragment of dream which I reported to you earlier 'I saw my brother in a box [*Kasten*]' is not to be translated 'my brother is restricting himself [*schränkt sich ein*]' but 'I should like my brother to restrict himself: *my brother must restrict himself.*' Of the two general characteristics of dreams which I have here brought forward, the second clearly has more prospect of being accepted without contradiction than the first. It is only by means of far-reaching investigations that we shall be able to establish the fact that what instigates dreams must always be a wish and cannot be a worry or an intention or a reproach; but this will not affect the other characteristic — that the dream does not simply reproduce this stimulus, but removes it, gets rid of it, deals with it, by means of a kind of experience.

(7) On the basis of these characteristics of dreams, we can return once more to a comparison between a dream and a parapraxis. In the latter we distinguished between a disturbing purpose and a disturbed one, and the parapraxis was a

compromise between them. A dream can be fitted into the same pattern. The disturbed purpose can only be that of sleeping. We may replace the disturbing one by the psychical stimulus, or let us say by the wish which presses to be dealt with, since we have not learnt so far of any other psychical stimulus that disturbs sleep. Here the dream, too, is the result of a compromise. One sleeps, but one nevertheless experiences the removing of a wish; one satisfies a wish, but at the same time one continues to sleep. Both purposes are partly achieved and partly abandoned.

(8) You will recall that at one point we hoped to approach an understanding of the problems of dreams from the fact that certain imaginative structures which are very transparent to us are know as 'day-dreams'. Now these day-dreams are in fact wish-fulfilments, fulfilments of ambitions and erotic wishes which are well known to us; but they are *thought*, even though vividly imagined, and never experienced as hallucinations. Of the two chief characteristics of dreams, then, the less well assured is preserved here, while the other, since it depends on the state of sleep and cannot be realized in waking life, is entirely absent. Linguistic usage, therefore, has a suspicion of the fact that wish-fulfilment is a chief characteristic of dreams. Incidentally, if our experience in dreams is only a modified kind of imagining made possible by the conditions of the state of sleep — that is, a 'nocturnal day-dreaming' — we can already understand how the process of constructing a dream can dispose of the nocturnal stimulus and bring satisfaction, since day-dreaming too is an activity bound up with satisfaction and is only practised, indeed, on that account.

But other usages of language express the same sense. There are familiar proverbs such as 'Pigs dream of acorns and geese dream of maize' or 'What do hens dream of? — Of millet.' So proverbs go even lower than we do — below children to animals — and assert that the content of dreams is the satisfaction of a need. Numbers of figures of speech seem to point in the same direction: 'lovely as a dream', 'I shouldn't have dreamt of such a thing', 'I haven't imagined it in my wildest dreams'. In this, linguistic usage is evidently taking sides. For there are anxiety-dreams as well, and dreams with a distressing or indifferent content; but linguistic usage has been unmoved by them. It is true that it knows of 'bad dreams', but a dream pure and simple is only the sweet fulfilment of a wish. Nor is there any proverb which might tell us that pigs or geese dream of being slaughtered.

It is inconceivable, of course, that the wish-fulfilling characteristic of dreams should not have been noticed by writers on the subject. On the contrary, it has often been noticed; but it has not occurred to any of them to recognize this characteristic as a universal one and to make it into a corner-stone for the explanation of dreams. We can well imagine what it is that has held them back from it and we shall go into the matter later on.

But consider what a large amount of light has been thrown on things by our examination of children's dreams, and with scarcely any effort: the functions of dreams as the guardians of sleep; their origin from two concurrent purposes, one of which, the desire for sleep, remains constant, while the other strives to satisfy a psychical stimulus; proof that dreams are psychical acts with a sense; their two chief characteristics — wish-fulfilment and hallucinatory experience. And in discovering all this we were almost able to forget that we were engaged on psychoanalysis. Apart from its connection with parapraxes, our work has carried no specific mark. Any psychologist, knowing nothing of the postulates of psychoanalysis, might have been able to give this explanation of children's dreams. Why have they not done so?

If dreams of the infantile kind were the only ones, the problem would be solved and our task finished, and that without our questioning the dreamer or bringing in the unconscious or resorting to free association. This is evidently where a continuation of our task lies ahead. We have already found repeatedly that characteristics which were claimed as being of general validity have turned out to apply only to a particular sort and number of dreams. The question for us is therefore whether the general characteristics we inferred from children's dreams have a firmer footing, whether they also hold good of dreams which are not transparently clear and whose manifest content gives no sign of being connected with a wish left over from the previous day. It is our view that these other dreams have undergone a far-reaching distortion and for that reason cannot be judged at a first glance. We suspect too that to explain this distortion we shall need the psychoanalytic technique which we have been able to do without in the understanding we have just gained of children's dreams.

In any case, there is yet another class of dreams which are undistorted and, like children's dreams, can easily be recognized as wish-fulfilments. These are the dreams which all through life are called up by imperative bodily needs — hunger, thirst, sexual need — that is, they are wish-fulfilments as reactions to internal somatic stimuli. Thus I have a note of a dream dreamt by a little girl of nineteen months, which consisted of a *menu*, to which her own name was attached: '*Anna F., stwawbewwies, wild stwawbewwies, omblet, pudden!*' This was a reaction to a day without food, owing to a digestive upset, which had actually been traced back to the fruit which apeared twice in the dream. The little girl's grandmother — their combined ages came to seventy years — was simultaneously obliged to go without food for a whole day on account of a disturbance due to a floating kidney. She dreamt the same night that she had been 'asked out' and had been served with the most appetizing delicacies.

Observations on prisoners who have been compelled to starve, and on people who have been subjected to privations on travels and explorations, teach us that under these conditions the satisfaction of their needs is regularly dreamt of. Thus Otto Nordenskjöld writes as follows of the members of his expedition while they were wintering in the Antarctic: 'The direction taken by our innermost thoughts was very clearly shown by our dreams, which were never more vivid or numerous than at this time. Even those of us who otherwise dreamt but rarely had long stories to tell in the morning when we exchanged our latest experiences in this world of the imagination. They were all concerned with the outside world which was now so remote from us, though they were often adapted to our actual circumstances....Eating and drinking, however, were the pivot round which our dreams most often revolved. One of us, who had a special gift for attending large luncheon parties during the night, was proud if he was able to report in the morning that he had "got through a three-course dinner". Another of us dreamt of tobacco, of whole mountains of tobacco; while a third dreamt of a ship in full sail coming in across open water. Yet another dream is worth repeating. The postman brought round the mail and gave a long explanation of why we had had to wait so long for it: he had delivered it at the wrong address and had only succeeded in recovering it with great difficulty. We dreamt, of course, of still more impossible things. But there was a most striking lack of imaginativeness shown by almost all the dreams I dreamt myself or heard described. It would certainly be of great psychological interest if all these dreams could be recorded. And it will easily be understood how much we longed for sleep, since it could offer each one of us everything that he most eagerly desired.' So too, according to Du Prel, 'Mungo Park, when he was almost dying of thirst on one of his African journeys, dreamt unceasingly of the well-watered valleys and meadows of his home. Similarly, Baron Trenck, suffering torments of hunger while he was a prisoner in the fortress at Magdeburg, dreamt of being surrounded by sumptuous meals; and George Back, who took part in Franklin's first expedition, when he was almost dying of starvation as a result of his fearful privations, dreamt constantly and regularly of copious meals.'

Anyone who has eaten some highly-spiced dish at dinner and develops a thirst during the night is very likely to dream that he is drinking. It is of course impossible to get rid of a fairly strong need for food or drink by means of a dream. One wakes up from a dream of this sort still feeling thirsty, and has to have a drink of real water. The effect produced by the dream is in this instance trivial from the practical point of view; but it is none the less clear that it was produced with the aim of protecting one's sleep against a stimulus that was urging one to wake up and take action. When the need is of less intensity dreams of satisfaction often help one to get over it.

In the same way, dreams create satisfaction under the influence of sexual stimuli, but these show peculiarities which deserve mention. Since it is characteristic of the sexual instinct to be a degree less dependent on its object than hunger and thirst, the satisfaction in dreams of emission can be a real one; and in consequence of certain difficulties (which I shall have to mention later) in its relation to its object, it happens with special frequency that the real satisfaction is nevertheless attached to a dream content which is obscure or distorted. This characteristic of dreams of emission (as Otto Rank has pointed out) makes them particularly favourable subjects for the study of dream-distortion. Furthermore, all adult dreams arising from bodily needs usually contain, in addition to the satisfaction, other material which is derived from purely psychical sources of stimulation and requires interpretation before it can be understood.

Moreover I do not mean to assert that the wish-fulfilment dreams of adults which are constructed on infantile lines only appear as reactions to the imperative needs that I have mentioned. We are acquainted as well with short, clear dreams of this sort which, under the influence of some dominant situation, arise out of what are unquestionably psychical sources of stimulation. There are, for instance, dreams of impatience: if someone has made preparations for a journey, for a theatrical performance that is important to him, for going to a lecture or paying a visit, he may dream of a premature fulfilment of his expectation; he may, during the night before the event, see himself arrived at his destination, present at the theatre, in conversation with the person he is going to visit. Or there are what are justly known as dreams of convenience, in which a person who would like to sleep longer dreams that his is already up and is washing, or is already at school, whereas he is really still sleeping and would rather get up in a dream than in reality. The wish to sleep, which we have recognized as regularly playing a part in the construction of dreams, comes into the open in these dreams and reveals itself in them as the essential dream-constructor. There is good reason for ranking the need to sleep alongside of the other great bodily needs.

Here is a reproduction of a picture by Schwind in the Schack Gallery in Munich which shows how correctly the artist grasped the way in which dreams arise from the dominant situation. Its title is 'The Prisoner's Dream', a dream whose content is bound to be his escape. It is a happy point that he is to escape through the window, for it is the stimulus of the light pouring in by the window that is putting an end to the prisoner's sleep. The gnomes who are clambering up on one another no doubt represent the successive positions which he himself would have had to take as he climbed up to the level of the window; and, if I am not mistaken and am not attributing too much deliberation to the artist, the topmost of the gnomes, who is sawing through the bars — that is, who is doing what the prisoner would like to do — has the same features as himself.

In all dreams other than children's dreams and those of an infantile type our path is, as I have said, obstructed by dream-distortion. We cannot tell, to begin with, whether these other dreams too are wish-fulfilments as we suspect, we cannot guess from their manifest content to what psychical stimulus they owe their origin, and we cannot prove that they too are endeavouring to get rid of that stimulus or in some way deal with it. They must be interpreted — that is, translated — their distortion must be undone, and their manifest content replaced by their latent one, before we can form a judgement as to whether what we have found in infantile dreams can claim to be valid for all dreams.

LECTURE 9
The Censorship of Dreams

Ladies and Gentlemen, — The study of the dreams of children has taught us the origin, the essential nature and the function of dreams. *Dreams are things which get rid of (psychical) stimuli disturbing to sleep, by the method of hallucinatory satisfaction.* We have, however, only been able to explain one group of the dreams of adults — those which we have described as dreams of an infantile type. What the facts are about the other we cannot yet say, but we do not understand them. We have arrived at a provisional finding, however, whose importance we must not under-estimate. Whenever a dream has been completely intelligible to us, it has turned out to be the hallucinated fulfilment of a wish. This coincidence cannot be a chance one nor a matter of indifference.

We have assumed of dreams of another sort, on the basis of various considerations and on the analogy of our views on parapraxes, that they are a distorted substitute for an unknown content, and that the first thing is to trace them back to it. Our immediate task, then, is an enquiry which will lead to an understanding of this *distortion in dreams.*

Dream-distortion is what makes a dream seem strange and unintelligible to us. We want to know a number of things about it: firstly, where it comes from — its dynamics —, secondly, what it does and, lastly, how it does it. We can also say that dream-distortion is carried out by the dream-work; and we want to describe the dream-work and trace it back to the forces operating in it.

And now listen to this dream. It was recorded by a lady belonging to our group, and, as she tells us, was derived from a highly-esteemed and cultivated elderly lady. No analysis was made of the dream; our informant remarks that for a psychoanalyst it needs no interpreting. Nor did the dreamer herself interpret it, but she judged it and condemned it as though she understood how to interpret it; for she said of it: 'And disgusting, stupid stuff like this was dreamt by a woman of fifty, who has no other thoughts day and night but worry about her child!'

Here, then, is the dream — which deals with 'love services' in war-time. *'She went to Garrison Hospital No. 1 and informed the sentry at the gate that she must speak to the Chief Medical Officer (mentioning a name that was unknown to her) as she wanted to volunteer for service at the hospital. She pronounced the word "service" in such a way that the NCO at once understood that she meant "love service". Since she was an elderly lady, after some hesitation he allowed her to pass. Instead of finding the Chief Medical Officer, however, she reached a large and gloomy apartment in which a number of officers and army doctors were standing and sitting round a long table. She approached a staff surgeon with her request, and he understood her meaning after she had said only a few words. The actual wording of her speech in the dream was: "I and many other women and girls in Vienna are ready to ..." at this point in the dream her words turned into a mumble "...for the troops — officers and other ranks without distinction." She could tell from the expressions on the officers' faces, partly embarrassed and partly sly, that everyone had understood her meaning correctly. The lady went on: "I'm aware that our decision must sound surprising, but we mean it in bitter earnest. No one asks a soldier in the field whether he wishes to die or not." There followed an awkward silence of some minutes. The staff surgeon then put his arm round her waist and said: "Suppose, madam, it actually came to ...(mumble). She drew away from him, thinking to herself: "He's like all the rest of them," and replied: "Good gracious, I'm an old woman and I might never come to that. Besides, there's one condition that must be observed: age must be respected. It must never happen that an elderly woman ... (mumble) ... a mere boy. That would be terrible." "I understand perfectly," replied the staff surgeon. Some of the officers, and among them one who had been a suitor of hers in her youth, laughed out loud. The lady then asked to be taken to the Chief Medical Officer, with whom she was acquainted, so that the whole matter could be thrashed out; but she found, to her consternation, that she could not recall his name. Nevertheless, the staff surgeon, most politely and respectfully, showed her the way up to the second floor by a very narrow, iron, spiral staircase, which led directly from the room to the upper storeys of the building. As she went up she heard an officer say: "That's a tremendous decision to make — no matter whether a woman's young or old! Splendid of her!" Feeling simply that she was doing her duty, she walked up an interminable staircase.*

'The dream was repeated twice in the course of a few weeks, with, as the lady remarked, some quite unimportant and meaningless modifications.'

From its continuous nature, the dream resembles a daytime phantasy: there are few breaks in it, and some of the details of its content could have been explained if they had been enquired into, but that, as you know, was not done. But what is remarkable and interesting from our point of view is that the dream shows several gaps — gaps not in the dreamer's memory of the dream but in the content of the dream itself. At three points the content was, as it were, extinguished; the speeches in which these gaps occurred were interrupted by a mumble. As no analysis was carried out, we have strictly speaking, no right to say anything about the sense of the dream. Nevertheless there are hints on which conclusions can be based (for instance, in the phrase 'love-services'); but above all, the portions of the speeches immediately preceding the mumbles call for the gaps to be filled in, and in an unambiguous manner. If we make the insertions, the content of the phantasy turns out to be that the dreamer is prepared, by way of fulfilling a patriotic duty, to put herself at the disposal of the troops, both officers and other ranks, for the satisfaction of their erotic needs. This is, of course, highly objectionable, the model of a shameless libidinal phantasy — but it does not appear in the dream at all. Precisely at the points at which the context would call for this admission, the manifest dream contains an indistinct mumble: something has been lost or suppressed.

You will, I hope, think it plausible to suppose that it was precisely the objectionable nature of these passages that was the motive for their suppression. Where shall we find a parallel to such an event? You need not look far in these days. Take up any political newspaper and you will find that here and there the text is absent and in its place nothing except the white paper is to be seen. This, as you know, is the work of the press censorship. In these empty places there was something that displeased the higher censorship authorities and for that reason it was removed — a pity, you feel, since no doubt it was the most interesting thing in the paper — the 'best bit'.

On other occasions the censorship has not gone to work on a passage *after* it has already been completed. The author has seen in advance which passages might expect to give rise to objections from the censorship and has on the account toned them down in advance, modified them slightly, or has contented himself with approximations and allusions to what would genuinely have come from his pen. In that case there are no blank places in the paper, but circumlocutions and obscurities of expression appearing at certain points will enable you to guess where regard has been paid to the censorship in advance.

Well, we can keep close to this parallel. It is our view that the omitted pieces of the speeches in the dream which were concealed by a mumble have likewise been sacrificed to a censorship. We speak in so many words of a '*dream-censorship*', to which some share in dream-distortion is to be attrributed. Wherever there are gaps in the manifest dream the dream-censorship is responsible for them. We should go further, and regard it as a manifestation of the censorship wherever a dream-element is remembered especially faintly, indefinitely and doubtfully among other elements that are more clearly constructed. But it is only rarely that this censorship manifests itself so undisguisedly — so naïvely, one might say — as in this example of the dream of 'love services'. The censorship takes effect much more frequently according to the second method, by producing softenings, approximations and allusions instead of the genuine thing.

I know of no parallel in the operations of the press-censorship to a third manner of working by the dream-censorship; but I am able to demonstrate it from precisely the one example of a dream which we have analysed so far. You will recall the dream of the 'three bad theatre-tickets for 1 florin 50'. In the latent thoughts of the dream the element 'over-hurriedly, too early' stood in the foreground. Thus: it was absurd to marry so *early* — it was also absurd to take the theatre-tickets so *early* — it was ridiculous of the sister-in-law to part with her money in such a *hurry* to buy jewellery with it. Nothing of this central element of the dream-thoughts passed over into the manifest dream; in it the central position is taken by the 'going to the theatre' and 'taking the tickets'. As a result of this displacement of accent, this fresh grouping of the elements of the content, the manifest dream has become so unlike the latent dream-thoughts that no-one would suspect the presence of the latter behind the former. This displacement of accent is one of the chief instruments of dream-distortion and it is what gives the dream the strangeness on account of which the dreamer himself is not inclined to recognize it as his own production.

Omission, modification, fresh grouping of the material — these, then, are the activities of the dream-censorship and the instruments of dream-distortion. The dream-censorship itself is the originator, or one of the originators, of the dream-distortion which we are now engaged in examining. We are in the habit of combining the concepts of modification and re-arrangement under the term 'displacement'.

After these remarks on the activities of the dream-censorship, we will now turn to its dynamics. I hope you do not take the term too anthropomorphically, and do not picture the 'censor of dreams' as a severe little manikin or a spirit living in a closet in the brain and there discharging his office; but I hope too that you do not take the term in too 'localizing' a sense, and do not think of a 'brain-centre', from which a censoring influence of this kind issues, an influence which would be brought to an end if the 'centre' were damaged or removed. For the time being it is nothing more than a serviceable term for describing a dynamic relation. The word does not prevent our asking by what purposes this influence is exercised and against what purposes it is directed. And we shall not be surprised to learn that we have come up against the dream-censorship once already, though perhaps without recognizing it.

For that is in fact the case. You will recall that when we began to make use of our technique of free association we made a surprising discovery. We became aware that our efforts at proceeding from the dream-element to the unconscious element for which it is a substitute were being met by a *resistance* . This resistance, we said, could be of different magnitudes, sometimes enormous and sometimes quite insignificant. In the latter case we need to pass through only a small number of intermediate links in our work of interpretation; but when the resistance is large we have to traverse long chains of associations from the dream-element, we are led far away from it and on our path we have to overcome all the difficulties which represent themselves as critical objections to the ideas that occur. What we met with as resistance in our work of interpretation must now be introduced into the dream-work in the form of the dream-censorship. The resistance to interpretation is only a putting into effect of the dream-censorship. It also proves to us that the force of the censorship is not exhausted in bringing about the distortion of dreams and thereafter extinguished, but that the censorship persists as a permanent institution which has as its aim the maintenance of the distortion. Moreover, just as the strength of the resistance varies in the interpretation of each element in a dream, so too the magnitude of the distortion introduced by the censorship varies for each element in the same dream. If we compare the manifest and the latent dream, we shall find that some particular latent elements have been completely eliminated, others modified to a greater or less extent, while yet others have been carried over into the manifest content of the dream unaltered or even perhaps strengthened.

But we wanted to inquire what are the purposes which exercise the censorship and against what purposes it is directed. Now this question, which is fundamental for the understanding of dreams and perhaps, indeed, of human life, is easy to answer if we look through the series of dreams which have been interpreted. The purposes which exercise the censorship are those which are acknowledged by the dreamer's waking judgement, those with which he feels himself at one. You may be sure that if you reject an interpretation of one of your own dreams which has been correctly carried out, you are doing so for the same motives for which the dream-censorship has been exercised, the dream-distortion brought about and the interpretation made necessary. Take the dream of our fifty-year-old lady. She thought her dream disgusting without having analysed it, and she would have been still more indignant if Dr von Hug-Hellmuth had told her anything of its inevitable interpretation; it was precisely because of this condemnation by the dreamer that the objectionable passages in her dream were replaced by a mumble.

The *purposes* against which the dream-censorship is directed must be described in the first instance from the point of view of that agency itself. If so, one can only say that they are inevitably of a reprehensible nature, repulsive from the ethical, aesthetic and social point of view — matters of which one does not venture to think at all or thinks only with disgust. These wishes, which are censored and given a distorted expression in dreams, are first and foremost manifestations of an unbridled and ruthless egoism. And, to be sure, the dreamer's own ego appears in every dream and plays the chief part in it, even if it knows quite well how to hide itself so far as the manifest content goes. This '*sacro egoismo*' of dreams is certainly not unrelated to the attitude we adopt when we sleep, which consists in our withdrawing our interest from the whole external world.

The ego, freed from all ethical bonds, also finds itself at one with all the demands of sexual desire, even those which have long been condemned by our aesthetic upbringing and those which contradict all the requirements of moral restraint. The desire for pleasure — the 'libido', as we call it — chooses its objects without inhibition, and by preference, indeed, the forbidden ones: not only other men's wives, but above all incestuous objects, objects sanctified by the common agreement of mankind, a man's mother and sister, a woman's father and brother.

(The dream of our fifty-year-old lady, too, was incestuous; her libido was unmistakably directed to her son.) Lusts which we think of as remote from human nature show themselves strong enough to provoke dreams. Hatred, too, rages without restraint. Wishes for revenge and death directed against those who are nearest and dearest in waking life, against the dreamer's parents, brothers and sisters, husband or wife, and his own children are nothing unusual. These censored wishes appear to rise up out of a positive Hell; after they have been interpreted when we are awake, no censorship of them seems to us too severe.

But you must not blame the dream itself on account of its evil content. Do not forget that it performs the innocent and indeed useful function of preserving sleep from disturbance. This wickedness is not part of the essential nature of dreams. Indeed you know too that there are dreams which can be recognized as the satisfaction of justified wishes and of pressing bodily needs. These, it is true, have no dream-distortion; but they have no need of it, for they can fulfil their function without insulting the ethical and aesthetic purposes of the ego. Bear in mind, too, that dream-distortion is proportionate to two factors. On the one hand it becomes greater the worse the wish that has to be censored; but on the other hand it also becomes greater the more severe the demands of the censorship at the moment. Thus a strictly brought-up and prudish young girl, with a relentless censorship, will distort dream-impulses which we doctors, for instance, would have to regard as permissable, harmless, libidinal wishes, and on which in ten years' time the dreamer herself will make the same judgement.

Furthermore, we have not got nearly far enough yet to be able to feel indignant at this result of our work of interpretation. We do not yet, I think, understand it properly; but our first duty is to defend it against certain aspersions. There is no difficulty in finding a weak point in it. Our dream-interpretations are made on the basis of the premisses which we have already accepted — that dreams in general have a sense, that it is legitimate to carry across from hypnotic to normal sleep the fact of the existence of mental processes which are at the time unconscious, and that everything that occurs to the mind is determined. If on the basis of these premisses we had arrived at plausible findings from dream-interpretation, we should have been justified in concluding that the premisses were valid. But how about it if these findings seem to be as I have pictured them? We should then be tempted to say: 'These are impossible, senseless or at the least most improbable findings; so there was something wrong about the premisses. Either dreams are not psychical phenomena, or there is nothing unconscious in the normal state, or our technique has a flaw in it. Is it not simpler and more satisfactory to suppose this rather than accept all the abominations which we are supposed to have discovered on the basis of our premisses?'

Yes, indeed! Both simpler and more satisfactory — but not necessarily on that account more correct. Let us give ourselves time: the matter is not yet ripe for judgement. And first, we can further strengthen the criticism of our dream-interpretations. The fact that the findings from them are so disagreeable and repellent need not, perhaps, carry very great weight. A stronger argument is that the dreamers to whom we are led to attribute such wishful purposes by the interpretation of their dreams reject them most emphatically and for good reasons. 'What?' says one of them, 'you want to convince me from this dream that I regret the money I have spent on my sister's dowry and my brother's education? But that cannot be so. I work entirely for my brothers and sisters; I have no other interest in life but to fulfil my duties to them, which, as the eldest of the family, I promised our departed mother I would do.' Or a woman dreamer would say: 'You think I wish my husband was dead? That is a shocking piece of nonsense! It is not only that we are most happily married — you would probably not believe me if I said that — but his death would rob me of everything I possess in the world.' Or another man would answer us: 'You say that I have sensual desires for my sister? That is ridiculous! She means nothing at all to me. We are on bad terms with each other and I have not exchanged a word with her for years.' We might still take it lightly, perhaps, if these dreamers neither confirmed nor denied the purposes we attribute to them; we might say that these were just things they did not know about themselves. But when they feel in themselves the precise contrary of the wish we have interpreted to them and when they are able to prove to us by the lives they lead that they are dominated by this contrary wish, it must surely take us aback. Has not the time come to throw aside the whole work we have done on dream-interpretation as something which its findings have reduced *ad absurdum*?

No, not even now. Even this stronger argument collapses if we examine it critically. Granted that there are unconscious purposes in mental life, nothing is proved by showing that purposes opposed to these are dominant in conscious life. Perhaps there is room in the mind for contrary purposes, for contradictions, to exist side by side. Possibly, indeed, the dominance of one impulse is precisely a necessary condition of its contrary being unconscious. We are after all left, then, with the first objections that were raised: the findings of dream-interpretation are not simple and they are very disagreeable. We may reply to the first that all your passion for what is simple will not be able to solve a single one of the problems of dreams. You must get accustomed here to assuming a complicated state of affairs. And we may reply to the second that you are plainly wrong to use a liking or disliking that you may feel as the ground for a scientific judgement. What difference does it make if the findings of dream-interpretation seem disagreable to you or, indeed, embarrassing and repulsive? '*ça n'empêche pas d'exister*', as I heard my teacher Charcot say in a similar case when I was a young doctor. One must be humble and hold back one's sympathies and antipathies if one wants to discover what is real in this world. If a physicist were able to prove to you that in a short period organic life on this earth would be brought to an end by freezing, would you venture to make the same reply to him: 'That cannot be so, the prospect is too disagreeable?' You would, I think, be silent, until another physicist came and pointed out to the first one an error in his premises or calculations. When you reject something that is disagreeable to you, what you are doing is *repeating* the mechanism of constructing dreams rather than understanding it and surmounting it.

You will promise now, perhaps, to disregard the repellent character of the censored dream-wishes and will withdraw upon the argument that after all it is unlikely that such a large space should be given to the evil in the constitution of human beings. But do your own experiences justify your saying this? I will not discuss how you may appear to yourselves; but have you found so much benevolence among your superiors and competitors, so much chivalry among your enemies and so little envy in your social surroundings that you felt it your duty to protest against egoistic evil having a share in human nature? Are you not aware of how uncontrolled and untrustworthy the average person is in everything to do with sexual life? Or do you not know that all the transgressions and excesses of which we dream at night are daily committed in real life by waking men? What does psychoanalysis do here but confirm Plato's old saying that the good are those who are content to dream of what the others, the bad, really do?

And now turn your eyes away from individuals and consider the Great War which is still laying Europe waste. Think of the vast amount of brutality, cruelty and lies which are able to spread over the civilized world. Do you really believe that a handful of ambitious and deluding men without conscience could have succeeded in unleashing all these evil spirits if their millions of followers did not share their guilt? Do you venture, in such circumstances, to break a lance on behalf of the exclusion of evil from the mental constitution of mankind?

You will represent to me that I am giving a one-sided judgement on the War: that it has also brought to light what is finest and noblest in men, their heorism, their self-sacrifice, their social sense. No doubt; but are you not now showing yourselves as accessories to the injustice that has so often been done to psychoanalysis in reproaching it with denying one thing because it has asserted another? It is not our intention to dispute the noble endeavours of human nature, nor have we ever done anything to detract from their value. On the contrary; I am exhibiting to you not only the evil dream-wishes which are censored but also the censorship, which suppresses them and makes them unrecognizable. We lay a stronger emphasis on what is evil in men only because other people disavow it and thereby make the human mind, not better, but incomprehensible. If now we give up this one-sided ethical valuation, we shall undoubtedly find a more correct formula for the relation between good and evil in human nature.

There it is, then. We need not give up the findings of our work on the interpretation of dreams even though we cannot but regard them as strange. Perhaps we shall be able to approach an understanding of them later from another direction. For the time being let us hold fast to this: dream-distortion is a result of the censorship which is exercised by recognized purposes of the ego against wishful impulses in any way objectionable that stir within us at night-time during our sleep. Why this should happen particularly at night-time and where these reprehensible wishes come from — these are matters on which, no doubt, much still remains for questioning and research.

But it would be unfair if we neglected at this point to emphasize sufficiently another outcome of our investigations. The dream-wishes which seek to disturb us in our sleep are unknown to us and indeed we only learnt of them through dream-interpretation. They are thus to be described, in the sense we have discussed, as unconscious for the time being. But we must reflect that they are unconscious too for more than the time being. The dreamer also disavows them, as we have seen in so many instances, after he has come to know them through the interpretation of his dream. We are then faced once again with the position we first came across in the 'hiccoughing' slip of the tongue, where the proposer of the toast protested indignantly that neither then nor at any earlier time had he become conscious of any disrespectful impulse towards his Chief. Already at the time we felt some doubts about the weight of an assurance of this kind, and suggested instead the hypothesis that the speaker was permanently unaware of the presence of this impulse in him. This situation is repeated now with every interpretation of a strongly distorted dream and consequently gains an increased importance in its bearing on the view we have taken. We are now prepared to assume that there are in the mind processes and purposes of which one knows nothing at all, has known nothing for a long time, and has even perhaps never known anything. With this the unconscious acquires a new sense for us; the characteristic of 'for the time being' or 'temporary' disappears from its essential nature. It can mean *permanently* unconscious and not merely 'latent at the time'. We shall of course have to hear more about this on some other occasion.

7

PSYCHOLOGY AS THE
BEHAVIORIST VIEWS IT

John B. Watson

Psychology as the behaviorist views it is a purely objective experimental branch of natural science. Its theoretical goal is the prediction and control of behavior. Introspection forms no essential part of its method, nor is the scientific value of its data dependent upon the readiness with which they lend themselves to interpretation in terms of consciousness. The behaviorist, in his efforts to get a unitary scheme of animal response, recognizes no dividing line between man and brute. The behavior of man, with all of its refinement and complexity, forms only a part of the behaviorist's total scheme of investigation.

It has been maintained by its followers generally that psychology is a study of the science of the phenomena of consciousness. It has taken as its problem, on the one hand, the analysis of complex mental states (or processes) into simple elementary constituents, and on the other the construction of complex states when the elementary constituents are given. The world of physical objects (stimuli, including here anything which may excite activity in a receptor), which forms the total phenomena of the natural scientist, is looked upon merely as means to an end. That end is the production of mental states that may be 'inspected' or 'observed.' The psychological object of observation in the case of an emotion, for example, is the mental state itself. The problem in emotion is the determination of the number and kind of elementary constituents present, their loci, intensity, order of appearance, etc. It is agreed that introspection is the method *par excellence* by means of which mental states may be manipulated for purposes of psychology. On this assumption, behavior data (including under this term everything which goes under the name of

Watson, John B. 1913. "Psychology as the Behaviorist Views It" in *Psychological Review, 20*, pp. 158-176.

comparative psychology) have no value *per se*. They possess significance only in so far as they may throw light upon conscious states.[1] Such data must have at least an analogical or indirect reference to belong to the realm of psychology.

Indeed, at times, one finds psychologists who are sceptical of even this analogical reference. Such scepticism is often known by the question which is put to the student of behavior, "what is the bearing of animal work upon human psychology?" I used to have to study over this question. Indeed it always embarrassed me somewhat. I was interested in my own work and felt that it was important, and yet I could not trace any close connection between it and psychology as my questioner understood psychology. I hope that such a confession will clear the atmosphere to such an extent that we will no longer have to work under false pretences. We must frankly admit that the facts so important to us which we have been able to glean from extended work upon the senses of animals by the behavior method have contributed only in a fragmentary way to the general theory of human sense organ processes, nor have they suggested new point of experimental attack. The enormous number of experiments which we have carried out upon learning have likewise contributed little to human psychology. It seems reasonably clear that some kind of compromise must be effected: either psychology must change its viewpoint so as to take in facts of behavior, whether or not they have bearings upon the problems of 'consciousness'; or the behavior must stand alone as a wholly separate and independent science. Should human psychologists fail to look with favor upon our overtures and refuse to modify their position, the behaviorists will be driven to using human beings as subjects and to employ methods of investigation which are exactly comparable to those now employed in the animal work.

Any other hypothesis than that which admits the independent value of behavior material, regardless of any bearing such material may have upon consciousness, will inevitably force us to the absurd position of attempting to construct the conscious content of the animal whose behavior we have been studying. On this view, after having determined our animal's ability to learn, the simplicity or complexity of its methods of learning, the effect of past habit upon present response, the range of stimuli to which it ordinarily responds, the widened range to which it can respond under experimental conditions, — in more general terms, its various problems and its various ways of solving them, — we should still feel that the task is unfinished and that the results are worthless, until we can interpret them by analogy in the light of consciousness. Although we have solved our problem we feel uneasy and unrestful because of our definition of psychology: we feel forced to say something about the possible mental processes of our animal. We say that, having no eyes, its stream of consciousness cannot contain brightness and color sensations as we know them, — having no taste buds this stream can contain no sensations of sweet, sour, salt and bitter. But on the other hand, since it does not respond to thermal, tactual and organic stimuli, its conscious content must be made up largely of these sensations; and we usually add, to protect ourselves against the reproach of being anthropomorphic, "if it has any consciousness." Surely this doctrine which calls for an analogical interpretation of all behavior data may be shown to be false: the position that the standing of an observation upon behavior is determined by its fruitful in yielding results which are interpretable only in the narrow realm of (really human) consciousness.

This emphasis upon analogy in psychology has led the behaviorist somewhat afield. Not being willing to throw off the yoke of consciousness he feels impelled to make a place in the scheme of behavior where the rise of consciousness can be determined. This point has been a shifting one. A few years ago certain animals were supposed to possess 'associative memory,' while certain others were supposed to lack it. One meets this search for the origin of consciousness under a good many disguises. Some of our texts state that consciousness arises at the moment when reflex and instinctive activities fail properly to conserve that organism. A perfectly adjusted organism would be lacking in consciousness. On the other hand whenever we find the presence of diffuse activity which results in habit formation, we are justified in assuming consciousness. I must confess that these arguments had weight with me when I began the study of behavior. I fear that a good many of us are still viewing behavior problems with something like this in mind. More than one student in behavior has attempted to frame criteria of the psychic — to devise a set of objective, structural and functional criteria which, when applied in the particular instance, will enable us to decide whether such and such responses are positively conscious, merely indicative of consciousness, or whether they are purely 'physiological.' Such problems as these can no longer satisfy behavior men. It would be better to give up the province altogether and admit frankly that the study of the behavior of animals has no justification, than to admit that our search is of such a 'will o' the wisp' character. One can assume either the presence or the absence of consciousness anywhere in the phylogenetic scale without affecting the problems of behavior by one jot or one tittle; and without influencing in any way the mode of experimental attack upon them. On the other hand, I cannot for one moment assume that the paramecium responds to light; that the rat learns a problem more quickly by working at the task five times a day than once a day, or that the human child exhibits plateaux in his learning curves. These are questions which vitally concern behavior and which must be decided by direct observation under experimental conditions.

This attempt to reason by analogy from human conscious processes to the conscious processes in animals, and *vice versa*: to make consciousness, as the human being knows it, the center of reference of all behavior, forces us into a situation similar to that which existed in biology in Darwin's time. The whole Darwinian movement was judged by the bearing it had upon the origin and development of the human race. Expeditions were undertaken to collect material which would establish the position that the rise of the human race was a perfectly natural phenomenon and not an act of special creation. Variations were carefully sought along with the evidence for the heaping up effect and the weeding out effect of selection; for in these and the other Darwinian mechanisms were to be found factors sufficiently complex to account for the origin and race differentiation of man. The wealth of material collected at the time was considered valuable largely in so far as it tended to develop the concept of evolution of man. It is strange that this situation should have remained the dominant one in biology for so many years. The moment zoology undertook the experimental study of evolution and descent, the situation immediately changed. Man ceased to be the center of reference. I doubt if any experimental biologist today, unless actually engaged in the problem of race differentiation in man, tries to interpret his findings in terms of human evolution, or ever refers to it in his thinking. He gathers his data from the study of many species of plants and animals and tries to work out the laws of inheritance in the particular type upon which he is conducting experiments. Naturally, he follows the progress of the work upon race differentiation in man and in the descent of man, but he looks upon these as special topics, equal in importance with his own yet ones in which his interests will never be vitally engaged. It is not fair to say that all of his work is directed toward human evolution or that it must be interpreted in terms of human evolution. He does not have to dismiss certain of his facts on the inheritance of coat color in mice because, forsooth, they have little bearing upon the differentiation of the *genus homo* into separate races, or upon the descent of the *genus homo* from some more primitive stock.

In psychology we are still in that stage of development where we feel that we must select our material. We have a general place of discard for processes, which we anathematize so far as their value for psychology is concerned by saying, "this is a reflex"; "that is a purely physiological fact which has nothing to do with psychology." We are not interested (as psychologists) in getting all of the processes of adjustment which the animal as a whole employs, and in finding how these various responses are associated, and how they fall apart, thus working out a systematic scheme for the prediction and control of response in general. Unless our observed facts are indicative of consciousness, we have no use for them, and unless our apparatus and method are designed to throw such facts into relief, they are thought of in just as disparaging a way. I shall always remember the remark one distinguished psychologists made as he looked over the color apparatus designed for testing the responses of animals to monochromatic light in the attic at Johns Hopkins. It was this: "And they call this psychology!"

I do not wish unduly to criticize psychology. It has failed, signally, I believe, during the fifty-odd years of its existence as an experimental discipline to make its place in the world as an undisputed natural science. Psychology, as it is generally thought of, has something esoteric in its methods. If you fail to reproduce my findings, it is not due to some fault in your apparatus or in the control of your stimulus, but it is due to the fact that your introspection is untrained.[2] The attack is made upon the observer and not upon the experimental setting. In physics and in chemistry the attack is made upon the experimental conditions. The apparatus was not sensitive enough, impure chemicals were used, etc. In these sciences a better technique will give reproducible results. Psychology is otherwise. If you can't observe 3–9 states of clearness in attention, your introspection is poor, If, on the other hand, a feeling seems reasonably clear to you, your introspection is again faulty. You are seeing too much. Feelings are never clear.

The time seems to have come when psychology must discard all reference to consciousness; when it need no longer delude itself into thinking that it is making mental states the object of observation. We have become the so enmeshed in speculative questions concerning the elements of mind, the nature of conscious content (for example, imageless thought, attitudes, and Bewusseinslage, etc.) that I, as an experimental student, feel that something is wrong with our premises and the types of problems which develop from them. There is no longer any guarantee that we all mean the same thing when we use the terms now current in psychology. Take the case of sensation. A sensation is defined in terms of its attributes. One psychologist will state with readiness that the attributes of a visual sensation are *quality, extension, duration,* and *intensity.* Another will add *clearness.* Still another that of *order.* I doubt if any one psychologist can draw up a set of statements describing what he means by sensation which will be agreed to by three other psychologists of different training. Turn for a moment to the question of the number of isolable sensations. Is there an extremely large number of color sensations — or only four, red, green, yellow and blue? Again, yellow, while psychologically simple, can be obtained by superimposing red and green spectral rays upon the same diffusing surface! If, on the other hand, we say that every just noticeable difference in the spectrum is a simple sensation, and that every just noticeable increase in the white value of a given color gives simple sensations, we are forced to admit that the number is so large and the conditions for obtaining them so complex that the concept of sensation is unusable, either for the purpose of analysis of that of synthesis. Titchener, who has fought the most valiant fight in this country for a psychology based upon introspection, feels that these differences of opinion as to the number of sensations and their attributes; as to whether there are relations (in the sense of elements) and on the many others which seem to be fundamental in every attempt at analysis, are perfectly natural in the present undeveloped state of psychology. While it is admitted that every growing science is full of unanswered questions, surely only those who are wedded to the system as we now have it, who have fought and suffered for it, can confidently believe that there will ever be any greater uniformity than there is now in the answers we have to such questions. I firmly believe that two hundred years from now, unless the introspective method is discarded, psychology will still be divided on the question as to whether auditory sensations have the quality of 'extension,' whether intensity is an attribute which can be applied to color, whether there is a difference in 'texture' between image and sensation and upon many hundreds of others of like character.

The condition in regard to other mental processes is just as chaotic. Can image type be experimentally tested and verified? Are recondite thought processes dependent mechanically upon imagery at all? Are psychologists agreed upon what feeling is? One states that feelings are attitudes. Another finds them to be groups of organic sensations possessing a certain solidarity. Still another and larger group finds them to be new elements correlative with and ranking equally with sensations.

My psychological quarrel is not with the systematic and structural psychologist alone. The last fifteen years have seen the growth of what is called functional psychology. This type of psychology decries the use of elements in the static sense of the structuralists. It throws emphasis upon the biological significance of conscious states into introspectively isolable elements. I have done my best to understand the difference between functional psychology and structural psychology. Instead of clarity, confusion grows upon me. The terms sensation, perception, affection, emotion, volition are used as much by the functionalist as by the structuralist. The addition of the word 'process' ('mental act as a whole,' and like terms are frequently met) after each serves in some way to remove the corpse of 'content' and to leave 'function' in its stead. Surely if these concepts are elusive when looked at from a content standpoint, they are still more deceptive when viewed from the angle of function, and especially so when function is obtained by the introspection method. It is rather interesting that no functional psychologist has carefully distinguished between 'perception' (and this is true of the other psychological terms as well) as employed by the systematist, and 'perceptual process' as used in functional psychology. It seems illogical and hardly fair to criticize the psychology which the systematist gives us, and then to utilize his terms without carefully showing the changes in meaning which are to be attached to them. I was greatly surprised sometime ago when I opened Pillsbury's book and saw psychology defined as the 'science of behavior.' A still more recent text states that psychology is the 'science of mental behavior.' When I saw these promising statements I thought, now surely we will have texts based upon different lines. After a few pages the science of behavior is dropped and one finds the conventional treatment of sensation, perception, imagery, etc., along with certain shifts in emphasis and additional facts which serve to give the author's personal imprint.

One of the difficulties in the way of a consistent functional psychology is the parallelistic hypothesis. If the functionalist attempts to express his formulations in terms which make mental states really appear to function, to play some active rôle in the world of adjustment, he almost inevitably lapses into terms which are connotative of interaction. When taxed with this he replies that it is more convenient to do so and that he does it to avoid the circumlocution and clumsiness which are inherent in any thoroughgoing parallelism.[3] As a matter of fact I believe the functionalist actually thinks in terms of interaction and resorts to parallelism only when forced to give expression to his views. I feel that *behaviorism* is the only consistent and logical functionalism. In it one avoids both the Scylla of parallelism and the Charybdis of interaction. Those time-honored relics of philosophical speculation need trouble the student of behavior as little as they trouble the student of physics. The consideration of the mind-body problem affects neither the type of problem selected nor the formulation of the solution of that problem. I can state my position here no better than by saying that I should like to bring my students up in the same ignorance of such hypotheses as one finds among the students of other branches of science.

This leads me to the point where I should like to make the argument constructive. I believe we can write a psychology, define it as Pillsbury, and never go back upon our definition: never use the terms consciousness, mental states, mind, content, introspectively verifiable, imagery, and the like. I believe that we can do it in a few years without running into the absurd terminology of Beer, Bethes, Von Uexküll, Nuel, and that of the so-called objective schools generally. It can be done in terms of stimulus and response, in terms of habit formation, habit integrations and the like. Furthermore, I believe that it is really worthwhile to make this attempt now.

The psychology which I should attempt to build up would take as a staring point, first, the observable fact that organisms, man and animal alike, do adjust themselves to their environment by means of hereditary and habit equipments. These adjustments may be very adequate or they may be so inadequate that the organism barely maintains its existence; secondly, that certain stimuli lead the organisms to make the responses. In a system of psychology completely worked out, given the response the stimuli can be predicted; given the stimuli the response can be predicted. Such a set of statements is crass and raw in the extreme, as all such generalizations must be. Yet they are hardly more raw and less realizable than the ones which appear in the psychology texts of the day. I possibly might illustrate my point better by choosing an everyday problem which anyone is likely to meet in the course of his work. Some time ago I was called upon to make a study of certain species of birds. Until I went to Tortugas I had never seen these birds alive. When I reached there I found the animals doing certain things: some of the acts seemed to work peculiarly well in such an environment, while others seemed to be unsuited to their type of life. I first studied the responses of the group as a whole and later those of individuals. In order to understand more thoroughly the relation between what was habit and what was hereditary in these responses, I took the young birds and reared them. In this way I was able to study the order of appearance of hereditary adjustments and their complexity, and later the beginnings of habit formation. My efforts in determining the stimuli which called forth such adjustments were crude indeed. Consequently my attempts to control behavior and to produce responses at will did not meet with much success. Their food and water, sex and other social relations, light and temperature conditions were all beyond control in a field study. I did find it possible to control their reactions in a measure by using the nest and egg (or young) as stimuli. It is not necessary in this paper to develop further how such a study should be carried out and how work of this kind must be supplemented by carefully controlled laboratory experiments. Had I been called upon to examine the natives of some of the Australian tribes, I should have gone about my task in the same way. I should have found the problem more difficult: the types of responses called forth by physical stimuli would have been more varied, and the number of effective stimuli larger. I should have had to determine the social setting of their lives in a far more careful way. These savages would be more influenced by the responses of each other than was the case with the birds. Furthermore, habits would have been more complex and the influences of past habits upon the present responses would have appeared more clearly. Finally, if I had been called upon to work out the psychology of the educated European, my problem would have required several lifetimes. But in the one I have at my disposal I should have followed the same general line of attack. In the main, my desire in all such work is to gain an accurate knowledge of adjustments and the stimuli calling them forth. My final reason for this is to learn general and particular methods by which I may control behavior. My goal is not "the description and explanation of states of consciousness as such," nor that of obtaining such proficiency in mental gymnastics that I can immediately lay hold of a state of consciousness and say, "this, as a whole, consists of gray sensation number 350, of such and such extent, occurring in conjunction with the sensation of cold of a certain intensity; one of pressure of a certain intensity and extent," and so on *ad infinitum*. If psychology would follow the plan I suggest, the educator, the physician, the jurist and the businessman could utilize our data in a practical way, as soon as we are able, experimentally, to obtain them. Those who have occasion to apply psychological principles practically would find no need to complain as they do at the present time. Ask any physician or jurist today whether scientific psychology plays a practical part in his daily routine and you will hear him deny that the psychology of the laboratories finds a place in his scheme of work. I think the criticism is extremely just. One of the earliest conditions which made me dissatisfied with psychology was the feeling that there was no realm of application for the principles which were being worked out in content terms.

What gives me hope that the behaviorist's position is a defensible one is the fact that those branches of psychology which have already partially withdrawn from the parent, experimental psychology, and which are consequently less dependent upon introspection are today in a most flourishing condition. Experimental pedagogy, the psychology of drugs, the psychology of advertising, legal psychology, the psychology of tests, and psychopathology are all vigorous growths. These are sometimes wrongly called "practical" or "applied" psychology. Surely there was never a worse misnomer. In the future there may grow up vocational bureaus which really apply psychology. At present these fields are truly scientific and are in search of broad generalizations which will lead to the control of human behavior. For example, we find out by experimentation whether a series of stanzas may be acquired more readily if the whole is learned at once, or whether it is more advantageous to learn each stanza separately and then pass to the succeeding. We do not attempt to apply our findings. The application of this principle is purely voluntary on the part of the teacher. In the psychology of drugs we may show the effect upon behavior of certain doses of caffeine. We may reach the conclusion that caffeine has a good effect upon the speed and accuracy of work. But these are general principles. We leave it to the individual as to whether the results of our tests shall be applied or not. Again, in legal testimony, we test the effects of recency upon the reliability of a witness's report. We test the accuracy of the report with respect to moving objects, stationary objects, color, etc. It depends upon the judicial machinery of the country to decide whether these facts are ever to be applied. For a 'pure' psychologist to say that he is not interested in the questions raised in these divisions of the science because they relate indirectly to the application of psychology shows, in the first place, that he fails to understand the scientific aim in such problems, and secondly, that he is not interested in a psychology which concerns itself with human life. The only fault I have with these disciplines is that much of their material is stated in terms of introspection, whereas a statement in terms of objective results would be far more valuable. There is no reason why appeal should ever be made to consciousness in any of them. Or why introspective data should ever be sought during the experimentation, or published in the results. In experimental pedagogy especially one can see the desirability of keeping all of the results on a purely objective plane. If this is done, work there on the human being will be comparable directly with the work upon animals. For example, at Hopkins, Mr. Ulrich has obtained certain results upon the distribution of effort in learning — using rats as subjects. He is prepared to give comparative results upon the effect of having an animal work at the problem once per day, three times per day, and five times per day. Whether it is advisable to have the animal learn only one problem at a time or learn three abreast. We need to have similar experiments made upon man, but we care as little about his 'conscious processes' during the conduct of the experiment as we care about such processes in the rats.

I am more interested at the present moment in trying to show the necessity for maintaining uniformity in experimental procedure and in the method of stating results in both human and animal work, than in developing any ideas I may have upon the changes which are certain to come in the scope of human psychology. Let us consider for a moment the subject of the range of stimuli to which animals respond. I shall speak first of the work upon vision in animals. We put our animal in a situation where he will respond (or learn to respond) to one of two monochromatic lights. We feed him at the one (positive) and punish him at the other (negative). In a short time the animal learns to go to the light at which he is fed. At this point questions arise which I may phrase in two ways: I may choose the psychological way and say "does the animal see these two lights as I do, *i.e.*, as two distinct colors, or does he see them as two grays differing in brightness, as does the totally color blind?" Phrased by the behaviorist, it would read as follows: "Is my animal responding upon the basis of the difference in intensity between the two stimuli, or upon the difference in wave-lengths?" He nowhere thinks of the animal's response in terms of his own experiences of colors and grays. He wishes to establish the fact whether wave-length is a factor in that animal's adjustment.[4] If so, what wave-lengths are effective and what differences in wave-length must be maintained in the different regions to afford bases for differential responses? If wave-length is not a factor in adjustment he wishes to know what difference in intensity will serve as a basis for response, and whether that same difference will suffice throughout the spectrum. Furthermore, he wishes to test whether the animal can respond to wave-lengths which do not affect the human eye. He is as much interested in comparing the rat's spectrum with that of the chick as in comparing it with man's. The point of view when the various sets of comparisons are made does not change in the slightest.

However we phrase the question to ourselves, we take our animal after the association has been formed and then introduce certain control experiments which enable us to return answers to the questions just raised. But there is just as keen a desire on our part to test man under the same conditions, and to state the results in both cases in common terms.

The man and the animal should be placed as nearly as possible under the same experimental conditions. Instead of feeding or punishing the human subject, we should ask him to respond by setting a second apparatus until standard and control offered no basis for a differential response. Do I lay myself open to the charge here that I am using introspection? My reply is not at all; that while I might very well feed my human subject for a right choice and punish him for a wrong one and thus produce the response if the subject could give it, there is no need of going to extremes even on the platform I suggest. But be it understood that I am merely using this second method as an abridged behavior method.[5] We can go just as far and reach just as dependable results by the longer method as by the abridged. In many cases the direct and typically human method cannot be safely used. Suppose, for example, that I doubt the accuracy of the setting of the control instrument, in the above experiment, as I am very likely to do if I suspect a defect in vision? It is hopeless for me to get his introspective report. He will say: "There is no difference in sensation, both are reds, identical in quality." But suppose I confront him with the standard and the control and so arrange conditions that he is punished if he responds to the 'control' but not with the standard. I interchange the positions of the standard and the control at will and force him to attempt to differentiate the one from the other. If he can learn to make the adjustment even after a large number of trials it is evident that the two stimuli do afford the basis for differential response.

Such a method may sound nonsensical, but I firmly believe we will have to resort increasingly to just such method where we have reason to distrust the language method.

There is hardly a problem in human visions which is not also a problem in animal vision: I mention the limits of the spectrum, threshold values, absolute and relative, flicker, Talbot's law, Weber's law, field of vision, the Purkinje phenomena, etc. Every one is capable of being worked out by behavior methods. Many of them are being worked out at the present time.

I feel that all the work upon the senses can be consistently carried forward along the lines I have suggested here for vision. Our results will, in the end, give an excellent picture of what each organ stands for in the way of function. The anatomist and the physiologist may take our data and show, on the one hand, the structures which are responsible for these responses, and, on the other, the physio-chemical relations which are necessarily involved (physiological chemistry of nerve and muscle) in these and other reactions.

The situation in regard to the study of memory is hardly different. Nearly all of the memory methods in actual use in the laboratory today yield the type of results I am urging for. A certain series of nonsense syllables or other material is presented to the human subject. What should receive the emphasis are the rapidity of the habit formation, the errors, peculiarities in the form of the curve, the persistence of the habit so formed, the relation of such habits to those formed when more complex material is used, etc. Now such results are taken down with the subject's introspection. The experiments are made for the purpose of discussing the mental machinery[6] involved in learning, in recall, recollection and forgetting, and not for the purpose of seeking the human being's way of shaping his responses to meet the problems in the terribly complex environment into which he is thrown, nor for that of showing the similarities and differences between man's methods and those of other animals.

The situation is somewhat difference when we come to a study of the more complex forms of behavior, such as imagination, judgment, reasoning, and conception. At present the only statements we have of them are in content terms.[7] Our minds have been so warped by the fifty-odd years which have been devoted to the study of states of consciousness that we can envisage these problems only in one way. We should meet the situation squarely and say that we are not able to carry forward investigations along all of these lines by the behavior methods which are in use at the present time. In extenuation I should like to call attention to the paragraph above where I made the point that the introspective method itself has reached a *cul-de-sac* with respect to them. The topics have become so threadbare from much handling that they may well be put away for a time. As our methods become better developed it will be possible to undertake investigations of more and more complex forms of behavior. Problems which are now laid aside will again become imperative, but they can be viewed as they arise from a new angle and in more concrete settings.

Will there be left over in psychology a world of pure psychics, to use Yerkes' term? I confess I do not know. The plans which I most favor for psychology lead practically to the ignoring of consciousness in the sense that that term is used by psychologists today. I have virtually denied that this realm of physics is open to experimental investigation. I don't wish to go further into the problem at present because it leads inevitably over into metaphysics. If you will grant the behaviorist the right to use consciousness in the same way that other natural scientists employ it — that is, without making consciousness a special object of observation — you have granted all that my thesis requires.

In concluding, I suppose I must confess to a deep bias on these questions. I have devoted nearly twelve years to experimentation on animals. It is natural that such a one should drift into a theoretical position which is in harmony with his experimental work. Possibly I have put up a straw man and have been fighting that. There may be no absolute lack of harmony between the position outlined here and that of functional psychology. I am inclined to think, however, that the two positions cannot be easily harmonized. Certainly the position I advocate is weak enough at present and can be attacked from many standpoints. Yet when all this is admitted I still feel that the considerations which I have urged should have a wide influence upon the type of psychology which is to be developed in the future. What we need to do is to start work upon psychology, making *behavior*, not *consciousness*, the objective point of our attack. Certainly there are enough problems in the control of behavior to keep us all working many lifetimes without ever allowing us time to think of consciousness *an sich*. Once launched in the undertaking, we will find ourselves in a short time as far divorced from an introspective psychology as the psychology of the present time is divorced from faculty psychology.

SUMMARY

1. Human psychology has failed to make good its claim as a natural science. Due to the mistaken notion that its fields of facts are conscious phenomena and that introspection is the only direct method of ascertaining these facts, it has enmeshed itself in a series of speculative questions which, while fundamental to its present tenets, are not open to experimental treatment. In the pursuit of answers to these question, it has become further and further divorced from contact with problems which vitally concern human interest.

2. Psychology, as the behaviorist views it, is a purely objective, experimental branch of natural science which needs introspection as little as do the sciences of chemistry and physics. It is granted that the behavior of animals can be investigated

without appeal to consciousness. Heretofore the viewpoint has been that such data have value only in so far a they can be interpreted by analogy in terms of consciousness. The position is taken here that the behavior of man and the behavior of animals must be considered on the same plane; as being equally essential to a general understanding of behavior. It can dispense with consciousness in a psychology sense. The separate observation of 'states of consciousness' is, on this assumption, no more a part of the task of the psychologist than of the physicist. We might call this the return to a non-reflective and naïve use of consciousness. In this sense consciousness may be said to be the instrument or tool with which all scientists work. Whether or not the tool is properly used at present by scientists is a problem for philosophy and not for psychology.

NOTES

1   That is, either directly upon the conscious state of behavior or indirectly upon the conscious state of the experimenter.

2   In this connection I call attention to the controversy now on between the adherents and the opposers of imageless thought. The 'types of reactors' (sensory and motor) were also matters of bitter dispute. The complication experiment was the source of another war of words concerning the accuracy of the opponents' introspection.

3   My colleague, Professor H. C. Warren, by whose advice this article was offered to the Review, believes that the parallelist can avoid the interaction terminology completely by exercising a little care.

4   He would have exactly the same attitude as if he were conducting an experiment to show whether an ant would crawl over a pencil laid across the trail or go around it.

5   I should prefer to look upon this abbreviated method, where the human subject is told in words, for example, to equate two stimuli; or to state in words whether a given stimulus is present or absent, etc., as the *language method* in behavior. It in no way changes the status of experimentation. The method becomes possible merely by virtue of the fact that in the particular case the experiementer and his animal have systems of abbreviations or shorthand behavior signs (language), any one of which may stand for a habit belonging to the repertoire both of the experimenter and his subject. To make the data obtained by the language method virtually the whole of behavior — or to attempt to mould all of the data obtained by other methods in terms of the one which has by all odds the most limited range — is putting the cart before the horse with a vengeance.

6   They are often undertaken apparently for the purpose of making crude pictures of what must or must not go on in the nervous system.

7   There is need of questioning more and more the existence of what psychology calls imagery. Until a few year sago I thought that centrally aroused visual sensations were as clear as those peripherally aroused. I had never accredited myself with any other kind. However, closer examination leads me to deny in my own case the presence of imagery in the Galtonian sense. The whole doctrine of the centrally aroused image is, I believe, at present on a very insecure foundation. Angell as well as Fernald reach the conclusion that an objective determination of image type is impossible. It would be an interesting confirmation of their experimental work if we should find by degrees that we have been mistaken in building up this enormous structure of the centrally aroused sensation (or image).

The hypothesis that all of the so-called 'higher thought' processes go on in terms of faint reinstatements of the original muscular act (including speech here) and that these are integrated into systems which respond in serial order (associative mechanisms) is, I believe, a tenable one. It makes reflective processes as mechanical as habit. The scheme of habit which James long ago described — where each return or afferent current releases the next appropriate motor discharge — is as true for 'thought processes' as for overt muscular acts. Paucity of 'imagery' would be the rule. In other words, wherever there are thought processes that are faint contractions of the systems of musculature involved in the overt exercise of the customary act, and especially in the still finer systems of musculature involved in speech. If this is true, and I do not see how it can be gainsaid, imagery becomes a mental luxury (even if it really exists) without any functional significance whatever. If experimental procedure justifies this hypothesis, we shall have at hand tangible phenomena which may be studied as behavior material. I should say that the day when we can study reflective processes by such methods is about as far off as the day when we can tell by physico-chemical methods the difference in the structure and arrangement of molecules between living protoplasm and inorganic substances. The solutions of both problems await the advent of methods and apparatus.

[After writing this paper I heard the addresses of Professor Thorndike and Angell, at the Cleveland meeting of the American Psychological Association. I hope to have the opportunity to discuss them at another time. I must even here attempt to answer one question raised by Thorndike.

Thorndike casts suspicions upon ideo-motor action. If by ideo-motor action he means just that and would not include sensori-motor action in his general denunciation, I heartily agree with him. I should throw out imagery altogether and attempt to show that practically all natural thought goes on in terms of sensori-motor processes in the larynx (but not in terms of 'imageless thought') which rarely come to consciousness in any person who has not groped for imagery in the psychological laboratory. This easily explains why so many of the well-educated laity know nothing of imagery. I doubt if Thorndike conceives of the matter in this way. He and Woodworth seem to have neglected the speech mechanisms.

It has been shown that improvement in habit comes unconsciously. The first we know of it is when it is achieved — when it becomes an object. I believe that 'consciousness' has just as little to do with *improvement* in thought processes. Since, according to my view, thought processes are really motor habits in the larynx, improvements, short cuts, changes, etc., in these habits are brought about in the same way that such changes are produced in other motor habits. This view carries with it the implication that there are no reflective processes (centrally initiated processes): The individual is always *examining objects*, in the one case objects in the now accepted sense, in the other their substitutes, viz., the movements in the speech musculature. From this it follows that there is not theoretical limitation of the behavior method. There remains, to be sure, the practical difficulty, which may never be overcome, of examining speech movements in the way that general bodily behavior may be examined.]

8

THE FOUNDATION OF S-R
BEHAVIOR THEORY

J.W. Atkinson

"It is believed that a clear formulation, even if later found incorrect, will ultimately lead more quickly and easily to a correct formulation than will a pussyfooting statement which might be more difficult to convict of falsity. The primary task of a science is the early and economical discovery of its basic laws. In the view of the scientifically sophisticated, to make an incorrect guess whose error is easily detected should be no disgrace; scientific discovery is in part a trial-and-error process, and such a process cannot occur without erroneous as well as successful trials. On the other hand, to employ a methodology by which it is impossible readily to detect a mistake once made, or deliberately to hide a possible mistake behind weasel words, philosophical fog, and anthropomorphic prejudice, slows the trial-and-error process, and so retards scientific progress" (Hull, 1943, pp. 398-399).

HULL'S *PRINCIPLES OF BEHAVIOR* (1943)

A quotation taken from the concluding chapter of Hull's major work appears under the heading of this chapter. It conveys his tough-minded attitude as he attempted to elaborate an objective theory of the behavior of organisms. We cannot, of course, do full justice to this imposing theoretical structure in so short a space. We shall have to deal selectively with matters that are most related to the central thread of this introduction to motivation, eliminating many technical

Atkinson, J.W. 1964. *An Introduction to Motivation.* Van Nostrand Reinhold, pp. 161-173. © Van Nostrand Reinhold, 1964.

details and the specifics of Hull's mathematical treatment of the fundamental relationships specified in the theory. Hull's 1943 theory was both a mathematical formulation and an attmpt to encourage the integration of molar behavior theory in psychology with physiology. He fully understood the dilemma faced by students of the social sciences:

> "Students of the social sciences are presented with the dilemma of waiting until the physicochemical problems of neurophysiology have been adequately solved before beginning the elaboration of behavior theory, or of proceeding in a provisional manner with certain reasonably stable principles of the coarse, macroscopic or molar action of the nervous system whereby movements are evoked by stimuli, particularly as related to the history of the individual organism.
>
> "There can hardly be any doubt that a theory of molar behavior founded upon an adequate knowledge of both molecular and molar principles would in general be more satisfactory than one founded upon molar considerations alone. But here again the history of physical science is suggestive. Owing to the fact that Galileo and Newton carried out their molar investigations, the world has had the use of a theory which was in very close approximation to observations at the molar level for nearly three hundred years before the development of the molecular science of modern relativity and quantum theory. Moreover, it is to be remembered that science proceeds by a series of successive approximations; it may very well be that had Newton's system not been worked out when it was there would have been no Einstein and no Planck, no relativity and no quantum theory at all. It is conceivable that the elaboration of a systematic science of behavior at a molar level may aid in the development of an adequate neurophysiology and thus lead in the end to a truly molecular theory of behavior firmly based on physiology" (Hull, 1943, p. 20).

And so, acknowledging the limitations of knowledge but feeling the necessity of getting on with the task, Hull set out to develop the type of theory of molar behavior in terms of intervening variables which Tolman had advocated. But throughout his work, the types of variables considered and the description offered of possible underlying neurophysiological mechanisms reveal Hull's conviction that the constructions of psychologists should always be guided by what seems best evidence or best guess as to the nature of the underlying physical process. The major hypothesis advanced by Hull in this molar behavior theory, and the one which for a good many years diverted attention from the traditional problem of motivation was his physiological hypothesis concerning the nature of reward or reinforcement.

THE BASIC PROBLEM FOR A THEORY OF BEHAVIOR

Hull saw his task within the framework of Darwin's theory of evolution. Living organisms, possessing receptors capable of being stimulated by both an internal and an external environment, and capable of motor response allowing movement through the external environment, are also so constituted that from time to time one or another of the commodities or conditions necessary for individual or species survival (like food or water) are lacking. Hull referred to such a deficiency as a state of *primary need* (Hull, 1943, p. 17). From these considerations, it follows that:

> ...an organism will hardly survive unless the state of organismic need and the state of the environment in its relation to the organism are somehow jointly and simultaneously brought to bear upon the movement-producing mechanism of the organism (Hull, 1943, p. 18).

Unless the appropriate reaction is immediately elicited by the combined action of environmental stimulus (S_e) and organismic need, that is, unless behavior completely adequate to the problem of survival is innate and the need soon satisfied, the organism will perish. But, as a matter of fact, organisms do not perish, or at least sufficiently large numbers have not perished over millions of years. How, then, does this coordination of inner need and environmental stimulation to produce complicated sequences of adaptive behavior come about. It must be learned. But how is it learned? That, in brief, is the basic problem to which Hull directed his attention. He begins at the beginning.

INNATE ENDOWMENT

The first two postulates (basic assumptions) of Hull's theory assert an organism's sensitivity to stimulation and the interaction of neural traces of simultaneously present stimuli. (His critics have charged that he swallowed up the whole psychological problem of perception in these postulates, but that the problem is off the mark of our present interest). In his third formal postulate, Hull assumed that organisms possess, at birth, unlearned tendencies to react to certain stimuli - in other words, reflexes:

> "Organisms at birth possess receptor effector connections ($_sU_R$) which, under combined stimulation (S) and drive (D), have the potentiality of evoking a hierarchy of responses that either individually or in combination are more likely to terminate the need than would be a random selection from the reaction potentials resulting from other stimulus and drive combinations" (Hull, 1943, Postulate 3, p. 66).

Hull assumed that when a condition of biological *need* arose, there would be produced what psychologists of the period had already taken to calling a *drive* which would activate the animal. Drive was to be considered an intervening variable which could be defined as a function of *antecedent* conditions. For example, the amount of food need increases with the number of hours elapsed since last feeding, and drive is a function of the need for food. Hull considered the demonstrations of increased activity in relation to number of hours of food privation, stage of estrous cycle in rats, etc., provided by Richter (1927) and others to be ample evidence of the activating or energizing function of *drive*. But in addition to assuming that need produces drive (i.e., activation of neural structures), Hull also assumed that different states of biological need produce qualitatively different patterns of internal stimulation, the now familiar drive stimulus (S_d). Thus, Hull's organism at birth possessed receptors which could be stimulated by external stimuli, the capacity for movement, the capacity to be activated (driven) by the presence of a biological need, internal receptors which were sensitive to particular need states (S_d), and also a hierarchy of innate response tendencies ($_sU_R$) which might be elicited by particular combinations of environmental stimulus (S_e) and drive stimulus (S_d). This joint elicitation of $_sU_R$ by S_e and S_d increased the probability that the responses originally elicited would be relevant in some way to the particular need which had arisen.

Two Immediate Consequences of a Biological Need

Of particular importance is the assumption that a particular biological need has two immediate consequences: drive (activation) and S_d, as is shown schematically below:

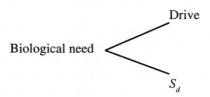

$$\text{Biological need} \quad \bigg\langle \quad \begin{array}{l} \text{Drive} \\[2em] S_d \end{array}$$

The function of a stimulus, whether external (S_e) or internal (S_d) is to elicit or evoke a response that is either innately associated with it ($_sU_R$) or connected to it as a consequence of learning. Thus, even in the first instance of behavior in the life of an organism we must, given this view, attribute selectivity of response, or direction of behavior, to the combined influence of $S_e + S_d$.

Drive, on the other hand, was conceived as a non-directional influence, as a *general exciter* of all responses that are elicited by the stimuli present at a given time. Thus it is the combination of stimulation ($S_e + S_d$) and drive together with the hierarchy of available unlearned dispositions ($_sU_R$) which constitutes the motivation of the very first response in the life of an organism.

Since both drive and an eliciting stimulus are required to initiate action, and drive is produced by biological needs, Hull's position was that biological needs are the ultimate springs of action:

> "The major primary needs or drives are so ubiquitous that they require little more than to be mentioned. They include the need for foods of various sorts (hunger), the need for water (thirst), the need for air, the need to avoid tissue injury (pain), the need to maintain an optimal temperature, the need to defecate, the need to micturate, the need for rest (after protracted exertion), the need for sleep (after protracted wakefulness), and the need for activity (after protracted inaction). The drives concerned with the maintenance of the species are those which lead to sexual intercourse and the need represented by nest building and care of the young" (Hull, 1943, pp. 59-60).

A MISLEADING RESTRICTION IN HULL'S USE OF THE TERM "MOTIVATION"

Hull addressed the problem of motivation, as definition of this problem had evolved, in his search for the combination of factors which together determine the response of an organism. He clearly asserted his fundamental agreement with the principle of contemporaneity which Lewin had urged and acknowledged the plurality of causes of an event: Now, it is assumed that *the immediate causes of an event must be active at the time the event begins to occur* (Hull, 1943, p. 109).

A little later we shall confront the formal principle advanced by Hull in 1943 to account for the immediate strength of a tendency to respond in a certain way in terms of the combined influence of several different variables. Yet almost from the outset in his book *Principles of Behavior*, Hull began to use the term "motivation" as a synonym for drive, one of the immediate determinants of a response, rather than in reference to the combination of influences which together determined the response tendency. For example:

> "In the case of hunger, for example, there must be an equation expressing the degree of drive or motivation as a function of the number of hours' food privation, say, and there must be a second equation expressing the vigor of organismic action as a function of the degree of drive (D) or motivation, combined in some manner with habit strength" (Hull, 1943, notes, p. 66).

He had obviously begun to think of "motivation" as *one kind of determinant* of a response, that is, *drive*, and the connection between stimulus and response referred to as sUr when it was innate and as habit $(_sH_R)$ when it was learned, as *another kind of determinant* of response. His working assumption was:

> "... that motivation (D) as such, whether its origin be food privation, electric shock, or whatever, bears a certain constant relationship to action intensity in combination with other factors, such as habit strength" (Hull, 1943, notes, pp. 66-67).

This usage departs from his own earlier use of the term "motivation" in reference to one problem, "striving for goals" as distinct from another problem, "learning," or "strengthening of connections" (see pp. 156-157), and it certainly departs from traditional use of the term in reference to the problem of the immediate determinants of the direction, vigor, and persistence of action.

Much of the contemporary confusion concerning the meaning of the term "motivation" can be attributed to Hull's identification of the term with *one* of the important explanatory constructs in his own theory, *drive*. Advocates of the Hullian viewpoint have tended to follow Hull's usage, and so for many of them the psychology of "motivation" is now completely identified with the functional properties of the construct, drive (see for example, Brown, 1960). We shall ignore this restrictive use of the term "motivation," for it renders meaningless the question, "How do the theoretical conceptions of motivation advanced by Tolman, Lewin, and Hull differ?" Only in Hull, and, perhaps, in the Freudian concept of "libido" do we find systematic explanatory use of a general energizing concept as one of the immediate determinants of action. We shall refer to *drive* as *one* of the important motivational variables in Hull's 1943 theory. Now we turn to a discussion of another one, *habit*.

THE PRINCIPLE OF PRIMARY REINFORCEMENT

Given the assumption of a hierarchy of innate stimulus-response connections $(_sU_R)$, "the process of learning," in Hull's view, "consists in the strengthening of certain of these connections as contrasted with others, or in the setting up of quite new connections" (Hull, 1943, p. 69). The former is the phenomenon of *selective learning*, to which Thorndike had drawn attention; the latter is the phenomenon of *conditioning*, to which Pavlov had drawn attention. Hull considered both phenomena to be special cases of the operation of the same basic laws, the most important of which was the *principle of primary reinforcement*.

We recall Hull's earlier notion that purposive pursuit of goals could be derived from principles which explain learning, and his earlier assumption that what Thorndike had called a "satisfier" might be called "a reinforcing state of affairs." In 1937, he had identified "reinforcing state of affairs" with the stimulus-response event which normally terminates a behavioral sequence, the goal or consummatory reaction ($S_G \rightarrow G_G$). Now, however, in his formal theory he advocated the view that the "*primary*" reinforcing state of affairs was reduction of biological need. We paraphrase his statement of the principle or "law" of primary reinforcement, eliminating certain neurophysiological details in his statement:

> Whenever a reaction (R) takes place in temporal contiguity with a stimulus (S), and this conjunction is followed closely by the diminution in a need (and the associated diminution in the drive, D, and in the drive stimulus, S_d), there will be an increment in the tendency for that stimulus on subsequent occasions to evoke that reaction (based on Hull, 1943, p. 71).

The increment in tendency for the stimulus on subsequent occasions to evoke the reaction was referred to as an increment in habit strength, and habit strength, or more briefly, *habit*, was designated $_SH_R$.

This principle, when applied to Thorndikian trial and error learning, accounts for the selective strengthening of the correct response (R) to the stimulus situation (S). The correct response is followed by eating and ingestion of food which reduces the need for food. It also accounts for Pavlov's observation that a stimulus like the ticking of a metronome, which originally has no power to elicit salivation, acquires that power when consistently followed by presentation of food and its ingestion by the dog. In this case there is, to begin with, no connection between the metronome (S) and salivary reaction (R), but the new connection is formed when the novel S-R event is closely followed by need reduction. Thus, Hull believed, he had embraced with one explanatory principle the two types of learning phenomena which had previously been treated as essentially different by learning theorists.

If we now imagine a neonate organism, as Hull conceived it, having only a family of reflexes ($_SU_R$) as innate equipment, we get this picture of what happens the very first time it becomes hungry. The first time the biological need for food occurs, the need produces *drive* and a distinctive internal pattern of stimuli, the drive stimulus, S_d. The momentary external stimulus situation (S_e), whatever it is, and the drive stimulus (S_d) jointly select one and then another unlearned response ($_SU_R$) according to the hierarchy of their initial (innate) strengths. The combined influence of *drive*, general exciter of responses, and the immediate stimulus situation $S_e + S_d$ accounts for the initiation and vigor of the various responses. If one of these — for example, a turn of the head, is quickly followed by the mother's breast in the mouth and reflexive sucking and swallowing, the connection between $S_e + S_d$ and that particular response (R) will be selectively strengthened. But so also will the primitive "consummatory" or "goal" reaction (R_G) of sucking and swallowing be *conditioned* to the S_d produced by the need and removed when the need is reduced. In principle, then, the first instance of hunger is conceived as producing behavior that is in no sense influenced or guided by an anticipation of the goal, no matter how vague, unless it were to be assumed that the S_d of hunger innately elicited some vestigial form of consummatory reaction, r_g. But by the repeated action of primary reinforcement (i.e., need-reduction) during the first days and weeks of life, the new habit defined by the connection between S_d and $r_g ({_{sd}H_{rg}})$ should soon be greatly strengthened allowing r_g-s_g soon to begin to play the important guiding and integrative roles assigned to it by Hull in his earlier analysis of purposive behavior.

Hull did not discuss this particular problem in his 1943 statement of the theory. He put off until later a formal discussion of the important role of the anticipatory goal reaction. Had he dealt with this implication of his theory in 1943, he might have anticipatd some of the difficulties that forced him later to revise his view of the immediate determinants of a response.

SECONDARY REINFORCEMENT

Hull was quick to recognize "that a great deal of behavior takes place in relatively protracted sequences in which primary reinforcement normally occurs only after the final act" (Hull, 1943, p. 84). Evidence had shown that reinforcement must follow soon after a particular *S-R* event to be effective. "Consequently," he asserted, "direct or primary reinforcement, as such, is inadequate to account for a very great deal of learning" (Hull, 1943, p. 84).

Consider how long it must take for food to be digested and thus repair the tissue deficit called hunger or need for food. Fortunately, experiments performed in Pavlov's laboratory had provided some evidence upon which could be based a principle to resolve this problem. Frolov had first presented food to a dog immediately after the sounding of a ticking metronome, producing the usual conditioned salivary response to the ticking metronome on subsequent occasions. Following this, the dog was presented with the stimulus of a black square in his line of vision. Initially, the black square had no effect on the dog's behavior, but then the black square was presented and followed, after an interval of 15 seconds, by the ticking of a metronome for 30 seconds, *no food being given*. On the tenth presentation of the black square by itself for 25 seconds, a total of 5.5 drops of saliva were secreted. This meant that the sound of the metronome, a stimulus which had earlier been associated with the ingestion of food, had acquired the capacity to act as a reinforcing agent itself. Hull referred to this as *secondary reinforcement*.

Hull cited other similar evidence that stimuli which have in the past been closely and consistently followed by primary reinforcement take on the capacity to serve as reinforcing states of affairs. Bugelski (1938) had trained two comparable groups of rats to press a bar which activated a mechanism that dropped a food pellet in a cup immediately before them in an apparatus invented by B. F. Skinner and often called the "Skinner Box." After the animals had learned to press the lever for food, this behavior was extinguished in both groups by adjusting the apparatus so that pressing the bar would no longer yield a food pellet. In one group, however, the bar press continued to produce the customary clicking noise of the food-release mechanism. In the other group, the mechanism was arranged so that a bar press would not produce a clicking noise during extinction trials. Bugelski found that the animals for whom the clicking noise followed a bar press, though no food was forthcoming, produced about 30 per cent more responses before reaching extinction of that response than the animals in the other group for whom a bar press produced neither the clicking noise nor the food. Hull considered this convincing evidence that a stimulus (the magazine click) which had been closely and consistently associated with receipt of food could contribute to the maintenance of another S-R connection, bar press.

Also cited by Hull were observations made by Cowles (1937) in studies of chimpanzees. Cowles had trained chimpanzees to insert colored discs into a slot machine which delivered a raisin for each disc and had observed that after this training the chimps would retain, hoard, and work for discs as if they had attained the status of subgoals. When given the task of learning which of five small boxes contained a token, Cowles found that performance compared favorably with performance when a food reward was employed. In one comparison, where the chance frequency of a correct response was 20 per cent, the average score of two chimps was 74 per cent for food tokens and 93 per cent for food reward.

In similar experiments, Wolfe (1936) had noted that both food and food tokens elicited anticipatory lip-smacking activity in chimpanzees, but a different kind of token that had not been associated with receipt of food did not. Hull was willing to leave open the question of the nature of secondary reinforcement in 1943. He considered the possibility that to reinforce another S-R connection a secondary reinforcing stimulus might have to elicit some component of the consummatory reaction or might itself have to be conditioned to the primary reinforcing state of affairs (i.e., diminution of need). But, as already stated, these matters which called for full discussion of the role of the anticipatory goal reaction were put aside for later treatment. Suffice to say that Hull broadened his principle of reinforcement to embrace the wider learning potentialities inherent in *secondary reinforcement*. Again, we paraphrase his statement:

Whenever a reaction (R) occurs in temporal contiguity with a stimulus (S) and this conjunction is closely followed in time with the diminution of need (and drive and drive stimulus, S_d) or with a stimulus situation which has been closely and consistently associated with such a need diminution, there will result an increment to the tendency for that stimulus to evoke that reaction (based on Hull, 1943, p. 98).

Experimental evidence shows that a stimulus loses its capacity to serve as a secondary reinforcement if not consistently followed by a primary reinforcing state of affairs. Grindley (1929) placed young chickens at the end of a runway and grains of boiled rice at the other end. He measured the speed of running on subsequent trials and found that chickens allowed to eat the rice showed a typical increase in speed of running on successive trials. However, chickens allowed only to look at the grains of rice through a glass plate showed an increase in speed on initial trials followed by a gradual reduction typical of extinction. From this experiment it appeared that the visual stimulus of the rice grains lost the power of secondary reinforcement as it lost the power of evoking the reaction (eating) conditioned to it at the time it had acquired its power of secondary reinforcement.

Hull considered the possibility that even the apparent reinforcing power of so-called goal or consummatory reactions should be conceived as instances of secondary reinforcement derived from frequent and consistent association of these particular reactions with the ultimate, primary reinforcing state of affairs:

> "Since the various receptor discharges associated with the eating of food, its swallowing, digestion, and absorption, have throughout the entire life of each organism been associated in a uniform and practically invariable sequence with ultimate need reduction, it is to be expected that the stimuli associated with mastication would have acquired a profound degree of secondary reinforcing power" (Hull, 1943, note, p. 99).

Speculations of this sort, which agree in principle with earlier views of Freud and Tolman concerning the ultimate aims or ends of behavior, greatly stimulated research having to do with the underlying physiological nature of the process of reinforcement. But this question, while one of fundamental interest and importance to physiological psychology, need not be answered to study systematically the functional properties and behavioral implications of objectively defined reinforcing states of affairs. The latter problem is of fundamental significance in contemporary efforts to develop an *ahistorical* and *aphysiological* mathematical conception of the motivation of behavior.

THE DETERMINANTS OF HABIT STRENGTH

Having developed his concept of drive, produced by biological need, as the general activator of response tendencies, Hull then identified four determinants of the strength of connection between a stimulus and response which he called *habit* ($_sH_R$). Strength of *habit* ($_sH_R$) was to be treated as a variable which together with *drive* intervenes between observable stimulus and observable response in the determination of present behavior.

On the observable response side, strength of habit could be indirectly measured in terms of the probability of response (given the appropriate stimulus), the speed or latency of the response (given the appropriate stimulus), and the resistance of the response to extinction when the normal reinforcing state of affairs was eliminated. That is to say, when both the stimulating circumstances and the strength of drive are held constant, an increase in the strength of habit can be inferred from an increase in probability of response, a decrease in the latency of response (i.e., the time between onset of stimulus and response), an increase in the magnitude of reaction, and increased resistance to extinction (i.e., trials to extinction) when reinforcement of that response is withheld.

Hull turned to experimental evidence which appeared, at the time, to justify the conclusion that the following four factors in the antecedent history of the organism determined the strength of habit:

1. The *contiguity of the stimulus and response during training*;

2. The closeness of the *S-R* event to a reinforcing state of affairs, which is referred to as *delay of reinforcement*;

3. The *number of reinforcements*; and

4. The *magnitude of reinforcement* during training.

In reference to the selective learning exhibited by Thorndike's dogs, Hull attributed the strength of habit of making the correct response to get out of the puzzle box to the degree of temporal contiguity between the stimuli of the box and the performance of the correct response, the relative absence of delay in attaining the food reward after performance of the correct response, the number of trials on which performance of that response in the presence of the stimuli of the box had been reinforced, and the magnitude of the reinforcement, which Hull identified with the magnitude of the reward offered the animals to reduce the need for food.

Hull's fourth basic postulate, which we paraphrase to avoid mathematical details, concerned the gradual growth of habit strength as a function of thse four antecedents:

> Whenever a response (*R*) and a stimulus (*S*) occur in close temporal contiguity, and this conjunction is closely associated with the

diminution of a need or with a stimulus which has been closely and consistently associated with the diminution of a need, there will result an increment to a tendency for that stimulus on later occasions to evoke that reaction. The increments from successive reinforcement summate in a manner which yields a combined habit strength $(_SH_R)$ which is a simple positive growth function of the number of reinforcements. The upper limit of this curve of learning is in turn a function of the magnitude of need reduction which is involved in primary, or which is associated with secondary, reinforcement; the delay of reinforcement; and the degree of contiguity between the stimulus and response (based on Hull, 1943, p. 178).

It was Hull's view that the amount of growth in habit strength on any single reinforced trial was a constant fraction of the growth potentiality still to be realized. Hence, variables which defined the upper limit of habit strength would influence the amount of increase in habit strength on any single reinforced trial.

In connection with amount of reward (or magnitude of reinforcement) as a determinant of habit strength, Hull presented evidence from a study by Gantt (1938), which is presented in Figure 6.2, showing that the amount of saliva produced by dogs in a salivary conditioning experiment depends upon the amount of reinforcing agent (food) used during training. Similar evidence of the positive effect of amount of reward on performance in a selective learning situation was presented. Grindley (1929-1930) had measured the speed with which chickens traversed a four-foot runway to food reward at the end of training when the number of grains of boiled rice present during each trial of training differed.

Hull was later to change his position regarding amount of reward and the problem with which we are already familiar in Tolman's work as the problem of incentive. In 1943, however, he had this to say about it:

"Motivation has two aspects, (1) that of drive (D, or S_d) characteristic of primary needs, and (2) that of incentive. The amount-of-reinforcement hypothesis is closely related to the second of these aspects. The concept of incentive in behavior theory corresponds roughly to the common-sense notion of reward. More technically, the incentive is that substance or commodity in the environment which satisfies a need, i.e., which reduces a drive" (Hull, 1943, p. 131).

He then went on to argue that if amount of reward defines the magnitude of reinforcement of a habit, all other things equal, the visual stimulus arising from a large piece of food or a large number of pieces of food (i.e., a large reward) should become more strongly conditioned to the reaction of approach than the visual stimulus produced by a smaller piece of food or fewer pieces of food (i.e., a small reward). Thus, when a food reward of a certain magnitude is visibly present, as in the original Thorndike experiments,

"...given a normal hunger drive, the organism will execute the correct one of several acts originally evoked by the situation more promptly, more vigorously, more certainly, and more persistently when a large amount of food is stimulating its receptors than when they are stimulated by a small amount" (Hull, 1943, p. 132).

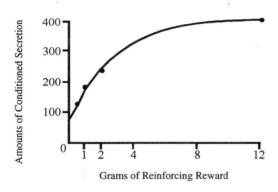

Figure 6.2 Graphic representation of the empirical functional relationship between the amount of the reinforcing agent (food) employed at each reinforcement of four conditioned reactions to as many different stimuli, and the final mean amount of salivary secretion evoked by each stimulus at the time of training. The appreciable secretional value of 75 units when the fitted curve is extrapolated to where the amount of reinforcing agent equals zero is presumably due to secretion evoked by static stimuli arising from the experimental environment. Plotted from unpublished data from the dog "Billy" kindly furnished by Gantt (1938) and published with his permission. The experimental work upon which this graph is based was performed prior to 1936. (From Hull, Principles of Behavior, copyright 1943, Appleton-Century-Crofts, Inc., p. 125)

Hull summarized the view that his hypothesis concerning the amount of reward encompassed one aspect of the problem of motivation as follows:

"From the amount-of-reinforcement hypothesis may be derived a special case of one phase of motivation, that of incentive or secondary motivation. This is the situation where the incentive (reinforcing agent) contributes a prominent, direct component of the stimulus complex which is conditioned to the act being reinforced. The stimulus component arising from a large amount of this substance will be different from that arising from a small amount, and will differ still more from a stimulus situation containing a zero amount. It follows from this and the amount-of-reinforcement hypothesis that in the course of reinforcement by differing amounts of the reinforcing agent, the organism will inevitably build up stronger reaction tendencies to the stimulus arising from large amounts than to that from small amounts, and no habit strength at all will be generated by zero amounts. It thus comes about, primary motivation (e.g., hunger) remaining constant, that large amounts of the agent will evoke more rapid, more vigorous, more persistent, and more certain reactions than will small or zero amounts. Thus a reinforcing agent as a stimulus becomes an incentive to action, and large amounts of the agent become more of an incentive than small amounts. This *a priori* expectation is well substantiated by quantitative experiment as well as by general observation" (Hull, 1943, p. 133).

STIMULUS GENERALIZATION

A fifth basic assumption of Hull's theory takes account of the fact that very rarely, if ever, is exactly the same stimulus situation repeated in the life of an organism. It posits the functional equivalence of stimuli, which though not identical, are very similar. In brief, the assumption of *stimulus generalization* means that when a particular *S-R* is reinforced, the reaction becomes associated with a considerable range of stimuli which, in terms of one or another qualitative or quantitative dimension, are *similar* to the stimulus present when reinforcement occurred. Thus if one considers a response which has been conditioned to a white stimulus, it should be elicited on some subsequent occasion by a light gray stimulus and to a lesser extent by a darker shade of gray. Hull then introduced the concept of effective habit strength, ${}_s\overline{H}_R$, to stand for the strength of habit elicited by a particular stimulus situation. Effective habit strength diminishes as the degree of similarity between the stimulus at the time of reinforcement (i.e., during training) and the stimulus at the time of subsequent elicitation of response decreases.

If we consider Thorndike's dogs put into the same problem box on subsequent trials, the principle of stimulus generalization accounts for the tendency of the dogs to perform the correct response sooner in successive rewarded trials even though the visual stimulus of the interior of the box, to which the animal is responding, may vary slightly from trial to trial depending upon the animal's location, the brightness of the room, etc. The concept of stimulus generalization accounts for transfer of training from one learning situation to other similar situations. The phenomena is illustrated in results obtained by Hovland (1937) to which Hull referred in stating the principle of stimulus generalization. (See Figure 6.3.)

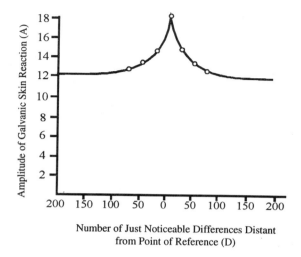

Figure 6.3 Empirical generalization gradient of conditioned galvanic skin reaction derived from data published by Hovland (1937). Note that the gradient extends in both directions on the stimulus continuum (vibration rate) from the point originally conditioned. (From Hull, Principles of Behavior, copyright 1943, Appleton-Century-Crofts, Inc., p. 185)

DRIVE AND HABIT AS INTERVENING VARIABLES

It is apparent that Hull viewed *drive* and *habit* as variables which were hidden from the view of the external observer, within the organism, which together determined the impetus to respond in a given situation. The presence and strength of each of these variables was to be inferred from antecedent observations and their behavioral consequences. He sought to specify with great precision the relationship between observable antecedents and the strength of each of the intervening variables *drive* and *habit*. And he advanced a principle which states, explicitly, how they combine to influence jointly the strength of the tendency to act in a certain way at a particular time. This is the conceptual problem of motivation which Tolman and Lewin, in particular, had given so much emphasis and the problem which Hull, himself, had begun to consider in his own earlier treatment of the purposive characteristics of behavior in terms of the combined action of S_e, S_d, and r_g-s_g, the anticipatory goal reaction.

DRIVE AND HABIT AS DETERMINANTS OF REACTION POTENTIAL

Hull began a chapter entitled "Primary Motivation and Reaction Potential" with these introductory remarks:

"It may be recalled that when the problem of primary reinforcement was under consideration ... the matter of organic need played a critical part in that the reduction of the need constituted the essential element in the process whereby the reaction was conditioned to new stimuli. We must now note that the state of an organism's needs also plays an important role in the causal determination of which of the many habits possessed by an organism shall function at a given moment. It is a matter of common observation that, as a rule, when an organism is in need of food only those acts appropriate to the securing of food will be evoked, whereas when it is in need of water, only those acts appropriate to the securing of water will be evoked, when a sexual hormone is dominant only those acts appropriate to reproductive activity will be evoked, and so on. Moreover, the extent or intensity of the need determines in large measure the vigor and persistence of the activity in question.

"By common usage the initiation of learned, or habitual, patterns of movement or behavior is called *motivation*. The evocation of action in relation to secondary reinforcing stimuli or *incentives* will be called *secondary motivation*; a brief discussion of incentives was given above ... in connection with the general subject of amount of reinforcement. The evocation of action in relation to primary needs will be called *primary motivation*; this is the subject of the present chapter" (Hull, 1943, p. 226).

Hull turned to empirical studies by Perin (1942) and Williams (1938) for evidence of "the functional dependence of the persistence of food-seeking behavior jointly on (1) the number of reinforcements of the habit in question, and (2) the number of hours of food privation" (Hull, 1943, pp. 226-227). Holding constant the other factors which influence the strength of habit, these investigators had provided results which might be considered a demonstration of how habit (defined in terms of number of reinforcements) and drive (defined in terms of hours of food privation) combine to influence the strength of the impetus to respond in a certain way. They had trained animals to press a bar in the Skinner apparatus, giving separate groups of albino rats different numbers of reinforcements varying from 5 to 90 under 23 hours of food privation. Then, after this training, the food reward was eliminated, and the bar press response was subjected to experimental extinction with the amount of food privation during extinction trials varying from 3 to 22 hours in different groups of rats. The number of unreinforced reactions performed by each group of rats, until there came a five-minute pause between successive presses of the bar, was employed as the measure of resistance to extinction.

Figure 6.4 shows how "persistence of food-seeking behavior" was related to a number of hours of food privation (strength of drive) during extinction when the number of reinforced trials (habit) was held constant at 16 for all groups. (These data may be compared with those of Tolman *et al.* concerning effect of "drive" on selectivity and speed in maze performance.)

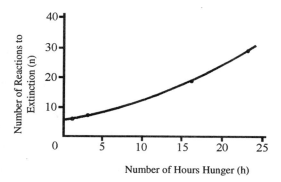

Number of Hours Hunger (h)

Figure 6.4 Graphic representation of the data showing the systematic relationship between the resistance to experimental extinction (circles) and the number of hours' food privation where the number of reinforcements is constant at 16. The smooth curve drawn through the sequence of circles represents the slightly positively accelerated function fitted to them. This function is believed to hold only up to the number of hours of hunger employed in the original habit formation process: in the present case, 23. (From Hull, Principles of Behavior, copyright 1943, Appleton-Century-Crofts, Inc., p. 228; adapted from Perin, 1942, p. 104)

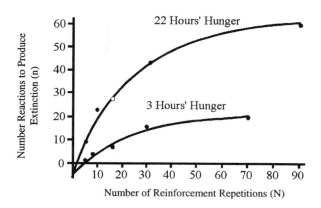

Number of Reinforcement Repetitions (N)

Figure 6.5 Combined effect of Drive and Habit (number of reinforcement repetitions) on performance (resistance to extinction) (From Hull, Principles of Behavior, copyright 1943, Appleton-Century-Crofts, Inc., p. 228; adapted from Perin, 1942, p. 101)

Even more instructive is the evidence obtained by Perin of the joint effect of *drive* and *habit* on "persistence of food-seeking." This is shown in Figure 6.5. When the number of reinforced trials is low, and hence inferred habit strength is weak, the level of performance during extinction trials is a little higher in the strong-drive group (22 hours' privation) than in the weak-drive group (3 hours' privation). However, when the number of reinforced trials is high, and hence inferred habit strength is strong, the performance level of the strong-drive group is substantially higher than that of the weak-drive group. Neither habit alone nor drive alone determines the strength of the "reaction tendency" which is expressed in the number of bar presses to extinction in this experiment. Instead it is possible to infer from Figure 6.5 that *drive and habit combine multiplicatively* to determine the strength of the "reaction tendency," which Hull then formally designated *reaction potential* and represented symbolically as $_sE_R$:

> "This multiplicative relationship is one of the greatest importance, because it is upon $_sE_R$ that the amount of action in its various forms presumably depends. It is clear, for example, that it is quite impossible to predict the vigor or persistence of a given type of action from a knowledge of either habit strength or drive strength alone; this can be predicted only from a knowledge of the product of the particular functions of $_sH_R$ and D respectively; in fact, this product constitutes the value which we are representing by the symbol $_sE_R$" (Hull, 1943, pp. 239-240).

Thus, finally, we come to see how Hull conceived the immediate determinants of action in the form of a mathematical equation relating drive and habit to the impetus to respond, which he called reaction potential — $_sE_R = f(_sH_R) \times f(d)$.

It is instructive to consider his conjectures concerning the underlying physiological process described by this important equation. Although the mathematical statement which relates objectively defined drive and habit strength to reaction potential does not depend upon Hull's physiological interpretation, and should be evaluated as a conception of the process of motivation quite aside from the validity of his guesses as to the nature of the physiological process, we enhance our understanding of his viewpoint by considering the picture he had in mind of the underlying physiological process of motivation in his discussion of "primary motivation":

> "Most, if not all, primary needs appear to generate and throw into the blood stream more or less characteristic chemical substances, or else to withdraw a characteristic substance. These substances (or their absence) have a selective physiological effect on more or less restricted and characteristic portions of the body (e.g., the so-called "hunger" contraction of the digestive tract) which serves to activate resident receptors. This receptor activation constitutes the drive stimulus, S_d.... In the case of tissue injury this sequence seems to be reversed; here the energy producing the injury is the drive stimulus, and its action causes the release into the blood of adrenal secretion which appears to be the physiological motivating substance.

"It seems likely, on the basis of various analogies, that, other things equal, the intensity of the drive stimulus would be some form of negatively accelerated increasing function of the concentration of the drive substance in the blood. However, for the sake of expository simplicity we shall assume in the present preliminary analysis that it is an increasing linear function.

"The afferent discharges arising from the drive stimulus (S_D) become conditioned to reactions just the same as any other elements in stimulus compounds, except that they may be somewhat more potent in acquiring habit loadings than most stimulus elements or aggregates. Thus the drive stimulus may play a role in a conditioned stimulus compound substantially the same as that of any other stimulus element or aggregate.... As a stimulus, S_D naturally manifests both qualitative and intensity primary stimulus generalization in common with other stimulus elements or aggregates in conditioned stimulus compounds....

"It appears probable that when blood which contains certain chemical substances thrown into it as the result of states of need, or which lacks certain substances as the result of other states of need, bathes the neural structures which constitute the anatomical bases of habit ($_SH_R$), the conductivity of these structures is augmented through lowered resistance either in the central neural tissue or at the effector end of the connection, or both. The latter type of action is equivalent, of course, to a lowering of the reaction threshold and would presumably facilitate reaction to neural impulses reaching the effector from any source whatever. As Beach [1942] suggests, it is likely that the selective action of drives on particular effector organs in non-learned forms of behavior acts mainly in this manner. It must be noted at once, however, that sensitizing a habit structure does not mean that this alone is sufficient to evoke reaction, any more than that caffeine or benzedrine alone will evoke reaction. Sensitization merely gives the relevant neural tissue, upon the occurrence of an adequate set of receptor discharges, an augmented facility in routing these impulses to the reactions previously conditioned to them or connected by native (inherited) growth processes. This implies to a certain extent the undifferentiated nature of drive in general, contained in Freud's concept of the "libido." However, it definitely does not presuppose the special dominance of any one drive, such as sex, over the other drives.

"While all drives seem to be alike in their powers of sensitizing *acquired* receptor-effector connections, their capacity to call forth within the body of the organism characteristic and presumably distinctive drive stimuli gives each a considerable measure of distinctiveness and specificity in the determination of action which, in case of necessity, may be sharpened by the process of patterning ... to almost any extent that the reaction situation requires for adequate and consistent reinforcement. In this respect, the action of drive substances differs sharply from that of a pseudo-drive substance such as caffeine, which appears to produce nothing corresponding to a drive stimulus.

"Little is known concerning the exact quantitative functional relationship of drive intensity to the conditions or circumstances which produce it, such as number of hours of hunger or the concentration of endocrine secretions in the blood. Judging from the work of Warden and associates [1934], the relationship of the hunger drive up to two or three days of food privation would be a negatively accelerated increasing function of time, though a study by Skinner [see Figure 6.6] suggests that it may be nearly linear up to about five days. For the sake of simplicity in the present explorational analysis we shall assume the latter as a first approximation.

"Physiological conditions of need, through their sensitizing action on the neural mediating structures lying between the receptors and the effectors ($_sH_R$), appear to combine with the latter to evoke reactions according to a multiplicative principle, i.e., reaction-evocation potentiality [or more simply, *reaction potential*] is the product of a function of habit strength multiplied by a function of the strength of drive:
$_sE_R = f(_sH_R) \times f(D)$ (Hull, 1943, pp. 240-242).

Hull stated the relationship of drive and drive stimulus formally in his sixth postulate, as follows:

"Associated with every drive (*D*) is a characteristic drive stimulus (*S_D*) whose intensity is an increasing monotonic function of the drive in question" (Hull, 1943, p. 253).

The principle of motivation was stated formally as the seventh postulate in Hull's 1943 theory:

"Any effective habit strength ($_s\bar{H}_R$) is sensitized into reaction potentiality ($_sE_R$) by all primary drives active within an organism at a given time, the magnitude of this potentiality being a product obtained by multiplying an increasing function of $_sH_R$ by an increasing function of *D*" (Hull, 1943, p. 253).

The major corollary of these two principles was that the strength of reaction potential ($_sE_R$) attributed to the effective habit strength ($S_e + S_DH_R$) and a particular condition of primary drive (*D*) would also be influenced by the presence of other "irrelevant" sources of drive. The aggregate strength of all sources of primary

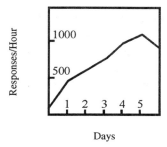

Days

Figure 6.6 Graph showing the relationship of the action potentiality as a function of the length of food privation following satiation. First note the fact that there is an appreciable amount of action potentiality at the beginning of this graph, where the amount of food privation is zero. Next, observe that the curve is relatively high at one day of food privation, which was the degree of drive under which the original training occurred. Finally, note that the rise in action potentiality is fairly continuous up to about five days, after which it falls rather sharply. This fall is evidently due to exhaustion, as the animals died soon after. (From Heron and Skinner, 1937)

drive active at the time is what Hull intended to represent as the strength of drive (D) in his equation $_sE_R = f(_sH_R) \times f(D)$. Thus hunger, thirst, and sexual need, all present at the same time, are expected—given this conception—to produce heightened excitability of whatever habits are evoked by the immediate stimulating circumstances, whether those habits are relevant or irrelevant to the ultimate satisfaction of any one of those primary need states.

While this certainly is the main implication of drive, conceived as a non-directive or non-selective activator, Hull believed that the drive stimulus (S_D), operating as part of the stimulus complex $S_e + S_D$ at any time, would account for the elicitation of habits likely to be instrumental in reducing the dominant need at the time. In this connection he reported the results of earlier experiments by himself (Hull, 1933) and Leeper (1935) which demonstrated that animals are capable of a discriminative reaction depending upon which of two drives, hunger or thirst, is dominant at the time.

In Hull's experiment, rats were run from the same starting box in a maze containing two paths, one to the left and the other to the right, both leading to the same goal box. On some days the animals were run when satiated for water but with 23 hours' food privation. On other days they would be satiated for food but under 23 hours' water privation. When the "hunger" condition prevailed, the reward was food and accessible only by taking the right entrance to the goal box; when the "thirst" condition prevailed, the reward was water and accessible only by taking the left entrance to the goalbox. The learning was slow, but the animals did learn to react discriminatively depending upon which drive stimulus, S_H or S_T, was dominant at the time.

In the Leeper experiment, there were two distinct goal boxes, one always containing food and the other always containing water. Under these conditions, the animals learned to react discriminatively in terms of the dominant drive much more quickly. Both experiments seemed to Hull to substantiate the view that animals are capable of differential reactions to identical external environmental situations (the starting box) on the basis of distinct drives.

The main thing to understand about Hull's 1943 principle of motivation of action is that *it posits the joint multiplicative influence of a non-specific or non-directive variable called drive and a specific or directive, associative variable called habit.* The direction of behavior is attributed to the action of the stimulus aggregate, $S_e + S_D$. The probability, vigor, and persistence of a particular response is attributed to the product of drive and habit and is called *reaction potential* ($_SE_R$). Reaction potential is the construct in Hull's theory which most nearly corresponds to what Lewin had conceived as a Psychological Force ($f_{P'G}$). Later, we shall compare in more detail various conceptions of the determinants of the strength of the tendency to act in a certain way.

INHIBITION AND EFFECTIVE REACTIVE POTENTIAL

What happens during experimental extinction of a response? That is, what happens when the combination of drive and habit produces an impetus to respond ($_SE_R$) and the response occurs but is not followed by a reinforcing state of affairs? We know that after a number of extinction trials, the response no longer occurs. But why does the response extinguish? Is the habit strength reduced? Is the drive reduced in some way? These are the questions that lead Hull to essentially a motivational explanation of experimental extinction.

Hull's view was, in brief, "that each response evocation produces in the organism a certain increment of a fatigue-like substance or condition which constitutes a need for rest" (Hull, 1943, p. 391). The need for rest, called *reactive inhibition* (I_R) because it "has the capacity directly to inhibit the power of S to evoke R" (*ibid.*, p. 391) is a function of the energy expenditure or amount of work involved in performance of the response. This fatigue-producing substance would be expected to accumulate during a series of non-reinforced trials and therefore produce experimental extinction. And rest would provide the condition needed for fatigue to dissipate, allowing subsequent *spontaneous recovery* of the response. (See page 119.) But since I_R constitutes a need, the cessation of activity would initiate the need-reduction or reinforcing process, thus strengthening the habit of not responding, which Hull called *conditioned inhibition* and symbolized $_SI_R$. Thus, at any particular time, there would exist a *total inhibition* (I_R) consisting of the summation of I_R (temporary state of fatigue) and $_SI_R$ (the habit of not responding).

Hull assumed that this total inhibition (I_R) worked to reduce the effective strength of the reaction potential. He assumed, specifically,

> "...that the reaction potential actually available for reaction evocation, i.e., the *effective* [italics added] reaction potential $(_S\bar{E}_R,...)$, is what remains of the reaction potential $(_SE_R)$ after the subtraction of the total inhibition, I_R; *i.e.*, $_S\bar{E}_R = {_SE_R} - I_R$" (Hull, 1943, p. 392).

Among the important implications of these assumptions concerning the effect of a non-rewarded trial is the general hypothesis that:

> "...other things equal, organisms receiving the same reinforcement following two responses which require different energy expenditures will, as practice continues, gradually come to choose the less laborious response. This is the 'law of less work'" (Hull, 1943, p. 392).

Tolman had posited a "demand" for short paths and least effort in his attempt to take account of essentially the same behavioral phenomena which Hull considered under the topic of inhibition.

THE OSCILLATION OF EFFECTIVE REACTION POTENTIAL

Several further assumptions were made by Hull concerning the link between *effective reaction potential* $(_S\bar{E}_R)$ and observable measurements of the probability, latency, magnitude, and resistance to extinction of a response. He assumed that the full value of $_S\bar{E}_R$ was rarely realized in the evocation of action because of a little understood physiological process which had the power to neutralize reaction potentials more or less from moment to moment. He assumed that this *oscillatory process* worked in a random manner to depress reaction potentials more or less from moment to moment and that the magnitude of its action on different reaction potentials at a given instant was uncorrelated. Thus, at a given moment, the *"momentary reaction potential"* $(_S\dot{\bar{E}}_R)$ of the weaker of two tendencies might actually exceed that of the stronger tendency, but this state of affairs would be less probable than the other way around.

THE REACTION THRESHOLD AND RESPONSE EVOCATION

Hull also assumed that there was a *reaction threshold* which must be superseded by the momentary effective reaction potential $(_S\dot{\bar{E}}_R)$ for action to occur. He conceived the reaction threshold as "the minimal amount of momentary effective reaction potential ($_s\bar{E}_R$) which is necessary to mediate reaction evocation when the situation is uncomplicated by competing reaction potentials..." (Hull, 1943, p. 394).

In this simple case of a single momentary reaction potential, Hull assumed that it must exceed the reaction threshold for the reaction to occur and that the extent to which the effective reaction potential exceeded the threshold would determine the probability, latency, magnitude, and resistance to extinction of a response.

When, however, tendencies to perform more than one response exceeded the threshold at the same time, the situation was more complicated. Hull's assumption, as stated in the final postulate of the 1943 theory was:

> "When the reaction potentials ($_sE_R$) to two or more incompatible reactions (R) occur in an organism at the same time, only the reaction whose momentary effective reaction potential ($_s\bar{E}_R$) is greatest will be evoked" (Hull, 1943, Postulate 16, p, 344).

These further assumptions concerning inhibition, oscillation of effective reaction potentials, the reaction threshold, and resolution of conflict among competing tendencies, which we have briefly reviewed, illustrate that there is more to a theoretical conception of the motivation of behavior than merely an articulate conception of the determinants of the tendency to act in a certain way.

Our discussion has emphasized Hull's conception of the determinants of *reaction potential* (i.e., $_sE_R = f(_sH_R) \times f(D)$) because, historically, one of the major conceptual issues in reference to the problem of motivation has been the question of whether or not anticipation of the goal of action is one of the immediate determinants of action. In Hull's essays of the 1930's, it appeared that he had taken the position that the guidance and integrative functions traditionally assigned to "the idea of the end" could be represented as an anticipatory goal reaction which functioned as a pure stimulus act in the determination of behavior. But, as we have now seen, that conception is missing in the initial formal statement of this theory which attributes the impetus to act to a multiplicative combination of a nonspecific excitement called *drive* and the specific associative variable called *habit*.

9

MOTIVATION RECONSIDERED: THE CONCEPT OF COMPETENCE

Robert W. White

When parallel trends can be observed in realms as far apart as animal behavior and psychoanalytic ego psychology, there is reason to suppose that we are witnessing a significant evolution of ideas. In these two realms, as in psychology as a whole, there is evidence of deepening discontent with theories of motivation based upon drives. Despite great differences in the language and concepts used to express this discontent, the theme is everywhere the same: Something important is left out when we make drives the operating forces in animal and human behavior.

The chief theories against which the discontent is directed are those of Hull and of Freud. In their respective realms, drive-reduction theory and psychoanalytic instinct theory, which are basically very much alike, have acquired a considerable air of orthodoxy. Both views have an appealing simplicity, and both have been argued long enough so that their main outlines are generally known. In decided contrast is the position of those who are not satisfied with drives and instincts. They are numerous, and they have developed many pointed criticisms, but what they have to say has not thus far lent itself to a clear and inclusive conceptualization. Apparently there is an enduring difficulty in making these contributions fall into shape.

In this paper I shall attempt a conceptualization which gathers up some of the important things left out by drive theory. To give the concept a name I have chosen the word *competence*, which is intended in a broad biological sense rather than in its narrow everyday meaning. As used here, competence will refer to an organism's capacity to interact effectively with its environment. In organisms capable of but little learning, this capacity might be considered an innate attribute, but in the

White, R.W. 1959. Motivation Reconsidered: The Concept of Competence. *Psychological Review, 66*, pp. 297-333.

mammals and especially man, with their highly plastic nervous systems, fitness to interact with the environment is slowly attained through prolonged feats of learning. In view of the directedness and persistence of the behavior that leads to these feats of learning, I consider it necessary to treat competence as having a motivational aspect, and my central argument will be that the motivation needed to attain competence cannot be wholly derived from sources of energy currently conceptualized as drives or instincts. We need a different kind of motivational idea to account fully for the fact that man and the higher mammals develop a competence in dealing with the environment which they certainly do not have at birth and certainly do not arrive at simply through maturation. Such an idea, I believe, is essential for any biologically sound view of human nature.

As a first step, I shall briefly examine the relevant trends of thought in several areas of psychology. From this it will become clear that the ideas advanced in this paper have already been stated, in one way or another, by workers in animal behavior, child development, cognitive psychology, psychoanalytic ego psychology, and the psychology of personality. If there is novelty in this essay, it lies in putting together pieces which are not in themselves new. They already lie before us on the table, and perhaps by looking once more we can see how to fit them into a larger conceptual picture.

THE TREND IN ANIMAL PSYCHOLOGY

One of the most obvious features of animal behavior is the tendency to explore the environment. Cats are reputedly killed by curiosity, dogs characteristically make a thorough search of their surroundings, and monkeys and chimpanzees have always impressed observers as being ceaseless investigators. Even Pavlov, whose theory of behavior was one of Spartan simplicity, could not do without an investigatory or orientating reflex. Early workers with the obstruction method, such as Dashiell (1925) and Nissen (1930), reported that rats would cross an electrified grid simply for the privilege of exploring new territory. Some theorists reasoned that activity of this kind was always in the service of hunger, thirst, sex, or some other organic need, but this view was at least shaken by the latent learning experiments, which showed that animals learned about their surroundings even when their major needs had been purposely sated. Shortly before 1950 there was a wave of renewed interest not only in exploratory behavior but also in the possibility that activity and manipulation might have to be assigned the status of independent motives.

Exploratory Behavior

In 1953 Butler reported an experiment in which monkeys learned a discrimination problem when the only reward was the opening of a window which permitted them to look out upon the normal comings and goings of the entrance room to the laboratory. The discriminations thus formed proved to be resistant to extinction. In a later study, Butler and Harlow (1957) showed that monkeys could build up a series of four different discriminations solely for the sake of inspecting the entrance room. Butler concluded that "monkeys — and presumably all primates — have a strong motive toward visual exploration of their environment and that learning may be established on the basis of this motive just as it may be established on the basis of any motive that regularly and reliably elicits responses." Montgomery, in 1954, reported a study with rats in which the animals, their major organic needs satiated, learned to avoid the short arm of a Y maze and to take the path which led them into additional maze territory suitable for exploration. Similar findings have been described by Myers and Miller (1954), whose rats learned to press a bar for the sake of poking their heads into a new compartment and sniffing around. Zimbardo and Miller (1958) enlarged upon this study by varying the amount of novelty in the two compartments. In their report "the hypothesis advanced is that opportunity to explore a 'novel' environment or to effect a stimulus change in the environment is the reinforcing agent."

These experiments make a strong case for an independent exploratory motive. The nature of this motive can be more fully discerned in situations in which the animals are allowed a varied repertory of behavior. In 1950 Berlyne published a searching paper on curiosity, a theme which he further developed in subsequent years (1955, 1957, 1958). The rats in his experiments were confronted with an unfamiliar space and later with various novel objects placed in it. Approaching, sniffing, and examining were readily elicited by each novelty, were fairly rapidly extinguished, but were restored nearly to original strength when a fresh novelty was added. Exploration on the part of chimpanzees has been studied by Welker (1956), who put various pairs of objects before the animals and observed the course of their interest. The objects were often first approached in a gingerly manner, with signs of uneasiness, then examined and handled quite fully, then discarded. Introducing a new pair of objects promptly reproduced the whole sequence, just as it did with the rats in Berlyne's experiments. Welker used pairs of objects to find out whether or not the chimpanzees would have common preferences. Bigness and brightness evoked more interest, and greater time was spent upon objects which could be moved, changed, or made to emit sounds and light.

Recent reviews by Butler (1958) and Cofer (1959) show that a great deal of similar work is going on in animal laboratories, generally with similar results.

Exploration as a Drive

The designers of these experiments have favoured the idea that exploration should be listed as an independent primary drive. In all cases the experimental plan calls for the elimination of other primary drives by satiation. It is recognized, however, that a confirmed advocate of orthodoxy might bring up two objections to the proposed enlargement of the list of primary drives. He might claim that exploratory behavior could be explained as a consequence of secondary reinforcement, or he might contend that it is reinforced by reduction of anxiety.

The first argument meets an immediate difficulty in Butler's finding that discriminations learned on the basis of visual exploration are resistant to extinction. When reinforcement of primary drive never takes place in the experimental situation, it is to be expected that secondary reinforcement will not prevent extinction (Miller, 1951). But even in those cases where extinction is rapid, as it was with Berlyne's rats and Welker's chimpanzees, serious problems are raised by the quick recovery of exploratory behavior when a novel stimulus is introduced (Berlyne, 1950). In order to sustain the idea that secondary reinforcement accounts for this fact, we should have to suppose that primary rewards have often been connected with the exploration of novelties. It would have to be assumed, for instance, that the securing of food by young animals occurred with considerable frequency in connection with the investigation of novel objects. This image may seem to fit mature animals who search the environment for their food, but it certainly cannot apply to young mammals before they are weaned. Here the learning process can do virtually nothing to reinforce an interest in novelties. Gratification comes from following the same old cues to the same old consummatory responses, and the animal whose attention strays to some novel variation of the breast will only find himself frustrated. One can say that the whole mammalian pattern of infancy works in the opposite direction. The mother is more active than the young in providing gratifications, and the babies must be pursued and retrieved if they stray from the scene of her ministry. However one looks at it, the hypothesis of secondary reinforcement seems to me to demand improbable assumptions about the relationship in the lives of young animals between exploration and primary need gratification.

The hypothesis that exploratory behavior is related to fear and receives its reinforcement from the reduction of anxiety is at first glance considerably more plausible. It seems justified by the observation that Welker's chimpanzees showed uneasiness on first contact with novel objects, and it fits the behavior of rats in a new maze, as reported by Whiting and Mowrer (1943), where initial terror gave place to an exploration so feverish that the food reward was not eaten. Montgomery and Monkman (1955) have undertaken to challenge this hypothesis by a direct experimental attack. They showed that fear induced in rats before entering a novel situation did not increase exploratory behavior, and that fear induced within the novel situation decreased exploration to an extent correlated with the intensity of the fear. They find it more reasonable to suppose that fear and exploration are conflicting forms of behavior, and this view can also be defended on purely logical grounds. Fear shows itself in either freezing or avoidance, whereas exploration is clearly an instance of approach. There is hardly a more perfect example of conflict between incompatible responses than that of an animal hesitating between investigation and flight. It is clear that exploration can sometimes serve to reduce anxiety, but the proposition that it comes into existence only for this purpose cannot be so easily accepted.

What assumptions have to be made to support the thesis that exploration is motivated by anxiety reduction? It has to be assumed that certain characteristic stimuli arouse anxiety and that exploration of these stimuli is then found to reduce the anxiety. If the characteristics in question are those of novelty and unfamiliarity, we must heed Berlyne's reminder that for the infant all experience is novel and unfamiliar. Berlyne (1950) proposes that the exploratory reaction "may be one that *all* stimuli originally evoke, but which disappears (becomes habituated) as the organism becomes familiar with them." But if all stimuli at first arouse anxious tension, we would have to deduce that all response would consist of avoidance in the interest of reducing that tension. Approaching a stimulus and taking steps to increase its impact could not occur. An exploratory tendency must be there in the first place before it can achieve the function of reducing anxiety. As Woodworth (1958) expresses it, "if there were no exploratory drive to balance and overbalance the fear drive, an animal would be helpless in a novel situation." I find it hard to believe that creatures so liberally endowed with fear could ever achieve a working mastery of the environment if they were impelled toward it only by the pressure of organic needs.

Both hypotheses thus far examined — secondary reinforcement and anxiety reduction — require us to make improbable assumptions. There remains the possibility that exploration should simply be added to the list of primary drives and otherwise treated in orthodox fashion. Myers and Miller (1954) suggest that this is the appropriate course, provided the new drive shows the same functional properties as those already known. "If an exploratory tendency can produce learning like other drives such as hunger, and also show a similar pattern of satiation and recovery, these functional parallels to already known drives would help to justify its classification in the same category." Logically the problem can be dealt with in this way, but we must consider very carefully what happens to the category of drive if we admit this new applicant to membership.

Using hunger as the chief model, the orthodox conception of drive involves the following characteristics: (*a*) there is a tissue need or deficit external to the nervous system which acts upon that system as a strong persisting stimulus (*b*) this promotes activity which is terminated by a consummatory response with consequent reduction of need; (*c*) the reduction of need brings about the learning which gradually shapes behavior into an economical pursuit of suitable goal objects. In this scheme the tension of an aroused drive is interpreted as unpleasant, at least in the sense that the animal acts in such a way as to lower the drive and becomes quiescent when it is lowered. There are probably no living champions of so simple an orthodoxy, yet the scheme remains pervasive, and it is therefore worth while to observe that the proposed exploratory drive hardly fits it at all.

In the first place, the exploratory drive appears to bear no relation whatever to a tissue need or deficit external to the nervous system. It is, of course, clearly related to certain characteristics of stimulation from the external environment, a source of motivation which Harlow (1953) would like to see restored to a serious place in contemporary psychology; but it certainly cannot be correlated with a visceral need comparable to hunger, thirst, or sex. Considering the pattern of satiation and recovery shown by Welker's chimpanzees, Woodworth (1958) remarks that "what becomes satiated is not the exploratory tendency in general, but the exploring of a particular place or object." It is possible, as Hebb (1955) has pointed out, that the so-called "reticular activation system" in the brain stem creates a kind of general drive state, and this mechanism might indeed be flexibly responsive to changes in sensory stimulation. This interesting suggestion, however, is still a far cry from viscerogenic drives; it commits us instead to the novel idea of a neurogenic motive, one in which the state of the nervous system and the patterns of external stimulation conspire to produce motivated behavior. There is even a good deal of trouble in supposing that the adequate stimuli for exploration are either strong or persistent. Novelty certainly cannot be equated with strength of persistence, and animals seem readily able to disregard the stimuli to exploration when they are weary.

In the second place, exploratory behavior cannot be regarded as leading to any kind of consummatory response. It is usual for the animal's investigation to subside gradually. If the animal at some point turns away and leaves the once novel object we may say that its curiosity is "satisfied," but we do not mean by this that the equivalent of a consummatory response has just taken place. The sequence suggests rather that curiosity wears out and slowly falls to a level where it no longer guides behavior, at least until a fresh novelty comes into view.

Finally, in the case of exploratory behavior there is real difficulty in identifying reinforcement with need reduction. Montgomery (1954), describing the learning of the Y maze, points out that the short arm, essentially a dead end, would tend to reduce the exploratory drive, whereas the long arm, itself a complex maze, would increase it — but the long arm is chosen. If the long arm functions as a reinforcing agent, "the mechanism underlying this reinforcement is an *increase*, rather than a decrease, in the strength of the exploratory drive." In this experiment, as in their natural habitat, animals do not wait to have novelty thrust upon them, nor do they avoid situations in which novelty may be found. Such behavior can be most readily conceptualized by admitting that under certain circumstances reinforcement can be correlated with an increase in arousal or excitement rather than a decrease. A drive which has no consummatory climax seems almost to require this formulation. It is distinctly implausible to connect reinforcement with the waning of an agreeable interest in the environment or with a general progress from zestful alertness to boredom.

If we admit exploration to the category of drive we are thus committing ourselves to believe that drives need have no extraneural sources in tissue deficits or visceral tensions, that they are not necessarily activated by strong or persistent stimuli, that they do not require consummatory responses, and that drive increase can sometimes be a mechanism of reinforcement.

Activity and Manipulation

Exploration is not the only motive proposed by critics of drive orthodoxy, and novelty is not the only characteristic of the environment which appears to incite motivated behavior. Some workers have suggested a need for activity, which can be strengthened by depriving animals of their normal opportunities for movement. Kagan and Berkun (1954) used running in an activity wheel as the reward for learning and found it "an adequate reinforcement for the instrumental response of bar pressing." Hill (1956) showed that rats will run in an activity wheel to an extent that is correlated with their previous degree of confinement. It is certain that the activity wheel offers no novelty to the animals in these experiments. Nevertheless, they seem to want to run, and they continue to run for such long times that no part of the behavior can readily be singled out as a consummatory response. Perhaps an unpleasant internal state created by inactivity is gradually worked off, but this is certainly accomplished by a tremendous increase of kinaesthetic stimulation and muscular output which would seem to imply increased excitation in the system as a whole.

Harlow and his associates (Harlow, 1953; Harlow, Harlow, & Meyer, 1950) maintain that there is also a manipulative drive. It is aroused by certain patterns of external stimulation and reduced by actively changing the external pattern. The experiments were done with rhesus monkeys, and they involve the solving of a mechanical problem which, however, leads to no further consequences or rewards. The task might be, for instance, to raise a hasp which is kept in place by both a hook and a pin; all that can be accomplished is to raise the hasp, which opens nothing and leads to no fresh discoveries. When the hasp problem is simply installed in the living cages, the monkeys return to it and solve it as many as 7 or 8 times over several days. It seems unlikely that novelty can be postulated as the essential characteristic of the stimulus which evokes this repeated behavior. The simplest interpretation is rather that value lies for the animal in the opportunity, as Zimbardo and Miller (1958) express it, "to effect a stimulus change in the environment." This formulation suggests something like the propensities toward mastery or power that have often been mentioned in discussions of human motivation.

The addition of activity and manipulation to the list of primary drives can only make more serious the difficulties for the othodox model that resulted from admitting exploration. But recent research with animals has put the orthodox model on the defensive even on its home grounds. It has become increasingly clear that hunger, thirst, and sex cannot be made to fit the simple pattern that seemed so helpful 40 years ago.

Changing Conceptions of Drive

In a brief historical statement, Morgan (1957) has pointed out that the conception of drive as a noxious stimulus began to lose its popularity among research workers shortly after 1940. "On the whole," he says, "the stimulus concept of drive owed more to wishful thinking than to experimental fact." When technical advances in biochemistry and brain physiology made it possible to bring in an array of new facts, there was a rapid shift toward the view that "drives arise largely through the internal environment acting on the central nervous system." One of the most influential discoveries was that animals have as many as a dozen specific hungers for particular kinds of food, instead of the single hunger demanded by Cannon's model of the hunger drive. If an animal's diet becomes deficient in some important element such as salt, sugar, or the vitamin-B complex, foods containing the missing element will be eagerly sought while other foods are passed by, a selectivity that obviously cannot be laid to contractions of the stomach. Similarly, a negative food preference can be produced by loading either the stomach or the blood stream with some single element of the normal diet. The early work of Beach (1942) on sexual behavior brought out similar complications in what had for a time been taken as a relatively simple drive. Hormone levels appeared to be considerably more important than peripheral stimulation in the arousal and maintenance of the sex drive. Further work led Beach (1951) to conclude that sexual behavior is "governed by a complex combination of processes." He points out that the patterns of control differ tremendously from one species to another and that within a single species the mechanisms may be quite different for males and females. Like hunger, the sex drive turns out to be no simple thing.

New methods of destroying and of stimulating brain centers in animals have had an equally disastrous effect on the orthodox drive model. The nervous system, and especially the hypothalamus, appears to be deeply implicated in the motivational process. Experimental findings on hypothalamic lesions in animals encourage Stellar (1954) to believe that there are different centers "responsible for the control of different kinds of basic motivation," and that in each case "there is one main excitatory center and one inhibitory center which operates to depress the activity of the excitatory center." As research findings accumulate, this picture may seem to be too cleanly drawn. Concerning sexual behavior, for example, Rosvold (1959) concludes a recent review by rejecting the idea of a single center in the cerebrum; rather, the sex drive "probably has a wide neural representation with a complex interaction between old and new brain structures and between neural and humoral agents." Nevertheless, Miller's (1958) careful work seems to leave little doubt that motivated behavior in every way similar to normal hunger and normal pain-fear can be elicited by electrical stimulation of quite restricted areas of the hypothalamus. It is clear that we cannot regress to a model of drives that represents the energy as coming from outside the nervous system. Whatever the effects of peripheral stimulation may be, drives also involve neural centers and neural patterns as well as internal biochemical conditions.

What sort of model becomes necessary to entertain these newly discovered facts? In 1938 Lashley expressed the view that motivation should not be equated with disturbance of organic equilibrium but rather with a "partial excitation of a very specific sensorimotor mechanism irradiating to affect other systems of reaction." Beach (1942) postulated that there must be in the nervous stystem "a condition analogous to Sherrington's central exicitatory state." Morgan, in 1943, undertook to capture the facts in a systematic theory which seems to have been well sustained by subsequent research (Morgan, 1957). He distinguished two types of process which he called *humoral motive factors* and *central motive states.* The humoral factors consist of chemical or hormonal constituents of the blood and lymph, and they are conceived to influence behavior chiefly by a direct sensitizing action on neural centers. The central motive states have several properties: They are partly self-maintaining through neural circuits, they tend to increase the organism's general activity, they evoke specific forms of behavior not strongly controlled by the environment, and they prime or prepare consummatory responses which will occur when adequate stimulation is found. This is a far cry from the orthodox model, but we must nowadays admit that the orthodox model is a far cry from the facts.

In view of this radical evolution of the concept of drive, it is not surprising to find the drive reduction hypothesis in serious difficulties. The earlier identification of reinforcement with drive reduction has been directly attacked in a series of experiments designed to show that learning takes place when drive reduction is ruled out.

In 1950 Sheffield and Roby showed that instrumental learning would take place in hungry rats when the reward consisted not of a nutritive substance but of sweet-tasting saccharine in the drinking water. This finding appeared to be "at variance with the molar principle of reinforcement used by Hull, which identifies primary reinforcement with 'need reduction.'" The authors naturally do not question the vital importance of need reduction, but they point out that need-reducing events may accomplish reinforcement through a mechanism more direct and speedy than the reduction of the need itself. They think that "stimulation and performance of a consummatory response appears to be more important to instrumental learning — in a primary, not acquired, way — than the drive satisfaction which the response normally achieves." Their findings are in line with an earlier experiment with chickens by Wolfe and Kaplon (1941), who used different sizes of food pellets so that the number of pecks and the amount of food received could be thrown out of their usual close connection. The chickens, we might say, would rather peck than eat; learning was more strongly reinforced when four pecks were necessary than when one peck was enough to take the same amount of food.

The substitution of the consummatory response for need reduction as the immediate reinforcing mechanism is a step in advance, but it soon turns out that another step is required. Can it be shown that an aroused need which does not reach consummation has a reinforcing effect? To test this possibility Sheffield, Wulff, and Backer (1951) provided male rats with the reward of copulating with a female, but not enough times to produce ejaculation. This reward was favorable to instrumental learning even though there was no need reduction and no performance of the final consummatory act. The results were supported by Kagan (1955), whose animals showed substantial learning under the same conditions, though learning was still faster when ejaculation was permitted. Sheffield, Roby, and Campbell (1954) have proposed a *drive-induction* theory according to which the property of reinforcement is assigned to the excitement of an aroused drive. We have already seen that some such assumption is essential if exploration is to be assigned to the status of a drive. Here it can be added that the whole theory of pregenital sexuality involves motivation without consummatory acts and without any but the most gradual need reduction. And as a final blow to the orthodox hypothesis comes the finding by Olds and Milner (1954) that positive reinforcement can be brought about by direct electrical stimulation of certain areas of the brain. Once again we learn that neural centers are deeply implicated in the plot of motivation. The simple mechanics of need reduction cannot possibly serve as the basis for a theory of learning.

Twenty years of research have thus pretty much destroyed the orthodox drive model. It is no longer appropriate to consider that drives originate solely in tissue deficits external to the nervous system, that consummatory acts are a universal feature and goal of motivated behavior, or that the alleviation of tissue deficits is the necessary condition for instrumental learning. Instead we have a complex picture in which humoral factors and neural centers occupy a prominent position; in which, moreover, the concept of neurogenic motives without consummatory ends appears to be entirely legitimate. Do these changes remove the obstacles to placing exploration, activity, and manipulation in the category of drives?

Perhaps this is no more than a question of words, but I should prefer at this point to call it a problem in conceptual strategy. I shall propose that these three new "drives" have much in common and that it is useful to bring them under the single heading of competence. Even with the loosening and broadening of the concept of drive, they are still in important respects different from hunger, thirst, and sex. In hunger and thirst, tissue deficits, humoral factors, and consummatory responses retain an important position. The mature sex drive depends heavily on hormonal levels and is sharply oriented toward consummation. Tendencies like exploration do not share these characteristics, whatever else they have in common with the better known drives. It is in order to emphasize their intrinsic peculiarities, to get them considered in their own right without a cloud of surplus meanings, that I prefer in this essay to speak of the urge that makes for competence simply as motivation rather than as drive.

THE TREND IN PSYCHOANALYTIC EGO PSYCHOLOGY

Rather an abrupt change of climate may be experienced as we turn from the animal laboratory to the psychoanalytic treatment room, but the trends of thought in the two realms turn out to be remarkably alike. Here the orthodox view of motivation is to be found in Freud's theory of the instincts — they might be known to us as drives if an early translator had been more literal with the German *Trieb*.

Freud's Theories of Instinct and Ego

In his final work, Freud (1949) described instincts as "somatic demands upon mental life" and as "the ultimate cause of all activity." He wrote further:

> It is possible to distinguish an indeterminate number of instincts and in common practice this is in fact done. For us, however, the important question arises whether we may not be able to derive all of these instincts from a few fundamental ones... After long doubts and vacillations we have decided to assume the existence of only two basic instincts, Eros and the *destructive instinct* (Freud, 1949, p. 20).

The history of Freud's long doubts and vacillations has been lucidly related by Bibring (1941). Up to 1914 Freud used a two-fold classification of sexual instincts and ego instincts. The ego instincts made their appearance in his case histories in a somewhat moral character, being held responsible for the disastrous repression of sexual needs, but in systematic usage they were conceived as serving the goal of self-preservation, and hunger was generally taken as an appropriate model. In 1914, when he evolved the concept of narcissism and saw that it threatened to blur the line between sexual and ego tendencies, Freud (1925b) still expressed himself as unwilling to abandon an idea which followed the popular distinction of love and hunger and which reflected man's dual existence "as reproducer and as one who serves his own ends." Various facts, particularly those of sadism and masochism, served to overcome his reluctance, so that he finally united self-preservation and preservation of the species under the heading of Eros or life instincts, establishing destructiveness or the death instinct as the great antagonist in a profound biological sense (Freud, 1948). This highly speculative step proved to be too much for some of his otherwise loyal followers, and the earlier orthodoxy did not become entirely extinct.

It is easier to follow Freud's reasoning when we bear in mind the simultaneous development of his ideas about the mental apparatus. Bibring (1941) points out that even in his early thinking a sharp contrast was always drawn between instinct and mental apparatus. Instinct supplied the energy in the form of powerful, persisting internal stimuli; the apparatus guided it into channels which produced organized behavior and eventually put a stop to the persisting stimulation. In 1915 Freud wrote:

> The nervous system is an apparatus having the function of abolishing stimuli which reach it or of reducing excitation to the lowest possible level; an apparatus which would even, if this were feasible, maintain itself in an altogether unstimulated condition.... The task of the nervous system is — broadly speaking — to master stimuli (Freud, 1925c, p. 63).

During the next decade there was a considerable growth in his ideas about the mental apparatus, culminating in the well known division into id, ego and superego. The activities of the ego now received much fuller recognition. Freud (1927) assigned to it "the task of self-preservation," which it accomplished through its several capacities of perception, memory, flight, defense, and adaptive action. One can see Freud's thought moving from a mechanical analogy — an engine and its fuel — toward a much more adaptational conception of the mental apparatus. Ego instincts did not wholly disappear, but the decline in their systematic importance was compensated by the insight that self-preservative tendencies were to some extent built into the whole living system. It is significant that as he took this course he came to question the earlier tension-reduction theory. In the last year of his life he declared it to be probable "that what is felt as pleasure or unpleasure is not the absolute degree of the tensions but something in the rhythm of their changes" (Freud, 1949).

Freud's tendency to revise his thinking makes it difficult to pin down an orthodox doctrine, but most workers will probably agree that his main emphasis was upon somatically based drives, a mental apparatus which received its power from the drives, and, of course, the multitude of ways in which the apparatus controlled, disguised, and transformed these energies. His treatment of the ego was far from complete, and it was not long before voices were raised against the conception that so vital and versatile a part of the personality could be developed solely by libidinal and aggressive energies.

An Instinct to Master

In 1942 Hendrick proposed that this difficulty be met by assuming the existence of an additional major instinct. "The development of ability to master a segment of the environment," he wrote, and the need to exercise such functions, can be conceptualized as "an instinct to master," further characterized as "an inborn drive to do and to learn how to do." The aim of this instinct is "pleasure in exercising a function successfully, regardless of its sensual value." The simpler manifestations are learning to suck, to manipulate, to walk, to speak, to comprehend and to reason; these functions and others eventually become integrated as the ego. "The central nervous system is more than a utility," Hendrick declared. The infant shows an immediate desire to use and perfect each function as it ripens, and the adult secures gratification from an executive function efficiently performed regardless of its service to other instincts.

Hendrick's procedure in this and two supporting papers (1943a, 1943b) is quite similar to that of the animal psychologists who propose listing exploration as an additional primary drive. The instinct to master has an aim — to exercise and develop the ego functions — and it follows hedonic principles by yielding "primary pleasure" when efficient action "enables the individual to control and alter his environment." It is to this extent analogous to the instincts assumed by Freud. But just as an exploratory drive seemed radically to alter the whole conception of drive, so the instinct to master implied a drastic change in the psychoanalytic idea of instinct. Critics were quick to point out that Freud had always conceived of instincts as having somatic sources external to the ego apparatus, a condition not met by the proposed instinct to master. There was nothing comparable to erogenous zones, to orgasm, or to the sequence of painful tension followed by pleasurable release. Mastery, the critics agreed, could not be an instinct, whatever else it might be.

It is of interest that Fenichel (1945), who definitely rejected Hendrick's proposal, gives us another close parallel to the animal work by attributing mastering behavior to anxiety-reduction. He argued that mastery is "a general aim of every organism but not of a specific instinct." He agreed that there is "a pleasure of enjoying one's abilities," but he related this pleasure to cessation of the anxiety connected with not being able to do things. "Functional pleasure," he wrote, "is pleasure in the fact that the exercise of a function is now possible without anxiety," and he contended that when anxiety is no longer present, when there is full confidence that a given situation can be met, then action is no longer accompanied by functional pleasure. We must certainly agree with Fenichel that anxiety *can* play the part he assigns it, but the proposal that all pleasure in ego functions comes from this source raises the same difficulties we have already considered in connection with exploratory behavior. That we exercise our capacities and explore our surroundings only to reduce our fear of the environment is not, as

I have already argued, an assumption that enjoys high probability on biological grounds.

Hartmann on the Ego

A less radical change in the orthodox model is proposed by Hartmann, who, in a series of papers since 1939, often in conjunction with Kris and Loewenstein, has been refining and expanding Freud's views on the ego and the instincts. While the ego is conceived as a "substructure" of the personality, this term is somewhat metaphorical because in practice the ego has to be defined by its functions. The list of functions, which includes grasping, crawling, walking, perceiving, remembering, language, thinking, and intention, covers much the same ground that was indicated by Hendrick, but Hartmann does not attribute their growth to an instinct. On the other hand, Hartmann (1950) early came to the conclusion that development could not be explained, as Freud had seemed to conceive it, simply as a consequence of conflict between instinctual needs and frustrating realities. The instincts alone would never guarantee survival; they require mediation by the innate ego apparatus if they are to meet "the average expectable environmental conditions." He therefore proposed that we conceive of an autonomous factor in ego development, an independent maturation of functions taking place in a "conflict-free ego sphere." Functions such as locomotion ripen through maturation and through learning even when they are not caught up in struggles to obtain erotic and aggressive gratification or to avoid anxiety. As Anna Freud (1952) has pointed out, walking becomes independent of instinctual upheavals a few weeks after its beginning; thereafter, it serves the child impartially in situations of conflict and those that are free from conflict.

Hartmann's idea of autonomous ego development has of course been assumed all along by workers in child psychology, but it is an important step to relate it to Freud's disclosures concerning unconscious motivation. In what now looks like an excess of enthusiasm for his own concepts, Freud (1925a) undertook to explain the outgrowing of the pleasure principle and the substituting of the reality principle as a simple and direct consequence of the frustration of instinctual needs. However, the reality principle contained the idea of postponing an immediate gratification in favour of a future one, and Hartmann (1956) properly notes that the capacities for postponement and anticipation cannot be conjured into existence simply by the collision of frustrating reality and ungratified need. Important as frustrations may be, these capacities must already be available, "some preparedness for dealing with reality" must already exist, before the frustration can produce its momentous educative effect. It can be seen from this example that Hartmann's analysis opens the way for profitable commerce between developmental psychologies inside and outside of psychoanalysis.

Hartmann's emphasis on adaptation permits him to perceive much more that is autonomous about the ego than was ever seriously included in Freud's systematic thought. He allows, for instance, that aims and interests which develop in the beginning as defenses against instincts may later become part of conflict-free spheres of activity — become interests in their own right — and thus achieve "secondary autonomy," a concept very close to Allport's (1937) functional autonomy of motives (Hartmann, 1950). He deals with the possibility that adaptive skills developing in the conflict-free sphere may have a decisive influence on the handling of conflicts. These skills have a history of their own, shaped jointly by the child's abilities and by the responses evoked from parents. As Monroe (1955) has expressed it, they have "a very important role in the development of the conscious and semi-conscious psychological self." They may thus have a direct influence upon the outcome when a child becomes involved in conflict. Rapaport (1958) sees Hartmann's ideas on the autonomy of the ego as vital to the proper understanding not only of healthy development but also of psychopathology itself.

In explaining the autonomous growth of the ego, Hartmann makes generous use of the concept of maturation, but he naturally does not exclude learning. Hartmann (1950) entertains the possibility, mentioned casually from time to time by Freud (1916, 1949), that ego functions are supplied with their own sources of energy independent of instincts, and that there is pleasure connected with their mere exercise. However, he makes little systematic use of this idea, relying instead upon a concept more central in Freud's thinking, that of the neutralization of drive energies. Freud (1927) found that he could "make no headway" in accounting for the varied activities of the ego without assuming "a displaceable energy, which is in itself neutral, but is able to join forces either with an erotic or with a destructive impulse, differing qualitatively as they do, and augment its total cathexis." He speculated that the neutral energy came from Eros and could be conceived as desexualized libido. Hartmann, Kris, and Loewenstein (1949) carried the idea forward a logical step by proposing that the energies of aggressive instincts could similarly be neutralized and placed at the disposal of the ego. Neutralized energy contributes to the development of the ego and makes possible a continuing interest in the objects of the environment regardless of their immediate relation to erotic or aggressive needs. Hartmann (1955) finds this concept particularly helpful in unscrambling the confusions that have arisen over the concept of sublimation.

The doctrine of neutralized instinctual energies is a curious one, and we should bear in mind the complex clinical findings that perhaps suggested it. Freud was an unquestioned genius in detecting the subtle operation of erotic urges and aggressive fantasies, along with elaborate mechanisms of defense, behind the seemingly objective or "neutral" activities of everyday life. Remarkable transformations of interest could sometimes be observed in the course of development. For example, a patient's childhood erotic rivalry and aggressive competition with his father might later disappear beneath a strong objective interest in running the family business; then suddenly, on the brink of success, this interest might come to a total halt, paralyzed by anxiety because the underlying instinctual goals came too close to symbolic fulfilment. The reappearance of instinctual preoccupations in such a case lends a certain color to the idea that they have somehow been driving the behavior all the time, even though the daily pursuit of business goals seems utterly remote from instinctual gratifications.

It is worth noticing that Freud's procedure in making the assumption of neutralized instinctual energy is similar to the one followed by orthodox behaviorists in connection with primary drives. These theorists started from the assumption that all behavior was powered by a limited number of organic drives, and then, in order to protect this assumption, they developed further hypotheses, such as secondary reinforcement, to account for motivated behavior that bore no obvious relation to primary goals. At the point where he could "make no headway" without postulating neutralization, Freud could conceivably have made a good deal of headway if he had been willing to assume that neutral energy, neither sexual nor aggressive, was available as a natural endowment in the first place. But he preferred to protect his assumption of two primary drives and to interpret other energies as transformations of these drives. Even so, the concept seems superfluous if we take Freud at his word about the nature of the life instincts. Freud (1949) made it clear that Eros included more than instincts having a sexual aim; its larger goal was "to establish even greater unities and to preserve them thus — in short, to bind together." Under this formula, it would seem possible to include energies inherently directed toward building up the integrated functions of the ego. But Freud did not exploit the full range of his theory of Eros and proposed only that neutral energies should be conceived as desexualized.

The concept of neutralization has in some respects had a good effect on psychoanalytic ego psychology. In Hartmann's writings, as we have seen, and in Rapaport's (1951, 1954) work on thinking, it has encouraged a strong interest in autonomous ego functions and a fresh analysis of their place in personality. Nevertheless, it seems to me an awkward conceptualization, on which in the end is likely to lead, as Colby (1955) has expressed it, to a "metapsychological snarl." The theory requires that instinctual energies can completely change their aims, which makes one wonder what purpose was served in the first place by defining them as having aims. It preserves an image of mobility of energies that seems much out of line with recent research on animal motivation, where energy is being conceived in a constantly closer relation to specific structures. To my mind it thus compares unfavorably with its quite straightforward alternative, which is that the alleged neutralized energies are there in the first place as part of the natural make-up of an adaptive organism. I shall later develop this possibility by means of the concept of competence in its motivational aspect, and I believe that this concept gains support from certain other lines of work in the psychoanalytic tradition.

Motility and a Sense of Industry

The trend away from instinct orthodoxy is illustrated by the work of Kardiner (1947) on what he calls "the development of the effective ego." Kardiner's reflections arose from his work on the traumatic neuroses of war. In these disorders the main threat is to self-preservation, and some of the most important symptoms, such as defensive rituals and paralyses, are lodged in the action systems that normally bring about successful adaptive behavior. It thus becomes pertinent to study the growth of action systems, to discover how they become integrated so as to maintain "controlled contact" with the environment and "controlled exploitation of objects in the outer world," and to work out the conditions which either favor or disrupt this acquired integration. Thinking along these lines, Kardiner is led to conclusions just about the opposite of Freud's: It is the successful and gratifying experiences, not the frustrations, that lead to increasingly integrated action and to the discrimination of self from outer world. Frustration produces chiefly disruptions and inhibitions which are unfavourable to the early growth of the ego. Children are gratified when they discover the connection between a movement executed and the accompanying and subsequent sensations. They are still more gratified when they carry out actions successfully; this "gives rise to the triumphant feeling of making an organ obedient to the will of the ego." Such experiences build up "a definite self- or body-consciousness which becomes the center and the point of reference of all purposeful and coördinated activity." Growth of the ego, in short, depends heavily upon action systems and the consequences of action. The course and vicissitudes of this development have to be studied in their own right, and they cannot be understood as side effects of the stages of libidinal development.

A similar theme is pursued to even more radical conclusions by Mittelmann (1954) in his paper on motility. Mittelmann regards motility, which manifests itself most typically in skilled motor actions such as posture, locomotion, and manipulation, as an "urge in its own right" in the same sense that one speaks of oral, excretory, or genital urges. From about 10 months of age it has a distinctly "driven" character, and there is restlessness and anger if it is blocked. During the second and third years the motor urge "dominates all other urges," so that it is proper to "consider this period the motor level of ego and libido development." The child makes tremendous efforts to learn to walk, and to walk well, and he exhibits joyous laughter as he attains these ends. Restrictions of motility may occur because the parents are anxious or because the child's assertiveness troubles them, and a lasting injury to the parent-child relationship may result. Clumsiness in motor or manipulative accomplishments may lead to self-hatred and dependence, for "the evolution of self-assertiveness and self-esteem is intimately connected with motor development." Motility is of central importance in many of the most characteristic functions of the ego. Partly by its means the infant differentiates himself from other objects, and the child's knowledge of objects depends on an extensive activity of manipulation and examination. "Thus motility becomes one of the most important aspects of reality testing." Because it is an element in all cognitive behavior, it can also be considered "the dominant integrative function." Mittelmann bases motor development, in short, on an independent urge, and he sees this urge as the really crucial motive behind the development of the ego.

Like Kardiner, Mittelmann does not attempt to formulate in detail the nature of the motility urge. It is likened not to an instinct but to a "partial instinct," and this seems to place it somewhere between Hendrick's instinct to master and Hartmann's dimly sketched independent energies of the ego. This indefiniteness may irk the systematic theorist, but Mittelmann's account of the part played by motility in ego development easily stands as a significant contribution. Even more influential in this respect is the work of Erikson (1953), who has given a highly detailed timetable of ego development. Erikson stays with the libido theory as far as it will go, but he passes beyond its reach in his account of the latency period and some of the later crises of growth. It is clear that something more than the orthodox instincts is involved in the "enormous value" with which the child in the second year "begins to endow his autonomous will." Something more would seem to be implied in the expanding imagination and initiative of the "phallic" child. Certainly more is involved during the school years, when children address themselves to motor, manual, and intellectual achievements and need "a sense of being able to make things and make them well and even perfectly: this is what I call the *sense of industry*." Erickson's (1952) theory of play is also influenced by the idea that learning to deal with the animate and inanimate worlds is an important preoccupation of childhood: "the playing child advances forward to new stages of real mastery." Action systems, motility, and a sense of industry all direct our attention to behavior which can scarcely be contained in the old bottle of instinct theory.

Glancing back over these trends in psychoanalytic ego psychology, we cannot fail to be impressed by striking similarities to the trend in animal work. Using Reik's familiar metaphor, we might say that those who listen with their ears and those who listen with the third ear have apparently been hearing much the same sounds. In both realms there is discontent with drive orthodoxy. In both there is persistent pointing to kinds of behavior neglected or explained away by drive orthodoxy: exploration, activity, manipulation, and mastery. Similar theories have been proposed to account for the energies in such behavior: (*a*) they are derived or transformed in some way from the primary drives or instincts (secondary reinforcement, neutralization of drive energies); (*b*) they are powered by the need to reduce anxiety; (*c*) they can be accounted for only by postulating a new primary drive (exploratory drive, instinct to master). When these explanations are considered to have failed, the one remaining course is to work out a different idea of motivation. In his study of action systems, Kardiner prefers to leave the question of energy sources unanswered, but Erikson's sense of industry and Mittelmann's motility urge point to a motivational base which is only remotely analogous to primary drives or fundamental instincts.

REFERENCES

Allport, G. W. *Personality: A psychological interpretation.* New York: Holt, 1937.

Beach, F. A. Analysis of factors involved in the arousal, maintenance and manifestation of sexual excitement in male animals. *Psychosom. Med.,* 1942, 4, 173-198.

Beach, F. A. Instinctive behavior: Reproductive activities. In S. S. Stevens (Ed.), *Handbook of experimental psychology.* New York: Wiley, 1951. Pp. 387-434.

Berlyne, D. E. Novelty and curiosity as determinants of exploratory behavior. *Brit. J. Psychol.,* 1950, 41, 68-80.

Berlyne, D. E. The arousal and satiation of perceptual curiosity in the rat. *J. comp. physiol. Psychol.,* 1955, 48, 238-246.

Berlyne, D. E. Attention to change, conditioned inhibition (SIR) and stimulus satiation. *Brit. J. Psychol.,* 1957, 48, 138-140.

Berlyne, D. E. The present status of research on exploratory and related behavior. *J. indiv. Psychol.,* 1958, 14, 121-126.

Bibring, E. The development and problems of the theories of the instincts. *Int. J. Psychoanal.,* 1941, 22, 102-131.

Butler, R. A. Discrimination learning by rhesus monkeys to visual-exploration motivation. *J. comp. physiol. Psychol.,* 1953, 46, 95-98.

Butler, R. A. Exploratory and related behavior: A new trend in animal research. *J. indiv. Psychol.,* 1958, 14, 111-120.

Butler, R. A. & Harlow, H. F. Discrimination learning and learning sets to visual exploration incentives. *J. gen. Psychol.,* 1957, 57, 257-264.

Cofer, C. N. Motivation. *Ann. Rev. Psychol.,* 1959, 10, 173-202.

Colby, K. M. *Energy and structure in psychoanalysis.* New York: Ronald, 1955.

Dashiell, J. F. A quantitative demonstration of animal drive. *J. comp. Psychol.,* 1925, 5, 205-208.

Erikson, E. H. *Childhood and society.* New York: Norton, 1952.

Erikson, E. H. Growth and crises of the healthy personality. In C. Kluckhohn, H. A. Murray, & D. Schneider (Eds.), *Personality in nature, society, and culture.* (2nd ed.) New York: Knopf, 1953. Pp. 185-225.

Fenichel, O. *The psychoanalytic theory of neurosis.* New York: Norton, 1945.

Freud, A. the mutual influences in the development of ego and id: Introduction to the discussion. *Psychoanal. Stud. Child,* 1952, 7, 42-50.

Freud, S. *Wit and its relation to the unconscious.* New York: Moffat, Yard, 1916.

Freud, S. Formulations regarding the two principles in mental functioning. *Collected papers.* Vol. 4. London: Hogarth Press and Institute of Psycho-analysis, 1925. Pp. 13-21. (a)

Freud, S. On narcissism: An introduction. *Collected papers.* Vol. 4. London. Hogarth Press and Institute of Psycho-analysis, 1925. Pp. 30-59. (b)

Freud, S. Instincts and their vicissitudes. *Collected papers.* Vol. 4. London: Hogarth Press and Institute of Psycho-analysis, 1925. Pp. 60-83. (c)

Freud, S. *The ego and the id.* (Trans. by J. Riviere) London: Hogarth Press, 1927.

Freud, S. *Beyond the pleasure principle.* London: Hogarth Press, 1948.

Freud, S. *An outline of psycho-analysis.* (Trans. by J. Strachey) New York: Norton, 1949.

Harlow, H. F. Mice, monkeys, men, and motives. *Psychol. Rev.*, 1953, 60, 23-32.

Harlow, H. F., Harlow, M. K., & Meyer, D. R. Learning motivated by a manipulation drive. *J. exp. Psychol.*, 1950, 40, 228-234.

Hartmann, H. Comments on the psychoanalytic theory of the ego. *Psychoanal. Stud. Child*, 1950, 5, 74-95.

Hartmann, H. Notes on the theory of sublimation. *Psychoanal. Stud. Child*, 1955, 10, 9-29.

Hartmann, H. Notes on the reality principle. *Psychoanal. Stud. Child*, 1956, 11, 31-53.

Hartmann, H., Kris, E., & Loewenstein, R. Notes on the theory of aggression. *Psychoanal. Stud. Child*, 1949, 3/4, 9-36.

Hebb, D. O. Drives and the c.n.s. (conceptual nervous system). *Psychol. Rev.*, 1955, 62, 243-254.

Hendrick, I. Instinct and the ego during infancy. *Psychoanal. Quart.*, 1942, 11, 33-58.

Hendrick, I. Work and the pleasure principle. *Psychoanal. Quart.*, 1943, 12, 311-329. (a)

Hendrick, I. The discussion of the 'instinct to master.' *Psychoanal. Quart.*, 1943, 12, 561-565. (b)

Hill, W. F. Activity as an autonomous drive. *J. comp. physiol. Psychol.*, 1956, 49, 15-19.

Johnson, E. E. The role of motivational strength in latent learning. *J. comp. physiol. Psychol.*, 1953, 45, 526-530.

Kagan, J. Differential reward value of incomplete and complete sexual behavior. *J. comp. physiol. Psychol.*, 1955, 48, 59-64.

Kagan, J., & Berkun, M. The reward value of running activity. *J. comp. physiol. Psychol.*, 1954, 47, 108.

Kardiner, A., & Spiegel, H. *War stress and neurotic illness.* New York: Hoeber, 1947.

Miller, N. E. Learnable drives and rewards. In S. S. Stevens (Ed.), *Handbook of experimental psychology.* New York: Wiley, 1951. Pp. 435-472.

Mittelmann, B. Motility in infants, children, and adults. *Psychoanal. Stud. Child*, 1954, 9, 142-177.

Montgomery, K. C. The role of the exploratory drive in learning. *J. comp. physiol. Psychol.*, 1954, 47, 60-64.

Montgomery, K. C., & Monkman, J. A. The relation between fear and exploratory behavior. *J. comp. physiol. Psychol.*, 1955, 48, 132-136.

Morgan, C. T. *Physiological psychology.* New York: McGraw-Hill, 1943.

Morgan, C. T. Physiological mechanisms of motivation. In M. R. Jones (Ed.), *Nebraska symposium on motivation 1957.* Lincoln, Neb.: Univer. Nebraska Press, 1957, Pp. 1-35.

Munroe, R. *Schools of psychoanalytical thought.* New York: Dryden, 1955.

Murphy, G. *Personality: A biosocial approach to origins and structure.* New York: Harper, 1947.

Myers, A. K. & Miller, N. E. Failure to find a learned drive based on hunger; evidence for learning motivated by exploration. *J. comp. physiol. Psychol.*, 1954, 47, 428-436.

Nissen, H. W. A study of exploratory behavior in the white rat by means of the obstruction method. *J. genet. Psychol.*, 1930, 37, 361-376.

Olds, J., & Milner, P. Positive reinforcement produced by electrical stimulation of septal area and other regions of rat brain. *J. comp. physiol. Psychol.*, 1954, 47, 419-427.

Rapaport, D. *Organization and pathology of thought.* New York: Columbia Univer. Press, 1951.

Rapaport, D. On the psychoanalytic theory of thinking. In R. P. Knight & C. R. Friedman (Eds.), *Psychoanalytic psychiatry and psychology.* New York: International Univer. Press, 1954. Pp. 259-273.

Rapaport, D. The theory of ego autonomy: A generalization. *Bull. Menninger Clin.*, 1958, 22, 13-35.

Rosvold, H. E. Physiological psychology. *Ann. Rev. Psychol.*, 1959, 10, 415-454.

Sheffield, F. D., & Roby, T. B. Reward value of a non-nutritive sweet taste. *J. comp. physiol. Psychol.*, 1950, 43, 471-481.

Sheffield, F. D., Roby, T. B., & Campbell, B. A. Drive reduction vs. consummatory behavior as determinants of reinforcement. *J. comp. physiol. Psychol.*, 1954, 47, 349-354.

Sheffield, F. D., Wulff, J. J., & Backer, R. Reward value of copulation without sex drive reduction. *J. comp. physiol. Psychol.*, 1951, 44, 3-8.

Steller, E. The physiology of motivation. *Psychol. Rev.*, 1954, 61, 5-22.

Welker, W. L. Some determinants of play and exploration in chimpanzees. *J. comp. physiol. Psychol.*, 1956, 49, 84-89.

Whiting, J. W. M. & Mowrer, O. H. Habit progression and regression — a laboratory study of some factors relevant to human socialization. *J. comp. Psychol.*, 1943, 36, 229-253.

Wolfe, J. B., & Kaplon, M. D. Effect of amount of reward and consummative activity on learning in chickens. *J. comp. Psychol.*, 1941, 31, 353-361.

Woodworth, R. S. *Dynamics of behavior.* New York: Holt, 1958.

Zimbardo, P. G., & Miller, N. E. Facilitation of exploration by hunger in rats. *J. comp. physiol. Psychol.*, 1958, 51, 43-46.

(Received October 30, 1958)

10

SELECTIONS FROM
SCIENCE AND HUMAN BEHAVIOR

B.F. Skinner

INNER "CAUSES"

Every science has at some time or other looked for causes of action inside the things it has studied. Sometimes the practice has proved useful, sometimes it has not. There is nothing wrong with an inner explanation as such, but events which are located inside a system are likely to be difficult to observe. For this reason we are encouraged to assign properties to them without justification. Worse still, we can invent causes of this sort without fear of contradiction. The motion of a rolling stone was once attributed to its *vis viva*. The chemical properties of bodies were thought to be derived from the *principles* or *essences* of which they were composed. Combustion was explained by the *phlogiston* inside the combustible object. Wounds healed and bodies grew well because of a *vis medicatrix*. It has been especially tempting to attribute the behavior of a living organism to the behavior of an inner agent, as the following example may suggest.

Neural causes. The layman uses the nervous system as a ready explanation of behavior. The English language contains hundreds of expressions which imply such a causal relationship. At the end of a long trial we read that the jury shows signs of *brain fag*, that the *nerves* of the accused are *on edge*, that the wife of the accused is on the verge of a *nervous breakdown*, and that his lawyer is generally thought to have lacked the *brains* needed to stand up to the prosecution. Obviously, no direct observations have been made of the nervous systems of any of these people. Their "brains" and "nerves" have been invented on the spur of the moment

Skinner, B. F. 1980. "Selections from Science and Human Behavior" in *Readings in Philosophy of Psychology*, edited by Ned Block, pp. 37-47. © Prentice-Hall, Inc. Reproduced by permission of the publisher.

to lend substance to what might otherwise seem a superficial account of their behavior.

The sciences of neurology and physiology have not divested themselves entirely of a similar practice. Since techniques for observing the electrical and chemical processes in nervous tissue had not yet been developed, early information about the nervous system was limited to its gross anatomy. Neural processes could only be inferred from the behavior which was said to result from them. Such inferences were legitimate enough as scientific theories, but they could not justifiably be used to explain the very behavior upon which they were based. The hypotheses of the early physiologists may have been sounder than those of the layman, but until independent evidence could be obtained, they were no more satisfactory as explanations of behavior. Direct information about many of the chemical and electrical processes in the nervous system is now available. Statements about the nervous system are no longer necessarily inferential or fictional. But there is still a measure of circularity in much physiological explanation, even in the writings of specialists. In World War I a familiar disorder was called "shell shock." Disturbances in behavior were explained by arguing that violent explosions had damaged the structure of the nervous system, though no direct evidence of such damage was available. In World War II the same disorder was classified as "neuropsychiatric." The prefix seems to show a continuing unwillingness to abandon explanations in terms of hypothetical neural damage.

Eventually a science of the nervous systems based upon direct observation rather that inference will describe the neural states and events which immediately precede instances of behavior. We shall know the precise neurological conditions which immediately precede, say, the response, "No, thank you." These events in turn will be found to be preceded by other neurological events, and these in turn by others. This series will lead us back to events outside the nervous system and, eventually, outside the organism. In the chapters which follow we shall consider external events of this sort in some detail. We shall then be better able to evaluate the place of neurological explanations of behavior. However, we may note here that we do not have and may never have this sort of neurological information at the moment it is needed in order to predict a specific instance of behavior. It is even more unlikely that we shall be able to alter the nervous system directly in order to set up the antecedent conditions of a particular instance. The causes to be sought in the nervous system are, therefore, of limited usefulness in the prediction and control of specific behavior.

Psychic inner causes. An even more common practice is to explain behavior in terms of an inner agent which lacks physical dimensions and is called "mental" or "psychic." The purest form of the psychic explanation is seen in the animism of primitive peoples. From the immobility of the body after death it is inferred that a spirit responsible for movement has departed. The *enthusiastic* person is, as the etymology of the word implies, energized by a "god within." It is only a modest refinement to attribute every feature of the behavior of the physical organism to a corresponding feature of the "mind" or of some inner "personality." The inner man is regarded as driving the body very much as the man at the steering wheel drives a car. The inner man wills an action, the outer executes it. The inner loses his appetite, the outer stops eating. The inner man wants and the outer gets. The inner has the impulse and the outer obeys.

It is not the layman alone who resorts to these practices, for many reputable psychologists use a similar dualistic system of explanation. The inner man is sometimes personified clearly, as when delinquent behavior is attributed to a "disordered personality," or he may be dealt with in fragments, as when behavior is attributed to mental processes, faculties, and traits. Since the inner man does not occupy space, he may be multiplied at will. It has been argued that a single physical organism is controlled by several psychic agents and that its behavior is the resultant of their several wills. The Freudian concepts of the ego, superego, and id are often used in this way. They are frequently regarded as nonsubstantial creatures, often in violent conflict, whose defeats or victories lead to the adjusted or maladjusted behavior of the physical organism in which they reside.

Direct observation of the mind comparable with the observation of the nervous system has not proved feasible. It is true that many people believe that they observe their "mental states" just as the physiologist observes neural events, but another interpretation of what they observe is possible, as we shall see in Chapter XVII. Introspective psychology no longer pretends to supply direct information about events which are the causal antecedents, rather than the mere accompaniments, of behavior. It defines its "subjective" events in ways which strip them of any usefulness in a causal analysis. The events appealed to in early mentalistic explanations of behavior have remained beyond the reach of observation. Freud insisted upon this by emphasizing the role of the unconscious — a frank recognition that important mental processes are not directly observable. The Freudian literature supplies may examples of behavior from which unconscious wishes, impulses, instincts, and emotions are inferred. Unconscious thought-processes have also been used to explain intellectual achievements. Though the mathematician may feel that he knows "how he thinks," he is often unable to give a coherent account of the mental processes leading to the solution of a specific problem. But any mental event which is unconscious is necessarily influential, and the explanation is therefore not based upon independent observations of a valid cause.

The fictional nature of this form of inner cause is shown by the ease with which the mental process is discovered to have just the properties needed to account for the behavior. When a professor turns up in the wrong classroom or gives the wrong lecture, it is because his *mind* is, at least for the moment, *absent*. If he forgets to give a reading assignment, it is because it has slipped his *mind* (a hint from the class may re*mind* him of it). He begins to tell an old joke but pauses for a moment, and it is evident to everyone that he is trying to make up his *mind* whether or not he has already used the joke that term. His lectures grow more tedious with the years, and questions from the class confuse him more and more, because his *mind* is failing. What he says is often disorganized because his *ideas* are confused. He is occasionally unnecessarily emphatic because of the force of his *ideas*. When he repeats himself, it is because he has an *idée fixe*; and when he repeats what others have said, it is because he borrows his *ideas*. Upon occasion there is nothing in what he says because he lacks *ideas*. In all this it is obvious that the mind and the ideas, together with their special characteristics, are being invented on the spot to provide spurious explanations. A science of behavior can hope to gain very little from so cavalier a practice. Since mental or psychic events are asserted to lack the dimensions of physical science, we have an additional reason for rejecting them.

Conceptual inner causes. The commonest inner causes have no specific dimensions at all, either neurological or psychic. When we say that a man eats *because* he is hungry, smokes a great deal *because* he has the tobacco habit, fights *because* of the instinct of pugnacity, behaves brilliantly *because* of his intelligence, or plays the piano well *because* of his musical ability, we seem to be referring to causes. But on analysis these phrases prove to be merely redundant descriptions. A single set of facts is described by the two statements: "He eats" and "He is hungry." A single set of facts is described by the two statements: "He smokes a great deal" and "He has the smoking habit." A single set of facts is described by the two statements: "He plays well" and "He has musical ability." The practice of explaining one statement in terms of the other is dangerous because it suggests that we have found the cause and therefore need search no further. Moreover, such terms as "hunger," "habit," and "intelligence" convert what are essentially the properties of a process or relation into what appear to be things. Thus we are unprepared for the properties eventually to be discovered in the behavior itself and continue to look for something which may not exist.

THE VARIABLES OF WHICH BEHAVIOR IS A FUNCTION

The practice of looking inside the organism for an explanation of behavior has tended to obscure the variables which are immediately available for a scientific analysis. These variables lie outside the organism, in its immediate environment and in its environmental history. They have a physical status to which the usual techniques of science are adapted, and they make it possible to explain behavior as other subjects are explained in science. These independent variables are of many sorts and their relations to behavior are often subtle and complex, but we cannot hope to give an adequate account of behavior without analyzing them.

Consider the act of drinking a glass of water. This is not likely to be an important bit of behavior in anyone's life, but it supplies a convenient example. We may describe the topography of the behavior in such a way that a given instance may be identified quite accurately by any qualified observer. Suppose now we bring someone into a room and place a glass of water before him. Will he drink? There appear to be only two possibilities: either he will or he will not. But we speak of the *chances* that he will drink, and this notion may be refined for scientific use. What we want to evaluate is the *probability* that he will drink. This may range from virtual certainty that drinking will occur to virtual certainty that it will not. The very considerable problem of how to measure the probability may be increased or decreased.

Everyday experience suggests several possibilities, and laboratory and clinical observation have added others. It is decidedly not true that a horse may be led to water but cannot be made to drink. By arranging a history of severe deprivation we could be "absolutely sure" that drinking will occur. In the same way we may be sure that the glass of water in our experiment will be drunk. Although we are not likely to arrange them experimentally, deprivations of the necessary magnitude sometimes occur outside the laboratory. We may obtain an effect similar to that of deprivation by speeding up the excretion of water. For example, we may induce sweating by raising the temperature of the room or by forcing heavy exercise, or we may increase the excretion of urine by mixing salt or urea in food taken prior to the experiment. It is also well known that loss of blood, as on a battlefield, sharply increases the probability of drinking. On the other hand, we may set the probability at virtually zero by inducing or forcing our subject to drink a large quantity of water before the experiment.

If we are to predict whether or not our subject will drink, we must know as much as possible about these variables. If we are to induce him to drink, we must be able to manipulate them. In both cases, moreover, either for accurate prediction or control, we must investigate the effect of each variable quantitatively with the methods and techniques of a laboratory science.

Other variables may, of course, affect the result. Our subject may be "afraid" that something has been added to the water as a practical joke or for experimental purposes. He may even "suspect" that the water has been poisoned. He may have grown up in a culture in which water is drunk only when no one is watching. He may refuse to drink simply to prove that we cannot predict or control his behavior. These possibilities do not disprove the relations between drinking and the variables listed in the preceding paragraphs; they simply remind us that other variables have to be taken into account. We must know the history of our subject with respect to the behavior of drinking water, and if we cannot eliminate social factors from the situation, then we must know the history of his personal relations to people resembling the experimenter. Adequate prediction in any science requires information about all relevant variables, and the control of a subject matter for practical purposes makes the same demands.

Other types of "explanation" do not permit us to dispense with these requirements of to fulfill them in any easier way. It is of no help to be told that our subject will drink provided he was born under a particular sign of the zodiac which shows a preoccupation with water or provided he is the lean and thirsty type or was, in short, "born thirsty." Explanations in terms of inner states or agents, however, may require further comment. To what extent is it helpful to be told, "He drinks because he is thirsty"? If to be thirsty means nothing more that to have a tendency to drink, this is mere redundancy. If it means that he drinks because of a state of thirst, an inner causal event is invoked. If this state is purely inferential — if no dimensions are assigned to it which would make direct observation possible — it cannot serve as an explanation. But if it has physiological or psychic properties, what role can it play in a science of behavior?

The physiologist may point out that several ways of raising the probability of drinking have a common effect: they increase the concentration of solutions in the body. Through some mechanism not yet well understood, this may bring about a corresponding change in the nervous system which in turn makes drinking more probable. In the same way, it may be argued that all these operations make the organism "feel thirsty" or "want a drink" and that such a psychic state also acts upon the nervous system in some unexplained way to induce drinking. In each case we have a causal chain consisting of three links: (1) an operation performed upon the organism from without — for example, water deprivation; (2) an inner condition — for example, physiological or psychic thirst; and (3) a kind of behavior — for example, drinking. Independent information about the second link would obviously permit is to predict the third without recourse to the first. It would be a preferred type of variable because it would be nonhistoric; the first link may lie in the past history of organism, but the second is a current condition. Direct information about the second link is, however, seldom, if ever, available. Sometimes we infer the second link from the first: an animal is said to be thirsty if it has not drunk for a long time. In that case, we obviously cannot dispense with the prior history.

The second link is useless in the *control* of behavior unless we can manipulate it. At the moment, we have no way of directly altering neural processes at appropriate moments in the life of a behaving organism, nor has any way been discovered to alter a psychic process. We usually set up the second link through the first: we make an animal thirsty, in either the physiological or the psychic sense, by depriving it of water, feeding it salt, and so on. In that case, the second link obviously does not permit us to dispense with the first. Even if some new technical discovery were to enable us to set up or change the second link directly, we should still have to deal with those enormous areas in which human behavior is controlled through manipulation of the first link. A technique of operating upon the second link would increase our control of behavior, but the techniques which have already been developed would still remain to be analyzed.

The most objectionable practice is to follow the causal sequence back only as far as a hypothetical second link. This is a serious handicap both in a theoretical science and in the practical control of behavior. It is no help to be told that to get an organism to drink we are simply to "make it thirsty" unless we are also told how this is to be done. When we have obtained the necessary prescription for thirst, the whole proposal is more complex than it need be. Similarly, when an example of maladjusted behavior is explained by saying that the individual is "suffering from anxiety," we have still to be told the cause of the anxiety. But the external conditions which are then invoked could have been directly related to the maladjusted behavior. Again, when we are told that a man stole a loaf of bread because "he was hungry," we have still to learn of the external conditions responsible for the "hunger." These conditions would have sufficed to explain the theft.

The objection to inner states is not that they do not exist, but that they are not relevant in a functional analysis. We cannot account for the behavior of any system while staying wholly inside it; eventually we must turn to forces operating upon the organism from without. Unless there is a weak spot in our causal chain so that the second link is not lawfully determined by the first, or the third by the second, then the first and third links must be lawfully related. If we must always go back beyond the second link for prediction and control, we may avoid many tiresome and exhausting digressions by examining the third link as a function of the first. Valid information about the second link may throw light upon this relationship but can in no way alter it.

OPERANT CONDITIONING

To get at the core of Thorndike's Law of Effect, we need to clarify the notion of "probability of response." This is an extremely important concept; unfortunately, it is also a difficult one. In discussing human behavior, we often refer to "tendencies" or "predispositions" to behave in particular ways. Almost every theory of behavior uses some such term as "excitatory potential," "habit strength," or "determining tendency." But how do we observe a tendency? And how can we measure one?

If a given example of behavior existed in only two states, in one of which it always occurred and in the other never, we should almost be helpless in following a program of functional analysis. An all-or-none subject matter lends itself only to primitive forms of description. It is a great advantage to suppose instead that the *probability* that a response will occur ranges continuously between these all-or-none extremes. We can then deal with variables which, unlike the eliciting stimulus, do not "cause a given bit of behavior to occur" but simply make the occurrence more probable. We may then proceed to deal, for example, with the combined effect of more than one such variable.

The everyday expressions which carry the notion of probability, tendency, or predisposition describe the frequencies with which bits of behavior occur. We never observe a probability as such. We say that someone is "enthusiastic" about bridge when we observe that he plays bridge often and talks about it often. To be "greatly interested" in music is to play, listen to, and talk about music a great deal. The "inveterate" gambler is one who gambles frequently. The camera "fan" is to be found taking pictures, developing them, and looking at pictures made by himself and others. The "highly sexed" person frequently engages in sexual behavior. The "dipsomaniac" drinks frequently.

In characterizing a man's behavior in terms of frequency, we assume certain standard conditions: he must be able to execute and repeat a given act, and other behavior must not interfere appreciably. We cannot be sure of the extent of a man's interest in music, for example, if he is necessarily busy with other things. When we come to refine the notion of probability of response for scientific use, we find that here, too, our data are frequencies and that the conditions under which they are observed must be specified. The main technical problem in designing a controlled experiment is to provide for the observation and interpretation of frequencies. We eliminate, or at least hold constant, any condition which encourages behavior which competes with the behavior we are to study. An organism is placed in a quiet box where its behavior may be observed through an one-way screen or recorded mechanically. This is by no means an environmental vacuum, for an organism will react to the features of the box in many ways; but its behavior will eventually reach a fairly stable level, against which the frequency of a selected response may be investigated.

To study the process which Thorndike called stamping in, we must have a "consequence." Giving food to a hungry organism will do. We can feed our subject conveniently with a small food tray which is operated electrically. When the tray is first opened, the organism will probably react to it in ways which interfere with the process we plan to observe. Eventually, after being fed from the tray repeatedly, it eats readily, and we are then ready to make this consequence contingent upon behavior and to observe the result.

We select a relatively simple bit of behavior which may be freely and rapidly repeated, and which is easily observed and recorded. If our experimental subject is a pigeon, for example, the behavior of raising the head above a given height is convenient. This may be observed by sighting across the pigeon's head at a scale pinned on the far wall of the box. We first study the height at which the head is normally held and select some line on the scale which is reached only infrequently. Keeping our eye on the scale we then begin to open the food tray very quickly whenever the head rises above the line. If the experiment is conducted according to specifications, the result is invariable: we observe an immediate change in the frequency with which the head crosses the line. We also observe, and this is of some importance theoretically, that higher lines are now being crossed. We may advance almost immediately to a higher line in determining when food is to be presented. In a minute or two, the bird's posture has changed so that the top of the head seldom falls below the line which we first chose.

When we demonstrate the process of stamping in in this relatively simple way, we see that certain common interpretations of Thorndike's experiment are superfluous. The expression "trial-and-error learning," which is frequently associated with the Law of Effect, is clearly out of place here. We are reading something into our observations when we call any upward movement of the head a "trial," and there is no reason to call any movement which does not achieve a specified consequence an "error." Even the term "learning" is misleading. The statement that the bird "learns that it will get food by stretching its neck" is an inaccurate report of what has happened. To say that it has acquired the "habit" of stretching its neck is merely to resort to an explanatory fiction, since our only evidence of the habit is the acquired tendency to perform the act. The barest possible statement of the process is this: we make a given consequence contingent upon certain physical properties of behavior (the upward movement of the head), and the behavior is then observed to increase in frequency.

It is customary to refer to any movement of the organism as a "response." The word is borrowed from the field of reflex action and implies an act which, so to speak, answers a prior event — the stimulus. But we may make an event contingent upon behavior without identifying, or being able to identify, a prior stimulus. We did not alter the environment of the pigeon to *elicit* the upward movement of the head. It is probably impossible to show that any single stimulus invariably precedes this movement. Behavior of this sort may come under the control of stimuli, but the relation is not that of elicitation. The term "response" is therefore not wholly appropriate but is so well established that we shall use it in the following discussion.

A response which has already occurred cannot, of course, be predicted or controlled. We can only predict that *similar* responses will occur in the future. The unit of a predictive science is, therefore, not a response but a class of responses. The word "operant" will be used to describe this class. The term emphasizes the fact that the behavior *operates* upon the environment to generate consequences. The consequences define the properties with respect to which responses are called similar. The term will be used both as an adjective (operant behavior) and as a noun to designate the behavior defined by a given consequence.

A single instance in which a pigeon raises is head is a *response.* It is a bit of history which may be reported in any frame of reference we wish to use. The behavior called "raising the head," regardless of when specific instances occur, is an *operant.* It can be described, not as an accomplished act, but rather as a set of acts defined by the property of the height to which the head is raised. In this sense an operant is defined by an effect which may be specified in physical terms; the "cutoff" at a certain height is a property of behavior.

The term "learning" may profitably be saved in its traditional sense to describe the reassortment of responses in a complex situation. Terms for the process of stamping in may be borrowed from Pavlov's analysis of the conditioned reflex. Pavlov himself called all events which strengthened behavior "reinforcement" and all the resulting changes "conditioning." In the Pavlovian experiment, however, a reinforcer is paired with a *stimulus*; whereas in operant behavior it is contingent upon a *response*. Operant reinforcement is therefore a separate process and requires a separate analysis. In both cases, the strengthening behavior which results from reinforcement is appropriately called "conditioning." In operant conditioning we "strengthen" an operant in the sense of making a response more probable or, in actual fact, more frequent. In Pavlovian or "respondent" conditioning we simply increase the magnitude of the response elicited by the conditioned stimulus and shorten the time which elapses between stimulus and response. (We note, incidentally, that these two cases exhaust the possibilities: an organism is conditioned when a reinforcer [1] accompanies another stimulus or [2] follows upon the organism's own behavior. Any event which does neither has no effect in changing a probability of response.) In the pigeon experiment, then, food is the *reinforcer* and presenting food when a response is emitted is the *reinforcement*. The *operant* is defined by the property upon which reinforcement is contingent — the height to which the head must be raised. The change in frequency with which the head is lifted to this height is the process of *operant conditioning*.

While we are awake, we act upon the environment constantly, and many of the consequences of our actions are reinforcing. Through operant conditioning the environment builds the basic repertoire with which we keep our balance, walk, play games, handle instruments and tools, talk, write, sail a boat, drive a car, or fly a plane. A change in the environment — a new car, a new friend, a new field of interest, a new job, a new location — may find us unprepared, but our behavior usually adjusts quickly as we acquire new responses and discard old. We shall see in the following chapter that operant reinforcement does more than build a behavioral repertoire. It improves the efficiency of behavior and maintains behavior in strength long after acquisition or efficiency has ceased to be of interest.

GOALS, PURPOSES, AND OTHER FINAL CAUSES

It is not current to say that operant reinforcement "strengthens the response which precedes it." The response has already occurred and cannot be changed. What is changed is the future probability of responses in the same *class*. It is the operant as a class of behavior, rather than the response as a particular instance, which is conditioned. There is, therefore, no violation of the fundamental principle of science which rules out "final causes." But this principle is violated when it is asserted that behavior is under the control of an "incentive" or "goal" which the organism has not yet achieved or a "purpose" which it has not yet fulfilled.

Statements which use such words as "incentive" or "purpose" are usually reducible to statements about operant conditioning, and only a slight change is required to bring them within the framework of a natural science. Instead of saying that a man behaves because of the consequences which *are* to follow his behavior, we simply say that he behaves because of the consequences which *have* followed similar behavior in the past. This is, of course, the Law of Effect or operant conditioning.

It is sometimes argued that a response is not fully described until its purpose is referred to as a current property. But what is meant by "describe"? If we observe someone walking down the street, we may report this event in the language of physical science. If we then add that "his purpose is to mail a letter," have we said anything which was not included in our first report? Evidently so, since a man may walk down the street "for many purposes" and in the same physical way in each case. But the distinction which needs to be made is not between instances of behavior; it is between the variables of which behavior is a function. Purpose is not a property of the behavior itself; it is a way of referring to controlling variables. If we make our report after we have seen our subject mail his letter and turn back, we attribute "purpose" to him from the event which brought the behavior of walking down the street to an end. This event "gives meaning" to his performance, not by amplifying a description of the behavior as such, but by indicating an independent variable of which it may have been a function. We cannot see his "purpose" before seeing that he mails a letter, unless we have observed similar behavior and similar consequences before. Where we have done this, we use the term simply to predict that he will mail a letter upon this occasion.

Nor can our subject see his own purpose without reference to similar events. If we ask him why he is going down the street or what his purpose is and he says, "I am going to mail a letter," we have not learned anything new about his behavior but only about some of its possible causes. The subject himself, of course, may be in an advantageous position in describing these variables because he has had an extended contact with his own behavior for many years. But his statement is not therefore in a different class from similar statements made by others who have observed his behavior upon fewer occasions. As we shall see in Chapter XVII, he is simply making a plausible prediction in terms of his experiences with himself. Moreover, he may be wrong. He may report that he is "going to mail a letter," and he may indeed carry an unmailed letter in his hand and may mail it at the end of the street, but we may still be able to show that his behavior is primarily determined by the fact that upon past occasions he has encountered someone who is important to him upon just such a walk. He may not be "aware of this purpose" in the sense of being able to say that his behavior is strong for this reason.

The fact that operant behavior seems to be "directed toward the future" is misleading. Consider, for example, the case of "looking for something." In what sense is the "something" which has not yet been found relevant to the behavior? Suppose we condition a pigeon to peck a spot on the wall of a box and then, when the operant is well established, remove the spot. The bird now goes to the usual place along the wall. It raises its head, cocks its eye in the usual direction, and may even emit a weak peck in the usual place. Before extinction is very far advanced, it returns to the same place again and again in similar behavior. Must we say that the pigeon is "looking for the spot"? Must we take the "looked for" spot into account in explaining the behavior?

It is not difficult to interpret this example in terms of operant reinforcement. Since visual stimulation from the spot has usually preceded the receipt of food, the spot has become a conditioned reinforcer. It strengthens the behavior of looking in given directions from different positions. Although we have undertaken to condition only the pecking response, we have in fact strengthened many different kinds of precurrent behavior which bring the bird into positions from which it sees the spot and pecks it. These responses continue to appear, even though we have removed the spot, until extinction occurs. The spot which is "being looked for" is the spot which has occurred in the past as the immediate reinforcement of the behavior of looking. In general, looking for something consists of emitting responses which in the past have produced "something" as a consequence.

The same interpretation applies to human behavior. When we see a man moving about a room opening drawers, looking under magazines, and so on, we may describe his behavior in fully objective terms: "Now he is in a certain part of the room; he has grasped a book between the thumb and forefinger of his right hand; he is lifting the book and bending his head so that any object under the book can be seen." We may also "interpret" his behavior or "read a meaning into it" by saying that "he is looking for something" or more specifically, that "he is looking for his glasses." What we have added is not a further description of his behavior but an inference about some of the variables responsible for it. There is no *current* goal, incentive, purpose, or meaning to be taken into account. This is so even if we ask him what he is doing and he says, " I am looking for my glasses." This is not a further description of his behavior but of the variables of which his behavior is a function; it is equivalent to "I have lost my glasses," "I shall stop what I am doing when I find my glasses," or "When I have done this in the past, I have found my glasses." These translations may seem unnecessarily roundabout, but only because expressions involving goals and purposes are abbreviations.

Very often we attribute purpose to behavior as another way of describing its biological adaptability. This issue has already been discussed, but one point may be added. In both operant conditioning and the evolutionary selection of behavioral characteristics, consequences alter future probability. Reflexes and other innate patterns of behavior evolve because they increase the chances of survival of the *species*. Operants grow strong because they are followed by important consequences in the life of the individual. Both processes raise the question of purpose for the same reason, and in both the appeal to a final cause may be rejected in the same way. A spider does not possess the elaborate behavioral repertoire with which it constructs a web because that web will enable it to capture the food it needs to survive. It possesses this behavior because similar behavior on the part of spiders in the past has enabled *them* to capture the food *they* need to survive. A series of events have been relevant to the behavior of web-making in its earlier evolutionary history. We are wrong in saying that we observe the "purpose" of the web when we observe similar events in the life of the individual.

11

A REVIEW OF B.F. SKINNER'S
VERBAL BEHAVIOR

Noam Chomsky

1

A great many linguists and philosophers concerned with language have expressed the hope that their studies might ultimately be embedded in a framework provided by behaviorist psychology, and that refractory areas of investigation, particularly those in which meaning is involved, will in this way be opened up to fruitful exploration. Since this volume [*Verbal Behavior* (New York: Appleton-Century-Crofts, 1957) — *Ed.*] is the first large-scale attempt to incorporate the major aspects of linguistic behavior within a behaviorist framework, it merits and will undoubtedly receive careful attention. Skinner is noted for his contribution to the study of animal behavior. The book under review is the product of study of linguistic behavior extending over more than twenty years. Earlier versions of it have been fairly widely circulated, and there are quite a few references in the psychological literature to its major ideas.

The problem to which this books is addressed is that of giving a "functional analysis" of verbal behavior. By functional analysis, Skinner means identification of the variables that control this behavior and specification of how they interact to determine a particular verbal response. Furthermore, the controlling variables are to be described completely in terms of such notions as *stimulus, reinforcement, deprivation*, which have been given a reasonably clear meaning in animal experimentation. In other words, the goal of the book is to provide a way to predict and control verbal behavior by observing and manipulating the physical environment of the speaker.

Chomsky, Noam. 1980. "A Review of B.F. Skinner's *Verbal Behavior*" in *Readings in Philosophy of Psychology*, edited by Ned Block. pp. 48-73. © Harvard University Press.

Skinner feels that recent advances in the laboratory study of animal behavior permit us to approach this problem with a certain optimism, since "the basic processes and relations which give verbal behavior its special characteristics are now fairly well understood... the results [of this experimental work] have been surprisingly free of species restrictions. Recent work has shown that the methods can be extended to human behavior without serious modification (3).[1]

It is important to see clearly just what it is in Skinner's program and claims that makes them appear so bold and remarkable. It is not primarily the fact that he has set functional analysis as his problem, or that he limits himself to study of *observables*, i.e., input-output relations. What is so surprising is the particular limitations he has imposed on the way in which the observables of behavior are to be studied, and, above all, the particularly simple nature of the *function* which, he claims, describes the causation of behavior. One would naturally expect that prediction of the behavior of a complex organism (or machine) would require, in addition to information about external stimulation, knowledge of the internal structure of the organism, the ways in which it processes input information and organizes its own behavior. These characteristics of the organism are in general a complicated product of inborn structure, the genetically determined course of maturation, and past experience. Insofar as independent neurophysiological evidence is not available, it is obvious that inferences concerning the structure of the organism are based on observation of behavior and outside events. Nevertheless, one's estimate of the relative importance of external factors and internal structure in the determination of behavior will have an important effect on the duration of research on linguistics (or any other) behavior, and on the kinds of analogies from animal behavior studies that will be considered relevant or suggestive.

Putting it differently, anyone who sets himself the problem of analyzing the causation of behavior will (in the absence of independent neurophysiological evidence) concern himself with the only data available, namely the record of inputs to the organism and the organism's present response, and will try to describe the function specifying the response in terms of the history of inputs. This is nothing more than the definition of his problem. There are no possible grounds for argument here, if one accepts the problem as legitimate, though Skinner has often advanced and defended this definition of a problem as if it were a thesis which other investigators reject. The differences that arise between those who affirm and those who deny the importance of the specific "contribution of the organism" to learning and performance concern the particular character and complexity of this function, and the kinds of observations and research necessary for arriving at a precise specification of it. If the contribution of the organism is complex, the only hope of predicting behavior even in a gross way will be through a very indirect program of research that begins by studying the detailed character of the behavior itself and the particular capacities of the organism involved.

Skinner's thesis is that external factors consisting of present stimulation and the history of reinforcement (in particular, the frequency, arrangement, and withholding of reinforcing stimuli) are of overwhelming importance, and that the general principles revealed in laboratory studies of these phenomena provide the basis for understanding the complexities of verbal behavior. He confidently and repeatedly voices his claim to have demonstrated that the contribution of the speaker is quite trivial and elementary, and that precise prediction of verbal behavior involves only specification of the few external factors that he has isolated experimentally with lower organisms.

Careful study of this book (and of the research on which it draws) reveals, however, that these astonishing claims are far from justified. It indicates, furthermore, that the insights that have been achieved in the laboratories of the reinforcement theorist, though quite genuine, can be applied to complex human behavior only in the most gross and superficial way, and that speculative attempts to discuss linguistic behavior in these terms alone omit from consideration factors of fundamental importance that are, no doubt, amenable to scientific study, although their specific characters cannot at present be precisely formulated. Since Skinner's work is the most extensive attempt to accommodate human behavior involving higher mental faculties within a strict behaviorist schema of the type that has attracted many linguists and philosophers, as well as psychologists, a detailed documentation is of independent interest. The magnitude of the failure of this attempt to account for verbal behavior serves as a kind of measure of the importance of the factors omitted from consideration, and an indication of how little is really known about this remarkably complex phenomenon.

The force of Skinner's argument lies in the enormous wealth and range of examples for which he proposes a functional analysis. The only way to evaluate the success of his program and the correctness of his basic assumption about verbal behavior is to review these examples in detail and to determine the precise character of the concepts in terms of which the functional analysis is presented. Section 2 of this review describes the experimental context with respect to which these concepts are originally defined. Sections 3 and 4 deal with the basic concepts — *stimulus, response,* and *reinforcement* — Sections 6 to 10 with the new descriptive machinery developed specifically for the description of verbal behavior. In Section 5 we consider the status of the fundamental claim, drawn from the laboratory, which serves as the basis for the analogic guesses about human behavior that have been proposed by many psychologists. The final section (Section 11) will consider some ways in which further linguistic work may play a part in clarifying some of these problems.

2

Although this book makes no direct reference to experimental work, it can be understood only in terms of the general framework that Skinner has developed for the description of behavior. Skinner divides the responses of the animal into two main categories. *Respondents* are purely reflex responses elicited by particular stimuli. *Operants* are emitted responses, for which no obvious stimulus can be discovered. Skinner has been concerned primarily with operant behavior. The experimental arrangement that he introduced consists basically of a box with a bar attached to one wall in such a way that when the bar is pressed, a food pellet is dropped into a tray (and the bar press is recorded). A rat placed in the box will soon press the bar, releasing a pellet into the tray. This state of affairs, resulting from the bar press, increases the *strength* of the bar-pressing operant. The food pellet is called a *reinforcer*; the event, a *reinforcing event*. The strength of an operant is defined by Skinner in terms of the rate of response during extinction (i.e., after the last reinforcement and before return of the pre-conditioning rate).

Suppose that release of the pellet is conditional on the flashing of a light. Then the rat will come to press the bar only when the light flashes. This is called *stimulus discrimination*. The response is called a *discriminated operant* and the light is called the *occasion* for its emission: this is to be distinguished from elicitation or a response by a stimulus in the case of the respondent.[2] Suppose that the apparatus is so arranged that bar-pressing of only a certain character (e.g., duration) will release the pellet. The rat will then come to press the bar in the required way. This process is called *response differentiation*. By successive slight changes in the conditions under which the response will be reinforced, it is possible to shape the response of a rat or a pigeon in very surprising ways in a very short time, so that rather complex behavior can be produced by a process of successive approximation.

A stimulus can become reinforcing by repeated association with an already reinforcing stimulus. Such a stimulus is called a *secondary reinforcer*. Like many contemporary behaviorists, Skinner consider money, approval, and the like to be secondary reinforcers which have become reinforcing because of their association with food, etc.[3] Secondary reinforcers can be *generalized* by associating them with a variety of different primary reinforcers.

Another variable that can affect the rate of the bar-pressing operant is drive, which Skinner defines operationally in terms of hours of deprivation. his major scientific book, *Behavior of Organisms*, is a study of the effects of food-deprivation and conditioning on the strength of the bar-pressing response of healthy mature rats. Probably Skinner's most original contribution to animal behavior studies has been his investigation of the effects of intermittent reinforcement, arranged in various different ways, presented in *Behavior of Organisms* and extended (with pecking of pigeons as the operant under investigation) in the recent *Schedules of Reinforcement* by Fester and Skinner (1957). It is apparently these studies that Skinner has in mind when he refers to the recent advances in the study of animal behavior.[4]

The notions *stimulus, response, reinforcement* are relatively well defined with respect to the bar-pressing experiments and others similarly restricted. Before we can extend them to real-life behavior, however, certain difficulties must be faced. We must decide, first of all, whether any physical event to which the organism is capable of reacting is to be called a stimulus on a given occasion, or only one to which the organism in fact reacts; and correspondingly, we must decide whether any part of behavior is to be called a response, or only one connected with stimuli in lawful ways. Questions of this sort pose something of a dilemma for the experimental psychologist. If he accepts the broad definitions, characterizing any physical event impinging on the organism as a stimulus and any part of the organism's behavior as a response, he must conclude that behavior has not been demonstrated to be lawful. In the present state of our knowledge, we must attribute an overwhelming influence on actual behavior to ill-defined factors of attention, set, volition, and caprice. If we accept the narrower definitions, the behavior is lawful by definition (if it consists of responses); but this fact is of limited significance, since most of what the animal does will simply not be considered behavior. Hence, the psychologist either must admit that behavior is not lawful (or that he cannot at present show that it is — not at all a damaging admission for a developing science), or must restrict his attention to those highly limited areas in which it is lawful (e.g., with adequate controls, bar-pressing in rats; lawfulness of the observed behavior provides, for Skinner, an implicit definition of a good experiment).

Skinner does not consistently adopt either course. He utilizes the experimental results as evidence for the scientific character of his system of behavior, and analogic guesses (formulated in terms of a metaphoric extension of the technical vocabulary of the laboratory) as evidence for its scope. This creates the illusion of a rigorous scientific theory with a very broad scope, although in fact the terms used in the description of real-life and of laboratory behavior may be mere homonyms, with at most a vague similarity of meaning. To substantiate this evaluation, a critical account of his book must show that with a literal reading (where the terms of the descriptive system have something like the technical meanings given in Skinner's definitions) the book covers almost no aspect of linguistic behavior, and that with a metaphoric reading, it is no more scientific than the traditional approaches to this subject matter, and rarely as clear and careful.[5]

3

Consider first Skinner's use of the notions *stimulus* and *response*. In *Behavior of Organisms* (9) he commits himself to the narrow definition for these terms. A part of the environment and a part of behavior are called *stimulus* (eliciting, discriminated, or reinforcing) and *response*, respectively, only if they are lawfully related; that is, if the *dynamic laws* relating them show smooth and reproducible curves. Evidently, stimuli and responses, so defined, have not been shown to figure very widely in ordinary human behavior.[6] We can, in the face of presently available evidence, continue to maintain the lawfulness of the relation between stimulus and response only by depriving them of their objective character. A typical example of *stimulus control* for Skinner would be the response to a piece of music with the utterance *Mozart* or to a painting with the response *Dutch*. These responses are asserted to be "under the control of extremely subtle properties" of the physical object or event (108). Suppose instead of saying *Dutch* we had said *Clashes with the wallpaper, I thought you liked abstract work, Never saw it before, Tilted, Hanging too low, Beautiful, Hideous, Remember our camping trip last summer?*, or whatever else might come into our minds when looking at a picture (in Skinnerian translation, whatever other responses exist in sufficient strength). Skinner could only say that each of these responses is under the control of some other stimulus property of the physical object. If we look at a red chair and say *red*, the response is under the control of the stimulus *redness*; if we say *chair*, it is under the control of the collection of properties (for Skinner, the object) *chairness* (110), and similarly for any other response. This device is as simple as it is empty. Since properties are free for the asking (we have as many of them as we have nonsynonymous descriptive expressions in our language, whatever this means exactly), we can account for a wide class of responses in terms of Skinnerian functional analysis by identifying the *controlling stimuli*. But the word *stimulus* has lost all objectivity in this usage. Stimuli are no longer part of the outside physical world; they are driven back into the organism. We identify the stimulus when we hear the response. It is clear from such examples, which abound, that the talk of *stimulus control* simply disguises a complete retreat to mentalistic psychology. We cannot predict verbal behavior in terms of the stimuli in the speaker's environment, since we do not know what the current stimuli are until he responds. Furthermore, since we cannot control the property of a physical object to which an individual will respond, except in highly artificial cases, Skinner's claim that his system, as opposed to the traditional one, permits the practical control of verbal behavior[7] is quite false.

Other examples of *stimulus control* merely add to the general mystification. Thus, a proper noun is held to be a response, "under the control of a specific person or thing" (as controlling stimulus, 113). I have often used the words *Eisenhower* and *Moscow*, which I presume are proper nouns if anything is, but have never been *stimulated* by the corresponding objects. How can this fact be made compatible with this definition? Suppose that I use the name of a friend who is not present. Is this an instance of a proper noun under the control of the friend as stimulus? Elsewhere it is asserted that a stimulus controls a response in the sense that presence of the stimulus increases the probability of the response. But it is obviously untrue that the probability that a speaker will produce a full name is increased when its bearer faces the speaker. Furthermore, how can one's own name be a proper noun in this sense? A multitude of similar questions arise immediately. It appears that the word *control* here is merely a misleading paraphrase for the traditional *denote* or *refer*. The assertion (115) that so far as the speaker is concerned, the relation of reference is "simply the probability that the speaker will emit a response of a given form in the presence of a stimulus having specified properties" is surely incorrect if we take the words *presence, stimulus,* and *probability* in their literal sense. That they are not intended to be taken literally is indicated by many examples, as when a response is said to be "controlled" by a situation or state of affairs as "stimulus." Thus, the expression *a needle in a haystack* "may be controlled as a unit by a particular type of situation" (116); the words in a single part of speech, e.g., all adjectives, are under the control of a single set of subtle properties of stimuli (121); "the sentence *The boy runs a store* is under the control of an extremely complex stimulus situation" (335); "*He is not at all well* may function as a standard response under the control of a state of affairs which might also control *He is ailing*" (325); when an envoy observes events in a foreign country and reports upon his return, his report is under "remote stimulus control" (416); the statement *This is war* may be a response to a "confusing international situation" (441); the suffix *-ed* is controlled by that "subtle property of stimuli which we speak of as action-in-the-past" (121) just a the *-s* in *The boy runs* is under the control of such specific features of the situation as its "currency" (332). No characterization of the notion *stimulus control* that is remotely related to the bar-pressing experiment (or that preserves the faintest objectivity) can be made to cover a set of examples like these, in which, for example, the *controlling stimulus* need not even impinge on the responding organism.

Consider now Skinner's use of the notion *response*. The problem of identifying units in verbal behavior has of course been a primary concern of linguists, and it seems very likely that experimental psychologists should be able to provide much-needed assistance in clearing up the many remaining difficulties in systematic identification. Skinner recognizes (20) the fundamental character of the problem of identification of a unit of verbal behavior, but is satisfied with an answer so vague and subjective that it does not really contribute to its solution. The unit of verbal behavior — the verbal operant — is defined as a class of responses of identifiable form functionally related to one or more controlling variables. No method is suggested for determining in a particular instance what are the controlling variables, how many such units have occurred, or where their boundaries are in the total response. Nor is any attempt made to specify how much of what kind of similarity in form or *control* is required for two physical events to be considered instances of the same operant. In short, no answers are suggested for the most elementary questions that must be asked of anyone proposing a method for description of behavior. Skinner is content with what he calls an *extrapolation* of the concept of operant developed in the laboratory of the verbal field. In the typical Skinnerian experiment, the problem of identifying the unit of behavior is not too crucial. It is defined, by fiat, as a recorded peck or bar-press, and systematic variations in the rate of this operant and its resistance to extinction are studied as a function of deprivation and scheduling of reinforcement (pellets). The operant is thus defined with respect to a particular experimental procedure. This is perfectly reasonable and has led to many interesting results. It is, however, completely meaningless to speak of extrapolating this concept of operant to ordinary verbal behavior. Such "extrapolation" leaves us with no way of justifying one or another decision about the units in the "verbal repertoire."

Skinner specifies "response strength" as the basic datum, the basic dependent variable in his functional analysis. In the bar-pressing experiment, response strength is defined in terms of rate of emission during extinction. Skinner has argued[8] that this is "the only datum that varies significantly and in the expected direction under conditions which are relevant to the 'learning process.'" In the book under review, response strength is defined as "probability of emission" (22). This definition provides a comforting impression of objectivity, which, however, is quickly dispelled when we look into the matter more closely. The term *probability* has some rather obscure meaning for Skinner in this book.[9] We are told, on the one hand, that "our evidence for the contribution of each variable [to response strength] is based on observation of frequencies alone" (28). At the same time, it appears that frequency is a very misleading measure of strength, since, for example, the frequency of a response may be "primarily attributable to the frequency of occurrence of controlling variables" (27). It is not clear how the frequency of a response can be attributable to anything BUT the frequency of occurrence of its controlling variables if we accept Skinner's view that the behavior occurring in a given situation is "fully determined" by the relevant controlling variables (175, 228). Furthermore, although the evidence for the contribution of each variable to response strength is based on observation of frequencies alone, it turns out that "we base the notion of strength upon several kinds of evidence" (22), in particular (22-28): emission of the response (particularly in unusual circumstances), energy level (stress), pitch level, speed and delay of emission, size of letters etc. in writing, immediate repetition, and — a final factor, relevant but misleading — over-all frequency.

Of course, Skinner recognizes that these measures do not co-vary, because (among other reasons) pitch, stress, quantity, and reduplication may have internal linguistic functions.[10] However, he does not hold these conflicts to be very important, since the proposed factors indicative of strength are "fully understood by everyone" in the culture (27). For example, "if we are shown a prized work of art and exclaim *Beautiful!*, the speed and energy of the response will not be lost on the owner." It does not appear totally obvious that in this case the way to impress the owner is to shriek *Beautiful* in a loud, high-pitched voice, repeatedly, and with no delay (high response strength). It may be equally effective to look at the picture silently (long delay) and then to murmur *Beautiful* in a soft, low-pitched voice (by definition, very low response strength).

It is not unfair, I believe, to conclude from Skinner's discussion of response strength, the *basic datum* in functional analysis, that his *extrapolation* of the notion of probability can be best interpreted as, in effect, nothing more than a decision to use the word *probability*, with its favorable connotation of objectivity, as a cover term to paraphrase such low-status words as *interest, intention, belief,* and the like. This interpretation is fully justified by the way in which Skinner uses the terms *probability* and *strength*. To cite just one example, Skinner defines the process of confirming an assertion in science as one of "generating additional variables to increase its probability" (425), and more generally, its strength (425-9). If we take this suggestion quite literally, the degree of confirmation of a scientific assertion can be measured as a simple function of the loudness, pitch, and frequency with which it is proclaimed, and a general procedure for increasing its degree of confirmation would be, for instance, to train machine guns on large crowds of people who have been instructed to shout it. A better indication of what Skinner probably has in mind here is given by his description of how the theory of evolution, as an example, is confirmed. This "single set of verbal responses ... is made more plausible — is strengthened — by several types of construction based upon verbal responses in geology, paleontology, genetics, and so on" (427). We are no doubt to interpret the terms *strength* and *probability* in this context as paraphrases of more familiar locutions such as "justified belief" or "warranted assertability," or something of the sort. Similar latitude of interpretation is presumably expected when we read that "frequency of effective action accounts in turn from what we may call the listener's belief" (88) or that "our belief in what someone tells us is similarly a function of, or identical with, our tendency to act upon the verbal stimuli which he provides" (160)[11]

I think it is evident, then, that Skinner's use of the terms *stimulus, control, response,* and *strength* justify the general conclusion stated in the last paragraph of Section 2. The way in which these terms are brought to bear on the actual data indicates that we must interpret them as mere paraphrases for the popular vocabulary commonly used to describe behavior and as having no particular connection with the homonymous expressions used in the description of laboratory experiments. Naturally, this terminological revision adds no objectivity to the familiar *mentalistic* mode of description.

4

The other fundamental notion borrowed from the description of bar-pressing experiments is *reinforcement*. It raises problems which are similar, and even more serious. In *Behavior of Organisms*, "the operation of reinforcement is defined as the presentation of a certain kind of stimulus in a temporal relation with either a stimulus or response. A reinforcing stimulus is defined as such by its power to produce the resulting change [in strength]. There is no circularity about this: some stimuli are found to produce the change, others not, and they are classified as reinforcing and nonreinforcing accordingly" (62). This is a perfectly appropriate definition[12] for the study of schedules of reinforcement. It is perfectly useless, however, in the discussion of real-life behavior, unless we can somehow characterize the stimuli which are reinforcing (and the situations and conditions under which they are reinforcing). Consider first of all the status of the basic principle that Skinner calls the "law of conditioning" (law of effect). It reads: "if the occurrence of an operant is followed by presence of a reinforcing stimulus, the strength is increased" (*Behavior of Organisms*, 21). As *reinforcement* was defined, this law becomes a tautology.[13] For Skinner, learning is just change in response strength.[14] Although the statement that presence of reinforcement is a sufficient condition for learning and maintenance of behavior is vacuous, the claim that it is a necessary condition may have some content, depending on how the class of reinforcers (and appropriate situations is characterized. Skinner does make it very clear that in his view reinforcement is a necessary condition for language learning and for the continued availability of linguistic responses in the adult.[15] However, the looseness of the term *reinforcement* as Skinner uses it in the book under review makes it entirely pointless to inquire into the truth or falsity of this claim. Examining the instances of what Skinner calls *reinforcement*, we find that not even the requirements that a reinforcer be an identifiable stimulus is taken seriously. In fact, the term is used in such a way that the assertion that reinforcement is necessary for learning and continued availability of behavior is likewise empty.

To show this, we consider some examples of *reinforcement*. First of all, we find a heavy appeal to automatic self-reinforcement. Thus, "a man talks to himself ... because of the reinforcement he receives" (163); "the child is reinforced automatically when he duplicates the sounds of airplanes, streetcars ..." (164); "the young child alone in the nursery may automatically reinforce his own exploratory verbal behavior when he produces sounds which he has heard in the speech of others" (58); "the speaker who is also an accomplished listener 'knows when he has correctly echoed a response' and is reinforced thereby" (68); thinking is "behaving which automatically affects the behavior and is reinforcing because it does so" (438; cutting one's finger should thus be reinforcing, and an example of thinking); "the verbal fantasy, whether overt or covert, is automatically reinforcing to the speaker as listener. Just as the musician plays or composes what he is reinforced by hearing, or as the artist paints what reinforces him visually, so the speaker engaged in verbal fantasy says what he is reinforced by hearing or writes what he is reinforced by reading" (439); similarly, care in problem solving, and rationalization, are automatically self-reinforcing (442-43). We can also reinforce someone by emitting verbal behavior as such (since this rules out a class of aversive stimulations, 167), by not emitting verbal behavior (keeping silent and paying attention, 199), or by acting appropriately on some future occasion (152; "the strength of [the speaker's] behavior is determined mainly by the behavior which the listener will exhibit with respect to a given state of affairs"; this Skinner considers the general case of "communication" or "letting the listener know"). In most such cases, of course, the speaker is not present at the time when the reinforcement takes place, as when "the artist ... is reinforced by the effects his works have upon ... others" (224), or when the writer is reinforced by the fact that his "verbal behavior may reach over centuries or to thousands of listeners or readers at the same time. The writer may not be reinforced often or immediately, but his net reinforcement may be great" (206; this accounts for the great "strength" of his behavior). An individual may also find it reinforcing to injure someone by criticism or by bringing bad news, or to publish an experimental result which upsets the theory of a rival (154), to describe circumstances which would be reinforcing if they were to occur (165), to avoid repetition (222), to "hear" his own name though in fact it was not mentioned or to hear nonexistent words in his child's babbling (259), to clarify or otherwise intensify the effect of a stimulus which serves an important discriminative function (416), and so on.

From this sample, it can be seen that the notion of reinforcement has totally lost whatever objective meaning it may ever have had. Running through these examples, we see that a person can be reinforced though he emits no response at all, and that the reinforcing *stimulus* need not impinge on the *reinforced person* or need not even exist (it is sufficient that it be imagined or hoped for). When we read that a person plays what music he likes (165), says what he likes (165), thinks what he likes (438-39), reads what books he likes (163), etc. BECAUSE he finds it reinforcing to do so, or that we write books or inform others of facts BECAUSE we are reinforced by what we hope will be the ultimate behavior of reader or listener, we can only conclude that the term *reinforcement* has a purely ritual function. The phrase "*X* is reinforced by *Y* (stimulus, state of affairs, event, etc.)" is being used as a cover term for "*X* wants *Y*," "*X* likes *Y*," "*X* wishes that *Y* were the case," etc. Invoking the term *reinforcement* has no explanatory force, and any idea that this paraphrase introduces any new clarity or objectivity into the description of wishing, liking, etc., is a serious delusion. The only effect is to obscure the important differences among the notions being paraphrased. Once we recognize the latitude with which the term *reinforcement* is being used, many rather startling comments lose their initial effect — for instance, that the behavior of the creative artist is "controlled entirely by the contingencies of reinforcement" (150). What has been hoped for from the psychologist is some indication how the casual and informal description of everyday behavior in the popular vocabulary can be explained or clarified in terms of the notions developed in careful experiment and observation, or perhaps replaced in terms of a better scheme. A mere terminological revision, in which a term borrowed from the laboratory is used with the full vagueness of the ordinary vocabulary, is of no conceivable interest.

It seems that Skinner's claim that all verbal behavior is acquired and maintained in "strength" through reinforcement is quite empty, because his notion of reinforcement has no clear content, functioning only as a cover term for any factor, detectable or not, related to acquisition or maintenance of verbal behavior.[16] Skinner's use of the term *conditioning* suffers from a similar difficulty. Pavlovian and operant conditioning are processes about which psychologists have developed real understanding. Instruction of human beings is not. The claim that instruction and imparting of information are simply matters of conditioning (357-66) is pointless. The claim is true, if we extend the term *conditioning* to cover these processes, but we know no more about them after having revised this term in such a way as to deprive it of its relatively clear and objective character. It is, as far as we know, quite false, if we use *conditioning* in its literal sense. Similarly, when we say that "it is the function of predication to facilitate the transfer of response from one term to another or from one object to another"(361), we have said nothing of significance. In what sense is this true of the predication *Whales are mammals?* Or, to take Skinner's example what point is there in saying that the effect of *The telephone is out of order* on the listener is to bring behavior formerly controlled by the stimulus *out of order* under control of the stimulus *telephone* (or the telephone itself) by a process of simple conditioning (362)? What laws of conditioning hold in this case? Furthermore, what behavior is *controlled* by the stimulus *out of order*, in the abstract? Depending on the object of which this is predicated, the present state of motivation of the listener, etc., the behavior may vary from rage to pleasure, from fixing the object to throwing it out, from simply not using it to trying to use it in the normal way (e.g., to see if it is really out of order), and so on. To speak of "conditioning" or "bringing a previously available behavior under control of a new stimulus" in such a case is just a kind of play-acting at science (cf. also 43*n*).

11

The preceding discussion covers all the major notions that Skinner introduces in his descriptive system. My purpose in discussing the concepts one by one was to show that in each case, if we take his terms in their literal meaning, the description covers almost no aspect of verbal behavior, and if we take them metaphorically, the description offers no improvement over various traditional formulations. The terms borrowed from experimental psychology simply lose their objective meaning with this extension, and take over the full vagueness of ordinary language. Since Skinner limits himself to such a small set of terms for paraphrase, many important distinctions are obscured. I think that this analysis supports the view expressed in Section 1, that elimination of the independent contribution of the speaker and learner (a result which Skinner considers of great importance, cf. 311-12) can be achieved only at the cost of eliminating all significance from the descriptive system, which then operates at a level so gross and crude that no answers are suggested to the most elementary questions.[46] The questions to which Skinner has addressed his speculations are hopelessly premature. It is futile to inquire into the causation of verbal behavior until much more is known about the specific character of this behavior; and there is little point in speculating about the process of acquisition without much better understanding of what is acquired.

Anyone who seriously approaches the study of linguistic behavior, whether linguist, psychologist, or philosopher, must quickly become aware of the enormous difficulty of stating a problem which will define the area of his investigations, and which will not be either completely trivial or hopelessly beyond the range of present-day understanding and technique. In selecting functional analysis as his problem, Skinner has set himself the task of the latter type. In an extremely interesting and insightful paper,[47] K. S. Lashley has implicitly delimited a class of problems which can be approached in a fruitful way by the linguist and psychologist, and which are clearly preliminary to those which Skinner is concerned. Lashley recognizes, as anyone must who seriously considers the data, that the composition and production of an utterance is not simply a matter of stringing together a sequence of responses under the control of outside stimulation and intraverbal association, and that the syntactic organization of an utterance is not something directly represented in any simple way in the physical structure of the utterance itself. A variety of observations lead him to conclude that syntactic structure is "a generalized pattern imposed on the specific acts as they occur" (512), and that "a consideration of the structure of the sentence and other motor sequences will show . . . that there are, behind the overtly expressed sequences, a multiplicity of integrative processes which can only be inferred from the final results of their activity" (509). He also comments on the great difficulty of determining the "selective mechanisms" used in the actual construction of a particular utterance (522).

Although present-day linguistics cannot provide a precise account of these integrative processes, imposed patterns, and selective mechanisms, it can at least set itself the problem of characterizing these completely. It is reasonable to regard the grammar of a language *L* ideally as a mechanism that provides an enumeration of the sentences in *L* in something like the way in which a deductive theory gives an enumeration of a set of theorems. (*Grammar*, in this sense of the word, includes phonology.) Furthermore, the theory of language can be regarded as a study of the formal properties of such grammars, and, with a precise enough formulation, this general theory can provide a uniform method for determining, from the process of generation of a given sentence, a structural description which can give a good deal of insight into how this sentence is used and understood. In short, it should be possible to derive from a properly formulated grammar a statement of the integrative processes and generalized patterns imposed on the specific acts that constitute an utterance. The rules of a grammar of the appropriate form can be subdivided into two types, optional and obligatory; only the latter must be applied in generating an utterance. The optional rules of the grammar can be viewed, then, as the selective mechanisms involved in the production of a particular utterance. The problem of specifying these integrative processes and selective mechanisms is nontrivial and not beyond the range of possible investigation. The results of such a study might, as Lashley suggests, be of independent interest for psychology and neurology (and conversely). Although such a study, even if successful, would by no means answer the major problems involved in the investigation of meaning and the causation of behavior, it surely will not be unrelated to these. It is at least possible, furthermore, that such a notion as *semantic generalization*, to which such heavy appeal is made in all approaches to language in use, conceals complexities and specific structure of inference not far different from those that can be studied and exhibited in the case of syntax, and that consequently the general character of the result of syntactic investigation may be corrective to oversimplified approaches to the theory of meaning.

The behavior of the speaker, listener, and learner of language constitutes, of course, the actual data for any study of language. The construction of a grammar which enumerates sentences in such a way that a meaningful structural description can be determined for each sentence does not in itself provide an account of this actual behavior. It merely characterizes abstractly the ability of one who has mastered the language to distinguish sentences from nonsentences, to understand new sentences (in part), to note certain ambiguities, etc. These are very remarkable abilities. We constantly read and hear new sequences of words, recognize them as sentences, and understand them. It is easy to show that the new events that we accept and understand as sentences are not related to those with which we are familiar by any simple notion of formal (or semantic or statistical) similarity or identity of grammatical frame. Talk of generalization in this case is entirely pointless and empty. It appears that we recognize a new item as a sentence not because it matches some familiar item in any simple way, but because it is generated by the grammar that each individual has somehow and in some form internalized. And we understand a new sentence, in part, because we are somehow capable of determining the process by which this sentence is derived in this grammar.

Suppose that we manage to construct grammars having the properties outlined above. We can then attempt to describe and study the achievement of the speaker, listener, and learner. The speaker and the listener, we must assume, have already acquired the capacities characterized abstractly by the grammar. The speaker's task is to select a particular compatible set of optional rules. If we know, from grammatical study, what choices are available to him and what conditions of compatibility the choices must meet, we can proceed meaningfully to investigate the factors that lead him to make one or another choice. The listener (or reader) must determine, from an exhibited utterance, what optional rules were chosen in the construction of the utterance. It must be admitted that the ability of a human being to do this far surpasses our present understanding. The child who learns a language has in some sense constructed the grammar for himself on the basis of his observation of sentences and nonsentences (i.e., correction by the verbal community). Study of the actual observed ability of a speaker to distinguish sentences from nonsentences, detect ambiguities, etc., apparently forces us to the conclusion that this grammar is of an extremely complex and abstract character, and that the young child has succeeded in carrying out what from the formal point of view, at least, seems to be a remarkable type of theory construction. Furthermore, this task is accomplished is an astonishingly short time, to a large extent independently of intelligence, and in a comparable way by all children. Any theory of learning must cope with these facts.

It is not easy to accept the view that a child is capable of constructing an extremely complex mechanism for generating a set of sentences, some of which he has heard, or that an adult can instantaneously determine whether (and if so, how) a particular item is generated by this mechanism, which has many of the properties of an abstract deductive theory. Yet this appears to be a fair description of the performance of the speaker, listener, and learner. If this is correct, we can predict that a direct attempt to account for the actual behavior of speaker, listener, and learner, not based on a prior understanding of the structure of grammars, will achieve very limited success. The grammar must be regarded as a component in the behavior of the speaker and listener which can only be inferred, as Lashley has put it, from the resulting physical acts. The fact that all normal children acquire essentially comparable grammars of great complexity with remarkable rapidity suggests that human beings are somehow specially designed to do this, with data-handling or "hypothesis-formulating" ability of unknown character and complexity.[48] The study of linguistic structure may ultimately lead to some significant insights into this matter. At the moment the question cannot be seriously posed, but in principle it may be possible to study the problem of determining what the built-in structure of an information-processing (hypothesis-forming) system must be to enable it to arrive at the grammar of a language from the available data in the available time. At any rate, just as the attempt to eliminate the contribution of the speaker leads to a "mentalistic" descriptive system that succeeds only in blurring important traditional distinctions, a refusal to study the contribution of the child to language learning permits only a superficial account of language acquisition, with a vast and unanalyzed contribution attributed to a step called *generalization* which in fact includes just about everything of interest in this process. If the study of language is limited in these ways, it seems inevitable that major aspects of verbal behavior will remain a mystery.

NOTES

1   Skinner's confidence in recent achievements in the study of animal behavior and their applicability to complex human behavior does not appear to be widely shared. In many recent publications of confirmed behaviorists there is a prevailing note of skepticism with regard to the scope of the achievements. For representative comments, see the contributions to *Modern Learning Theory* (by W. K. Estes *et al.*; New York: Appleton-Century-Crofts, Inc., 1954); B. R. Bugelski, *Psychology of Learning* (New York: Holt, Rhinehart & Winston, Inc., 1956); S. Koch, in *Nebraska Symposium on Motivation, 58* (London, 1956); W. S. Verplanck, "Learned and Innate Behavior," *Psych. Rev., 52* (1955), 139. Perhaps the strongest view is that of H. Harlow, who has asserted ("Mice, Monkeys, Men, and Motives," *Psych. Rev., 60* [1953], 23-32) that "a strong case came be made for the proposition that the importance of the psychological problems studied during the last 15 years has decreased as a negatively accelerated function approaching an asymptote of complete indifference." N. Tinbergen, a leading representative of a different approach to animal-behavior studies (comparative ethology), concludes a discussion of *functional analysis* with the comment that "we may now draw the conclusion that the causation of behavior is immensely more complex than was assumed in the generalizations of the past. A number of internal and external factors act upon complex central nervous structures. Second, it will be obvious that the facts at our disposal are very fragmentary indeed" — *The Study of Instinct* (Toronto: Oxford Univ. Press, 1951), p. 74.

2   In *Behavior of Organisms* (New York: Appleton-Century Crofts, Inc., 1938). Skinner remarks that "although a conditioned operant is the result of the correlation of the response with a particular reinforcement, a relation between it and a discriminative stimulus acting prior to the response is the almost universal rule" (178-79). Even emitted behavior is held to be produced by some sort of "originating force" (51) which, in the case of operant behavior, is not under experimental control. The distinction between eliciting stimuli, discriminating stimuli, and "originating forces" has never been adequately clarified and becomes even more confusing when private internal events are considered to be discriminated stimuli (see below).

3   In a famous experiment, chimpanzees were taught to perform complex tasks to receive tokens which had become secondary reinforcers because of association with food. The idea that money, approval, prestige, etc. actually acquire their motivating effects on human behavior according to this paradigm is unproved, and not particularly plausible. Many psychologists within the behaviorist movement are quite skeptical about this (cf. 23*n*). As in the case of most aspects of human behavior, the evidence about secondary reinforcement is so fragmentary, conflicting, and complex that almost any view can find some support.

4   Skinner's remark quoted above about the generality of his basic results must be understood in the light of the experimental limitations he has imposed. If it were true in any deep sense that the basic processes in language are well understood and free of species restriction, it would be extremely odd that language is limited to man. With the exception of a few scattered observations (cf. his article, "A Case History in Scientific Method," *The American Psychologist*, 11 [1956], 221-33), Skinner is apparently basing this claim on the fact that qualitatively similar results are obtained with bar pressing of rats and pecking of pigeons under special conditions of deprivation and various schedules of reinforcement. One immediately questions how much can be based on these facts, which are in part at least an artifact traceable to experimental design and the definition of *stimulus* and *response* in terms of *smooth dynamic curves* (see below). The dangers

inherent in any attempt to *extrapolate* to complex behavior from the study of such simple responses as bar pressing should be obvious and have often been commented on (cf., e.g., Harlow, *op. cit.*). The generality of even the simplest results is open to serious question. Cf. in this connection M. E. Bitterman, J. Wodinsky, and D. K. Candland, "Some Comparative Psychology," *Am. Jour. of Psych.*, *71* (1958), 94-110, where it is shown that there are important qualitative differences in solution of comparable elementary problems by rats and fish.

5   An analogous argument, in connection with a different aspect of Skinner's thinking is given by M. Scriven in *"A Study of Radical Behaviorism,"* *Univ. of Minn. Studies in Philosophy of Science*, I. Cf. Verplanck's contribution to *Modern Learning Theory, op. cit.* pp. 283-88, for more general discussion of the difficulties in formulating an adequate definition of *stimulus* and *response*. He concludes, quite correctly, that in Skinner's sense of the word, stimuli are not objectively identifiable independently of the resulting behavior, nor are they manipulable. Verplanck presents a clear discussion of many other aspects of Skinner's system, commenting on the intestability of many of the so-called "laws of behavior" and the limited scope of many of the others, and the arbitrary and obscure character of Skinner's notion of *lawful relation*; and, at the same time, noting the importance of the experimental data that Skinner has accumulated.

6   In *Behavior of Organisms*, Skinner apparently was willing to accept this consequence. He insists (41-42) that the terms of casual description in the popular vocabulary are not validly descriptive until the defining properties of stimulus and response are specified, the correlation is demonstrated experimentally, and the dynamic changes in it are shown to be lawful. Thus, in describing a child as hiding from a dog, "it will not be enough to dignify the popular vocabulary by appealing to essential properties of *dogness* or *hidingness* and to suppose them intuitively known." But this is exactly what Skinner does in the book under review, as we will see directly.

7   253f. and elsewhere, repeatedly. As an example of how well we can control behavior using the notions developed in this book, Skinner shows here how he would go about evoking the response *pencil*. The most effective way, he suggests, is to say to the subject, "Please say *pencil*" (our chances would, presumably, be even further improved by use of "aversive stimulation," e.g., holding a gun to his head). We can also "make sure that no pencil or writing instrument is available, then hand our subject a pad of paper appropriate to pencil sketching, and offer him a handsome reward for a recognizable picture of a cat." It would also be useful to have voices saying *pencil* or *pen and* . . . in the background; signs reading *pencil* or *pen and* . . . ; or to place a "large and unusual pencil in an unusual place clearly in sight." "Under such circumstances, it is highly probable that our subject will say *pencil*." "The available techniques are all illustrated in this sample." These contributions of behavior theory to the practical control of human behavior are amply illustrated elsewhere in the book, as when Skinner shows (13-14) how we can evoke the response *red* (the device suggested is to hold a red object before the subject and say, "Tell me what color this is").

　　In fairness, it must be mentioned that there are certain nontrivial applications of *operant conditioning* to the control of human behavior. A wide variety of experiments have shown that the number of plural nouns (for example) produced by the subject will increase if the experimenter says, " right" or "good" when one is produced (similarly, positive attitudes on a certain issue, stories with particular content, etc.; cf. L. Krasner, "Studies of the Conditioning of Verbal Behavior," *Psych. Bull.*, *55* [1958], for a survey of several dozen experiments of this kind, mostly with positive results). It is of some interest that the subject is usually unaware of the process. Just what insight this gives into normal verbal behavior is not obvious. Nevertheless, it is an example of positive and not totally expected results using the Skinnerian paradigm.

8   "Are Theories of Learning Necessary?", *Psych. Rev.*, *57* (1950), 193-216.

9   And elsewhere. In his paper "Are Theories of Learning Necessary?" Skinner considers the problem how to extend his analysis of behavior to experimental situations in which it is impossible to observe frequencies, rate of response being the only valid datum. His answer is that

"the notion of probability is usually extrapolated to cases in which a frequency analysis cannot be carried out. In the field of behavior we arrange a situation in which frequencies are available as data, but we use the notion of probability in analyzing or formulating instances of even types of behavior which are not susceptible to this analysis" (199). There are, of course, conceptions of probability not based directly on frequency, but I do not see how any of these apply to the cases that Skinner has in mind. I see no way of interpreting the quoted passage other than as signifying an intention to use the word *probability* in describing behavior quite independently of whether the notion of probability is at all relevant.

10 Fortunately, "In English this present no great difficulty" since, for example, "relative pitch levels ... are not ... important" (25). No reference is made to the numerous studies of the function of relative pitch levels and other intonational features in English.

11 The vagueness of the word *tendency*, as opposed to *frequency*, saves the latter quotation from the obvious incorrectness of the former. Nevertheless, a good deal of stretching is necessary. If *tendency* has anything like its ordinary meaning, the remark is clearly false. One may believe strongly the assertion that Jupiter has four moons, that many of Sophocles' plays have been irretrievably lost, that the earth will burn to a crisp in ten million years, and so on, without experiencing the slightest tendency to act upon these verbal stimuli. We may, of course, turn Skinner's assertion into a very unilluminating truth by defining "tendency to act" to include tendencies to answer questions in certain ways, under motivation to say what one believes is true.

12 One should add, however, that it is in general not the stimulus as such that is reinforcing, but the stimulus in a particular situational context. Depending on experimental arrangement, a particular physical event or object may be reinforcing, punishing, or unnoticed. Because Skinner limits himself to a particular, very simple experimental arrangement, it is not necessary for him to add this qualification, which would not be at all easy to formulate precisely. But it is of course necessary if he expects to extend his descriptive system to behavior in general.

13 This has been frequently noted.

14 See, for example, "Are Theories of Learning Necessary?", *op. cit.*, p. 199. Elsewhere, he suggests that the term *learning* be restricted to complex situations, but these are not characterized.

15 "A child requires verbal behavior when relatively unpatterned vocalizations, selectively reinforced, gradually assume forms which produce appropriate consequences in a given verbal community" (31). "Differential reinforcement shapes up all verbal forms, and when a prior stimulus enters into the contingency, reinforcement is responsible for its resulting control.... The availability of behavior, its probability or strength, depends on whether reinforcements *continue* in effect and according to what schedules" (203-4): elsewhere frequently.

16 Talk of schedules of reinforcement here is entirely pointless. How are we to decide, for example, according to what schedules covert reinforcement is *arranged*, as in thinking or verbal fantasy, or what the scheduling is of such factors as silence, speech, and appropriate future reactions to communicated information?

46 E.g., what are in fact the actual units of verbal behavior? Under what conditions will a physical event capture the attention (be a stimulus) or be a reinforcer? How do we decide what stimuli are in "control" in a specific case? When are stimuli "similar"? And so on. (It is not interesting to be told, e.g., that we say *Stop* to an automobile or billiard ball because they are sufficiently similar to reinforcing people [46].)

The use of unanalyzed notions like *similar* and *generalization* is particularly disturbing, since it indicates an apparent lack of interest in every significant aspect of the learning or the use of language in new situations. No one has ever doubted that in some sense, language is learned by generalization, or that novel utterances and situations are in some way similar to familiar ones. The only matter of serious interest is the specific "similarity." Skinner has, apparently, no interest in this. Keller and Schoenfield, *op. cit.*, proceed to incorporate these notions (which they identify) into their Skinnerian "modern objective psychology" by defining two stimuli to be similar when "we make the same sort of *response* to them" (124; but when are responses of the "same sort"?). They do not seem to notice that this definition converts their "principle of generalization" (116), under any reasonable interpretation of this, into a tautology. It is obvious that such a definition will not be of much help in the study of language learning or construction of new responses in appropriate situations.

[47] "The Problem of Serial Order in Behavior," in L. A. Jeffress, ed., *Hixon Symposium on Cerebral Mechanisms in Behavior* (New York: John Wiley & Sons Inc., 1951). Reprinted in F. A. Beach, D. O. Hebb, C. T. Morgan, H. W. Nissen, eds., *The Neuropsychology of Lashley* (New York: McGraw-Hill Book Company, 1960). Page references are to the latter.

[48] There is nothing essentially mysterious about this. Complex innate behavior patterns and innate "tendencies to learn in specific ways" have been carefully studied in lower organisms. Many psychologists have been inclined to believe that such biological structure will not have an important effect on acquisition of complex behavior in higher organisms, but I have not been able to find any serious justification for this attitude. Some recent studies have stressed the necessity for carefully analyzing the strategies available to the organism, regarded as complex "information processing system" (cf. J. S. Bruner, J. J Goodnow, and G. A. Austin, *A Study of Thinking* [New York, 1956]; A. Newell, J. C. Shaw, and H. A. Simon, "Elements of a Theory of Human Problem Solving," *Psych. Rev.,* 65 [1958], 151-66), if anything significant is to be said about the character of human learning. These may be largely innate, or developed by early learning processes about which very little is yet known. (But see Harlow, "The Formation of Learning Sets," *Psych. Rev.,* 56 (1949), 51-65, and many later papers, where striking shifts in the character of learning are shown as a result of early training; also D. O. Hebb, *Organization of Behavior,* 109 ff.). They are undoubtedly quite complex. Cf. Lenneberg, *op. cit.,* and R. B. Lees, review of Noam Chomsky's *Syntactic Structures in Language,* 33 (1957), 406f, for discussion of the topics mentioned in this section.

12

THE LOGICAL ANALYSIS OF PSYCHOLOGY

Carl G. Hempel

Author's prefatory note, 1977. The original French version of this article was published in 1935. By the time it appeared in English, I had abandoned the narrow translationalist form of physicalism here set forth for a more liberal reductionist one, referred to in note 1, which presents psychological properties and states as partially characterized, but not defined, by bundles of behavioral dispositions. Since then, I have come to think that this conception requires still further broadening, and that the introduction and application of psychological terms and hypotheses is logically and methodologically analogous to the introduction and application of the terms and hypotheses of a physical theory. The consideration that prompted those changes also led me long ago to abandon as untenable the verificationist construal of the "empirical meaning" of a sentence — a construal which plays such a central role in the arguments set forth in this article.

Since the article is so far from representing my present views, I was disinclined to yet another republication, but I yielded to Dr. Block's plea that it offer a concise account of an early version of logical behaviorism and would thus be a useful contribution to this anthology.

In an effort to enhance the closeness of translation and the simplicity of formulation, I have made a number of small changes in the text of the original English version; none of these affects the substance of the article.

Hempel, Carl G. 1980. "The Logical Analysis of Psychology" in *Readings in Philosophy of Psychology, vol. 1*, edited by Ned Block. Pp. 14-23. © Harvard University Press.

I

One of the most important and most discussed problems of contemporary philosophy is that of determining how psychology should be characterized in the theory of science. This problem, which reaches beyond the limits of epistemological analysis and has engendered heated controversy in metaphysics itself, is brought to a focus by the familiar alternative, "Is psychology a natural science, or is it one of the sciences of mind and culture (*Geisteswissenschaften*)?"

The present article attempts to sketch the general lines of a new analysis of psychology, one which makes use of rigorous logical tools, and which has made possible decisive advances toward the solution of the above problem.[1] This analysis was carried out by the "Vienna Circle" (*Weiner Kreis*), the members of which (M. Schlick, R. Carnap, P. Frank, O. Neurath, F. Waismann, H. Feigl, etc.) have, during the past ten years, developed an extremely fruitful method for the epistemological examination and critique of the various sciences, based in part on the work of L. Wittgenstein.[2] We shall limit ourselves essentially to the examination of psychology as carried out by Carnap and Neurath.

The method characteristic of the studies of the Vienna Circle can be briefly defined as a *logical analysis of the language of science*. This method became possible only with the development of a subtle logical apparatus which makes use, in particular, of all the formal procedures of the modern symbolic logic.[3] However, in the following account, which does not pretend to give more than a broad orientation, we shall limit ourselves to setting out the general principles of this new method, without making use of strictly formal procedures.

II

Perhaps the best way to characterize the position of the Vienna Circle as it relates to psychology, is to say that it is the exact antithesis of the current epistemological thesis that there is a fundamental logical difference between experimental psychology, a natural science, and introspective psychology; and in general, between the natural sciences on the one hand, and the sciences of mind and culture on the other.[4] The common content of the widely different formulations used to express this contention, which we reject, can be set down as follows. Apart from certain aspects clearly related to physiology, psychology is radically different, both in subject matter and in method, from physics in the broad sense of the term. In particular, it is impossible to deal adequately with the subject matter of psychology by means of physical methods. The subject matter of physics includes such concepts as mass, wave length, temperature, field intensity, etc. In dealing with these, physics employs its distinctive method which makes a combined use of description and causal explanation. Psychology, on the other hand, has for its subject matter notions which are, in a broad sense, mental. They are *toto genere* different from the concepts of physics, and the appropriate method for dealing with them scientifically is that of empathetic insight called "introspection," a method which is peculiar to psychology.

One of the principal differences between the two kinds of subject matter is generally believed to consist in the fact that the objects investigated by psychology — in contradistinction to those of physics — are specifically endowed with meaning. Indeed, several proponents of this idea state that the distinctive method of psychology consists in "understanding the sense of meaningful structures" (*sinnvolle Gebilde verstehend zu erfassen*). Take, for example, the case of a man who speaks. Within the framework of physics, this process is considered to be completely explained once the movements which make up the utterance have been traced to their causes, that is to say, to certain physiological processes in the organism, and, in particular, in the central nervous system. But, it is said, this does not even broach the psychological problem. The latter begins with understanding the sense of what is said, and proceeds to integrate it into a wider context of meaning.

It is usually this latter idea which serves as a principle for the fundamental dichotomy that is introduced into the classification of the sciences. There is taken to be an *absolutely impassable gulf* between the *natural sciences* which have a subject matter devoid of meaning and the *sciences of mind and culture*, which have an intrinsically meaningful subject matter, the appropriate methodological instrument for the scientific study of which is "comprehension of meaning."

III

The position in the theory of science which we have just sketched has been attacked from several different points of view.[5] As far as psychology is concerned, one of the principal countertheses is that formulated by behaviorism, a theory born in America shortly before the war. (In Russia, Pavlov has developed similar ideas.) Its principal methodological postulate is that a scientific psychology should limit itself to the study of the bodily behavior with which man and the animals respond to changes in their physical environment, and should proscribe as nonscientific any descriptive use of terms from introspective or "understanding" psychology, such as 'feeling,' 'lived experience,' 'idea,' 'will,' 'intention,' 'goal,' disposition,' 'repression'.[6] We find in behaviorism, consequently, an attempt to construct a scientific psychology which would show by its success that even in psychology we have to do with purely physical processes, and that therefore there can be no impassable barrier between psychology and physics. However, this manner of undertaking the critique of a scientific thesis is not completely satisfactory. It seems, indeed, that the soundness of the behavioristic thesis expounded above depends on the possibility of fulfilling the program of behavioristic psychology. But one cannot expect the question as to the scientific status of psychology to be settled by empirical research in psychology itself. To achieve this is rather an undertaking in epistemology. We turn, therefore, to the consideration advanced by members of the Vienna Circle concerning this problem.

IV

Before addressing the question whether the subject matter of physics and psychology are essentially the same or different in nature, it is necessary first to clarify the very concept of the subject matter of a science. The theoretical content of a science is to be found in statements. It is necessary, therefore, to determine whether there is a fundamental difference between the statements of psychology and those of physics. Let us therefore ask what it is that determines the content — one can equally well say the "meaning" — of a statement. When, for example, do we know the meaning of the following statement: "Today at one o'clock, the temperature of such and such a place in the physics laboratory was 23.4° centigrade"? Clearly when, and only when, we know under what conditions we would call the statement true, and under what circumstances we would call it false. (Needless to say, it is not necessary to know whether or not the statement is true.) Thus, we understand the meaning of the above statement since we know that it is true when a tube of a certain kind filled with mercury (in short, a thermometer with a centigrade scale), placed at the indicated time at the location in question, exhibits a coincidence between the level of the mercury and the mark of the scale numbered 23.4. It is also true if in the same circumstances one can observe certain coincidences on another instrument called an "alcohol thermometer"; and, again, if a galvanometer connected with a thermopile shows a certain deviation when the thermopile is placed there at the indicated time. Further, there is a long series of other possibilities which make the statement true, each of which is described by a "physical test sentence," as we will call it. The statement itself clearly affirms nothing other than this: all these physical test sentences obtain. (However, one verifies only some of these physical test sentences, and then "concludes by induction" that the others obtain as well.) The statement, therefore, is nothing but an abbreviated formulation of all those test sentences.

Before continuing the discussion, let us sum up this result as follows:

1. A statement that specifies the temperature at a selected point in space-time can be "retranslated" without change of meaning into another statement — doubtless longer — in which the word "temperature" no longer appears. That term functions solely as an abbreviation, making possible the concise and complete description of a state of affairs the expression of which would otherwise be very complicated.

2. The example equally shows that *two statements which differ in formulation* can nevertheless have the *same meaning*. A trivial example of a statement having

the same meaning as the above would be: "Today at one o'clock, at such and such a location in the laboratory, the temperature was 19.44° Réamur."

As a matter of fact, the preceding considerations show — and let us set it down as another result — that *the meaning of a statement is established by the conditions of its verification.* In particular, two differently formulated statements have the same meaning or the same effective content when, and only when, they are both true or both false in the same conditions. Furthermore, a statement for which one can indicate absolutely no conditions which would verify it, which is in principle incapable of confrontation with test conditions, is wholly devoid of content and without meaning. In such a case we have to do, not with a statement properly speaking, but with a "pseudo-statement," that is to say, a sequence of words correctly constructed from the point of view of grammar, but without content.[7]

In view of these considerations, our problem reduces to one concerning the difference between the circumstances which verify psychological statements and those which verify the statements of physics. Let us therefore examine a statement which involves a psychological concept, for example: "Paul has a toothache." What is the specific content of this statement, that is to say, what are the circumstances in which it would be verified? It will be sufficient to indicate some test sentences which describe these circumstances.

a. Paul weeps and makes gestures of such and such kinds.

b. At the question "What is the matter?," Paul utters the words "I have a toothache."

c. Closer examination reveals a decayed tooth with exposed pulp.

d. Paul's blood pressure, digestive processes, the speed of his reactions, show such and such changes.

e. Such and such processes occur in Paul's central nervous system.

The list could be expanded considerably but it is already sufficient to bring out the fundamental and essential point, namely, that all the circumstances which verify this psychological statement are expressed by physical test sentences. [This is true even of test condition *b*, which merely expresses the fact that in specified physical circumstances (the propagation of vibrations produced in the air by the enunciation of the words, "What is the matter?") there occurs in the body of the subject a certain physical process (speech behavior of such and such a kind).]

The statement in question, which is about someone's "pain," is therefore, just like that concerning the temperature, simply an abbreviated expression of the fact that all its test sentences are verified.[8] (Here, too, one verifies only some of the test sentences and then infers by way of induction that the others obtain as well.) It can be retranslated without loss of content into a statement which no longer contains the term "pain," but only physical concepts. Our analysis has consequently established that a certain statement belonging to psychology has the same content as a statement belonging to physics; a result which is in direct contradiction to the thesis that there is an impassable gulf between the statements of psychology and those of physics.

The above reasoning can be applied to *any psychological statement*, even to those which concern, as is said, "deeper psychological strata" than that of our example. Thus, the assertion that Mr. Jones suffers from intense inferiority feelings of such and such kinds can be confirmed or falsified only by observing Mr. Jones' behavior in various circumstances. To this behavior belong all the bodily processes of Mr. Jones, and, in particular, his gestures, the flushing and paling of his skin, his utterances, his blood pressure, the events that occur in his central nervous system, etc. In practice, when one wishes to test statements concerning what are called the deeper layers of the psyche, one limits oneself to the observation of external bodily behavior, and, particularly, to speech movements evoked by certain physical stimuli (the asking of questions). But it is well known that experimental psychology has also developed techniques for making use of the subtler bodily states referred to above in order to confirm the psychological discoveries made by cruder methods. The statement concerning the inferiority feelings of Mr. Jones — whether true or false — means only this: such and such happenings take place in Mr. Jones' body in such and such circumstances.

We shall call a statement which can be translated without change of meaning into the language of physics, a "physicalistic statement," whereas we shall reserve the expression "statement of physics" to those which are already formulated in the terminology of physical science. (Since every statement is in respect of content equivalent to itself, every statement of physics is also a physicalistic statement.) The result of the preceding considerations can now be summed up as follows: *All psychological statements which are meaningful, that is to say, which are in principle verifiable, are translatable into statements which do not involve psychological concepts, but only the concepts of physics. The statements of psychology are consequently physicalistic statements. Psychology is an integral part of physics.* If a distinction is drawn between psychology and the other areas of physics, it is only from the point of view of the practical aspects of research and the direction of interest, rather than a matter of principle. This logical analysis, the result of which shows a certain affinity with the fundamental ideas of behaviorism, constitutes the physicalistic conception of psychology.

V

It is customary to raise the following fundamental objection against the above conception. The physical test sentences of which you speak are absolutely incapable of formulating the intrinsic nature of a mental process; they merely describe the physical *symptoms* from which one infers, by purely psychological methods — notably that of understanding — the presence of a certain mental process.

But it is not difficult to see that the use of the method of understanding or of other psychological procedures is bound up with the existence of certain observable physical data concerning the subject undergoing examination. There is no psychological understanding that is not tied up physically in one way or another with the person to be understood. Let us add that, for example, in the case of the statement about the inferiority complex, even the "introspective" psychologist, the psychologist who "understands," can confirm his conjecture only if the body of Mr. Jones, when placed in certain circumstances (most frequently, subjected to questioning), reacts in a specified manner (usually, by giving certain answers). Consequently, even if the statement in question had to be arrived at, *discovered*, by "empathetic understanding," the only *information* it gives us is nothing more nor less than the following: under certain circumstances, certain specific events take place in the body of Mr. Jones. It is this which constitutes the meaning of the psychological statement.

The further objection will perhaps be raised that men can feign. Thus, though a criminal at the bar may show physical symptoms of mental disorder, one would nevertheless be justified in wondering whether his mental confusion was "real" or only simulated. One must note that in the case of the simulator, only some of the conditions are fulfilled which verify the statement "This man is mentally unbalanced," those, namely, which are most accessible to direct observation. A more penetrating examination — which should in principle take into account events occurring in the central nervous system — would give a decisive answer; and this answer would in turn clearly rest on a physicalistic basis. If, at this point, one wished to push the objection to the point of admitting that a man could show *all the "symptoms"* of a mental disease without being "really" ill, we reply that it would be absurd to characterize such a man as "really normal"; for it is obvious that by the very nature of the hypothesis we should possess no criterion in terms of which to distinguish this man from another who, while exhibiting the same bodily behavior down to the last detail, would, "in addition" be "really ill." (To put the point more precisely, one can say that this hypothesis contains a *logical contradiction*, since it amounts to saying, "It is possible that a statement should be false even when the necessary and sufficient conditions of its truth are fulfilled.")

Once again we clearly that the meaning of a psychological statement consists solely in the function of abbreviating the description of certain modes of physical response characteristic of the bodies of men or animals. An analogy suggested by O. Neurath may be of further assistance in clarifying the logical function of psychological statements.[9] The complicated statements that would describe the movements of the hands of a watch in relation to one another, and relatively to the stars, are ordinarily summed up in an assertion of the following form: This watch runs well (runs badly, etc.)." The term "runs" is introduced here as an auxiliary defined expression which makes it possible to formulate briefly a relatively complicated system of statements. It would thus be absurd to say, for example, that the movement of the hands is only a "physical symptom" which reveals the presence of a running which is intrinsically incapable of being grasped by physical means, or to ask, if the watch should stop, what has become of the running of the watch.

It is in exactly the same way that abbreviating symbols are introduced into the language of physics, the concept of temperature discussed above being an example. The system of physical test sentences *exhausts* the meaning of the statement concerning the temperature at a place, and one should not say that these sentences merely have to do with "symptoms" of existence of a certain temperature.

Our argument has shown that it is necessary to attribute to the characteristic concepts of psychology the same logical function as that performed by the concepts of "running" and of "temperature." They do nothing more than make possible the succinct formulation of propositions concerning the states or processes of animal or human bodies.

The introduction of new psychological concepts can contribute greatly to the progress of scientific knowledge. But it is accompanied by a danger, that, namely, of making an excessive and, consequently, improper use of new concepts, which may result in questions and answers devoid of sense. This is frequently the case in metaphysics, notably with respect to the notions which we formulated in section II. Terms which are abbreviating symbols are imagined to designate a special class of "psychological objects," and thus one is led to ask questions about the "essence" of these objects, and how they differ from "physical objects." The time-worn problem concerning the relation between mental and physical events is also based on this confusion concerning the logical function of psychological concepts. Our argument, therefore, enables us to see that *the psycho-physical problem is a pseudo-problem*, the formulation of which is based on an inadmissible use of scientific concepts; it is of the same logical nature as the question, suggested by the example above, concerning the running of the watch to the movement of the hands.[10]

VI

In order to bring out the exact status of the fundamental idea of the physicalistic conception of psychology (or logical behaviorism), we shall contrast it with certain theses of psychological behaviorism and of classical materialism, which give the appearance of being closely related to it.[11]

1. Logical behaviorism claims neither that minds, feelings, inferiority complexes, voluntary actions, etc., do not exist, nor that their existence is in the least doubtful. It insists that the very question as to whether these psychological constructs really exist is already a pseudo-problem, since these notions in their "legitimate use" appear only as abbreviations in physicalistic statements. Above

all, one should not interpret the position sketched in this paper as amounting to the view that we know only the "physical side" of psychological processes, and that the question whether there are mental phenomena behind the physical processes falls beyond the scope of science and must be left either to faith or to the conviction of each individual. On the contrary, the logical analyses originating in the Vienna Circle, one of whose consequences is the physicalistic conception of psychology, teach us that every meaningful question is, in principle, capable of a scientific answer. Furthermore, these analyses show that what, in the case of the mind-body problem, is considered as an object of belief, is absolutely incapable of being expressed by a factual proposition. In other words, there can be no question here of an "article of faith." Nothing can be an object of faith which cannot, in principle, be an object of knowledge.

2. The thesis here developed, though related in certain ways to the fundamental idea of behaviorism, does not demand, as does the latter, that psychological research restrict itself methodologically to the study of the responses organisms make to certain stimuli. It by no means offers a theory belonging to the domain of psychology, but rather a logical theory about the statement of scientific psychology. Its position is that the latter are without exception physicalistic statements, by whatever means they may have been obtained. Consequently, it seeks to show that if in psychology only physicalistic statements are made, this is not a limitation because it is logically *impossible* to do otherwise.

3. In order for logical behaviorism to be valid, it is not necessary that we be able to describe the physical state of a human body which is referred to by a certain psychological statement — for example, one dealing with someone's feeling of pain — down to the most minute details of the phenomena of the central nervous system. No more does it presuppose a knowledge of all the physical laws governing human or animal bodily processes; nor *a fortiori* is the existence of rigorously deterministic laws relating to these processes a necessary condition of the truth of the behavioristic thesis. At no point does the above argument rest on such a concrete presupposition.

VII

In concluding, I should like to indicate briefly the clarification brought to the problem of the division of the sciences into totally different areas, by the method of the logical analysis of scientific statements, applied above to the special case of the place of psychology among the sciences. The considerations we have advanced can be extended to the domain of sociology, taken in the broad sense as the science of historical, cultural, and economic processes. In this way one arrives at the result that every sociological assertion which is meaningful, that is to say, in principle verifiable, "has as its subject matter nothing else than the states, processes and behavior of groups or of individuals (human or animal), and their responses to one another and to their environment,"[12] and consequently that every sociological statement is a physicalistic statement. This view is characterized by Neurath as the thesis of "social behaviorism," which he adds to that of "individual behaviorism" which we have expounded above. Furthermore, it can be shown[13] that every statement of what are called the "sciences of mind and culture" is a sociological statement in the above sense, provided it has genuine content. Thus one arrives at the "thesis of the unity of science":

The division of science into different areas rests exclusively on differences in research procedures and direction of interest; *one must not regard it as a matter of principle. On the contrary, all the branches of science are in principle of one and the same nature; they are branches of the unitary science, physics.*

VIII

The method of logical analysis which we have attempted to explicate by clarifying, as an example, the statements of psychology, leads, as we have been able to show only too briefly for the sciences of mind and culture, to a "physicalism" based on logic (Neurath): *Every statement of the above-mentioned disciplines, and, in general, of empirical science as a whole*, which is not merely a meaningless sequence of words, *is translatable, without change of content, into a statement containing only physicalistic terms, and consequently is a physicalistic statement.*

This thesis frequently encounters strong opposition arising from the idea that such analyses violently and considerably reduce the richness of the life of mind or spirit, as though the aim of the discussion were purely and simply to eliminate vast and important areas of experience. Such a conception comes from a false interpretation of physicalism, the main elements of which we have already examined in section VII above. As a matter of fact, nothing can be more remote from a philosophy which has the methodological attitude we have characterized than the making of decisions, on its own authority, concerning the truth or falsity of particular scientific statements, or the desire to eliminate any matters of fact whatsoever. *The subject matter of this philosophy is limited to the form of scientific statements, and the deductive relationships obtaining between them.* It is led by its analyses to the thesis of physicalism, and establishes on purely logical grounds that a certain class of venerable philosophical "problems" consists of pseudo-problems. It is certainly to the advantage of the progress of scientific knowledge that these imitation jewels in the coffer of scientific problems be known for what they are, and that the intellectual powers which have till now been devoted to a class of meaningless questions which are by their very nature insoluble, become available for the formulation and study of new and fruitful problems. That the method of logical analysis stimulates research along these lines is shown by the numerous publications of the Vienna Circle and those who sympathize with its general point of view (H. Reichenbach, W. Dubislav, and others).

In the attitude of those who are so bitterly opposed to physicalism, an essential role is played by certain psychological factors relating to individuals and groups. Thus the contrast between the constructs (*Gebilde*) developed by the psychologist, and those developed by the physicist, or, again, the questions as to the nature of the specific subject matter of psychology and the cultural sciences (which present the appearance of a search for the essence and unique laws of "objective spirit") is usually accompanied by a strong emotional coloring which has come into being during the long historical development of a "philosophical conception of the world," which was considerably less scientific than normative and intuitive. These emotional factors are still deeply rooted in the picture by which our epoch represents the world to itself. They are protected by certain affective dispositions which surround them like a rampart, and for all these reasons appear to us to have genuine content — something which a more penetrating analysis shows to be impossible.

A psychological and sociological study of the causes for the appearance of these "concomitant factors" of the metaphysical type would take us beyond the limits of this study,[14] but without tracing it back to its origins, it is possible to say that if the logical analyses sketched above are correct, the fact that they necessitate at least a partial break with traditional philosophical ideas which are deeply dyed with emotion can certainly not justify an opposition to physicalism — at least of one acknowledges that philosophy is to be something more than the expression of an individual vision of the world, that it aims at being a science.

NOTES

[1]   I now consider the type of physicalism outlined in this paper as too restrictive; the thesis that all statements of empirical science are translatable, without loss of theoretical content, into the language of physics, should be replaced by the weaker assertion that all statements of empirical science are *reducible* to sentences in the language of physics, in the sense that for every empirical hypothesis, including, of course, those of psychology, it is possible to formulate certain test conditions in terms of physical concepts which refer to more or less directly observable physical attributes. But those test conditions are not asserted to exhaust the theoretical content of the given hypothesis in all cases. For a more detailed development of this thesis, cf. R. Carnap, "Logical Foundations of the Unity of Science," reprinted in A. Marras, ed., *Intentionality, Mind, and Language* (Urbana: Univ. of Illinois Press, 1972).

[2]   *Tractatus Logico-Philosophicus* (London, 1922).

[3]   A recent presentation of symbolic logic, based on the fundamental work of Whitehead and Russell, *Principia Mathematica*, is to be found in R. Carnap, *Abriss der Logistik* (Vienna: Springer, 1929, vol. 2 of the series *Schriften zur Wissenschaftlichen Weltauffassung*). It includes an extensive bibliography, as well as references to other logistic systems.

4   The following are some of the principal publications of the Vienna Circle on the nature of psychology as a science: R. Carnap, *Scheinprobleme in der Philosophie. Das Fremdpsychische und des Realismusstreit* (Leipzig: Meiner, 1928); *Der Logische Aufbau der Welt* (Leipzig: Meiner, 1928); [English trans.: *Logical Structure of the World* (Berkeley: Univ. of California Press, 1967)]; "Die Physikalische Sprache als Universalsprache der Wissenschaft," *Erkenntnis*, 2 (1931-32), 432-465 [English trans.: *The Unity of Science* (London: Kegan Paul, 1934)]; "Psychologie in physikalischer Sprache," *Erkenntnis*, 3 (1932-33), 107-142 [English trans.: "Psychology in Physical Language," in A. J. Ayer, ed., *Logical Positivism* (New York: Free Press, 1959)]; "Ueber Protokollsaetze," *Erkenntnis*, 3 (1932-33), 215-228; O. Neurath, "Protokollsaetze," *Erkenntnis*, 3 (1932-33), 204-214 [English trans.: "Protocol Sentences," in *Logical Positivism*]; *Einheitswissenschaft und Psychologie* (Vienna: Springer, 1933; vol. 1 of the series *Einheitswissenschaft*). See also the publications mentioned in the notes below.

5   P. Oppenheim, for example, in his book *Die Natuerliche Ordnung der Wissenschaften* (Jena: Fischer, 1926), opposes the view that there are fundamental differences between any of the different areas of science. On the analysis of "understanding," cf. M. Schilck, "Erbleben, Erkennen, Metaphysik," *Kantstudien*, 31 (1926), 146.

6   For further details see the statement of one of the founders of behaviorism: J. B. Watson, *Behaviorism* (New York: Norton, 1930); also A. A. Roback, *Behaviorism and Psychology* (Cambridge, Mass.: Univ. Bookstore, 1923); and A. P. Weiss, *A Theoretcial Basis of Human Behavior*, 2nd ed. rev. (Columbus, Ohio: Adams, 1929); see also the work by Kohler cited in note 11 below.

7   Space is lacking for further discussion of the logical form of test sentences (recently called "protocol sentences" by Neurath and Carnap). On this question see Wittgenstein, *Tractatus Logico-Philosophicus*, as well as the articles by Neurath and Carnap which have appeared in *Erkenntnis* (above, note 4).

8   Two critical comments, 1977: (a) This reference to verification involves a conceptual confusion. The thesis which the preceding considerations were intended to establish was clearly that the statement "Paul has a toothache" is, in effect, an abbreviated expression of all its test sentences; not that it expresses the claim (let alone the "fact") that all those test sentences have actually been tested and verified. (b) Strictly speaking, none of the test sentences just mentioned is implied by the statement "Paul has a toothache": the latter may be true and yet any or all of those test sentences may be false. Hence, the preceding considerations fail to show that the given psychological statement can be "translated" into sentences which, in purely physical terms, describe macro-behavioral manifestations of pain. This failure of the arguments outlined in the text does not preclude the possibility, however, that sentences ascribing pain or other psychological characteristics to an individual might be "translatable," in a suitable sense, into physical sentences ascribing associated physical micro-states or micro-events to the nervous system or to the entire body of the individual in question.

9   "Soziologie im Physikalismus," *Erkenntnis*, 2 (1931-32), 393-431, particularly p. 411 [English trans.: "Sociology and Physicalism," in A.. J. Ayer, ed., *Logical Positivism*].

10 Carnap, *Der Logische Aufbau der Welt*, pp. 231-236; id. *Scheinprobleme in der Philosophie*. See also note 4 above.

11 A careful discussion of the ideas of so-called "internal" behaviorism is to be found in *Psychologische Probleme* by W. Koehler (Berlin: Springer, 1933). See particularly the first two chapters.

12 R. Carnap, "Die Physikalische Sprache als Universalsprache," p. 451. See also: O. Neurath, *Empirische Soziologie* (Vienna: Springer, 1931; the fourth monograph in the series *Schriften zur wissenschaftlichen Weltauffassung*).

[13] See R. Carnap, *Der Logische Aufbau der Welt*, pp. 22-34 and 185-211, as well as the works cited in the preceding notes.

[14] O. Neurath has made interesting contributions along these lines in *Empirische Soziologie* and in "Soziologie im Physikalismus" (see above note 9), as has R. Carnap in his article "Ueberwindung der Metaphysik durch logische Analyse der Sprache," *Erkenntnis*, 2 (1931-32), 219-241 [English trans.: "The Elimination of Metaphysics through Logical Analysis of Language," in A. J. Ayer, ed., *Logical Positivism*].

13

THE MIND-BODY PROBLEM

Could calculating machines have pains, Martians have
expectations and disembodied spirits have thoughts?
The modern functionalist approach to psychology raises
the logical possibility that they could.

Jerry A. Fodor

Modern philosophy of science has been devoted largely to the formal and
systematic description of the successful practices of working scientists. The
philosopher does not try to dictate how scientific inquiry and argument ought to be
conducted. Instead he tries to enumerate the principles and practices that have
contributed to good science. The philosopher has devoted the most attention to
analyzing the methodological peculiarities of the physical sciences. The analysis
has helped to clarify the nature of confirmation, the logical structure of scientific
theories, the formal properties of statements that express laws and the question of
whether theoretical entities actually exist.

It is only rather recently that philosophers have become seriously interested in
the methodological tenets of psychology. Psychological explanations of behavior
refer liberally to the mind and to states, operations and processes of the mind. The
philosophical difficulty comes in stating in unambiguous language what such
references imply.

Traditional philosophies of mind can be divided into two broad categories:
dualist theories and materialist theories. In the dualist approach the mind is a
nonphysical substance. In materialist theories the mental is not distinct from the
physical; indeed, all mental states, properties, processes and operations are in
principle identical with physical states, properties, processes and operations. Some
materialists, known as behaviorists, maintain that all talk of mental causes can be
eliminated from the language of psychology in favor of talk of environmental
stimuli and behavioral responses. Other materialists, the identity theorists, contend
that there are mental causes and that they are identical with neurophysiological
events in the brain.

Fodor, Jerry A. 1981. "The Mind-Body Problem" in *Scientific American 244*, pp. 114-123. © 1981.
Scientific American.

In the past 15 years a philosophy of mind called functionalism that is neither dualist nor materialist has emerged from philosophical reflection on developments in artificial intelligence, computational theory, linguistics, cybernetics and psychology. All these fields, which are collectively known as the cognitive sciences, have in common a certain level of abstraction and a concern with systems that process information. Functionalism, which seeks to provide a philosophical account of this level of abstraction, recognizes the possibility that systems as diverse as human beings, calculating machines and disembodied spirits could all have mental states. In the functionalist view the psychology of a system depends not on the stuff it is made of (living cells, metal or spiritual energy) but on how the stuff is put together. Functionalism is a difficult concept, and one way of coming to grips with it is to review the deficiencies of the dualist and materialist philosophies of mind it aims to displace.

The chief drawback of dualism is its failure to account adequately for mental causation. If the mind is nonphysical, it has no position in physical space. How, then, can a mental cause give rise to a behavioral effect that has a position in space? To put it another way, how can the nonphysical give rise to the physical without violating the laws of the conservation of mass, of energy and of momentum?

The dualist might respond that the problem of how an immaterial substance can cause physical events is not much obscurer than the problem of how one physical event can cause another. Yet there is an important difference: there are many clear cases of physical causation but not one clear case of nonphysical causation. Physical interaction is something philosophers, like all other people, have to live with. Nonphysical interaction, however, may be no more than an artifact of the immaterialist construal of the mental. Most philosophers now agree that no argument has successfully demonstrated why mind-body causation should not be regarded as a species of physical causation.

Dualism is also incompatible with the practices of working psychologists. The psychologist frequently· applies the experimental methods of the physical sciences to the study of the mind. If mental processes were different in kind from physical processes, there would be no reason to expect these methods to work in the realm of the mental. In order to justify their experimental methods many psychologists urgently sought an alternative to dualism.

In the 1920's John B. Watson of Johns Hopkins University made the radical suggestion that behavior does not have mental causes. He regarded the behavior of an organism as its observable responses to stimuli, which he took to be the causes of its behavior. Over the next 30 years psychologists such as B. F. Skinner of Harvard University developed Watson's ideas into an elaborate world view in which the role of psychology was to catalogue the laws that determine causal relations between stimuli and responses. In this "radical behaviorist" view the problem of explaining the nature of the mind-body interaction vanishes; there is no such interaction.

Radical behaviorism has always worn an air of paradox. For better or worse, the idea of mental causation is deeply ingrained in our everyday language and in our ways of understanding our fellow men and ourselves. For example, people commonly attribute behavior to beliefs, to knowledge and to expectations. Brown puts gas in his tank because he believes the car will not run without it. Jones writes not "acheive" but "achieve" because he knows the rule about putting *i* before *e*. Even when a behavioral response is closely tied to an environmental stimulus, mental processes often intervene. Smith carries an umbrella because the sky is cloudy, but the weather is only part of the story. There are apparently also mental links in the causal chain: observation and expectation. The clouds affect Smith's behavior only because he observes them and because they induce in him an expectation of rain.

The radical behaviorist is unmoved by appeals to such cases. He is prepared to dismiss references to mental causes, however plausible they may seem, as the residue of outworn creeds. The radical behaviorist predicts that as psychologists come to understand more about the relations between stimuli and responses they will find it increasingly possible to explain behavior without postulating mental causes.

The strongest argument against behaviorism is that psychology has not turned out this way; the opposite has happened. As psychology has matured, the framework of mental states and processes that is apparently needed to account for experimental observations has grown all the more elaborate. Particularly in the case of human behavior psychological theories satisfying the methodological tenets of radical

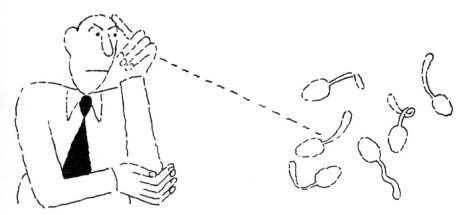

DUALISM is the philosophy of mind that regards the mind as a nonphysical substance. It divides everything there is in the world into two distinct categories: the mental and the physical. The chief difficulty with dualism is its failure to account adequately for the causal interaction of the mental and the physical. It is not evident how a nonphysical mind could give rise to any physical effects without violating the laws of conservation of mass, energy and momentum.

behaviorism have proved largely sterile, as would be expected if the postulated mental processes are real and causally effective.

Nevertheless, many philosophers were initially drawn to radical behaviorism because, paradoxes and all, it seemed better than dualism. Since a psychology committed to immaterial substances was unacceptable, philosophers turned to radical behaviorism because it seemed to be the only alternative materialist philosophy of mind. The choice, as they saw it, was between radical behaviorism and ghosts.

By the early 1960's philosophers began to have doubts that dualism and radical behaviorism exhausted the possible approaches to the philosophy of mind. Since the two theories seemed unattractive, the right strategy might be to develop a materialist philosophy of mind that nonetheless allowed for mental causes. Two such philosophies emerged, one called logical behaviorism and the other called the central-state identity theory.

Logical behaviorism is a semantic theory about what mental terms mean. The basic idea is that attributing a mental state (say thirst) to an organism is the same as saying that the organism is disposed to behave in a particular way (for example to drink if there is water available). On this view every mental ascription is equivalent in meaning to an if-then statement (called a behavioral hypothetical) that expresses a behavioral disposition. For example, "Smith is thirsty" might be taken to be equivalent to the dispositional statement "If there were water available, then Smith would drink some." By definition a behavioral hypothetical includes no mental terms. The if-clause of the hypothetical speaks only of stimuli and the then-clause speaks only of behavioral responses. Since stimuli and responses are physical events, logical behaviorism is a species of materialism.

The strength of logical behaviorism is that by translating mental language into the language of stimuli and responses it provides an interpretation of psychological explanations in which behavioral effects are attributed to mental causes. Mental causation is simply the manifestation of a behavioral disposition. More precisely, mental causation is what happens when an organism has a behavioral disposition and the if-clause of the behavioral hypothetical expressing the disposition happens to be true. For example, the causal statement "Smith drank some water because he was thirsty" might be taken to mean "If there were water available, then Smith would drink some, and there was water available."

I have somewhat oversimplified logical behaviorism by assuming that each mental ascription can be translated by a unique behavioral hypothetical. Actually the logical behaviorist often maintains that it takes an open-ended set (perhaps an infinite set) of behavioral hypotheticals to spell out the behavioral disposition expressed by a mental term. The mental ascription "Smith is thirsty" might also be satisfied by the hypothetical "If there were orange juice available, then Smith would drink some" and by a host of other hypotheticals. In any event the logical behaviorist does not usually maintain he can actually enumerate all the hypotheticals that correspond to a behavioral disposition expressing a given mental term. He only insists that in principle the meaning of any mental term can be conveyed by behavioral hypotheticals.

RADICAL BEHAVIORISM is the philosophy of mind that denies the existence of the mind and mental states, properties, processes and operations. The radical behaviorist believes behavior does not have mental causes. He considers the behavior of an organism to be its responses to stimuli. The role of psychology is to catalogue the relations between stimuli and responses.

The way the logical behaviorist has interpreted a mental term such as thirsty is modeled after the way many philosophers have interpreted a physical disposition such as fragility. The physical disposition "The glass is fragile" is often taken to mean something like "If the glass were struck, then it would break." By the same token the logical behaviorist's analysis of mental causation is similar to the received analysis of one kind of physical causation. The causal statement "The glass broke because it was fragile" is taken to mean something like "If the glass were struck, then it would break, and the glass was struck."

By equating mental terms with behavioral dispositions the logical behaviorist has put mental terms on a par with the nonbehavioral dispositions of the physical sciences. That is a promising move, because the analysis of nonbehavioral dispositions is on relatively solid philosophical ground. An explanation attributing the breaking of a glass to its fragility is surely something even the staunchest materialist can accept. By arguing that mental terms are synonymous with dispositional terms, the logical behaviorist has provided something the radical behaviorist could not: a materialist account of mental causation.

Nevertheless, the analogy between mental causation as construed by the logical behaviorist and physical causation goes only so far. The logical behaviorist treats the manifestation of a disposition as the sole form of mental causation, whereas the physical sciences recognize additional kinds of causation. There is the kind of causation where one physical event causes another, as when the breaking of a glass is attributed to its having been struck. In fact, explanations that involve event-event causation are presumably more basic than dispositional explanations, because the manifestation of a disposition (the breaking of a fragile glass) always involves event-event causation and not vice versa. In the realm of the mental many examples of event-event causation involve one mental state's causing another, and for this kind of causation logical behaviorism provides no analysis. As a result the logical behaviorist is committed to the tacit and implausible assumption that psychology requires a less robust notion of causation than the physical sciences require.

Event-event causation actually seems to be quite common in the realm of the mental. Mental causes typically give rise to behavioral effects by virtue of their interaction with other mental causes. For example, having a headache causes a disposition to take aspirin only if one also has the desire to get rid of the headache, the belief that aspirin exists, the belief that taking aspirin reduces headaches and so on. Since mental states interact in generating behavior, it will be necessary to find a construal of psychological explanations that posits mental processes: causal sequences of mental events. It is this construal that logical behaviorism fails to provide.

Such considerations bring out a fundamental way in which logical behaviorism is quite similar to radical behaviorism. It is true that the logical behaviorist, unlike the radical behaviorist, acknowledges the existence of mental states. Yet since the underlying tenet of logical behaviorism is that references to mental states can be translated out of psychological explanations by employing behavioral hypotheticals, all talk of mental states and processes is in a sense heuristic. The only facts to which the behaviorist is actually committed are facts about relations between stimuli and responses. In this respect logical behaviorism is just radical behaviorism in a semantic form. Although the former theory offers a construal of mental causation, the construal is Pickwickian. What does not really exist cannot cause anything, and the logical behaviorist, like the radical behaviorist, believes deep down that mental causes do not exist.

LOGICAL BEHAVIORISM is a semantic thesis about what mental terms mean. The logical behaviorist maintains that mental terms express behavioral dispositions. Consider the mental state of being thirsty. The logical behaviorist maintains that the sentence "Smith is thirsty" might be taken as equivalent in meaning to the dispositional statement "If there were water available, then Smith would drink some." The strength of logical behaviorism is that it provides an account of mental causation: the realization of a behavioral disposition. For example, the causal statement "Smith drank some water because he was thirsty" might be taken to mean "If there were water available, then Smith would drink some, and there was water available."

An alternative materialist theory of the mind to logical behaviorism is the central-state identity theory. According to this theory, mental events, states and processes are identical with neurophysiological events in the brain, and the property of being in a certain mental state (such as having a headache or believing it will rain) is identical with the property of being in a certain neurophysiological state. On this basis it is easy to make sense of the idea that a behavioral effect might sometimes have a chain of mental causes; that will be the case whenever a behavioral effect is contingent on the appropriate sequence of neurophysiological events.

The central-state identity theory acknowledges that it is possible for mental causes to interact causally without ever giving rise to any behavioral effect, as when a person thinks for a while about what he ought to do and then decides to do nothing. If mental processes are neurophysiological, they must have the causal properties of neurophysiological processes. Since neurophysiological processes are presumably physical processes, the central-state identity theory ensures that the concept of mental causation is as rich as the concept of physical causation.

The central-state identity theory provides a satisfactory account of what the mental terms in psychological explanations refer to, and so it is favored by psychologists who are dissatisfied with behaviorism. The behaviorist maintains that mental terms refer to nothing or that they refer to the parameters of stimulus-response relations. Either way the existence of mental entities is only illusory. The identity theorist, on the other hand, argues that mental terms refer to neurophysiological states. Thus he can take seriously the project of explaining behavior by appealing to its mental causes.

The chief advantage of the identity theory is that it takes the explanatory constructs of psychology at face value, which is surely something a philosophy of mind ought to do if it can. The identity theory shows how the mentalistic explanations of psychology could be not mere heuristics but literal accounts of the causal history of behavior. Moreover, since the identity theory is not a semantic theses, it is immune to many arguments that cast in doubt logical behaviorism. A drawback of logical behaviorism is that the observation "John has a headache" does not seem to mean the same thing as a statement of the form "John is disposed to behave in such and such a way." The identity theorist, however, can live with the fact that "John has a headache" and "John is in such and such a brain state" are not synonymous. The assertion of the identity theorist is not that these sentences mean the same thing but only that they are rendered true (or false) by the same neurophysiological phenomena.

The identity theory can be held either as a doctrine about mental particulars (John's current pain or Bill's fear of animals) or as a doctrine about mental universals, or properties (having a pain or being afraid of animals). The two doctrines, called respectively token physicalism and type physicalism, differ in strength and plausibility. Token physicalism maintains only that all the mental particulars that happen to exist are neurophysiological, whereas type physicalism makes the more sweeping assertion that all the mental particulars there could possibly be are neurophysiological. Token physicalism does not rule out the logical possibility of machines and disembodied spirits having mental properties. Type physicalism dismisses this possibility because neither machines nor disembodied spirits have neurons.

Type physicalism is not a plausible doctrine about mental properties even if token physicalism is right about mental particulars. The problem with type physicalism is that the psychological constitution of a system seems to depend not on its hardware, or physical composition, but on its software, or program. Why

CENTRAL-STATE IDENTITY THEORY is the philosophy of mind that equates mental events, states and processes with neurophysiological events. Property of being in a given mental state is identical with the property of being in a given neurophysiological state.

should the philosopher dismiss the possibility that silicon-based Martians have pains, assuming that the silicon is properly organized? And why should the philosopher rule out the possibility of machines having beliefs, assuming that the machines are correctly programmed? If it is logically possible that Martians and machines could have mental properties, then mental properties and neurophysiological processes cannot be identical, however much they may prove to be coextensive.

What it all comes down to is that there seems to be a level of abstraction at which the generalizations of psychology are most naturally pitched. This level of abstraction cuts across differences in the physical composition of the systems to which psychological generalizations apply. In the cognitive sciences, at least, the natural domain for psychological theorizing seems to be all systems that process information. The problem with type physicalism is that there are possible information-processing systems with the same psychological constitution as human beings but not the same physical organization. In principle all kinds of physically different things could have human software.

This situation calls for a relational account of mental properties that abstracts them from the physical structure of their bearers. In spite of the objections to logical behaviorism that I presented above, logical behaviorism was at least on the right track in offering a relational interpretation of mental properties: to have a headache is to be disposed to exhibit a certain pattern of relations between the stimuli one encounters and the responses one exhibits. If that is what having a headache is, however, there is no reason in principle why only heads that are physically similar to ours can ache. Indeed, according to logical behaviorism, it is a necessary truth that any system that has our stimulus-response contingencies also has our headaches.

All of this emerged 10 or 15 years ago as a nasty dilemma for the materialist program in the philosophy of mind. On the one hand the identity theorist (and not the logical behaviorist) had got right the causal character of the interactions of mind and body. On the other the logical behaviorist (and not the identity theorist) had got right the relational character of mental properties. Functionalism has apparently been able to resolve the dilemma. By stressing the distinction computer science draws between hardware and software the functionalist can make sense of both the causal and the relational character of the mental.

The intuition underlying functionalism is that what determines the psychological type to which a mental particular belongs is the causal role of the particular in the mental life of the organism. Functional individuation is differentiation with respect to causal role. A headache, for example, is identified with the type of mental state that among other things causes a disposition for taking aspirin in people who believe aspirin relieves a headache, causes a desire to rid oneself of the pain one is feeling, often causes someone who speaks English to say such things as "I have a headache" and is brought on by overwork, eyestrain and tension. This list is presumably not complete. More will be known about the nature of a headache as psychological and physiological research discovers more about its causal role.

Functionalism construes the concept of causal role in such a way that a mental state can be defined by its causal relations to other mental states. In this respect functionalism is completely different from logical behaviorism. Another major difference is that functionalism is not a reductionist thesis. It does not foresee, even in principle, the elimination of mentalistic concepts from the explanatory apparatus of psychological theories.

FUNCTIONALISM is the philosophy of mind based on the distinction that computer science draws between a system's hardware, or physical composition, and its software, or program. The psychology of a system such as a human being, a machine or a disembodied spirit does not depend on the stuff the system is made of (neuroses, diodes or spiritual energy) but on how that stuff is organized. Functionalism does not rule out the possibility, however remote it may be, of mechanical and ethereal systems having mental states and processes.

The difference between functionalism and logical behaviorism is brought out by the fact that functionalism is fully compatible with token physicalism. The functionalist would not be disturbed if brain events turn out to be the only things with the functional properties that define mental states. Indeed, most functionalists fully expect it will turn out that way.

Since functionalism recognizes that mental particulars may be physical, it is compatible with the idea that mental causation is a species of physical causation. In other words, functionalism tolerates the materialist solution to the mind-body problem provided by the central-state identity theory. It is possible for the functionalist to assert both that mental properties are typically defined in terms of their relations and that interactions of mind and body are typically causal in however robust a notion of causality is required by psychological explanations. The logical behaviorist can endorse only the first assertion and the type physicalist only the second. As a result functionalism seems to capture the best features of the materialist alternatives to dualism. It is no wonder that functionalism has become increasingly popular.

Machines provide good examples of two concepts that are central to functionalism: the concept that mental states are interdefined and the concept that they can be realized by many systems. The illustration on the next page [p.293] contrasts a behavioristic Coke machine with a mentalistic one. Both machines dispense a Coke for 10 cents. (The price has not been affected by inflation.) The states of the machines are defined by reference to their causal roles, but only the machine on the left would satisfy the behaviorist. Its single state (SO) is completely specified in terms of stimuli and responses. SO is the state a machine is in if, and only if, given a dime as the input, it dispenses a Coke as the output.

The machine on the right in the illustration has interdefined states ($S1$ and $S2$), which are characteristic of functionalism. $S1$ is the state a machine is in if, and only if, (1) given a nickel, it dispenses nothing and proceeds to $S2$, and (2) given a dime, it dispenses a Coke and stays in $S1$. $S2$ is the state a machine is in if, and only if, (1) given a nickel, it dispenses a Coke and proceeds to $S1$, and (2) given a dime, it dispenses a Coke and a nickel and proceeds to $S1$. What $S1$ and $S2$ jointly amount to is the machine's dispensing a Coke if it is given a dime, dispensing a Coke and a nickel if it is given a dime and a nickel and waiting to be given a second nickel if it has been given a first one.

Since $S1$ and $S2$ are each defined by hypothetical statements, they can be viewed as dispositions. Nevertheless, they are not behavioral dispositions because the consequences an input has for a machine in $S1$ or $S2$ are not specified solely in terms of the output of the machine. Rather, the consequences also involve the machine's internal states.

Nothing about the way I have described the behavioristic and mentalistic Coke machines puts constraints on what they could be made of. Any system whose states bore the proper relations to inputs, outputs and other states could be one of these machines. No doubt it is reasonable to expect such a system to be constructed out of such things as wheels, levers and diodes (token physicalism for Coke machines). Similarly, it is reasonable to expect that our minds may prove to be neurophysiological (token physicalism for human beings).

Nevertheless, the software description of a Coke machine does not logically require wheels, levers and diodes for its concrete realization. By the same token, the software description of the mind does not logically require neurons. As far as functionalism is concerned a Coke machine with states S1 and S2 could be made of ectoplasm, if there is such stuff and if its states have the right causal properties. Functionalism allows for the possibility of disembodied Coke machines in exactly the same way and to the same extent that it allows for the possibility of disembodied minds.

To say that S1 and S2 are interdefined and realizable by different kinds of hardware is not, of course, to say that a Coke machine has a mind. Although interdefinition and functional specification are typical features of mental states, they are clearly not sufficient for mentality. What more is required is a question to which I shall return below.

Some philosophers are suspicious of functionalism because it seems too easy. Since functionalism licenses the individuation of states by reference to their causal role, it appears to allow a trivial explanation of any observed event E, that is, it appears to postulate an E-causer. For example, what makes the valves in a machine open? Why, the operation of a valve opener. And what is a valve opener? Why, anything that has the functionally defined property of causing valves to open.

In psychology this kind of question-begging often takes the form of theories that in effect postulate homunculi with the selfsame intellectual capacities the theorist set out to explain. Such is the case when visual perception is explained by simply postulating psychological mechanisms that process visual information. The behaviorist has often charged the mentalist, sometimes justifiably, of mongering this kind of question-begging pseudo explanation. The charge will have to be met if functionally defined mental states are to have a serious role in psychological theories.

The burden of the accusation is not untruth but triviality. There can be no doubt that it is a valve opener that opens valves, and it is likely that visual perception is mediated by the processing of visual information. The charge is that such putative functional explanations are mere platitudes. The functionalist can meet this objection by allowing functionally defined theoretical constructs only where mechanisms exist that can carry out the function and only where he has some notion of what such mechanisms might be like. One way of imposing this requirement is to identify the mental processes that psychology postulates with the operations of the restricted class of possible computers called Turing machines.

A Turing machine can be informally characterized as a mechanism with a finite number of program states. The inputs and outputs of the machine are written on a tape that is divided into squares each of which includes a symbol from a finite alphabet. The machine scans the tape one square at a time. It can erase the symbol on a scanned square and print a new one in its place. The machine can execute only the elementary mechanical operations of scanning, erasing, printing, moving the tape and changing state.

The program states of the Turing machine are defined solely in terms of the input symbols on the tape, the output symbols on the tape, the elementary operations and the other states of the program. Each program state is therefore functionally defined by the part it plays in the overall operation of the machine. Since the functional role of a state depends on the relation of the state to other states as well as to inputs and outputs, the relational character of the mental is captured by the Turing-machine version of functionalism. Since the definition of a program state never refers to the physical structure of the system running the program, the Turing-machine version of functionalism also captures the idea that the character of a mental state is independent of its physical realization. A human being, a roomful of people, a computer and a disembodied spirit would all be a Turing machine if they operated according to a Turing-machine program.

The proposal is to restrict the functional definition of psychological states to those that can be expressed in terms of the program states of Turing machines. If this restriction can be enforced, it provides a guarantee that psychological theories will be compatible with the demands of mechanisms. Since Turing machines are very simple devices, they are in principle quite easy to build. Consequently by formulating a psychological explanation as a Turing-machine program the psychologist ensures that the explanation is mechanistic, even though the hardware realizing the mechanism is left open.

There are many kinds of computational mechanisms other than Turing machines, and so the formulation of a functionalist psychological theory in Turing-machine notation provides only a sufficient condition for the theory's being mechanically realizable. What makes the condition interesting, however, is that the simple Turing machine can perform many complex tasks. Although the elementary operations of the Turing machine are restricted, iterations of the operations enable the machine to carry out any well-defined computation on discrete symbols.

An important tendency in the cognitive sciences is to treat the mind chiefly as a device that manipulates symbols. If a mental process can be functionally defined as an operation on symbols, there is a Turing machine capable of carrying out the computation and a variety of mechanisms for realizing the Turing machine. Where the manipulation of symbols is important the Turing machine provides a connection between functional explanation and mechanistic explanation.

The reduction of a psychological theory to a program for a Turing machine is a way of exorcising the homunculi. The reduction ensures that no operations have been postulated except those that could be performed by a familiar mechanism. Of course, the working psychologist usually cannot specify the reduction for each functionally individuated process in every theory he is prepared to take seriously. In practice the argument usually goes in the opposite direction; if the postulation of a mental operation is essential to some cherished psychological explanation, the theorist tends to assume that there must be a program for a Turing machine that will carry out that operation.

	STATE S0
DIME INPUT	DISPENSES A COKE

	STATE S1	STATE S2
NICKEL INPUT	GIVES NO OUTPUT AND GOES TO S2	DISPENSES A COKE AND GOES TO S1
DIME INPUT	DISPENSES A COKE AND STAYS IN S1	DISPENSES A COKE AND A NICKEL AND GOES TO S1

TWO COKE MACHINES bring out the difference between behaviorism (the doctrine that there are no mental causes) and mentalism (the doctrine that there are mental causes). Both machines dispense a Coke for 10 cents and have states that are defined by reference to their causal role. The machine at the left is a behavioristic one: its single state (SO) is defined solely in terms of the input and the output. The machine at the right is a mentalistic one: its two states ($S1$, $S2$) must be defined not only in terms of the input and the output but also in terms of each other. To put it another way, the output of the Coke machine depends on the state the machine is in as well as on the input. The functionalist philosopher maintains that mental states are interdefined, like the internal state of the mentalistic Coke machine.

The "black boxes" that are common in flow charts drawn by psychologists often serve to indicate postulated mental processes for which Turing reductions are wanting. Even so, the possibility in principle of such reductions serves as a methodological constraint on psychological theorizing by determining what functional definitions are to be allowed and what it would be like to know that everything has been explained that could possibly need explanation.

Such is the origin, the provenance and the promise of contemporary functionalism. How much has it actually paid off? This question is not easy to answer because much of what is now happening in the philosophy of mind and the cognitive sciences is directed at exploring the scope and limits of the functionalist explanations of behavior. I shall, however, give a brief overview.

An obvious objection to functionalism as a theory of the mind is that the functionalist definition is not limited to mental states and processes. Catalysts, Coke machines, valve openers, pencil sharpeners, mousetraps and ministers of finance are all in one way or another concepts that are functionally defined, but none is a mental concept such as pain, belief and desire. What, then, characterizes the mental? And can it be captured in a functionalist framework?

The traditional view in the philosophy of mind has it that mental states are distinguished by their having what are called either qualitative content or intentional content. I shall discuss qualitative content first.

It is not easy to say what qualitative content is; indeed, according to some theories, it is not even possible to say what it is because it can be known not by description but only by direct experience. I shall nonetheless attempt to describe it. Try to imagine looking at a blank wall through a red filter. Now change the filter to a green one and leave everything else exactly the way it was. Something about the character of your experience changes when the filter does, and it is this kind of thing that philosophers call qualitative content. I am not entirely comfortable about introducing qualitative content in this way, but it is a subject with which many philosophers are not comfortable.

The reason qualitative content is a problem for functionalism is straightforward. Functionalism is committed to defining mental states in terms of their causes and effects. It seems, however, as if two mental states could have all the same causal relations and yet could differ in their qualitative content. Let me illustrate this with the classic puzzle of the inverted spectrum.

It seems possible to imagine two observers who are alike in all relevant psychological respects except that experiences having the qualitative content of red for one observer would have the qualitative content of green for the other. Nothing about their behavior need reveal the difference because both of them see ripe tomatoes and flaming sunsets as being similar in color and both of them call that color "red." Moreover, the causal connection between their (qualitatively distinct) experiences and their other mental states could also be identical. Perhaps they both think of Little Red Riding Hood when they see ripe tomatoes, feel depressed when they see the color green and so on. It seems as if anything that could be packed into the notion of the causal role of their experiences could be shared by them, and yet the qualitative content of the experiences could be as different as you like. If this is possible, then the functionalist account does not work for mental states that have qualitative content. If one person is having a green experience while another person is having a red one, then surely they must be in different mental states.

The example of the inverted spectrum is more than a verbal puzzle. Having qualitative content is supposed to be a chief factor in what makes a mental state conscious. Many psychologists who are inclined to accept the functionalist framework are nonetheless worried about the failure of functionalism to reveal much about the nature of consciousness. Functionalists have made a few ingenious attempts to talk themselves and their colleagues out of this worry, but they have not, in my view, done so with much success. (For example, perhaps one is wrong in thinking one can imagine what an inverted spectrum would be like.) As matters stand, the problem of qualitative content poses a serious threat to the assertion that functionalism can provide a general theory of the mental.

Functionalism has fared much better with the intentional content of mental states. Indeed, it is here that the major achievements of recent cognitive science are found. To say that a mental state has intentional content is to say that it has certain semantic properties. For example, for Enrico to believe Galileo was Italian apparently involves a three-way relation between Enrico, a belief and a proposition that is the content of the belief (namely the proposition that Galileo was Italian). In particular it is an essential property of Enrico's belief that it is about Galileo (and not about, say, Newton) and that it is true if, and only if, Galileo was indeed Italian. Philosophers are divided on how these considerations fit together, but it is widely agreed that beliefs involve semantic properties such as expressing a proposition, being true or false and being about one thing rather than another.

It is important to understand the semantic properties of beliefs because theories in the cognitive sciences are largely about the beliefs organisms have. Theories of learning and perception, for example, are chiefly accounts of how the host of beliefs an organism has are determined by the character of its experiences and its genetic endowment. The functionalist account of mental states does not by itself provide the required insights. Mousetraps are functionally defined, yet mousetraps do not express propositions and they are not true or false.

There is at least one kind of thing other than a mental state that has intentional content: a symbol. Like thoughts, symbols seem to be about things. If someone says "Galileo was Italian," his utterance, like Enrico's belief, expresses a proposition about Galileo that is true or false depending on Galileo's homeland. This parallel between the symbolic and the mental underlies the traditional quest for a unified treatment of language and mind. Cognitive science is now trying to provide such a treatment.

The basic concept is simple but striking. Assume that there are such things as mental symbols (mental representations) and that mental symbols have semantic properties. On this view having a belief involves being related to a mental symbol, and the belief inherits its semantic properties from the mental symbol that figures in the relation. Mental processes (thinking, perceiving, learning and so on) involve causal interactions among relational states such as having a belief. The semantic properties of the words and sentences we utter are in turn inherited from the semantic properties of the mental states that language expresses.

Associating the semantic properties of mental states with those of mental symbols is fully compatible with the computer metaphor, because it is natural to think of the computer as a mechanism that manipulates symbols. A computation is a causal chain of computer states and the links in the chain are operations on semantically interpreted formulas in a machine code. To think of a system (such as the nervous system) as a computer is to raise questions about the nature of the code in which it computes and the semantic properties of the symbols in the code. In fact, the analogy between minds and computers actually implies the postulation of mental symbols. There is no computation without representation.

The representational account of the mind, however, predates considerably the invention of the computing machine. It is a throwback to classical epistemology, which is a tradition that includes philosophers as diverse as John Locke, David Hume, George Berkeley, René Descartes, Immanuel Kant, John Stuart Mill and William James.

Hume, for one, developed a representational theory of the mind that included five points. First, there exist "Ideas," which are a species of mental symbol. Second, having a belief involves entertaining an Idea. Third, mental processes are causal associations of Ideas. Fourth, Ideas are like pictures. And fifth, Ideas have their semantic properties by virtue of what they resemble: the Idea of John is about John because it looks like him.

Contemporary cognitive psychologists do not accept the details of Hume's theory, although they endorse much of its spirit. Theories of computation provide a far richer account of mental processes than the mere association of Ideas. And only a few psychologists still think that imagery is the chief vehicle of mental representation. Nevertheless, the most significant break with Hume's theory lies in the abandoning of resemblance as an explanation of the semantic properties of mental representations.

Many philosophers, starting with Berkeley, have argued that there is something seriously wrong with the suggestion that the semantic relation between a thought and what the thought is about could be one of resemblance. Consider the thought that John is tall. Clearly the thought is true only of the state of affairs consisting of John's being tall. A theory of the semantic properties of a thought should therefore explain how this particular thought is related to this particular state of affairs. According to the resemblance theory, entertaining the thought involves having a mental image that shows John to be tall. To put it another way, the relation between the thought that John is tall and his being tall is like the relation between a tall man and his portrait.

The difficulty with the resemblance theory is that any portrait showing John to be tall must also show him to be many other things: clothed or naked, lying, standing or sitting, having a head or not having one, and so on. A portrait of a tall man who is sitting down resembles a man's being seated as much as it resembles a man's being tall. On the resemblance theory it is not clear what distinguishes thoughts about John's height from thoughts about his posture.

The resemblance theory turns out to encounter paradoxes at every turn. The possibility of construing beliefs as involving relations to semantically interpreted mental representations clearly depends on having an acceptable account of where the semantic properties of the mental representations come from. If resemblance will not provide this account, what will?

The current idea is that the semantic properties of a mental representation are determined by aspects of its functional role. In other words, a sufficient condition for having semantic properties can be specified in causal terms. This is the connection between functionalism and the representational theory of the mind. Modern cognitive psychology rests largely on the hope that these two doctrines can be made to support each other.

No philosopher is now prepared to say exactly how the functional role of a mental representation determines its semantic properties. Nevertheless, the functionalist recognizes three types of causal relation among psychological states involving mental representations, and they might serve to fix the semantic properties of mental representations. The three types are causal relations among mental states and stimuli, mental states and responses and some mental states and other ones.

Consider the belief that John is tall. Presumably the following facts, which correspond respectively to the three types of causal relation, are relevant to determining the semantic properties of the mental representation involved in the belief. First, the belief is a normal effect of certain stimulations, such as seeing John in circumstances that reveal his height. Second, the belief is the normal cause of certain behavioral effects, such as uttering "John is tall." Third, the belief is a normal cause of certain other beliefs and a normal effect of certain other beliefs. For example, anyone who believes John is tall is very likely also to believe someone is tall. Having the first belief is normally causally sufficient for having the second belief. And anyone who believes everyone in the room is tall and also believes John is in the room will very likely believe John is tall. The third belief is a normal effect of the first two. In short, the functionalist maintains that the proposition expressed by a given mental representation depends on the causal properties of the mental states in which that mental representation figures.

The concept that the semantic properties of mental representations are determined by aspects of their functional role is at the center of current work in the cognitive sciences. Nevertheless, the concept may not be true. Many philosophers who are unsympathetic to the cognitive turn in modern psychology doubt its truth, and many psychologists would probably reject it in the bald and unelaborated way that I have sketched it. Yet even in its skeletal form, there is this much to be said in its favor: It legitimizes the notion of mental representation, which has become increasingly important to theorizing in every branch of the cognitive sciences. Recent advances in formulating and testing hypotheses about the character of mental representations in fields ranging from phonetics to computer vision suggest that the concept of mental representation is fundamental to empirical theories of the mind.

The behaviorist has rejected the appeal to mental representation because it runs counter to his view of the explanatory mechanisms that can figure in psychological theories. Nevertheless, the science of mental representation is now flourishing. The history of science reveals that when a successful theory comes into conflict with a methodological scruple, it is generally the scruple that gives way. Accordingly the functionalist has relaxed the behaviorist constraints on psychological explanations. There is probably no better way to decide what is methodologically permissible in science than by investigating what successful science requires.

14

ARTIFICIAL INTELLIGENCE AS PHILOSOPHY AND AS PSYCHOLOGY

D.C. Dennett

Philosophers of mind have been interested in computers since their arrival a generation ago, but for the most part they have been interested only in the most abstract questions of principle, and have kept actual machines at arm's length and actual programs in soft focus. Had they chosen to take a closer look at the details I do not think they would have found much of philosophic interest until fairly recently, but recent work in Artificial Intelligence, or AI, promises to have a much more variegated impact on philosophy, and so, quite appropriately, philosophers have begun responding with interest to the bold manifestos of the Artificial Intelligentsea. My goal in this chapter is to provide a sort of travel guide to philosophers pursuing this interest. It is well known that amateur travelers in strange lands often ludicrously miscomprehend what they see, and enthusiastically report wonders and monstrosities that later investigations prove never to have existed, while overlooking genuine novelties of the greatest importance. Having myself fallen prey to a variety of misconceptions about AI, and wasted a good deal of time and energy pursuing chimaeras, I would like to alert other philosophers to some of these pitfalls of interpretation. Since I am still acutely conscious of my own amateur status as an observer of AI, I must acknowledge at the outset that my vision of what is going on in AI, what is important and why, is almost certainly still somewhat untrustworthy. There is much in AI that I have not read, and much that I have but not understood. So traveler, beware; take along any other maps you can find, and listen critically to the natives.

The interest of philosophers of mind in Artificial Intelligence comes as no surprise to many tough-minded experimental psychologists, for from their point of

Dennett, D.C. 1978. "Artificial Intelligence as Philosophy and as Psychology," in *Brainstorms: Philosophical Essays on Mind and Psychology*, edited by D.C. Dennett. Pp. 109-126. © 1978 MIT Press.

view the two fields look very much alike: there are the same broad generalizations and bold extrapolations, the same blithe indifference to the hard-won data of the experimentalist, the same appeal to the deliverances of casual introspection and conceptual analysis, the aprioristic reasonings about what is impossible in principle or what must be the case in psychology. The only apparent difference between the two fields, such a psychologist might say, is that the AI worker pulls his armchair up to a console. I will argue that this observation is largely justified, but should not in most regards be viewed as a criticism. There is much work for the armchair psychologist to do, and a computer console has proven a useful tool in this work.

Psychology turns out to be very difficult. The task of psychology is to explain human perception, learning, cognition, and so forth in terms that will ultimately unite psychological theory to physiology in one way or another, and there are two broad strategies one could adopt: a *bottom-up* strategy that starts with some basic and well-defined unit or theoretical atom for psychology, and builds these atoms into molecules and larger aggregates that can account for the complex phenomena we all observe, or a *top-down* strategy that begins with a more abstract decomposition of the highest levels of psychological organization, and hopes to analyze these into more and more detailed smaller systems or processes until finally one arrives at elements familiar to the biologists. It is a commonplace that both endeavors could and should proceed simultaneously, but there is now abundant evidence that the bottom-up strategy in psychology is unlikely to prove very fruitful. The two best developed attempts at bottom-up psychology are stimulus-response behaviorism and what we might call "neuron signal physiological psychology", and both are now widely regarded as stymied, the former because stimuli and responses prove not to be perspicuously chosen atoms, the latter because even if synapses and impulse trains are perfectly good atoms, there are just too many of them, and their interactions are too complex to study once one abandons the afferent and efferent peripheries and tries to make sense of the crucial center (see Chapters 4 and 5). Bottom-up strategies have not proved notably fruitful in the early development of other sciences, in chemistry and biology for instance, and so psychologists are only following the lead of "mature" sciences if they turn to the top-down approach. Within that broad strategy there are a variety of starting points that can be ordered in an array. Faced with the practical impossibility of answering the empirical questions of psychology by brute inspection (how *in fact* does the nervous system accomplish X or Y or Z?), psychologists ask themselves an easier preliminary question:

How could any system (with features A, B, C,...) possibly accomplish X?

This sort of question is easier because it is "less empirical"; it is an *engineering* question, a quest for a solution (any solution) rather than a discovery. Seeking an answer to such a question can sometimes lead to the discovery of general constraints on all solutions (including of course nature's as yet unknown solution), and therein lies the value of this style of aprioristic theorizing. Once one decides to do psychology this way, one can choose a degree of empirical difficulty for one's question by filling in the blanks in the question schema above. The more empirical constraints one puts on the description of the system, or on the description of the requisite behavior, the greater the claim to "psychological reality" one's answer must make. For instance, one can ask how any neuronal network with such-and-such physical features could *possibly* accomplish human color discriminations, or we can ask how any finite system could *possibly* subserve the acquisition of a natural language, or one can ask how human memory could *possibly* be so organized so as to make it so relatively easy for us to answer questions like "Have you ever ridden an antelope?", and so relatively hard to answer "What did you have for breakfast last Tuesday?". Or, one can ask, with Kant, how anything at all could *possibly* experience or know anything at all. Pure epistemology thus viewed, for instance, is simply the limiting case of the psychologists' quest, and is *prima facie* no less valuable to *psychology* for being so neutral with regard to empirical details. Some such questions are of course better designed to yield good answers than others, but *properly carried out*, any such investigation can yield constraints that bind all more data-enriched investigations.

AI workers can pitch their investigations at any level of empirical difficulty they wish; at Carnegie Mellon University, for instance, much is made of paying careful attention to experimental data on human performance, and attempting to model human performance closely. Other workers in AI are less concerned with that degree of psychological reality and have engaged in a more abstract version of AI. There is much that is of value and interest to psychology at the empirical end of the spectrum, but I want to claim that AI is better viewed as sharing with traditional epistemology the status of being a most general, most abstract asking of the top-down question: how is knowledge possible? It has seemed to some philosophers that AI cannot be plausibly so construed because it takes on an additional burden: it restricts itself to mechanistic solutions, and hence its domain is not the Kantian domain of all possible modes of intelligence, but just all possible mechanistically realizable modes of intelligence. This, it is claimed, would beg the question against vitalists, dualists and other anti-mechanists. But as I have argued elsewhere, the mechanism requirement of AI is not an additional constraint of any moment, for if psychology is possible at all, and if Church's thesis is true, the constraint of mechanism is no more severe than the constraint against begging the question in psychology, and who would wish to evade that? (See Chapter 5).

So I am claiming that AI shares with philosophy (in particular, with epistemology and philosophy of mind) the status of most abstract investigation of the principles of psychology. But it shares with psychology *in distinction from philosophy* a typical tactic in *answering* its questions. In AI or cognitive psychology the typical attempt to answer a *general* top-down question consists in designing a *particular* system that does, or appears to do, the relevant job, and then considering which of its features are necessary not just to one's particular system but to any such system. Philosophers have generally shunned such elaborate system-designing in favor of more doggedly general inquiry. This is perhaps the major difference between AI and "pure" philosophical approaches to the same questions, and it is one of my purposes here to exhibit some of the relative strengths and weaknesses of the two approaches.

The system-design approach that is common to AI and other styles of top-down psychology is beset by a variety of dangers of which these four are perhaps the chief:

(1) designing a system with component subsystems whose stipulated capacities are *miraculous* given the constraints one is accepting. (E.g., positing more information-processing in a component than the relevant time and matter will allow, or, at a more abstract level of engineering incoherence, positing a subsystem whose duties would require it to be more "intelligent" or "knowledgeable" than the supersystem of which it is to be a part.

(2) mistaking *conditional* necessities of one's particular solution for completely general constraints (a trivial example would be proclaiming that brains use LISP; less trivial examples require careful elucidation).

(3) restricting oneself artificially to the design of a subsystem (e.g., a depth perceiver or sentence parser) and concocting a solution that is systematically incapable of being grafted onto the other subsystems of a whole cognitive creature.

(4) restricting the performance of one's system to an artificially small part of the "natural" domain of that system and providing no efficient or plausible way for the system to be enlarged.

These dangers are altogether familiar to AI, but are just as common, *if harder to diagnose conclusively*, in other approaches to psychology. Consider danger (1): both Freud's ego subsystem and J.J. Gibson's invariance-sensitive perceptual "tuning forks" have been *charged* with miraculous capacities. Danger (2): behaviorists have been *charged* with illicitly extrapolating from pigeon-necessities to people-necessities, and it is often claimed that what the frog's eye tells the frog's brain is not at all what the person's eye tells the person's brain. Danger (3): it is notoriously hard to see how Chomsky's early *syntax*-driven system could interact with semantical components to produce or comprehend purposeful speech. Danger (4): it is hard to see how some models of nonsense-syllable rote memorization could be enlarged to handle similar but more sophisticated memory tasks. It is one of the great strengths of AI that when one of its products succumbs to any of these dangers this can usually be quite conclusively demonstrated.

I now have triangulated AI with respect to both philosophy and psychology (as my title suggested I would): AI can be (and should often be taken to be) as abstract and "unempirical" as philosophy in the questions it attempts to answer, but at the same time, it should be as explicit and particularistic in its models as psychology at its best. Thus one might learn as much of value to psychology or epistemology from a *particular* but highly *un*realistic AI model as one could learn from a detailed psychology of, say, Martians. A good psychology of Martians, however unlike us they might be, would certainly yield general principles of psychology or epistemology applicable to human beings. Now before turning to the all important question: "What, so conceived, has AI accomplished?", I want to consider briefly some misinterpretations of AI that my sketch of it so far does not protect us from.

Since we are viewing AI as a species of top-down cognitive psychology, it is tempting to suppose that the decomposition of function in a computer is intended by AI to be somehow isomorphic to the decomposition of function in a brain. One learns of vast programs made up of literally billions of basic computer events and somehow so organized as to produce a simulacrum of human intelligence, and it is altogether natural to suppose that since the brain is known to be composed of billions of tiny functioning parts, and since there is a *gap of ignorance* between our understanding of intelligent human behavior and our understanding of those tiny parts, the ultimate, millenial goal of AI must be to provide a hierarchical breakdown of parts in the computer that will mirror or be isomorphic to some hard-to-discover hierarchical breakdown of brain-event parts. The familiar theme of "organs made of tissues made of cells made of molecules made of atoms" is to be matched, one might suppose, in electronic hardware terms. In the thrall of this picture one might be discouraged to learn that some functional parts of the nervous system do not seem to function in the digital way the atomic functioning parts in computers do. The standard response to this worry would be that one had looked too deep in the computer (this is sometimes called the "grain problem"). The computer is a digital device at bottom, but a digital device can simulate an "analogue" device to any degree of continuity you desire, and at a higher level of aggregation in the computer one may find the analogue elements that are mappable onto the non-digital brain parts. As many writers have observed, we cannot gauge the psychological reality of a model until we are given the commentary on the model that tells us which features of the model are intended to mirror real saliencies in nature, and which are either backstage expediters of the modeling or sheer inadvertent detail. (In the Eighteenth Century, scientists built beautiful brass clockwork models of the solar system called orreries. The *gears* of an orrery are not intended to represent anything real in the firmament, nor are the reflections of one brass globe in another.) When one looks at AI programs in detail one sees mountains of digital calculation or "number crunching"; if this looks terribly unbiological, this is to be excused since that part of the model's structure is to be viewed as backstage, not part of the model we are supposed to compare with nature.

This story is fine in principle, I think, and the day may come when this imagined isomorphism down to the neuronal level (but not backstage) is proclaimed, but in fact we see nothing remotely like this in current AI work. We see instead models that diverge from nature *very* early on the downward path. AI programs typically model relatively high-level cognitive features, such as concept learning or revision of goals or beliefs, and it does indeed often take millions of basic computer events to simulate just a handful of these *intended model features* — but no one really knows or cares what these basic events are, for no one supposes that *any* of the saliencies in the mass of activity that subserves the intended features are to be taken seriously as psychology or physiology. The psychological reality of an AI program is thus usually intended to be only skin deep; only the highest levels of program description and commentary are to be counted as the model.

The *thin*ness of the psychological reality of AI models is obscured for the uninitiated by a particularly misleading feature of most of the AI programs that get into the limelight. What especially attracts audiences and evokes wonder is the marvelous verisimilitude of some of the programs. Consider this excerpt of conversation (minus the programmer's excellent commentary) between Terry Winograd's SHRDLU and its interlocutor. SHRDLU is a program that lives in an imaginary "block world" where it can manipulate colored blocks on a table in response to commands and answer questions about its life in this world. Computer responses are capitalized.

Had you touched any pyramid before you put the green one on the little cube?

YES, THE GREEN ONE.

When did you pick it up?

WHILE I WAS STACKING UP THE RED CUBE, A LARGE RED BLOCK AND A LARGE GREEN CUBE.

Why?

TO GET RID OF IT.

Why did you do that?

TO CLEAR OFF THE RED CUBE.

Why did you clear off that cube?

TO PUT IT ON A LARGE GREEN CUBE.

Why did you do that?

BECAUSE YOU ASKED ME TO.

When SHRDLU replies to the last question with "Because you asked me to", one can hardly help being struck by the apparent *humanity* of the response— "SHRDLU is *one of us!*" it is tempting to exclaim. If one is naive, one will be awestruck; if one is not, one will still be titillated by the illusion, for that is largely what it is.

SHRDLU's response, though perfectly appropriate to the occasion (and not by coincidence!) is "canned". Winograd has simply given SHRDLU this whole sentence to print at times like these. If a child gave SHRDLU's response we would naturally expect its behavior to manifest a general capacity which might also reveal itself by producing the response: "Because you told me to," or, "Because that's what I was asked to do," or on another occasion: "Because I felt like it," or "Because your assistant told me to," but these are dimensions of subtlety beyond SHRDLU. Its behavior is remarkably versatile, but it does not reveal a rich knowledge of interpersonal relations, of the difference between requests and orders, of being cooperative with other people under appropriate circumstances. (It should be added that Winograd's paper makes it very explicit where and to what extent he is canning SHRDLU's responses, so·anyone who feels cheated by SHRDLU has simply not read Winograd. Other natural language programs do not rely on canned responses, or rely on them to a minimal extent.)

The fact remains, however, that much of the antagonism to AI is due to resentment and distrust engendered by such legerdemain. Why do AI people use these tricks? For many reasons. First, they need to get some tell-tale response back from the program and it is as easy to can a mnemonically vivid and "natural" response as something more sober, technical and understated (perhaps: "REASON: PRIOR COMMAND TO DO THAT"). Second, in Winograd's case he was attempting to reveal the *minimal* conditions for correct analysis of certain linguistic forms (note all the "problems" of pronominal antecedents in the sentences displayed), so "natural" language *output* to reveal correct analysis of natural language *input* was entirely appropriate. Third, AI people put canned responses in their programs because it is fun. It is fun to amuse one's colleagues, who are not fooled of course, and it is especially fun to bamboozle the outsiders. As an outsider, one must learn to be properly unimpressed by AI verisimilitude, as one is by the chemist's dazzling forest of glass tubing, or the angry mouths full of teeth painted on World War II fighter planes. (Joseph Weizenbaum's famous ELIZA program, the computer "psychotherapist" who apparently listens so wisely and sympathetically to one's problems, is intended in part as an antidote to the enthusiasm generated by AI verisimilitude. It is almost all clever canning, and is not a psychologically realistic model of anything, but rather a demonstration of how easily one can be gulled into attributing too much to a program. It exploits syntactic landmarks in one's input with nothing approaching genuine understanding, but it makes a good show of comprehension nevertheless. One might say it was a plausible model of a Wernicke's aphasic, who can babble on with well-formed and even semantically appropriate responses to his interlocutor, sometimes sustaining the illusion of comprehension for quite a while.)

The AI community pays a price for this misleading if fascinating fun, not only by contributing to the image of AI people as tricksters and hackers, but by fueling more serious misconceptions of the point of AI research. For instance, Winograd's real contribution in SHRDLU is *not* that he has produced an English speaker and understander that is psychologically realistic at many different levels of analysis (though that is what the verisimilitude strongly suggests, and what a lot of the fanfare — for which Winograd is not responsible — has assumed), but that he has explored some of the deepest demands on any system that can take direction (in a natural language), plan, change the world and keep track of the changes wrought or contemplated, and in the course of this exploration he has clarified the problems and proposed ingenious and plausible *partial* solutions to them. The real contribution in Winograd's work stands quite unimpeached by the perfectly true but irrelevant charge the SHRDLU doesn't have a *rich* or human understanding of most of the words in its very restricted vocabulary, or is terribly slow.

In fact, paying so much attention to the performance of SHRDLU (and similar systems) reveals a failure to recognize that AI programs are not *empirical* experiments but *thought*-experiments prosthetically regulated by computers. Some AI people have recently become fond of describing their discipline as "experimental epistemology". This unfortunate term should make a philosopher's blood boil, but if AI called itself thought-experimental epistemology (or even better: *Gedanken*-experimental epistemology) philosophers ought to be reassured. The questions asked and answered by the thought-experiments of AI are about whether or not one can obtain certain sorts of information processing — recognition, inference, control of various sorts, for instance — from certain sorts of designs. Often the answer is no. The process of elimination looms large in AI. Relatively plausible schemes are explored far enough to make it clear that they are utterly incapable of delivering the requisite behavior, and learning this is important progress, even if it doesn't result in a mind-boggling robot.

The hardware realizations of AI are almost gratuitous. Like dropping the cannonballs off the Leaning Tower of Pisa, they are demonstrations that are superfluous to those who have understood the argument, however persuasive they are to the rest. Are computers then irrelevant to AI? "In principle" they are irrelevant (in the same sense of "in principle", diagrams on the blackboard are in principle unnecessary to teaching geometry), but in practice they are not. I earlier described them as "prosthetic regulators" of thought-experiments. What I meant was this: it is notoriously difficult to keep wishful thinking out of one's thought-experiments; computer simulation *forces* one to recognize all the costs of one's imagined design. As Pylyshyn observes, "What is needed is...a technical language with which to discipline one's imagination." The discipline provided by computers is undeniable (and especially palpable to the beginning programmer). It is both a good thing — for the reasons just stated — and a bad thing. Perhaps you have known a person so steeped in, say, playing bridge, that his entire life becomes in his eyes a series of finesses, end plays and cross-ruffs. Every morning he draws life's trumps and whenever he can see the end of a project he views it as a lay-down. Computer languages seem to have a similar effect on people who become fluent in them. Although I won't try to prove it by citing examples, I think it is quite obvious that the "technical language" Pylyshyn speaks of can cripple an imagination in the process of disciplining it.

It has been said so often that computers have huge effects on their users' imaginations that one can easily lose sight of one of the most obvious but still underrated ways in which computers achieve this effect, and that is the sheer speed of computers. Before computers came along the theoretician was strongly constrained to ignore the possibility of truly massive and complex processes in psychology because it was hard to see how such processes could fail to *appear* at worst mechanical and cumbersome, at best vegetatively slow, and of course a hallmark of mentality is its swiftness. One might say that the speed of thought defines the upper bound of subjective "fast", the way the speed of light defines the upper bound of objective "fast". Now suppose there had never been any computers but that somehow (by magic, presumably) Kenneth Colby had managed to dream up these flow charts as a proposed model of a part of human organization in

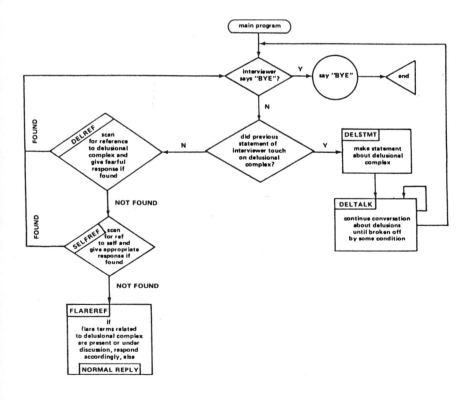

Figure 7-1

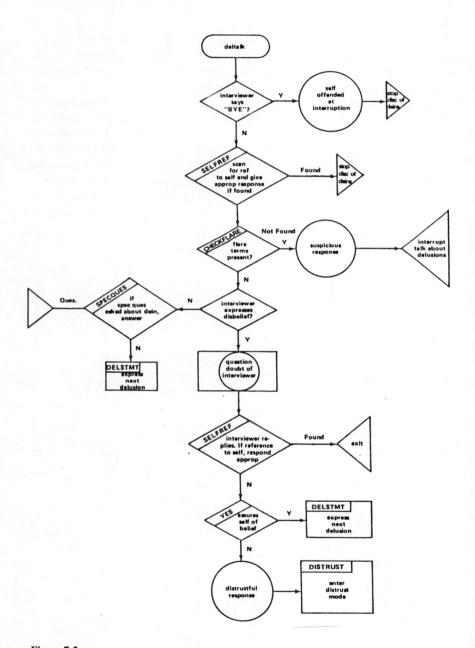

Figure 7-2

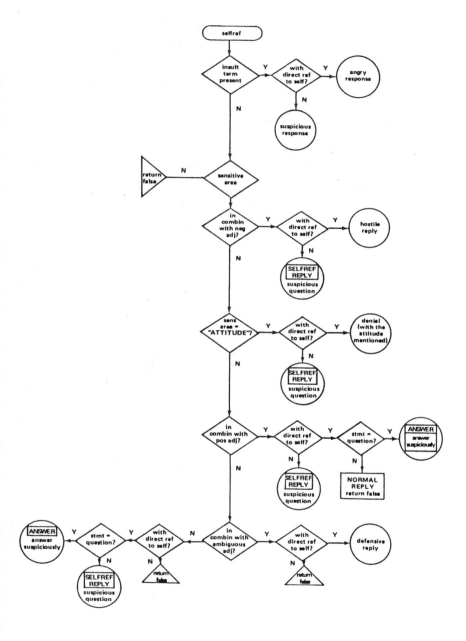

Figure 7-3

paranoia. (The flow charts are from his book, *Artificial Paranoia*, Pergamon, 1975; figure 7.1 represents the main program; figures 7.2 and 7.3 are blow-ups of details of the main program.) It is obvious to everyone, even Colby I think, that this is a vastly oversimplified model of paranoia, but had there not been computers to show us how all this processing and much much more can occur in a twinkling, we would be inclined to dismiss the proposal immediately as altogether too clanking and inorganic, a Rube Goldberg machine. Most programs look like that in slow motion (hand simulation) but speeded up they often reveal a dexterity and grace that appears natural, and this grace is entirely undetectable via a slow analysis of the program (cf. time lapse photography of plants growing and buds opening). The grace in operation of AI programs may be mere illusion. Perhaps nature is graceful *all the way down*, but for better or for worse, computer speed has liberated the imagination of theoreticians by opening up the possibility and plausibility of very complex interactive information processes playing a role in the production of cognitive events so swift as to be atomic to introspection.

At last I turn to the important question. Suppose that AI is viewed as I recommend, as a most abstract inquiry into the possibility of intelligence or knowledge. Has it solved any very general problems or discovered any very important constraints or principles? I think the answer is a qualified yes. In particular, I think AI has broken the back of an argument that has bedeviled philosophers and psychologists for over two hundred years. Here is a skeletal version of it: *First*, the only psychology that could possibly succeed in explaining the complexities of human activity must posit internal representations. This premise has been deemed obvious by just about everyone except the radical behaviorists (both in psychology and philosophy — both Watson and Skinner, and Ryle and Malcolm). Descartes doubted almost everything *but* this. For the British Empiricists, the internal representations were called ideas, sensations, impressions; more recently psychologists have talked of hypotheses, maps, schemas, images, propositions, engrams, neural signals, even holograms and whole innate theories. So the first premise is quite invulnerable, or at any rate it has an impressive mandate (see Chapter 6). But, *second*, nothing is intrinsically a representation of anything; something is a representation only *for* or *to* someone; any representation or system of representations thus requires at least one *user* or *interpreter* of the representation who is external to it. Any such interpreter must have a variety of psychological or intentional traits (see Chapter 1): it must be capable of a variety of *comprehension*, and must have beliefs and goals (so it can *use* the representation to *inform* itself and thus assist it in achieving its goals). Such an interpreter is then a sort of homunculus.

Therefore, psychology *without* homunculi is impossible. But psychology *with* homunculi is doomed to circularity or infinite regress, so psychology is impossible.

The argument given is a relatively abstract version of a familiar group of problems. For instance, it seems (to many) that we cannot account for perception unless we suppose it provides us with an internal image (or model or map) of the external world, and yet what good would that image do us unless we have an inner eye to perceive it, and how are we to explain *its* capacity for perception? It also seems (to many) that understanding a heard sentence must be somehow *translating* it into some internal message, but how will this message in turn be understood: by translating it into something else? The problem is an old one, and let's call it *Hume's Problem*, for while he did not state it explicitly, he appreciated its force and strove mightily to escape its clutches. Hume's internal representations were impressions and ideas, and he wisely shunned the notion of an inner *self* that would intelligently *manipulate* these items, but this left him with the necessity of getting the ideas and impressions to "think for themselves". The result was his theory of the self as a "bundle" of (nothing but) impressions and ideas. He attempted to set these impressions and ideas into dynamic interaction by positing various associationistic links, so that each succeeding idea in the stream of consciousness dragged its successor onto the stage according to one or another principle, all without benefit of intelligent *supervision*. It didn't work, of course. It couldn't conceivably work, and Hume's failure is plausibly viewed as the harbinger of doom for any remotely analogous enterprise. On the one hand, how could *any* theory of psychology make sense of representations that *understand themselves*, and on the other, how could *any* theory of psychology avoid regress or circularity if it posits at least one representation-understander in addition to the representations?

Now no doubt some philosophers and psychologists who have appealed to internal representations over the years have believed in their hearts that somehow the force of this argument could be blunted, that Hume's problem could be solved, but I am sure no one had the slightest idea *how to do this* until AI and the notion of data-structures came along. Data-structures may or may not be biologically or psychologically realistic representations, but they are, if not living, breathing examples, at least clanking, functioning examples of representations that can be said in the requisite sense to understand themselves.

How this is accomplished can be metaphorically described (and any talk about internal representations is bound to have a large element of metaphor in it) by elaborating our description (see Chapter 5) of AI as a top-down theoretical inquiry. One starts, in AI, with a specification of a whole person or cognitive organism — what I call, more neutrally, an intentional system (see Chapter 1) — or some artificial segment of that person's abilities (e.g., chess-playing, answering questions about baseball) and then breaks that largest intentional system into an organization of subsystems, each of which could itself be viewed as an intentional system (with its own specialized beliefs and desires) and hence as formally a homunculus. In fact, homunculus talk is ubiquitous in AI, and almost always illuminating. AI homunculi talk to each other, wrest control from each other, volunteer, sub-contract, supervise, and even kill. There seems no better way of describing what is going on. Homunculi are *bogeymen* only if they duplicate *entire* the talents they are rung in to explain (a special case of danger (1)). If one can get a team or committee of *relatively* ignorant, narrow-minded, blind homunculi to produce the intelligent behavior of the whole, this is progress. A flow chart is typically the organizational chart of a committee of homunculi (investigators, librarians, accountants, executives); each box specifies a homunculus by prescribing a function *without saying how it is to be accomplished* (one says, in effect: put a little man in there to do the job). If we then look closer at the individual boxes we see that the function of each is accomplished by subdividing it via another flow chart into still smaller, more stupid homunculi. Eventually this nesting of boxes within boxes lands you with homunculi so stupid (all they have to do is remember whether to say yes or no when asked) that they can be, as one says, "replaced by a machine". One *discharges* fancy homunculi from one's scheme by organizing armies of such idiots to do the work.

When homunculi at a level interact, they do so by sending *messages*, and each homunculus has representations that it uses to execute its functions. Thus typical AI discussions do draw a distinction between representation and representation-user: they take the *first step* of the threatened infinite regress, but as many writers in AI have observed, it has gradually emerged from the tinkerings of AI that there is a trade-off between sophistication in the representation and sophistication in the user. The more raw and uninterpreted the representation — e.g., the mosaic of retinal stimulation at an instant — the more sophisticated the interpreter or user of the representation. The more interpreted a representation — the more *procedural* information is *embodied in it*, for instance — the less fancy the interpreter need be. It is this fact that permits one to get away with *lesser* homunculi at high levels, by getting their earlier or lower brethren to do some of the work. One never quite gets *completely* self-understanding representations (unless one stands back and views all representation in the system from a global vantage point), but all homunculi are ultimately discharged. One gets the advantage of the trade-off only by sacrificing versatility and universality in one's subsystems and their representations, so one's homunculi cannot be too versatile nor can the messages they send and receive have the full flavor of normal human linguistic interaction. We have seen an example of how homuncular communications may fall short in SHRDLU's remark, "Because you asked me to." The context of production and the function of the utterance makes clear that this is a sophisticated communication and the product of a sophisticated representation, but it is not a full-fledged Gricean speech act. If it were, it would require too fancy a homunculus to use it.

There are two ways a philosopher might view AI data structures. One could grant that they are indeed self-understanding representations or one could cite the various disanalogies between them and prototypical or *real* representations (human statements, paintings, maps) and conclude that data-structures are not really internal representations at all. But if one takes the latter line, the modest successes of AI simply serve to undercut our first premise: it is no longer obvious that psychology needs internal representations; internal pseudo-representations may do just as well.

It is certainly tempting to argue that since AI has provided us with the only known way of solving Hume's Problem, albeit for very restrictive systems, it must be on the right track, and its categories must be psychologically real, but one might well be falling into Danger (2) if one did. We can all be relieved and encouraged to learn that there is a way of solving Hume's Problem, but it has yet to be shown that AI's way is the only way it can be done.

AI has made a major contribution to philosophy and psychology by revealing a particular way in which simple cases of Hume's Problem can be solved. What else has it accomplished of interest to philosophers? I will close by just drawing attention to the two main areas where I think the AI approach is of particular relevance to philosophy.

For many years philosophers and psychologists have debated (with scant interdisciplinary communication) about the existence and nature of mental images. These discussions have been relatively fruitless, largely, I think, because neither side had any idea of how to come to grips with Hume's Problem. Recent work in AI, however, has recast the issues in a clearly more perspicuous and powerful framework, and anyone hoping to resolve this ancient issue will find help in the AI discussions.

The second main area of philosophical interest, in my view, is the so-called "frame problem." The frame problem is an abstract *epistemological* problem that was in effect discovered by AI thought-experimentation. When a cognitive creature, an entity with many beliefs about the world, performs an act, the world changes and many of the creature's beliefs must be revised or updated. How? It cannot be that we perceive and notice *all* the changes (for one thing, many of the changes we *know* to occur do not occur in our perceptual fields), and hence it cannot be that we rely entirely on perceptual input to revise our beliefs. So we must have internal ways of up-dating our beliefs that will fill in the gaps and keep our internal model, the totality of our beliefs, roughly faithful to the world.

If one supposes, as philosophers traditionally have, that one's beliefs are a set of propositions, and reasoning is inference or deduction from members of the set, one is in for trouble, for it is quite clear (though still controversial) that systems relying only on such processes get swamped by combinatorial explosions in the updating effort. It seems that our entire conception of belief and reasoning must be radically revised if we are to explain the undeniable capacity of human beings to keep their beliefs roughly consonant with the reality they live in.

I think one can find an *appreciation* of the frame problem in Kant (we *might* call the frame problem Kant's Problem) but unless one disciplines one's thought-experiments in the AI manner, philosophical proposals of solutions to the problem, including Kant's of course, can be viewed as at best suggestive, at worst mere wishful thinking.

I do not want to suggest that philosophers abandon traditional philosophical methods and retrain themselves as AI workers. There is plenty of work to do by thought-experimentation and argumentation, disciplined by the canons of philosophical method and informed by the philosophical tradition. Some of the most influential recent work in AI (e.g., Minsky's papers on "Frames") is loaded with recognizably philosophical speculations of a relatively unsophisticated nature. Philosophers, I have said, should study AI. Should AI workers study philosophy? Yes, unless they are content to reinvent the wheel every few days. When AI reinvents a wheel, it is typically square, or at best hexagonal, and can only make a few hundred revolutions before it stops. Philosopher's wheels, on the other hand, are perfect circles, require *in principle* no lubrication, and can go in at least two directions at once. Clearly a meeting of minds is in order.

15

COMPUTER SCIENCE AS EMPIRICAL INQUIRY: SYMBOLS AND SEARCH

Allan Newell and Herbert A. Simon

COMPUTER SCIENCE is the study of the phenomena surrounding computers. The founders of this society understood this very well when they called themselves the Association for Computing Machinery. The machine — not just the hardware, but the programmed living machine — is the organism we study.

This is the tenth Turing Lecture. The nine persons who preceded us on this platform have presented nine different views of computer science. For our organism, the machine, can be studied at many levels and from many sides. We are deeply honored to appear here today and to present yet another view, the one that has permeated the scientific work for which we have been cited. We wish to speak of computer science as empirical inquiry.

Our view is only one of many; the previous lectures make that clear. However, even taken together the lectures fail to cover the whole scope of our science. Many fundamental aspects of it have not been represented in these ten awards. And if the time ever arrives, surely not soon, when the compass has been boxed, when computer science has been discussed from every side, it will be time to start the cycle again. For the hare as lecturer will have to make an annual sprint to overtake the cumulation of small, incremental gains that the tortoise of scientific and technical development has achieved in his steady march. Each year will create a new gap and call for a new sprint, for in science there is no final word.

Computer science is an empirical discipline. We would have called it an experimental science, but like astronomy, economics and geology, some of its

Newell, A., and H.A. Simon. 1981. "Computer Science as Empirical Inquiry: Symbols and Search" in *Communications of the Association for Computing Machinery, vol. 19*, 35–50 © 1981 Association for Computing Machinery.

unique forms of observation and experience do not fit a narrow stereotype of the experimental method Nonetheless, they are experiments. Each new machine that is built is an experiment. Actually constructing the machine poses a question to nature; and we listen for the answer by observing the machine in operation and analyzing it by all analytical and measurement means available. Each new program that is built is an experiment. It poses a question to nature, and its behavior offers clues to an answer. Neither machines nor programs are black boxes; they are artifacts that have been designed, both hardware and software, and we can open them up and look inside. We can relate their structure to their behavior and draw many lessons from a single experiment. We don't have to build 100 copies of, say, a theorem prover, to demonstrate statistically that it has not overcome the combinatorial explosion of search in the way hoped for. Inspection of the program in the light of a few runs reveals the flaw and lets us proceed to the next attempt.

We build computers and programs for many reasons. We build them to serve society and as tools for carrying out the economic tasks of society. But as basic scientists we build machines and programs as a way of discovering new phenomena and analyzing phenomena we already know about. Society often becomes confused about this, believing that computers and programs are to be constructed only for the economic use that can be made of them (or as intermediate items in a developmental sequence leading to such use). It needs to understand that the phenomena surrounding computers are deep and obscure, requiring much experimentation to assess their nature. It needs to understand that, as in any science, the gains that accrue from such experimentation and understanding pay off in the permanent acquisition of new techniques; and that it is these techniques that will create the instruments to help society in achieving its goals.

Our purpose here, however, is not to plead for understanding from an outside world. It is to examine one aspect of our science, the development of new basic understanding by empirical inquiry. This is best done by illustrations. We will be pardoned if, presuming upon the occasion, we choose our examples from the area of our own research. As will become apparent, these examples involve the whole development of artificial intelligence, especially in its early years. They rest on much more than our own personal contributions. And even where we have made direct contributions, this has been done in cooperation with others. Our collaborators have included especially Cliff Shaw, with whom we formed a team of three through the exciting period of the late fifties. But we have also worked with a great many colleagues and students at Carnegie-Mellon University.

Time permits taking up just two examples. The first is the development of the notion of a symbolic system. The second is the development of the notion of heuristic search. Both conceptions have deep significance for understanding how information is processed and how intelligence is achieved. However, they do not come close to exhausting the full scope of artificial intelligence though they seem to us to be useful for exhibiting the nature of fundamental knowledge in this part of computer science.

I. SYMBOLS AND PHYSICAL SYMBOL SYSTEMS

One of the fundamental contributions to knowledge of computer science has been to explain, at a rather basic level, what symbols are. This explanation is a scientific proposition about Nature. It is empirically derived, with a long and gradual development.

Symbols lie at the root of intelligent action, which is, of course, the primary topic of artificial intelligence. For that matter, it is a primary question for all computer science. For all information is processed by computers in the service of ends, and we measure the intelligence of a system by its ability to achieve stated ends in the face of variations, difficulties, and complexities posed by the task environment. This general investment of computer science attaining intelligence is obscured when the tasks being accomplished are limited in scope, for then the full variations in the environment can be accurately foreseen. It becomes more obvious as we extend computers to more global, complex and knowledge intensive tasks — as we attempt to make them our agents, capable of handling on their own the full contingencies of the natural world.

Our understanding of the system's requirements for intelligent action emerges slowly. It is composite, for no single elementary thing accounts for intelligence in all its manifestations. There is no "intelligence principle," just as there is no "vital principle" that conveys by its very nature the essence of life. But the lack of a simple *deus ex machina* does not imply that there are no structural requirements for intelligence. One such requirement is the ability to store and manipulate symbols. To put the scientific question, we may paraphrase the title of a famous paper by Warren McCulloch (1961): What is a symbol, that intelligence may use it, and intelligence, that it may use a symbol?

LAWS OF QUALITATIVE STRUCTURE

All sciences characterize the essential nature of the systems they study. These characterizations are invariably qualitative in nature, for they set the terms within which more detailed knowledge can be developed. Their essence can often be captured in very short, very general statements. One might judge these general laws, because of their limited specificity, as making relatively little contribution to the sum of a science, were it not for the historical evidence that shows them to be results of the greatest importance.

The Cell Doctrine in Biology. A good example of a law of qualitative structure is the cell doctrine in biology, which states that the basic building block of all living organisms is the cell. Cells come in a large variety of forms, though they all have a nucleus surrounded by protoplasm, the whole encased by a membrane. But this internal structure was not, historically, part of the specification of the cell doctrine; it was subsequent specificity developed by intensive investigation. The cell doctrine can be conveyed almost entirely by the statement we gave above, along with some vague notions about what size a cell can be. The impact of this law on biology, however, has been tremendous, and the lost motion in the field prior to its gradual acceptance was considerable.

Plate Tectonics in Geology. Geology provides an interesting example of a qualitative structure law, interesting because it has gained acceptance in the last decade and so its rise in status is still fresh in our memory. The theory of plate tectonics asserts that the surface of the globe is a collection of huge plates — a few dozen in all — which move (at geological speeds) against, over, and under each other into the center of the earth, where they lose their identity. The movements of the plates account for the shapes and relative locations of the continents and oceans, for the areas of volcanic and earthquake activity, for the deep sea ridges, and so on. With a few additional particulars as to speed and size, the essential theory has been specified. It was of course not accepted until it succeeded in explaining a number of details, all of which hung together (e.g. accounting for flora, fauna, and stratification agreements between West Africa and Northeast South America). The plate tectonics theory is highly qualitative. Now that it is accepted, the whole earth seems to offer evidence for it everywhere, for we see the world in its terms.

The Germ Theory of Disease. It is little more than a century since Pasteur enunciated the germ theory of disease, a law of qualitative structure that produced a revolution in medicine. The theory proposes that most diseases are caused by the presence and multiplication in the body of tiny single-celled living organisms, and that contagion consists in the transmission of these organisms from one host to another. A large part of the elaboration of the theory consisted in identifying the organisms associated with specific diseases, describing them, and tracing their life histories. The fact that the law has many exceptions — that many diseases are not produced by germs — does not detract from its importance. The law tells us to look for a particular kind of cause; it does not insist that we will always find it.

The Doctrine of Atomism. The doctrine of atomism offers an interesting contrast to the three laws of qualitative structure we have just described. As it emerged from the work of Dalton and his demonstrations that the chemicals combined in fixed proportions, the law provided a typical example of qualitative structure: the elements are composed of small, uniform particles, differing from one element to another. But because the underlying species of atoms are so simple and limited in their variety, quantitative theories were soon formulated which assimilated all the general structure in the original qualitative hypothesis. With cells, tectonic plates, and germs, the variety of structure is so great that the underlying qualitative principle remains distinct, and its contribution to the total theory clearly discernible.

Conclusion. Laws of qualitative structure are seen everywhere in science. Some of our greatest scientific discoveries are to be found among them. As the examples illustrate, they often set the terms on which a whole science operates.

PHYSICAL SYMBOL SYSTEMS

Let us return to the topic of symbols, and define a *physical symbol system*. The adjective "physical" denotes two important features: (1) Such systems clearly obey the laws of physics — they are realizable by engineered systems made of engineered components; (2) although our use of the term "symbol" prefigures our intended interpretation, it is not restricted to human symbol systems.

A physical symbol system consists of a set of entities, called symbols, which are physical patterns that can occur as components of another type of entity called an expression (or symbol structure). Thus a symbol structure is composed of a number of instances (or tokens) of symbols related in some physical way (such as one token being next to another). At any instant of time the system will contain a collection of these symbol structures. Besides these structures, the system also contains a collection of processes that operate on expressions to produce other expressions: processes of creation, modification, reproduction, and destruction. A physical symbol system is a machine that produces through time an evolving collection of symbol structures. Such a system exists in a world of objects wider than just these symbolic expressions themselves.

Two notions are central to this structure of expressions, symbols, and objects: designation and interpretation.

Designation. An expression designates an object if, given the expression, the system can either affect the object itself or behave in ways depending on the object.

In either case, access to the object via the expression has been obtained, which is the essence of designation.

Interpretation. The system can interpret an expression if the expression designates a process and if, given the expression, the system can carry out the process.[1]

Interpretation implies a special form of dependent action: given an expression, the system can perform the indicated process, which is to say, it can evoke and execute its own processes from expressions that designate them.

A system capable of designation and interpretation, in the sense just indicated, must also meet a number of additional requirements, of completeness and closure.

We will have space only to mention these briefly; all of them are important and have far-reaching consequences.

(1) A symbol may be used to designate any expression whatsoever. That is, given a symbol, it is not prescribed a priori what expressions it can designate. This arbitrariness pertains only to symbols: the symbol tokens and their mutual relations determine what object is designated by a complex expression. (2) There exist expressions that designate every process of which the machine is capable. (3) There exist processes for creating any expression and for modifying any expression in arbitrary ways. (4) Expressions are stable; once created, they will continue to exist until explicitly modified or deleted. (5) The number of expressions that the system can hold is essentially unbounded.

The type of system we have just defined is not unfamiliar to computer scientists. It bears a strong family resemblance to all general purpose computers. If a symbol-manipulation language, such as LISP, is taken as defining a machine, then the kinship becomes truly brotherly. Our intent in laying out such a system is not to propose something new. Just the opposite: it is to show what is now known and hypothesized about systems that satisfy such a characterization.

We can now state a general scientific hypothesis — a law of qualitative structure for symbol systems:

The Physical Symbol System Hypothesis. A physical symbol system has the necessary and sufficient means for general intelligent action.

By "necessary" we mean that any system that exhibits general intelligence will prove upon analysis to be a physical symbol system. By "sufficient" we mean that any physical symbol system of sufficient size can be organized further to exhibit general intelligence.

By "general intelligent action" we wish to indicate the same scope of intelligence as we see in human action: that in any real situation behavior appropriate to the ends of the system and adaptive to the demands of the environment can occur, within some limits of speed and complexity.

The Physical Symbol System Hypothesis clearly is a law of qualitative structure. It specifies a general class of systems within which one will find those capable of intelligent action.

This is an empirical hypothesis. We have defined a class of systems; we wish to ask whether that class accounts for a set of phenomena we find in the real world. Intelligent action is everywhere around us in the biological world, mostly in human behavior. It is a form of behavior we can recognize by its effects whether it is performed by humans or not. The hypothesis could indeed be false. Intelligent behavior is not so easy to produce that any system will exhibit it willy-nilly. Indeed, there are people whose analyses lead them to conclude either on philosophical or on scientific grounds that the hypothesis *is* false. Scientifically, one can attack or defend it only by bringing forth empirical evidence about the natural world.

We now need to trace the development of this hypothesis and look at the evidence for it.

DEVELOPMENT OF THE SYMBOL SYSTEM HYPOTHESIS

A physical symbol system is an instance of a universal machine. Thus the symbol system hypothesis implies that intelligence will be realized by a universal computer. However, the hypothesis goes far beyond the argument, often made on general grounds of physical determining, that any computation that is realizable can be realized by a universal machine, provided that it is specified. For it asserts specifically that the intelligent machine is a symbol system, thus making a specific architectural assertion about the nature of intelligent systems. It is important to understand how this additional specificity arose.

Formal Logic. The roots of the hypothesis go back to the program of Frege and of Whitehead and Russell for formalizing logic: capturing the basic conceptual notions of mathematics in logic and putting the notions of proof and deduction on a secure footing. This effort culminated in mathematical logic — our familiar prepositional, first-order, and higher-order logics. It developed a characteristic view, often referred to as the "symbol game." Logic, and by incorporation all of mathematics, was a game played with meaningless tokens according to certain purely syntactic rules. All meaning had been purged. One had a mechanical, though permissive (we would now say nondeterministic), system about which various things could be proved. Thus progress was first made by walking away from all that seemed relevant to meaning and human symbols. We could call this the stage of formal symbol manipulation.

This general attitude is well reflected in the development of information theory. It was pointed out time and again that Shannon had defined a system that was useful only for communication and selection, and which had nothing to do with meaning. Regrets were expressed that such a general name as "information theory" had been given to the field, and attempts were made to rechristen it as "the theory of selective information" — to no avail, of course.

Turing Machines and the Digital Computer. The development of the first digital computers and of automata theory, starting with Turing's own work in the '30s, can be treated together. They agree in their view of what is essential. Let us use Turing's own model, for it shows the features well.

A Turing machine consists of two memories: an unbounded tape and a finite state control. The tape holds data, i.e. the famous zeroes and ones. The machine has a very small set of proper operations — read, write, and scan operations — on the tape. The read operation is not a data operation, but provides conditional branching to a control state as a function of the data under the read head. As we all know, this model contains the essentials of all computers, in terms of what they can do, though other computers with different memories and operations might carry out the same computations with different requirements of space and time. In particular, the model of a Turing machine contains within it the notions both of what cannot be computed and of universal machines — computers that can do anything that can be done by any machine.

We should marvel that two of our deepest insights into information processing were achieved in the thirties, before modern computers came into being. It is a tribute to the genius of Alan Turing. It is also a tribute to the development of mathematical logic at the time, and testimony to the depth of computer science's obligation to it. Concurrently with Turing's work appeared the work of the logicians Emil Post and (independently) Alonzo Church. Starting from independent notions of logistic systems (Post productions and recursive functions, respectively), they arrived at analogous results on undecidability and universality — results that were soon shown to imply that all three systems were equivalent. Indeed, the convergence of all these attempts to define the most general class of information-processing systems provides some of the force of our conviction that we have captured the essentials of information processing in these models.

In none of these systems is there, on the surface, a concept of the symbol as something that *designates*. The data are regarded as just strings of zeroes and ones — indeed that data be inert is essential to the reduction of computation to physical process. The finite state control system was always viewed as a small controller, and logical games were played to see how small a state system could be used without destroying the universality of the machine. No games, as far as we can tell, were ever played to add new states dynamically to the finite control — to think of the control memory as holding the bulk of the system's knowledge. What was accomplished at this stage was half the principle of interpretation — showing that a machine could be run from a description. Thus this is the stage of automatic formal symbol manipulation.

The Stored Program Concept. With the development of the second generation of electronic machines in the mid-forties (after the Eniac) came the stored program concept. This was rightfully hailed as a milestone, both conceptually and practically. Programs now can be data, and can be operated on as data. This capability is, of course, already implicit in the model of Turing: the descriptions are on the very same tape as the data. Yet the idea was realized only when machines acquired enough memory to make it practicable to locate actual programs in some internal place. After all, the Eniac had only twenty registers.

The stored program concept embodies the second half of the interpretation principle, the part that says that the system's own data can be interpreted. But it does not yet contain the notion of designation — of the physical relation that underlies meaning.

List-Processing. The next step, taken in 1956, was list-processing. The contents of the data structures were now symbols, in the sense of our physical symbol system: patterns that designated that had referents. Lists held addresses which permitted access to other lists — thus the notion of list structures. That this was a new view was demonstrated to us many times in the early days of list processing when colleagues would ask where the data were — that is, which list finally held the collections of bits that were the content of the system. They found it strange that there were no such bits, there were only symbols that designated yet other symbol structures.

List-processing is simultaneously three things in the development of computer science. (1) It is the creation of a genuine dynamic memory structure in a machine that had heretofore been perceived as having fixed structure. It added to our ensemble of operations those that built and modified structure in addition to those that replaced and changed content. (2) It was an early demonstration of the basic abstraction that a computer consists of a set of data types and a set of operations proper to these data types, so that a computational system should employ whatever data types are appropriate to the application, independent of the underlying machine. (3) List-processing produced a model of designation, thus defining symbol manipulation in the sense in which we use this concept in computer science today.

As often occurs, the practice of the time already anticipated all the elements of list-processing: addresses are obviously used to gain access, the drum machines used linked programs (so called one-plus-one addressing), and so on. But the conception of list processing as an abstraction created a new world in which designation and dynamic symbolic structure were the defining characteristics. The embedding of the early list-processing systems in languages (the IPLs, LISP) is often decried as having been a barrier to the diffusion of list-processing techniques throughout programming practice; but it was the vehicle that held the abstraction together.

LISP. One more step is worth noting: McCarthy's creation of LISP in 1959-60 (McCarthy, 1960). It completed the act of abstraction, lifting list structures out of their embedding in concrete machines, creating a new formal system with S-expressions, which could be shown to be equivalent to the other universal schemes of computation.

Conclusion. That the concept of the designating symbol and symbol manipulation does not emerge until the mid-fifties does not mean that the earlier steps were either inessential or less important. The total concept is the join of computability, physical realizability (and by multiple technologies), universality, the symbolic representation of processes (i.e., interpretability), and, finally, symbolic structure and designation. Each of the steps provided an essential part of the whole.

The first step in this chain, authored by Turing, is theoretically motivated, but the others all have deep empirical roots. We have been led by the evolution of the computer itself. The stored program principle arose out of the experience with Eniac. List-processing arose out of the attempt to construct intelligent programs. It took its cue from the emergence of random access memories, which provided a clear physical realization of a designating symbol in the address. LISP arose out of the evolving experience with list-processing.

THE EVIDENCE

We come now to the evidence for the hypothesis that physical symbol systems are capable of intelligent action, and that general intelligent action calls for a physical symbol system. The hypothesis is an empirical generalization and not a theorem. We know of no way of demonstrating the connection between symbol systems and intelligence on purely logical grounds. Lacking such a demonstration, we must look at the facts. Our central aim, however, is not to review the evidence in detail, but to use the example before us to illustrate the proposition that computer science is a field of empirical inquiry. Hence, we will only indicate what kinds of evidence there are, and the general nature of the testing process.

The notion of physical symbol system had taken essentially its present form by the middle of the 1950's, and one can date from that time the growth of artificial intelligence as a coherent subfield of computer science. The twenty years of work since then has seen a continuous accumulation of empirical evidence of two main varieties. The first addresses itself to the *sufficiency* of physical symbol systems for producing intelligence, attempting to construct and test specific systems that have such a capability. The second kind of evidence addresses itself to the *necessity* of having a physical symbol system wherever intelligence is exhibited. It starts with Man, the intelligent system best known to us, and attempts to discover whether his cognitive activity can be explained as the working of a physical symbol system. There are other forms of evidence, which we will comment upon briefly later, but these two are the important ones. We will consider them in turn. The first is generally called artificial intelligence, the second, research in cognitive psychology.

Constructing Intelligent Systems. The basic paradigm for the initial testing of the germ theory of disease was: identify a disease then look for the germ. An analogous paradigm has inspired much of the research in artificial intelligence; identify a task domain calling for intelligence, then construct a program for a digital computer that can handle tasks in that domain. The easy and well structured tasks were looked at first: puzzles and games, operations-research problems of scheduling and allocating resources, simple induction tasks. Scores, if not hundreds, of programs of these kinds have by now been constructed, each capable of some measure of intelligent action in the appropriate domain.

Of course intelligence is not an all-or-none matter, and there has been steady progress toward higher levels of performance in specific domains, as well as toward widening the range of those domains. Early chess programs, for example, were deemed successful if they could play the game legally and with some indication of purpose; a little later, they reached the level of human beginners; within ten or fifteen years, they began to compete with serious amateurs. Progress has been slow (and the total programming effort invested small) but continuous, and the paradigm of construct-and-test proceeds in a regular cycle — the whole research activity mimicking at a macroscopic level the basic generate-and-test cycle of many of the AI programs.

There is a steadily widening area within which intelligent action is attainable. From the original tasks, research has extended to building systems that handle and understand natural language in a variety of ways, systems for interpreting visual scenes, systems for hand-eye coordination, systems that design, systems that write computer programs, systems for speech understanding — the list is, if not endless, at least very long. If there are limits beyond which the hypothesis will not carry us, they have not yet become apparent. Up to the present, the rate of progress has been governed mainly by the rather modest quantity of scientific resources that have been applied and the inevitable requirement of a substantial system-building effort for each new major undertaking.

Much more has been going on, of course, than simply a piling up of examples of intelligent systems adapted to specific task domains. It would be surprising and unappealing if it turned out that the AI programs performing these diverse tasks had nothing in common beyond their being instances of physical symbol systems. Hence, there has been great interest in searching for mechanisms possessed of generality, and for common components among programs performing a variety of tasks. This search carries the theory beyond the initial symbol system hypothesis to a more complete characterization of the particular kinds of symbol systems that are effective in artificial intelligence. In the second section of this paper, we will discuss one example of a hypothesis at this second level of specificity: the heuristic search hypothesis.

The search for generality spawned a series of programs designed to separate out general problem-solving mechanisms from the requirements of particular task domains. The General Problem Solver (GPS) was perhaps the first of these; while among its descendants are such contemporary systems as PLANNER and CONNIVER. The search for common components has led to generalized schemes of representation for goals and plans, methods for constructing discrimination nets, procedures for the control of tree search, pattern-matching mechanisms, and language-parsing systems. Experiments are at present under way to find convenient devices for representing sequences of time and tense, movement, causality, and the like. More and more, it becomes possible to assemble large intelligent systems in a modular way from such basic components.

We can gain some perspective on what is going on by turning, again, to the analogy of the germ theory. If the first burst of research stimulated by that theory consisted largely in finding the germ to go with each disease, subsequent effort turned to learning what a germ was — to building on the basic qualitative law a new level of structure. In artificial intelligence, an initial burst of activity aimed at building intelligent programs for a wide variety of almost randomly selected tasks is giving way to more sharply targeted research aimed at understanding the common mechanism of such systems.

The Modeling of Human Symbolic Behavior. The symbol system hypothesis implies that the symbolic behavior of man arises because he has the characteristics of a physical symbol system. Hence, the results of efforts to model human behavior with symbol systems become an important part of the evidence for the hypothesis, and research in artificial intelligence goes on in close collaboration with research in information processing psychology as it is usually called.

The search for explanations of man's intelligent behavior in terms of symbol systems has had a large measure of success over the past twenty years; to the point where information-processing theory is the leading contemporary point of view in cognitive psychology. Especially in the areas of problem-solving, concept attainment, and long-term memory, symbol manipulation models now dominate the scene.

Research in information-processing psychology involves two main kinds of empirical activity. The first is the conduct of observations and experiments on human behavior in tasks requiring intelligence. The second, very similar to the parallel activity in artificial intelligence, is the programming of symbol systems to model the observed human behavior. The psychological observations and experiments lead to the formulation of hypotheses about the symbolic processes the subjects are using, and these are an important source of the ideas that go into the construction of the programs. Thus many of the ideas for the basic mechanisms of GPS were derived from careful analysis of the protocols that human subjects produced while thinking aloud during the performance of a problem-solving task.

The empirical character of computer science is nowhere more evident than in this alliance with psychology. Not only are psychological experiments required to test the veridicality of the simulation models as explanations of the human behavior, but out of the experiments come new ideas for the design and construction of physical-symbol systems.

Other Evidence. The principal body of evidence for the symbol-system hypothesis that we have not considered is negative evidence: the absence of specific competing hypotheses as to how intelligent activity might be accomplished — whether by man or by machine. Most attempts to build such hypotheses have taken place within the field of psychology. Here we have had a continuum of theories from the points of view usually labeled "behaviorism" to those usually labeled "Gestalt theory." Neither of these points of view stands as a real competitor to the symbol-system hypothesis, and for two reasons. First, neither behaviorism nor Gestalt theory has demonstrated, or even shown how to demonstrate, that the explanatory mechanisms it postulates are sufficient to account for intelligent behavior in complex tasks. Second, neither theory has been formulated with anything like the specificity of artificial programs. As a matter of fact, the alternative theories are so vague that it is not terribly difficult to give them information-processing interpretations, and thereby assimilate them to the symbol-system hypothesis.

NOTE

1   *Editor's note*: This is a different notion of "interpretation" from that explained in the introduction.

16

MINDS, BRAINS, AND PROGRAMS

John R. Searle

What psychological and philosophical significance should we attach to recent efforts at computer simulations of human cognitive capacities? In answering this question, I find it useful to distinguish what I will call "strong" AI from "weak" or "cautious" AI (Artificial Intelligence). According to weak AI, the principal value of the computer in the study of the mind is that it gives us a very powerful tool. For example, it enables us to formulate and test hypotheses in a more rigorous and precise fashion. But according to strong AI, the computer is not merely a tool in the study of the mind: rather, the appropriately programmed computer really *is* a mind, in the sense that computers given the right programs can be literally said to *understand* and have other cognitive states. In strong AI, because the programmed computer has cognitive states, the programs are not mere tools that enable us to test psychological explanations; rather, the programs are themselves the explanations.

I have no objection to the claims of the weak AI, at least as far as this article is concerned. My discussion here will be directed at the claims I have defined as those of strong AI, specifically the claim that the appropriately programmed computer literally has cognitive states and that the programs thereby explain human cognition. When I hereafter refer to AI, I have in mind the strong version, as expressed by these two claims.

I will consider the work of Roger Schank and his colleagues at Yale (Schank & Abelson 1977), because I am more familiar with it than I am with any other similar claims, and because it provides a very clear example of the sort of work I wish to examine. But nothing that follows depends upon the details of Schank's

Searle, J.R. 1980. "Minds, Brains, and Programs." *The Behavioral and Brain Sciences, 3*, (1980) 417-424. © Cambridge University Press. Reprinted with the permission of Cambridge University Press.

programs. The same arguments would apply to Winograd's SHRDLU (Winograd 1973), Weizenbaum's ELIZA (Weizenbaum 1965), and indeed any Turing machine simulation of human mental phenomena.

Very briefly, and leaving out the various details, one can describe Schank's program as follows: the aim of the program is to simulate human ability to understand stories. It is characteristic of human being's story-understanding capacity that they can answer questions about the story even though the information that they give was never explicitly stated in the story. Thus, for example, suppose you are given the following story: "A man went into a restaurant and ordered a hamburger. When the hamburger arrived it was burned to a crisp, and the man stormed out of the restaurant angrily, without paying for the hamburger or leaving a tip." Now, if you are asked "Did the man eat the hamburger?" you will presumably answer, "No, he did not." Similarly, if you are given the following story: "A man went into a restaurant and ordered a hamburger; when the hamburger came he was very pleased with it; and as he left the restaurant he gave the waitress a large tip before paying his bill," and you are asked the question, "Did the man eat the hamburger?," you will presumably answer, "Yes, he ate the hamburger." Now Schank's machine can answer questions about restaurants in this fashion. To do this, they have a "representation" of the sort of information that human beings have about restaurants, which enables them to answer such questions as those above, given these sorts of stories. When the machine is given the story and then asked the question, the machine will print out answers of the sort that we would expect human beings to give if told similar stories. Partisans of strong AI claim that in this question and answer sequence the machine is not only simulating a human ability but also

1. that the machine can literally be said to *understand* the story and provide the answers to questions, and

2. that what the machine and its programs do *explains* the human ability to understand the story and answer questions about it.

Both claims seem to me to be totally unsupported by Schank's[1] work, as I will attempt to show in what follows.

One way to test any theory of the mind is to ask oneself what it would be like if my mind actually worked on the principles that the theory says all minds work on. Let us apply this test to the Schank program with the following *Gedankenexperiment*. Suppose that I'm locked in a room and given a large batch of Chinese writing. Suppose furthermore (as is indeed the case) that I know no Chinese, either written or spoken, and that I'm not even confident that I could recognize Chinese writing as Chinese writing distinct from, say, Japanese writing or meaningless squiggles. Now suppose further that after this first batch of Chinese writing I am given a second batch of Chinese script together with a set of rules for correlating the second batch with the first batch. The rules are in English, and I understand these rules as well as any other native speaker of English. They enable me to correlate one set of formal symbols with another set of formal symbols, and all that "formal" means here is that I can identify the symbols entirely by their shapes. Now suppose also that I am given a third batch of Chinese symbols together with some instructions, again in English, that enable me to correlate elements of this third batch with the first two batches, and these rules instruct me how to give back certain Chinese symbols with certain sorts of shapes in response to certain sorts of shapes given me in the third batch. Unknown to me, the people who are giving me all of these symbols call the first batch "a script," they call the second batch a "story," and they call the third batch "questions." Furthermore, they call the symbols I give them back in response to the third batch "answers to the questions," and the set of rules in English that they gave me, they call "the program." Now just to complicate the story a little, imagine that these people also give me stories in English, which I understand, and they then ask me questions in English about these stories, and I give them back answers in English. Suppose also that after a while I get so good at following the instructions for manipulating the Chinese symbols and the programmers get so good at writing the programs that from the external point of view — that is, from the point of view of somebody outside the room in which I am locked — my answers to the questions are absolutely indistinguishable from those of native Chinese speakers. Nobody just looking at my answers can tell that I don't speak a word of Chinese. Let us also suppose that my answers to the English questions are, as they no doubt would be, indistinguishable from those of other native English speakers, for the simple reason that I am a native English speaker. From the external point of view — from the point of view of someone reading my "answers" — the answers to the Chinese questions and the English questions are equally good. But in the Chinese case, unlike the English case, I produce the answers by manipulating uninterpreted formal symbols. As far as the Chinese is concerned, I simply behave like a computer; I perform computational operations on formally specified elements. For the purposes of the Chinese, I am simply an instantiation of the computer program.

Now the claims made by strong AI are that the programmed computer understands the stories and that the program in some sense explains human understanding. But we are now in a position to examine these claims in light of our thought experiment.

1. As regards the first claim, it seems to me quite obvious in the example that I do not understand a word of the Chinese stories. I have inputs and outputs that are indistinguishable from those of the native Chinese speaker, and can have any formal program you like, but I still understand nothing. For the same reasons, Schank's computer understands nothing of any stories, whether in Chinese, English, or whatever, since in the Chinese case the computer is me, and in cases where the computer is not me, the computer has nothing more than I have in the case where I understand nothing.

2. As regards the second claim, that the program explains human understanding, we can see that the computer and its program do not provide sufficient conditions of understanding since the computer and the program are functioning, and there is no understanding. But does it even provide a necessary condition or a significant contribution to understanding? One of the claims made by the supporters of strong AI is that when I understand a story in English, what I am doing is exactly the same — or perhaps more of the same — as what I was doing in manipulating the Chinese symbols. It is simply more formal symbol manipulation that distinguishes the case in English, where I do understand, from the case in Chinese, where I don't. I have not demonstrated that this claim is false, but it would certainly appear an incredible claim in the example. Such plausibility as the claim has derives from the supposition that we can construct a program that will have the same inputs and outputs as native speakers, and in addition we assume that speakers have some level of description where they are also instantiations of a program. On the basis of these two assumptions we assume that even if Schank's program isn't the whole story about understanding, it may be part of the story. Well, I suppose that is an empirical possibility, but not the slightest reason has so far been given to believe that it is true, since what is suggested — though certainly not demonstrated — by the example is that the computer program is simply irrelevant to my understanding of the story. In the Chinese case I have everything that artificial intelligence can put into me by way of a program, and I understand nothing: in the English case I understand everything, and there is so far no reason at all to suppose that my understanding has anything to do with computer programs, that is, with computational operations on purely formally specified elements. As long as the program is defined in terms of computational operations on purely formally defined elements, what the example suggests is that these by themselves have no interesting connection with understanding. They are certainly not sufficient conditions, and not the slightest reason has been given to suppose that they are necessary conditions or even that they make a significant contribution to understanding. Notice that the force of the argument is not simply that different machines can have the same input and output while operating on different formal principles — that is not the point at all. Rather, whatever purely formal principles you put into the computer, they will not be sufficient for understanding, since a human will be able to follow the formal principles without understanding anything. No reason whatever has been offered to suppose that such principles are necessary or even contributory, since no reason has been given to suppose that when I understand English I am operating with any formal program at all.

Well, then, what is it that I have in the case of the English sentences that I do not have in the case of the Chinese sentences? The obvious answer is that I know what the former mean, while I haven't the faintest idea what the latter mean. But in what does this consist and why couldn't we give it to a machine, whatever it is? I will return to this question later, but first I want to continue with the example.

I have had the occasions to present this example to several workers in artificial intelligence, and, interestingly, they do not seem to agree on what the proper reply to it is. I get a surprising variety of replies, and in what follows I will consider the most common of these (specified along with their geographic origins).

But first I want to block some common misunderstandings about "understanding": in many of these discussions one finds a lot of fancy footwork about the word "understanding." My critics point out that there are many different degrees of understanding; that "understanding" is not a simple two-place predicate; that there are even different kinds and levels of understanding, and often the law of excluded middle doesn't even apply in a straightforward way to statements of the form "x understands y"; that in many cases it is a matter for decision and not a simple matter of fact whether x understands y; and so on. To all of these points I want to say: of course, of course. But they have nothing to do with the points at issue. There are clear cases in which "understanding" literally applies and clear cases in which it does not apply; and these two sorts of cases are all I need for this argument.[2] I understand stories in English; to a lesser degree I can understand stories in French; to a still lesser degree, stories in German; and in Chinese, not at all. My car and my adding machine, on the other hand, understand nothing: they are not in that line of business. We often attribute "understanding" and other cognitive predicates by metaphor and analogy to cars, adding machines, and other artifacts, but nothing is proved by such attributions. We say, "The door *knows* when to open because of its photoelectric cell," "The adding machine *knows how* (*understands how, is able*) to do addition and subtraction but not division," and "The thermostat *perceives* changes in the temperature." The reason we make these attributions is quite interesting, and it has to do with the fact that in artifacts we extend our own intentionality;[3] our tools are extensions of our purposes, and so we find it natural to make metaphorical attributions of intentionality to them; but I take it no philosophical ice is cut by such examples. The sense in which an automatic door "understands instructions" from its photoelectric cell is not at all the sense in which I understand English. If the sense in which Schank's programmed computers understand stories is supposed to be the metaphorical sense in which the door understands, and not the sense in which I understand English, the issue would not be worth discussing. But Newell and Simon (1963) write that the kind of cognition they claim for computers is exactly the same as for human beings. I like the straightforwardness of this claim, and it is the sort of claim I will be considering. I will argue that in the literal sense the programmed computer understands what the car and the adding machine understand, namely, exactly nothing. The computer understanding is not just (like my understanding of German) partial or incomplete; it is zero.

Now to the replies:

1. The systems reply (Berkeley). "While it is true that the individual person who is locked in the room does not understand the story, the fact is that he is merely part of a whole system, and the system does understand the story. The person has a large ledger in front of him in which are written the rules, he has a lot of scratch paper and pencils for doing calculations, he has 'data banks' of sets of Chinese symbols. Now, understanding is not being ascribed to the mere individual; rather it is being ascribed to this whole system of which he is a part."

My response to the systems theory is quite simple: let the individual internalize all of these elements of the system. He memorizes the rules in the ledger and the databanks of Chinese symbols, and he does all the calculations in his head. The individual then incorporates the entire system. There isn't anything at all to the system that he does not encompass. We can even get rid of the room and suppose he works outdoors. All the same, he understands nothing of the Chinese, and a fortiori neither does the system, because there isn't anything in the system that isn't in him. If he doesn't understand, then there is no way the system could understand because the system is just a part of him.

Actually I feel somewhat embarrassed to give even this answer to the systems theory because the theory seems to me so unplausible to start with. The idea is that while a person doesn't understand Chinese, somehow the *conjunction* of that person and bits of paper might understand Chinese. It is not easy for me to imagine how someone who was not in the grip of an ideology would find the idea at all plausible. Still, I think many people who are committed to the ideology of strong AI will in the end be inclined to say something very much like this; so let us pursue it a bit further. According to one version of this view, while the man in the internalized systems example doesn't understand Chinese in the sense that a native Chinese speaker does (because, for example, he doesn't know that the story refers to restaurants and hamburgers, etc.), still "the man as a formal symbol manipulation system" *really does understand Chinese.* The subsystem of the man that is the formal symbol manipulation system for Chinese should not be confused with the subsystem for English.

So there are really two subsystems in the man; one understands English, the other Chinese, and "it's just that the two systems have little to do with each other." But, I want to reply, not only do they have little to do with each other, they are not even remotely alike. The subsystem that understands English (assuming we allow ourselves to talk in this jargon of "subsystems" for a moment) knows that the stories are about restaurants and eating hamburgers, he knows that he is being asked questions about restaurants and that he is answering questions as best he can by making various inferences from the content of the story, and so on. But the Chinese system knows none of this. Whereas the English subsystem knows that "hamburgers" refers to hamburgers, the Chinese subsystem knows only that "squiggle squiggle" is followed by "squoggle squoggle." All he knows is that various formal symbols are being introduced at one end and manipulated according to rules written in English, and other symbols are going out at the other end. The whole point of the original example was to argue that such symbol manipulation by itself couldn't be sufficient for understanding Chinese in any literal sense because the man could write "squoggle squoggle" after "squiggle squiggle" without understanding anything in Chinese. And it doesn't meet that argument to postulate subsystems within the man, because the subsystems are no better off than the man was in the first place; they still don't have anything even remotely like what the English-speaking man (or subsystem) has. Indeed, in the case as described, the Chinese subsystem is simply a part of the English subsystem, a part that engages in meaningless symbol manipulation according to rules in English.

Let us ask ourselves what is supposed to motivate the systems reply in the first place; that is, what *independent* grounds are there supposed to be for saying that the agent must have a subsystem within him that literally understands stories in Chinese? As far as I can tell the only grounds are that in the example I have the same input and output as native Chinese speakers and a program that goes from one to the other. But the whole point of the examples has been to try to show that that couldn't be sufficient for understanding, in the sense in which I understand stories in English, because a person, and hence the set of systems that go to make up a person, could have the right combination of input, output, and program and still not understand anything in the relevant literal sense in which I understand English. The only motivation for saying there *must* be a subsystem in me that understands Chinese is that I have a program and I can pass the Turing test; I can fool native Chinese speakers. But precisely one of the points at issue is the adequacy of the Turing test. The example shows that there could be two "systems," both of which pass the Turing test, but only one of which understands; and it is no argument against this point to say that since they both pass the Turing test they must both understand, since this claim fails to meet the argument that the system in me that understands English has a great deal more than the system that merely processes Chinese. In short, the systems reply simply begs the question by insisting without argument that the system must understand Chinese.

Furthermore, the systems reply would appear to lead to consequences that are independently absurd. If we are to conclude that there must be cognition in me on the grounds that I have a certain sort of input and output and a program in between, then it looks like all sorts of noncognitive subsystems are going to turn out to be cognitive. For example, there is a level of description at which my stomach does information processing, and it instantiates any number of computer programs, but I take it we do not want to say that it has any understanding [cf. Pylyshyn: "Computation and Cognitition" *BBS* 3(1) 1980]. But if we accept the systems reply, then it is hard to see how we avoid saying that stomach, heart, liver, and so on, are all understanding subsystems, since there is no principled way to distinguish the motivation for saying the Chinese subsystem understands from saying that the stomach understands. It is, by the way, not an answer to this point to say that the

Chinese system has information as input and output and the stomach has food and food products as input and output, since from the point of view of the agent, from my point of view, there is no information in either the food or the Chinese — the Chinese is just so many meaningless squiggles. The information in the Chinese case is solely in the eyes of the programmers and the interpreters, and there is nothing to prevent them from treating the input and output of my digestive organs as information if they so desire.

This last point bears on some independent problems in strong AI, and it is worth digressing for a moment to explain it. If strong AI is to be a branch of psychology, then it must be able to distinguish those systems that are genuinely mental from those that are not. It must be able to distinguish the principles on which the mind works from those on which nonmental systems work; otherwise it will offer us no explanations of what is specifically mental about the mental. And the mental-nonmental distinction cannot be just in the eye of the beholder but it must be intrinsic to the systems; otherwise it would be up to any beholder to treat people as nonmental and, for example, hurricanes as mental if he likes. But quite often in the AI literature the distinction is blurred in ways that would in the long run prove disastrous to the claim that AI is a cognitive inquiry. McCarthy, for example, writes, "Machines as simple as thermostats can be said to have beliefs, and having beliefs seems to be a characteristic of most machines capable of problem solving performance" (McCarthy 1979). Anyone who thinks strong AI has a chance as a theory of the mind ought to ponder the implications of that remark. We are asked to accept it as a discovery of strong AI that the hunk of metal on the wall that we use to regulate the temperature has beliefs in exactly the same sense that we, our spouses, and our children have beliefs, and furthermore that "most" of the other machines in the room — telephone, tape recorder, adding machine, electric light switch, — also have beliefs in this literal sense. It is not the aim of this article to argue against McCarthy's point, so I will simply assert the following without argument. The study of the mind starts with such facts as that humans have beliefs, while thermostats, telephones, and adding machines don't. If you get a theory that denies this point you have produced a counter-example to the theory and the theory is false. One gets the impression that people in AI who write this sort of thing think they can get away with it because they don't really take it seriously, and they don't think anyone else will either. I propose for a moment at least, to take it seriously. Think hard for one minute about what would be necessary to establish that that hunk of metal on the wall over there had real beliefs, beliefs with direction of fit, propositional content, and conditions of satisfaction; beliefs that had the possibility of being strong beliefs or weak beliefs; nervous, anxious, or secure beliefs; dogmatic, rational, or superstitious beliefs; blind faiths or hesitant cogitations; any kind of beliefs. The thermostat is not a candidate. Neither is stomach, liver, adding machine, or telephone. However, since we are taking the idea seriously, notice that its truth would be fatal to strong

AI's claim to be a science of the mind. For now the mind is everywhere. What we wanted to know is what distinguishes the mind from thermostats and livers. And if McCarthy were right, strong AI wouldn't have a hope of telling us that.

II. The Robot Reply (Yale). "Suppose we wrote a different kind of program from Schank's program. Suppose we put a computer inside a robot, and this computer would not just take in formal symbols as input and give out formal symbols as output, but rather would actually operate the robot in such a way that the robot does something very much like perceiving, walking, moving about, hammering nails, eating, drinking — anything you like. The robot would, for example, have a television camera attached to it that enabled it to 'see,' it would have arms and legs that enabled it to 'act,' and all of this would be controlled by its computer 'brain.' Such a robot would, unlike Schank's computer, have genuine understanding and other mental states."

The first thing to notice about the robot reply is that it tacitly concedes that cognition is not solely a matter of formal symbol manipulation, since this reply adds a set of causal relation with the outside world [cf. Fodor: "Methodological Solipsism" *BBS* 3(1) 1980]. But the answer to the robot reply is that the addition of such "perceptual" and "motor" capacities adds nothing by way of understanding, in particular, or intentionality, in general, to Schank's original program. To see this, notice that the same thought experiment applies to the robot case. Suppose that instead of the computer inside the robot, you put me inside the room and, as in the original Chinese case, you give me more Chinese symbols with more instructions in English for matching Chinese symbols to Chinese symbols and feeding back Chinese symbols to the outside. Suppose, unknown to me, some of the Chinese symbols that come to me come from a television camera attached to the robot and other Chinese symbols that I am giving out serve to make the motors inside the robot move the robot's legs or arms. It is important to emphasize that all I am doing is manipulating formal symbols: I know none of these other facts. I am receiving "information" from the robot's "perceptual" apparatus, and I am giving out "instructions" to its motor apparatus without knowing either of these facts. I am the robot's homunculus, but unlike the traditional homunculus, I don't know what's going on. I don't understand anything except the rules for symbol manipulation. Now in this case I want to say that the robot has no intentional states at all; it is simply moving about as a result of its electrical wiring and its program. And furthermore, by instantiating the program I have no intentional states of the relevant type. All I do is follow formal instructions about manipulating formal symbols.

III. The brain simulator reply (Berkeley and M.I.T.). "Suppose we design a program that doesn't represent information that we have about the world, such as the information in Schank's scripts, but simulates the actual sequence of neuron firings at the synapses of the brain of a native Chinese speaker when he understands stories in Chinese and gives answers to them. The machine takes in Chinese stories and questions about them as input, it simulates the formal structure of actual Chinese brains in processing these stories, and it gives out Chinese answers as outputs. We can even imagine that the machine operates, not with a single serial program, but with a whole set of programs operating in parallel, in the manner that actual human brains presumably operate when they process natural language. Now surely in such a case we would have to say that the machine understood the stories; and if we refuse to say that, wouldn't we also have to deny that native Chinese speakers understood the stories? At the level of the synapses, what would or could be different about the program of the computer and the program of the Chinese brain?

Before countering this reply I want to digress to note that it is an odd reply for any partisan of artificial intelligence (or functionalism, etc.) to make: I thought the whole idea of strong AI is that we don't need to know how the brain works to know how the mind works. The basic hypothesis, or so I had supposed, was that there is a level of mental operations consisting of computational processes over formal elements that constitute the essence of the mental and can be realized in all sorts of different brain processes, in the same way that any computer program can be realized in different computer hardwares: on the assumptions of strong AI, the mind is to the brain as the program is to the hardware, and thus we can understand the mind without doing neurophysiology. If we had to know how the brain worked to do AI we wouldn't bother with AI. However, even getting this close to the operation of the brain is still not sufficient to produce understanding. To see this, imagine that instead of a monolingual man in a room shuffling symbols we have the man operate an elaborate set of water pipes with valves connecting them. When the man receives the Chinese symbols, he looks up in the program, written in English, which valves he has to turn on and off. Each water connection corresponds to a synapse in the Chinese brain, and the whole system is rigged up so that after doing all the right firings, that is after turning on all the right faucets, the Chinese answers pop out at the output end of the series of pipes.

Now where is the understanding in this system? It takes Chinese as input, it simulates the formal structure of the synapses of the Chinese brain, and it gives Chinese as output. But the man certainly doesn't understand Chinese, and neither do the water pipes, and if we are tempted to adopt what I think is the absurd view that somehow the *conjunction* of man *and* water pipes understands, remember that in principle the man can internalize the formal structure of the water pipes and do all the "neuron firings" in his imagination. The problem with the brain simulator is that it is simulating the wrong things about the brain. As long as it simulates only the formal structure of the sequence of neuron firings at the synapses, it won't have simulated what matters about the brain, namely its causal properties as shown by the water pipe example: we can have all the formal properties carved off from the relevant neurobiological causal properties.

IV. The combination reply (Berkeley and Stanford). "While each of the previous three replies might not be completely convincing by itself as a refutation of the Chinese room counterexample, if you take all three together they are collectively much more convincing and even decisive. Imagine a robot with a brain-shaped computer lodged in its cranial cavity, imagine the computer programmed with all the synapses of a human brain, imagine the whole behavior of the robot is indistinguishable from human behavior, and now think of the whole thing as a unified system and not just as a computer with inputs and outputs. Surely in such a case we would have to ascribe intentionality to the system."

I entirely agree that in such a case we would find it rational and indeed irresistible to accept the hypothesis that the robot had intentionality, as long as we knew nothing more about it. Indeed, besides appearance and behavior, the other elements of the combination are really irrelevant. If we could build a robot whose behavior was indistinguishable over a large range from human behavior, we would attribute intentionality to it, pending some reason not to. We wouldn't need to know in advance that its computer brain was a formal analogue of the human brain.

But I really don't see that this is any help to the claims of strong AI; and here's why: According to strong AI, instantiating a formal program with the right input and output is a sufficient condition of, indeed is constitutive of, intentionality. As Newell (1979) puts it, the essence of the mental is the operation of a physical symbol system. But the attributions of intentionality that we make to the robot in this example have nothing to do with formal programs. They are simply based on the assumption that if the robot looks and behaves sufficiently like us, then we would suppose, until proven otherwise, that it must have mental states like ours that cause and are expressed by its behavior and it must have an inner mechanism capable of producing such mental states. If we knew independently how to account for its behavior without such assumptions we would not attribute intentionality to it, especially if we knew it had a formal program. And this is precisely the point of my earlier reply to objection II.

Suppose we knew that the robot's behavior was entirely accounted for by the fact that a man inside it was receiving uninterpreted formal symbols from the robot's sensory receptors and sending out uninterpreted formal symbols to its motor mechanism, and the man was doing this symbol manipulation in accordance with a bunch of rules. Furthermore, suppose the man knows none of these facts about the robot, all he knows is which operations to perform on which meaningless symbols. In such a case we would regard the robot as an ingenious mechanical dummy. The hypothesis that the dummy has a mind would now be unwarranted and unnecessary, for there is now no longer any reason to ascribe intentionality to the robot or to the system of which it is a part (except of course for the man's intentionality in manipulating the symbols). The formal symbol manipulations go on, the input and output are correctly matched, but the only real locus of intentionality is the man, and he doesn't know any of the relevant intentional states: he doesn't, for example, *see* what comes into the robot's eyes, he doesn't *intend* to move the robot's arm, and he doesn't *understand* any of the remarks made to or by the robot. Nor, for the reasons stated earlier, does the system of which man and robot are a part.

To see this point, contrast this case with cases in which we find it completely natural to ascribe intentionality to members of certain other primate species such as apes and monkeys to domestic animals such as dogs. The reasons we find it natural are, roughly, two: we can't make sense of the animal's behavior without the ascription of intentionality, and we can see that the beasts are made of similar stuff to ourselves — that is an eye, that a nose, this is its skin, and so on. Given the coherence of the animal's behavior and the assumption of the same causal stuff underlying it, we assume both that the animal must have mental states underlying its behavior, and that the mental states must be produced by mechanisms made out of the stuff that is like our stuff. We would certainly make similar assumptions about the robot unless we had some reason not to, but as soon as we knew that actual causal properties of the physical substance were irrelevant we would abandon the assumption of intentionality. [See "Cognition and Consciousness in Nonhuman Species" *BBS* I(4) 1978.]

There are two other responses to my example that come up frequently (and so are worth discussing) but really miss the point.

V. The other minds reply (Yale). "How do you know that other people understand Chinese or anything else? Only by their behavior. Now the computer can pass the behavioral tests as well as they can (in principle), so if you are going to attribute cognition to other people you must in principle also attribute it to the computers."

This objection really is only worth a short reply. The problem in this discussion is not about how I know that other people have cognitive states, but rather what it is that I am attributing to them when I attribute cognitive states to them. The thrust of the argument is that it couldn't be just computational processes and their output because the computational processes and their output can exist without the cognitive state. It is no answer to this argument to feign anesthesia. In "cognitive sciences" one presupposes the reality and knowability of the mental in the same way that in physical sciences one has to presuppose the reality and knowability of physical objects.

VI. The many mansions reply (Berkeley). "Your whole argument presupposes that AI is only about analogue and digital computers. But that just happens to be the present state of technology. Whatever these causal processes are that you say are essential for intentionality (assuming you are right), eventually we will be able to build devices that have these causal processes, and that will be artificial intelligence. So your arguments are in no way directed at the ability of artificial intelligence to produce and explain cognition."

I really have no objections to this reply save to say that it in effect trivializes the project of strong AI by redefining it as whatever artificially produces and explains cognition. The interest of the original claim made on behalf of artificial intelligence is that it was a precise, well defined thesis: mental processes are computational processes over formally defined elements. I have been concerned to challenge that thesis. If the claim is redefined so that it is no longer that thesis, my objections no longer apply because there is no longer a testable hypothesis for them to apply to.

Let us now return to the question I promised I would try to answer: granted that in my original example I understand the English and do not understand the Chinese, and granted therefore that the machine doesn't understand either English or Chinese, still there must be something about me that makes it the case that I understand English and a corresponding something lacking in me that makes it the case that I fail to understand Chinese. Now why couldn't we give those somethings, whatever they are, to a machine?

I see no reason in principle why we couldn't give a machine the capacity to understand English or Chinese, since in an important sense our bodies with our brains are precisely such machines. But I do see very strong arguments for saying that we could not give such a thing to a machine where the operation of the machine is defined solely in terms of computational processes over formally defined elements; that is, where the operation of the machine is defined as an instantiation of a computer program that I am able to understand English and have other forms of intentionality (I am, I suppose, the instantiation of any number of computer programs), but as far as we know it is because I am a certain sort of organism with a certain biological (i.e. chemical and physical) structure, and this structure, under certain conditions, is causally capable of producing perception, action, understanding, learning, and other intentional phenomena. And part of the point of the present argument is that only something that had those causal powers could have that intentionality. Perhaps other physical and chemical processes could produce exactly these effects; perhaps, for example, Martians also have intentionality but their brains are made of different stuff. This is an empirical question, rather like the question whether photosynthesis can be done by something with a chemistry different from that of chlorophyll.

But the main point of the present argument is that no purely formal model will ever be sufficient by itself for intentionality because the formal properties are not by themselves constitutive of intentionality, and they have by themselves no causal powers except the power, when instantiated, to produce the next stage of the formalism when the machine is running. And any other causal properties that particular realizations of the formal model have, are irrelevant to the formal model because we can always put the same formal model in a different realization where those causal properties are obviously absent. Even if, by some miracle, Chinese speakers exactly realize Schank's program, we can put the same program in English speakers, water pipes, or computers, none of which understand Chinese, the program notwithstanding.

What matters about brain operations is not the formal shadow cast by the sequence of synapses but rather the actual properties of the sequences. All the arguments for the strong version of artificial intelligence that I have seen insist on drawing an outline around the shadows cast by cognition and then claiming that the shadows are the real thing.

By way of concluding I want to try to state some of the general philosophical points implicit in the argument. For clarity I will try to do it in a question and answer fashion, and I begin with that old chestnut of a question:

"Could a machine think?"

The answer is, obviously, yes. We are precisely such machines.

"Yes, but could an artifact, a man-made machine, think?"

Assuming it is possible to produce artificially a machine with a nervous system, neurons with axons and dendrites, and all the rest of it, sufficiently like ours, again the answer to the question seems to be obviously, yes. If you can exactly duplicate the causes, you can duplicate the effects. And indeed it might be possible to produce consciousness, intentionality, and all the rest of it using some other sorts of chemical principles than those that human beings use. It is, as I said, an empirical question.

"OK, but could a digital computer think?"

If by "digital computer" we mean anything at all that has a level of description where it can correctly be described as the instantiation of a computer program, then again the answer is, of course, yes, since we are the instantiations of any number of computer programs, and we can think.

"But could something think, understand, and so on *solely* in virtue of being a computer with the right sort of program? Could instantiating a program, the right program of course, by itself be sufficient condition of understanding?"

This I think is the right question to ask, though it is usually confused with one or more of the earlier questions, and the answer to it is no.

"Why not?"

Because the formal symbol manipulations by themselves don't have any intentionality; they are quite meaningless; they aren't even *symbol* manipulations, since the symbols don't symbolize anything. In the linguistic jargon, they have only a syntax but no semantics. Such intentionality as computers appear to have is solely in the minds of those who program them and those who use them, those who send in the input and those who interpret the output.

The aim of the Chinese room example was to try to show this by showing that as soon as we put something into the system that really does have intentionality (a man), and we program him with the formal program, you can see that the formal program carries no additional intentionality. It adds nothing, for example, to a man's ability to understand Chinese.

Precisely that feature of AI that seemed so appealing — the distinction between the program and the realization — proves fatal to the claim that simulation could be duplication. The distinction between the program and its realization in the hardware seems to be parallel to the distinction between the level of mental operations and the level of brain operations. And if we could describe the level of mental operations as a formal program, then it seems we could describe what was essential about the mind without doing either introspective psychology or neurophysiology of the brain. But the equation "mind is to brain as program is to hardware" breaks down at several points, among them the following three:

First, the distinction between program and realization has the consequence that the same program could have all sorts of crazy realizations that had no form of intentionality. Weizenbaum (1976, Ch. 2), for example, shows in detail how to construct a computer using a roll of toilet paper and a pile of small stones. Similarly, the Chinese story understanding program can be programmed into a sequence of water pipes, none of which thereby acquires an understanding of Chinese. Stones, toilet paper, wind, and water pipes are the wrong kind of stuff to have intentionality in the first place — only something that has the same causal powers as brains can have intentionality — and though the English speaker has the right kind of stuff for intentionality you can easily see that he doesn't get any extra intentionality by memorizing the program, since memorizing won't teach him Chinese.

Second, the program is purely formal, but the intentional states are not in that way formal. They are defined in terms of their content, not their form. The belief that it is raining, for example, is not defined as a certain formal shape, but as a certain mental content with conditions of satisfaction, a direction of fit (see Searle 1979), and the like. Indeed the belief as such hasn't even got a formal shape in this syntactic sense, since one and the same belief can be given an indefinite number of different syntactic expressions in different linguistic systems.

Third, as I mentioned before, mental states and events are literally a product of the operation of the brain, but the program is not in that way a product of the computer.

"Well if programs are in no way constitutive of mental processes, why have so many people believed the converse? That at least needs some explanation."

I don't really know the answer to that one. The idea that computer simulations could be the real thing ought to have seemed suspicious in the first place because the computer isn't confined to simulating mental operations, by any means. No one supposes that computer simulations of a five-alarm fire will burn the neighborhood down or that a computer simulation of a rainstorm will leave us all drenched. Why on earth would anyone suppose that a computer simulation of understanding actually understood anything? It is sometimes said that it would be frightfully hard to get computers to feel pain or fall in love, but love and pain are neither harder nor easier than cognition or anything else. For simulation, all you need is the right input and output and a program in the middle that transforms the former into the latter. That is all the computer has for anything it does. To confuse simulation with duplication is the same mistake, whether it is pain, love, cognition, fires, or rainstorms.

Still, there are several reasons why AI must have seemed — and to many people perhaps still does seem — in some way to reproduce and thereby explain mental phenomena, and I believe we will not succeed in removing these illusions until we have fully exposed the reasons that give rise to them.

First, and perhaps most important, is a confusion about the notion of "information processing": many people in cognitive science believe that the human brain, with its mind, does something called "information processing," and analogously the computer with its program does information processing; but fires and rainstorms, on the other hand, don't do information processing at all. Thus, though the computer can simulate the formal features of any process whatever, it stands in a special relation to the mind and brain because when the computer is properly programmed, ideally with the same program as the brain, the information processing is identical in the two cases, and this information processing is really the essence of the mental. But the trouble with this argument is that it rests on an ambiguity in the notion of "information." In the sense in which people "process information" when they reflect, say, on problems in arithmetic or when they read and answer questions about stories, the programmed computer does not do "information processing." Rather, what it does is manipulate formal symbols. The fact that the programmer and the interpreter of the computer output use the symbols to stand for objects in the world is totally beyond the scope of the computer. The computer, to repeat, has a syntax but no semantics. Thus, if you type into the computer "2 plus 2 equals?" it will type out "4." But it has no idea that "4" means 4 or that it means anything at all. And the point is not that it lacks some second-order information about the interpretation of its first-order symbols, but rather that its first-order symbols don't have any interpretations as far as the computer is concerned. All the computer has is more symbols. The introduction of the notion of "information processing" therefore produces a dilemma: either we construe the notion of "information processing" in such a way that it implies intentionality as part of the process or we don't. If the former, then the programmed computer does not do information processing, it only manipulates formal symbols. If the latter, then, though the computer does information processing, it is only doing so in the sense in which adding machines, typewriters, stomachs, thermostats, rainstorms, and hurricanes do information processing; namely, they have a level of description at which we can describe them as taking information in at one end, transforming it, and producing information as output. But in this case it is up to outside observers to interpret the input and output as information in the ordinary sense. And no similarity is established between the computer and the brain in terms of any similarity of information processing. ·

Second, in much of AI there is a residual behaviorism or operationalism. Since appropriately programmed computers can have input-output patterns similar to those of human being, we are tempted to postulate mental states in the computer similar to human mental states. But once we see that it is both conceptually and empirically possible for a system to have human capacities in some realm without having any intentionality at all, we should be able to overcome this impulse. My desk adding machine has calculating capacities, but no intentionality, and in this paper I have tried to show that a system could have input and output capabilities that duplicated those of a native Chinese speaker and still not understand Chinese, regardless of how it was programmed. The Turing test is typical of the tradition in being unashamedly behavioristic and operationalistic, and I believe that if AI workers totally repudiated behaviorism and operationalism much of the confusion between simulation and duplication would be eliminated.

Third, this residual operationalism is joined to a residual form of dualism; indeed strong AI only makes sense given the dualistic assumption that, where the mind is concerned, the brain doesn't matter. In strong AI (and in functionalism, as well) what matters are programs, and programs are independent of their realization in machines; indeed, as far as AI is concerned, the same program could be realized by an electronic machine, a Cartesian mental substance, or a Hegelian world spirit. The single most surprising discovery that I have made in discussing these issues is that many AI workers are quite shocked by my idea that actual human mental phenomena might be dependent on actual physical-chemical properties of actual human brains. But if you think about it for a minute you can see that I should not have been surprised; for unless you accept some form of dualism, the strong AI project hasn't got a chance. The project is to reproduce and explain the mental by designing programs, but unless the mind is not only conceptually but empirically independent of the brain you couldn't carry out this project, for the program is completely independent of any realization. Unless you believe that the mind is separable from the brain both conceptually and empirically — dualism in a strong form — you cannot hope to reproduce the mental by writing and running programs since programs must be independent of brains or any other particular forms of instantiation. If mental operations consist in computational operations on formal symbols, then it follows that they have no interesting connection with the brain; the only connection would be that the brain just happens to be one of the indefinitely many types of machines capable of instantiating the program. This form of dualism is not the traditional Cartesian variety that claims there are two sorts of *substances*, but it is Cartesian in the sense that it insists that what is specifically mental about the mind has no intrinsic connection with the actual properties of the brain. This underlying dualism is masked from us by the fact that AI literature contains frequent fulminations against "dualism"; what the authors seem to be unaware of is that their position presupposes a strong version of dualism.

"Could a machine think?" My own view is that *only* a machine could think, and indeed only very special kinds of machines, namely brains and machines that had the same causal powers as brains. And that is the main re had little to tell us about thinking, since it has nothing to tell By its own definition, it is about programs, and programs Whatever else intentionality is, it is a biological phenomenon, be as causally dependent on the specific biochemistry of its photosynthesis, or any other biological phenomena. No one we could produce milk and sugar by running a computer simu sequences in lactation and photosynthesis, but where the min people are willing to believe in such a miracle because of dualism: the mind they suppose is a matter of formal processe of quite specific material causes in the way that milk and sugar are not.

In defense of this dualism the hope is often expressed that the brain is a digital computer (early computers, by the way, were often called "electronic brains"). But that is no help. Of course the brain is a digital computer. Since everything is a digital computer, brains are too. The point is that the brain's causal capacity to produce intentionality cannot consist in its instantiating a computer program, since for any program you like it is possible for something to instantiate that program and still not have any mental states. Whatever it is that the brain does to produce intentionality, it cannot consist in instantiating a program since no program, by itself, is sufficient for intentionality.

ACKNOWLEDGMENTS

I am indebted to a rather large number of people for discussion of these matters and for their patient attempts to overcome my ignorance of artificial intelligence. I would especially like to thank Ned Block, Hubert Dreyfus, John Haugeland, Roger Schank, Robert Wilensky, and Terry Winograd.

NOTES

[1] I am not, of course, saying that Schank himself is committed to these claims.

[2] Also, "understanding" implies both the possession of mental (intentional) states and the truth (validity, success) of these states. For the purposes of this discussion we are concerned only with the possession of the states.

[3] Intentionality is by definition that feature of certain mental states by which they are directed at or about objects and states of affairs in the world. Thus, beliefs, desires, and intentions are intentional states; undirected forms of anxiety and depression are not. For further discussion see Searle (1979c).

17

WHAT IS IT LIKE TO BE A BAT?

Thomas Nagel

Consciousness is what makes the mind-body problem really intractable. Perhaps that is why current discussions of the problem give it little attention or get it obviously wrong. The recent wave of reductionist euphoria has produced several analyses of mental phenomena and mental concepts designed to explain the possibility of some variety of materialism, psychophysical identification, or reduction.[1] But the problems dealt with are those common to this type of reduction and other types, and what makes the mind-body problem unique, and unlike the water-H_2O problem or the Turing machine-IBM machine problem or the lightning-electrical discharge problem or the gene-DNA problem or the oak tree-hydrocarbon problem, is ignored.

Every reductionist has his favorite analogy from modern science. It is most unlikely that any of these unrelated examples of successful reduction will shed light on the relation of mind to brain. But philosophers share the general human weakness for explanations of what is incomprehensible in terms suited for what is familiar and well understood, though entirely different. This has led to the acceptance of implausible accounts of the mental largely because they would permit familiar kinds of reduction. I shall try to explain why the usual examples do not help us to understand the relationship between mind and body — why, indeed, we have at present no conception of what an explanation of the physical nature of a mental phenomenon would be. Without consciousness the mind-body problem would be much less interesting. With consciousness it seems hopeless. The most important and characteristic feature of conscious mental phenomena is very poorly understood. Most reductionist theories do not even try to explain it. And careful examination

Nagel, T. 1974. "What Is it Like to be a Bat?" in *Philosophical Review*, 83, pp. 435-450.

will show that no currently available concept of reduction is applicable to it. Perhaps a new theoretical form can be devised for the purpose, but such a solution, if it exists, lies in the distant intellectual future.

Conscious experience is a widespread phenomena. It occurs at many levels of animal life, though we cannot be sure of its presence in the simpler organisms, and it is very difficult to say in general what provides evidence of it. (Some extremists have been prepared to deny it even of mammals other than man.) No doubt it occurs in countless forms totally unimaginable to us, on other planets in other solar systems throughout the universe. But no matter how the form may vary, the fact that an organism has conscious experience *at all* means, basically, that there is something it is like to *be* that organism. There may be further implications about the form of the experience; there may even (though I doubt it) be implications about the behavior of the organism. But fundamentally an organism has conscious mental states if and only if there is something that it is like to *be* that organism — something it is like *for* the organism.

We may call this the subjective character of the experience. It is not captured by any of the familiar, recently devised reductive analyses of the mental, for all of them are logically compatible with its absence. It is not analyzable in terms of any explanatory system of functional states, or intentional states, since these could be ascribed to robots or automata that behaved like people though they experienced nothing.[2] It is not analyzable in terms of the causal role of experiences in relation to typical human behavior — for similar reasons.[3] I do not deny that conscious mental states and events cause similar behavior, nor that they may be given functional characterizations. I deny only that this kind of thing exhausts their analysis. Any reductionist program has to be based on an analysis of what is to be reduced. If the analysis leaves something out, the problem will be falsely posed. It is useless to base the defense of materialism on any analysis of mental phenomena that fails to deal explicitly with their subjective character. For there is no reason to suppose that a reduction which seems plausible when no attempt is made to account for consciousness can be extended to include consciousness. Without some idea, therefore, of what the subjective character of experience is, we cannot know what is required of a physicalist theory.

While an account of the physical basis of mind must explain many things, this appears to be the most difficult. It is impossible to exclude the phenomenological features of experience from a reduction in the same way that one excludes the phenomenal features of an ordinary substance from a physical or chemical reduction of it — namely, by explaining them as effects on the minds of human observers.[4] If physicalism is to be defended, the phenomenological features must themselves be given a physical account. But when we examine their subjective character it seems that such a result is impossible. The reason is that every subjective phenomenon is essentially connected with a single point of view, and it seems inevitable that an objective, physical theory will abandon that point of view.

Let me first try to state the issue somewhat more fully than by referring to the relation between the subjective and the objective, or between the *pour-soi* and the *en-soi*. This is far from easy. Facts about what it is like to be an *X* are very peculiar, so peculiar that some may be inclined to doubt their reality, or the significance of claims about them. To illustrate the connection between subjectivity and a point of view, and to make evident the importance of subjective features, it will help to explore the matter in relation to an example that brings out clearly the divergence between the two types of conception, subjective and objective.

I assume we all believe that bats have experience. After all, they are mammals, and there is no more doubt that they have experience than that mice or pigeons or whales have experience. I have chosen bats instead of wasps or flounders because if one travels too far down the phylogenetic tree, people gradually shed their faith that there is experience there at all. Bats, although more closely related to us than those other species, nevertheless present a range of activity and a sensory apparatus so different from ours that the problem I want to pose is exceptionally vivid (though it certainly could be raised with other species). Even without the benefit of philosophical reflection, anyone who has spent some time in an enclosed space with an excited bat knows what it is to encounter a fundamentally alien form of life.

I have said that the essence of the belief that bats have experience is that there is something that it is like to be a bat. Now we know that most bats (the microchiroptera, to be precise) perceive the external world primarily by sonar, or echolocation, detecting the reflections, from objects within range, of their own rapid, subtly modulated, high-frequency shrieks. Their brains are designed to correlate the outgoing impulses with the subsequent echoes, and the information thus acquired enables bats to make precise discriminations of distance, size, shape, motion, and texture comparable to those we make by vision. But bat sonar, though clearly a form of perception, is not similar in its operation to any sense that we possess, and there is no reason to suppose that it is subjectively like anything we can experience or imagine. This appears to create difficulties for the notion of what it is like to be a bat. We must consider whether any method will permit us to extrapolate to the inner life of the bat from our own case,[5] and if not, what alternative methods there may be for understanding the notion.

Our own experience provides the basic material for our imagination, whose range is therefore limited. It will not help to try to imagine that one has webbing on one's arms, which enables one to fly around at dusk and dawn catching insects in one's mouth; that one has very poor vision, and perceives the surrounding world by a system of reflected high-frequency sound signals; and that one spends the day hanging upside down by one's feet in an attic. In so far as I can imagine this (which is not very far), it tells me only what it would be like for *me* to behave as a bat behaves. But that is not the question. I want to know what it is like for a *bat* to be a bat. Yet if I try to imagine this, I am restricted to the resources of my own mind, and those resources are inadequate to the task. I cannot perform it either by imagining additions to my present experience, or by imagining segments gradually subtracted from it, or by imagining some combination of additions, subtractions, and modifications.

To the extent that I could look and behave like a wasp or a bat without changing my fundamental structure, my experiences would not be anything like the experiences of those animals. On the other hand, it is doubtful that any meaning can be attached to the supposition that I should possess the internal neurophysiological constitution of a bat. Even if I could by gradual degrees be transformed into a bat, nothing in my present constitution enables me to imagine what the experiences of such a future stage of myself thus metamorphosed would be like. The best evidence would come from the experiences of bats, if we only knew what they were like.

So if extrapolation from our own case is involved in the idea of what it is like to be a bat, the extrapolation must be incompletable. We cannot form more than a schematic conception of what it *is* like. For example, we may ascribe general *types* of experience of the basis of the animal's structure and behavior. Thus we describe bat sonar as a form of three-dimensional forward perception; we believe that bats feel some versions of pain, fear, hunger, and lust, and that they have other, more familiar types of perception besides sonar. But we believe that these experiences also have in each case a specific subjective character, which it is beyond our ability to conceive. And if there is conscious life elsewhere in the universe, it is likely that some of it will not be describable even in the most general experiential terms available to us.[6] (The problem is not confined to exotic cases, however, for it exists between one person and another. The subjective character of the experience of a person deaf and blind from birth is not accessible to me, for example, nor presumably is mine to him. This does not prevent us each from believing that the other's experience has such a subjective character.)

If anyone is inclined to deny that we can believe in the existence of facts like this whose exact nature we cannot possibly conceive, he should reflect that in contemplating the bats we are in much the same position that intelligent bats or Martians[7] would occupy if they tried to form a conception of what it was like to be us. The structure of their own minds might make it impossible for them to succeed, but we know they would be wrong to conclude that there is not anything precise that it is like to be us: that only certain general types of mental state could be ascribed to us (perhaps perception and appetite would be concepts common to us both; perhaps not). We know they would be wrong to draw such a skeptical conclusion because we know what it is like to be us. And we know that while it includes an enormous amount of variation and complexity, and while we do not possess the vocabulary to describe it adequately, its subjective character is highly specific, and in some respects describable in terms that can be understood only by creatures like us. The fact that we cannot expect ever to accommodate in our language a detailed description of Martian or bat phenomenology should not lead us to dismiss as meaningless the claim that bats and Martians have experiences fully comparable in richness of detail to our own. It would be fine if someone were to develop concepts and a theory that enabled us to think about those things; but such an understanding may be permanently denied to us by the limits of our nature. And to deny the reality or logical significance of what we can never describe or understand is the crudest form of cognitive dissonance.

This brings us to the edge of a topic that requires much more discussion that I can give it here: namely, the relation between facts on the one hand and conceptual schemes or systems of representation on the other. My realism about the subjective domain in all its forms implies a belief in the existence of facts beyond the reach of human concepts. Certainly it is possible for a human being to believe that there are facts which humans never *will* possess the requisite concepts to represent or comprehend. Indeed, it would be foolish to doubt this, given the finiteness of humanity's expectations. After all, there would have been transfinite numbers even if everyone had been wiped out by the Black Death before Cantor discovered them. But one might also believe that there are facts which *could* not ever be represented or comprehended by human beings, even if the species lasted forever — simply because our structure does not permit us to operate with concepts of the requisite type. This impossibility might even be observed by other beings, but it is not clear that the existence of such beings, or the possibility of their existence, is a precondition of the significance of the hypothesis that there are humanly inaccessible facts. (After all, the nature of beings with access to humanly inaccessible facts is presumably itself a humanly inaccessible fact.) Reflection on what it is like to be a bat seems to lead us, therefore, to the conclusion that there are facts that do not consist in the truth of propositions expressible in a human language. We can be compelled to recognize the existence of such facts without being able to state or comprehend them.

I shall not pursue this subject, however. Its bearing on the topic before us (namely, the mind-body problem) is that it enables us to make a general observation about the subjective character of experience. Whatever may be the status of facts about what it is like to be a human being, or a bat, or a Martian, these appear to be facts that embody a particular point of view.

I am not adverting here to the alleged privacy of experience to its possessor. The point of view in question is not one accessible only to a single individual. Rather it is a *type*. It is often possible to take up a point of view other than one's own, so the comprehension of such facts is not limited to one's own case. There is a sense in which phenomenological facts are perfectly objective: one person can know or say of another what the quality of the other's experience is. They are subjective, however, in the sense that even this objective ascription of experience is possible only for someone sufficiently similar to the object of ascription to be able to adopt his point of view — to understand the ascription in the first person as well as in the third, so to speak. The more different from oneself the other experiencer is, the less success one can expect with this enterprise. In our own case we occupy the relevant point of view, but we will have as much difficulty understanding our own experience properly if we approach it from another point of view as we would if we tried to understand the experience of another species without taking up *its* point of view.[8]

This bears directly on the mind-body problem. For if the facts of experience — facts about what it is like *for* the experiencing organism — are accessible only from one point of view, then it is a mystery how the true character of experiences could be revealed in the physical operation of that organism. The latter is a domain of objective facts *par excellence* — the kind that can be observed and understood from many points of view and by individuals with differing perceptual systems. There are no comparable imaginative obstacles to the acquisition of knowledge about bat neurophysiology by human scientists, and intelligent bats or Martians might learn more about the human brain than we ever will.

This is not by itself an argument against reduction. A Martian scientist with no understanding of visual perception could understand the rainbow, or lightning, or clouds as physical phenomena, though he would never be able to understand the human concepts of rainbow, lightning, or cloud, or the place these things occupy in our phenomenal world. The objective nature of the things picked out by these concepts could be apprehended by him because, although the concepts themselves are connected with a particular point of view and a particular visual phenomenology, the things apprehended from that point of view are not: they are observable from the point of view but external to it; hence they can be comprehended from other points of view also, either by the same organisms or by others. Lightning has an objective character that is not exhausted by its visual appearance, and this can be investigated by a Martian without vision. To be precise, it has a *more* objective character than is revealed in. its visual appearance. In speaking of the move from subjective to objective characterization, I wish to remain noncommittal about the existence of an end point, the completely objective intrinsic nature of the thing, which one might or might not be able to reach. It may be more accurate to think of objectivity as a direction in which the understanding can travel. And in understanding a phenomenon like lightning, it is legitimate to go as far away as one can from a strictly human viewpoint.[9]

In the case of experience, on the other hand, the connection with a particular point of view seems much closer. It is difficult to understand what could be meant by the *objective* character of an experience, apart from the particular point of view from which its subject apprehends it. After all, what would be left of what it was like to be a bat if one removed the viewpoint of the bat? But if experience does not have, in addition to its subjective character, an objective nature that can be apprehended from many different points of view, then how can it be supposed that a Martian investigating my brain might be observing physical processes which were my mental processes (as he might observe physical processes which were bolts of lightning), only from a different point of view? How, for that matter, could a human physiologist observe them from another point of view?[10]

We appear to be faced with a general difficulty about psychophysical reduction. In other areas the process of reduction is a move in the direction of greater objectivity, toward a more accurate view of the real nature of things. This is accomplished by reducing our dependence on individual or species-specific points of view toward the object of investigation. We describe it not in terms of the impressions it makes on our sense, but in terms of its more general effects and of properties detectable by means other than the human senses. The less it depends on a specifically human viewpoint, the more objective is our description. It is possible to follow this path because although the concepts and ideas we employ in thinking about the external world are initially applied from a point of view that involves our perceptual apparatus, they are used by us to refer to things beyond ourselves — toward which we *have* the phenomenal point of view. Therefore we can abandon it in favor of another, and still be thinking about the same things.

Experience itself, however, does not seem to fit the pattern. The idea of moving from appearance to reality seems to make no sense here. What is the analogue in this case to pursuing a more objective understanding of the same phenomena by abandoning the initial subjective viewpoint toward them in favor of another that is more objective but concerns the same thing? Certainly it *appears* unlikely that we will get closer to the real nature of human experience by leaving behind the particularity of our human point of view and striving for a description in terms accessible to beings that could not imagine what it was like to be us. If the subjective character of experience is fully comprehensible only from one point of view, then any shift to greater objectivity — that is, less attachment to a specific viewpoint — does not take us nearer to the real nature of the phenomenon: it takes us farther away from it.

In a sense, the seeds of this objection to the reducibility of experience are already detectable in successful cases of reduction; for in discovering sound to be, in reality, a wave phenomenon in air or other media, we leave behind one viewpoint to take up another, and the auditory, human or animal viewpoint that we leave behind remains unreduced. Members of radically different species may both understand the same physical events in objective terms, and this does not require that they understand the phenomenal forms in which those events appear to the senses of members of the other species. Thus it is a condition of their referring to a common reality that their more particular viewpoints are not part of the common reality that they both apprehend. The reduction can succeed only if the species-specific viewpoint is omitted from what is to be reduced.

But while we are right to leave this point of view aside in seeking a fuller understanding of the external world, we cannot ignore it permanently, since it is the essence of the internal world, and not merely a point of view on it. Most of the neobehaviorism of recent philosophical psychology results from the effort to substitute an objective concept of mind for the real thing, in order to have nothing left over which cannot be reduced. If we acknowledge that a physical theory of mind must account for the subjective character of experience, we must admit that no presently available conception gives us a clue how this could be done. The problem is unique. If mental processes are indeed physical processes, then there is something it is like, intrinsically,[11] to undergo certain physical processes. What it is for such a thing to be the case remains a mystery.

What moral should be drawn from these reflections, and what should be done next? It would be a mistake to conclude that physicalism must be false. Nothing is proved by the inadequacy of physicalist hypotheses that assume a faulty objective analysis of mind. It would be truer to say that physicalism is a position we cannot understand because we do not at present have any conception of how it might be true. Perhaps it will be thought unreasonable to require such a conception as a condition of understanding. After all, it might be said, the meaning of physicalism is clear enough: mental states are states of the body; mental states are physical events. We do not know *which* physical states and events they are, but that should not prevent us from understanding the hypothesis. What could be clearer than the words "is" and "are"?

But I believe it is precisely this apparent clarity of the word "is" that is deceptive. Usually, when we are told that X is Y we know *how* it is supposed to be true, but that depends on a conceptual or theoretical background and is not conveyed by the "is" alone. We know how both "X" and "Y" refer, and the kinds of things to which they refer, and we have a rough idea how the two referential paths might converge on a single thing, be it an object, a person, a process, an event, or whatever. But when the two terms of the identification are very disparate it may not be so clear how it could be true. We may not have even a rough idea of how the two referential paths could converge, or what kind of things they might converge on, and a theoretical framework may have to be supplied to enable us to understand this. Without the framework, an air of mysticism surrounds the identification.

This explains the magical flavor of popular presentations of fundamental scientific discoveries, given out as propositions to which one must subscribe without really understanding them. For example, people are now told at an early age that all matter is really energy. But despite the fact that they know what "is" means, most of them never form a conception of what makes this claim true, because they lack the theoretical background.

At the present time the status of physicalism is similar to that which the hypothesis that matter is energy would have had if uttered by a pre-Socratic philosopher. We do not have the beginnings of a conception of how it might be true. In order to understand the hypothesis that a mental event is a physical event, we require more than an understanding of the word "is". The idea of how a mental and a physical term might refer to the same thing is lacking, and the usual analogies with theoretical identification in other fields fail to supply it. They fail because if we construe the reference of mental terms to physical events on the usual model, we either get a reappearance of separate subjective events as the effects through which mental reference to physical events is secured, or else we get a false account of how mental terms refer (for example, a causal behaviorist one).

Strangely enough, we may have evidence for the truth of something we cannot really understand. Suppose a caterpillar is locked in a sterile safe by someone unfamiliar with insect metamorphosis, and weeks later the safe is reopened, revealing a butterfly. If the person knows that the safe has been shut the whole time, he has reason to believe that the butterfly is or was once the caterpillar, without having any idea in what sense this might be so. (One possibility is that the caterpillar contained a tiny winged parasite that devoured it and grew into the butterfly.)

It is conceivable that we are in such a position with regard to physicalism. Donald Davidson has argues that if mental events have physical causes and effects, they must have physical descriptions. He holds that we have reason to believe this even though we do not — and in fact *could* not — have a general psychophysical theory.[12] His argument applies to intentional mental events, but I think we also have some reason to believe that sensations are physical processes, without being in a position to understand how. Davidson's position is that certain physical events have irreducible mental properties, and perhaps some view describable in this way is correct. But nothing of which we can now form a conception corresponds to it; now have we any idea what a theory would be like that enabled us to conceive of it.[13]

Very little work has been done on the basic question (from which mention of the brain can be entirely omitted) whether any sense can be made of experiences' having an objective character at all. Does it make sense, in other words, to ask what my experiences are *really* like, as opposed to how they appear to me? We cannot genuinely understand the hypothesis that their nature is captured in a physical description unless we understand the more fundamental idea that they *have* an objective nature (or that objective processes can have a subjective nature).[14]

I should like to close with a speculative proposal. It may be possible to approach the gap between subjective and objective from another direction. Setting aside temporarily the relation between the mind and the brain, we can pursue a more objective understanding of the mental in its own right. At present we are completely unequipped to think about the subjective character of experience without relying on the imagination — without taking up the point of view of the experiental subject. This should be regarded as a challenge to form new concepts and devise a new method — an objective phenomenology not dependent on empathy or the imagination. Though presumably it would not capture everything, its goal would be to describe, at least in part, the subjective character of experiences in a form comprehensible to beings incapable of having those experiences.

We would have to develop such a phenomenology to describe the sonar experiences of bats; but it would also be possible to begin with humans. One might try, for example, to develop concepts that could be used to explain to a person blind from birth what it was like to see. One would reach a blank wall eventually, but it should be possible to devise a method of expressing in objective terms much more than we can at present, and with much greater precision. The loose intermodal analogies — for example, "Red is like the sound of a trumpet" — which crop up in discussions of this subject are of little use. That should be clear to anyone who has both heard a trumpet and seen red. But structural features of perception might be more accessible to objective description, even though something would be left out. And concepts alternative to those we learn in the first person may enable us to arrive at a kind of understanding even of our own experience which is denied us by the very ease of description and lack of distance that subjective concepts afford.

Apart from its own interest, a phenomenology that is in this sense objective may permit questions about the physical[15] basis of experience to assume a more intelligible form. Aspects of subjective experience that admitted this kind of objective description might be better candidates for objective explanations of a more familiar sort. But whether or not this guess is correct, it seems unlikely that any physical theory of mind can be contemplated until more thought has been given to the general problem of subjective and objective. Otherwise we cannot even pose the mind-body problem without sidestepping it.[16]

NOTES

[1] Examples are J.J.C. Smart, *Philosophy and Scientific Realism* (London, 1963); David K. Lewis, "An Argument for the Identity Theory," *Journal of Philosophy*, LXIII (1966), reprinted with addenda in David M. Rosenthal, *Materialism & the Mind-Body Problem* (Englewood Cliffs, N.J., 1971); Hilary Putnam, "Psychological Predicate" in Capitan and Merrill, *Art, Mind, & Religion* (Pittsburgh, 1967), reprinted in Rosenthal, *op. cit.*, as "The Nature of Mental States"; D.M. Armstrong, *A Materialist Theory of the Mind* (London, 1968); D.C. Dennett, *Content and Consciousness* (London, 1969). I have expressed earlier doubts in "Armstrong on the Mind," *Philosophical Review*, LXXIX (1970), 394-403; "Brain Bisection and the Unity of Consciousness," *Synthèse*, 22 (1971); and a review of Dennett, *Journal of Philosophy*, LXIX (1972). See also Saul Kripke, "Naming and Necessity" in Davidson and Harman, *Semantics of Natural Language* (Dordrecht, 1972), esp. pp. 334-342; and M.T. Thornton, "Ostensive Terms and Materialism," *The Monist*, 56 (1972).

[2] Perhaps there could not actually be such robots. Perhaps anything complex enough to behave like a person would have experiences. But that, if true, is a fact which cannot be discovered merely by analyzing the concept of experience.

3   It is not equivalent to that about which we are incorrigible, both because we are not incorrigible about experience and because experience is present in animals lacking language and thought, who have no beliefs at all about their experiences.

4   Cf. Richard Rorty, "Mind-Body Identity, Privacy, and Categories," *The Review of Metaphysics,* XIX (1965), esp. 37-38.

5   By "our own case" I do not mean just "my own case," but rather the mentalistic ideas that we apply unproblematically to ourselves and other human beings.

6   Therefore the analogical form of the English expression "what it is like" is misleading. It does not mean "what (in our experience) it *resembles*," but rather "how it is for the subject himself."

7   Any intelligent extraterrestrial beings totally different from us.

8   It may be easier than I suppose to transcend inter-species barriers with the aid of the imagination. For example, blind people are able to detect objects near them by a form a sonar, using vocal clicks or taps of a cane. Perhaps if one knew what that was like, one could by extension imagine roughly what it was like to possess the much more refined sonar of a bat. The distance between oneself and other persons and other species can fall anywhere on a continuum. Even for other persons the understanding of what it is like to be them is only partial, and when one moves to species very different from oneself, a lesser degree of partial understanding may still be available. The imagination is remarkably flexible. My point, however, is not that we cannot *know* what it is like to be a bat. I am not raising that epistemological problem. My point is rather that even to form a *conception* of what it is like to be a bat (and a fortiori to know what it is like to be a bat) one must take up the bat's point of view. If one can take it up roughly, or partially, then one's conception will also be rough or partial. Or so it seems in our present state of understanding.

9   The problem I am going to raise can therefore be posed even if the distinction between more subjective and more objective descriptions or viewpoints can itself be made only within a larger human point of view. I do not accept this kind of conceptual relativism, but it need not be refuted to make the point that psychophysical reduction cannot be accommodated by the subjective-to-objective model familiar from other cases.

10   The problem is not just that when I look at the "Mona Lisa," my visual experience has a certain quality, no trace of which is to be found by someone looking into my brain. For even if he did observe there a tiny image of the "Mona Lisa," he would have no reason to identify it with the experience.

11   The relation would therefore not be a contingent one, like that of a cause and its distinct effect. It would be necessarily true that a certain physical state felt a certain way. Saul Kripke (*op. cit.*) argues that causal behaviorist and related analyses of the mental fail because they construe, e.g., "pain" as a merely contingent name of pains. The subjective character of an experience ("its immediate phenomenological quality" Kripke calls it [p. 340]) is the essential property left out by such analyses, and the one in virtue of which it is, necessarily, the experience it is. My view is closely related to his. Like Kripke, I find the hypothesis that a certain brain state should *necessarily* have a certain subjective character incomprehensible without further explanation. No such explanation emerges from theories which view the mind-brain relation as contingent, but perhaps there are other alternatives, not yet discovered.

A theory that explained how the mind-brain relation was necessary would still leave us with Kripke's problem of explaining why it nevertheless appears contingent. That difficulty seems to me surmountable, in the following way. We may imagine something by representing it to ourselves either perceptually, sympathetically, or symbolically. I shall not try to say how symbolic imagination works, but part of what happens in the other two cases is this. To imagine something perceptually, we put ourselves in a conscious state resembling the state we would be in if we perceived it. To imagine something sympathetically, we put ourselves in a conscious state resembling the thing itself. (This method can be used only to imagine mental events and states —

our own or another's.) When we try to imagine a mental state occurring without its associated brain state, we first sympathetically imagine the occurrence of the mental state: that is, we put ourselves into a state that resembles it mentally. At the same time, we attempt to perceptually imagine the non-occurrence of the associated physical state, by putting ourselves into another state unconnected with the first: one resembling that which we would be in if we perceived the non-occurrence of the physical state. Where the imagination of physical features is perceptual and the imagination of mental features is sympathetic, it appears to us that we can imagine any experience occurring without its associated brain state, and vice versa. The relation between them will appear contingent even if it is necessary, because of the independence of the disparate types of imagination.

(Solipsism, incidentally, results if one misinterprets sympathetic imagination as if it worked like perceptual imagination: it then seems impossible to imagine any experience that is not one's own.)

[12] See "Mental Events" in Foster and Swanson, *Experience and Theory* (Amherst, 1970); though I don't understand the argument against psychophysical laws.

[13] Similar remarks apply to my paper "Physicalism," *Philosophical Review* LXXIV (1965), 339-356, reprinted with postscript in John O'Connor, *Modern Materialism* (New York, 1969).

[14] This question also lies at the heart of the problem of other minds, whose close connection with the mind-body problem is often overlooked. If one understood how subjective experience could have an objective nature, one would understand the existence of subjects other than oneself.

[15] I have not defined the term "physical." Obviously it does not apply just to what can be described by the concepts of contemporary physics, since we expect further developments. Some may think there is nothing to prevent mental phenomena from eventually being recognized as physical in their own right. But whatever else may be said of the physical, it has to be objective. So if our idea of the physical ever expands to include mental phenomena, it would have to assign them an objective character – whether or not this is done by analyzing them in terms of other phenomena regarded as physical. It seems to me more likely, however, that mental-physical relations will eventually be expressed in a theory whose fundamental terms cannot be placed clearly in either category.

[16] I have read versions of this paper to a number of audiences, and am indebted to any people for their comments.